Praise for *Winning the Knowledge Transfer Race*

"There is no substitute for experience. Bill Baker and Michael English, pioneers in benchmarking best practices, have synthesized their practical insights and tested approaches into a fresh new perspective for managing and expanding *intellectual capital*. This comprehensive guide brings the concept of knowledge-based enterprise *down to earth* with straightforward frameworks, tools, processes and methods for accelerating knowledge sharing and kicking value creation into high gear."

—**Verna Allee**, Author, *The Future of Knowledge*

"*Winning the Knowledge Transfer Race* is a well-crafted and well-thought addition to the field of best practices benchmarking. It effectively conveys the importance of *speed*, learning, sharing, transfer, and *reuse* of knowledge as forms of *intellectual capital*. These authors are practitioners, colleagues, thought-leaders and early-adopters of best practices benchmarking. They deliver a clear roadmap, inspiring stories, useful illustrations, and an actionable strategy for creating value and profitability as well as sustaining a competitive advantage."

—**Christopher E. Bogan**, President and CEO,
Best Practices, LLC

"After a preview, I cannot wait to get my copy of *Winning the Knowledge Transfer Race*; and not for my bookcase—for my briefcase. Baker and English have compiled the hitchhiker's guide to navigating the world of performance improvement for organizations savvy enough to leverage their knowledge assets to gain competitive advantage. The book, loaded with illustrations, is an integrated collection of overviews, tools, and models that provide a powerful, but compact reference, not just for knowledge professionals, but for anyone who wants their enterprise to excel. Companies, large and small, will be providing this to employees as a handbook to support their internal programs."

—**Fred D. Bowers**, President, *Bowers Enterprise*,
early pioneer of benchmarking, and former head of
benchmarking for *Digital Equipment Corp*

"Baker and English's book is a new look at the evolving nature of the competitive landscape and the importance of continued learning to meet the significant challenges. *Speed* of learning and applying new found knowledge to benefit the customers has certainly become the mantra of successful organizations worldwide. Their recommended use of Benchmarking to discover new Best Practices and Lessons Learned and motivate change agents supports my own findings and belief in this process. This involves a process which requires the capture, exchange, and adoption of Best Practices to achieve excellence. *Winning the Knowledge Transfer Race* takes the reader on a systematic journey to achieve higher performance in a way that we can all relate."

—**Robert C. Camp**, Ph.D., P. E., Principal,
Best Practice Institute, Ithaca, NY

WINNING
THE
KNOWLEDGE
TRANSFER
RACE

Michael J. English
William H. Baker, Jr.

McGraw-Hill

New York Chicago San Francisco Lisbon
London Madrid Mexico City Milan New Delhi
San Juan Seoul Singapore Sydney Toronto

Copyright © 2006 by The McGraw-Hill Companies, Inc. All rights reserved. Printed in the United States of America. Except as permitted under the United States Copyright Act of 1976, no part of this publication may be reproduced or distributed in any form or by any means, or stored in a data base or retrieval system, without the prior written permission of the publisher.

1 2 3 4 5 6 7 8 9 0   DOC/DOC   0 9 8 7 6 5

ISBN 0-07-145794-1

This publication is designed to provide accurate and authoritative information in regard to the subject matter covered. It is sold with the understanding that the publisher is not engaged in rendering legal, accounting, or other professional service. If legal advice or other expert assistance is required, the services of a competent professional person should be sought.
> —*From a declaration of principles jointly adopted by a committee of the American Bar Association and a committee of publishers.*

McGraw-Hill books are available at special quantity discounts to use as premiums and sales promotions, or for use in corporate training programs. For more information, please write to the Director of Special Sales, McGraw-Hill Professional, Two Penn Plaza, New York, NY 10121-2298. Or contact your local bookstore.

This book is printed on recycled, acid-free paper containing a minimum of 50% recycled, de-inked fiber.

Contents

Contents

Preface

A question haunting modern mankind is, why did the Neanderthals disappear from the earth about 28,000 years ago after inhabiting it for 170,000 years? The answer is a sobering illustration of how what is *not* known can have deadly consequences. Despite coexisting with the Neanderthals for 70,000 years, *Homo sapiens* survived because they were able to communicate in a fully developed spoken language that enabled them to transfer knowledge and share it with one another. In contrast, the Neanderthals, not having language, were extremely limited in how they could pass on knowledge to one another.

Thus, Neanderthals froze to death near plenty of wood because they didn't have the knowledge that others in their clans did about how to start a fire. Flintlike stones were nearby, too. But they didn't know how to use them. Many Neanderthals died needlessly because they did not know how to use sparks or the friction from sticks to create a flame. Knowledge transfer was the issue, not fire building. Each new generation of Neanderthals often had to "reinvent the wheel" and relearn what was already known. Anthropologists have a saying that one does not have to fail to become extinct, just succeed a little less often. The Neanderthals were disadvantaged and just succeeded a little less often competing for food, water, and shelter. Neanderthals perished in many other ways that would have been preventable had they been able to transfer knowledge. Ever since, however, *Homo sapiens* have used language to educate and pass on knowledge to their future generations, and because of this, they have survived and prospered. *Homo sapiens* can take knowledge acquired through individual experiences, share it, and transmit it from generation to generation.[1]

Reverting to the present day, this book examines twenty-first-century *Homo sapiens* organized in business enterprises and shows how, in order to win in the face of fierce competition, they must transfer new forms of knowledge, described as intellectual capital. Just like their ancestors of 28,000 years before, they can take and share knowledge. But the key word is *can*. It doesn't happen automatically. This is now an information age. Today, knowledge transfers have to be done in deliberate and systematic ways if the wisdom involved is to be converted into profits.

Before the introduction, it must be made clear that this book addresses only the kinds of knowledge used in business and industry. Because knowledge is the sum of what is known, there are bodies of it for other fields: science, mathematics, technology, history, politics, literature, theater, religion, philosophy, and so on. The discussion in this book is limited to the kinds of knowledge that are involved in the conduct of business and industry. So there won't be references to such scientific disciplines as physics, where Albert Einstein's famous equation $E = MC^2$ expresses the theory of relativity. Instead, the chapters that follow will examine intellectual capital and how it can be used to shape markets and deliver products and services. Technological advances, to the extent that they are convertible into customer value and profits, will also be a part of the conversation.

Endnotes

1. Patrick K. O'Brien (ed.), *Atlas of World History* (New York: Oxford University Press, 2002), p. 17.

Acknowledgments

This book codifies the knowledge, insights, skills, experiences, and creativity that we've learned and developed from many colleagues, practitioners, and thought leaders, and from each other. Since we've come from different industries, it has amazed us how often we could see the same mistakes being made over and over in every industry. And so, we've converted our combined human capital into intellectual assets and shared them in this book, so that organizations can become leaders in the knowledge transfer race and achieve sustainable competitive advantages.

First, we thank our life partners: Martha Rea Baker and Paula Arlene English. They have been our inspiration. They have encouraged us and given us the time and space to see this through. We are grateful and thankful.

We are grateful to others as well. Our special thanks and appreciation go to Jeanne Glasser, our senior editor at McGraw-Hill. Thank you, Jeanne, for believing in our project and helping to give it life. Our thanks also go to Crystal McCage for her editorial assistance and for making many valuable suggestions. Our sincere appreciation also goes to Daina Penikas, editing supervisor at McGraw-Hill and to Alice Manning, copyeditor. This group of special people helped us make this a book more valuable, and every bit worth buying, reading, using, and reusing. Thank you one and all.

Others we wish to thank for help and inspiration are Verna Allee, John D. Adams, Christopher Bogan, Marilynn Brennan, Irving Briks, Suzie Bruin, Rachel Buckley, Bob Camp, Paul Cherrett, Rory Chase, Tom Davenport, Nancy Dixon, Justin English, Theresa Esposto, Bob Frost, Jerry Gass, Anthony Glaude, C. Jackson Grayson, Jr., Susan Grow, Bob Hawiszczak, John Hendricks, David Hogg, Cindy Hubert, Kay Hunn, Alison Indergard, Joe Ivers, Constantine Kazakos, Art Kleimer, Marsha Krashoc, Jeffrey Liker, Claudia Loffler, Laura Longmire,

Roze Lotz, Joseph Martucci, Richard McDermott, Phil McDonald, Neal Mackertich, Dave Rawles, Jon McKenzie, Barbara Newell, Carla O'Dell, William O'Connor, Mark Palla, Rusty Patterson, Dan Pinkney, Jack Pompeo, Ross Robson, Phil Roether, Don Ronchi, Melissie Rumizen, Holger Sbrzesny, Peter Senge, Kristen Smithwick, Susan Silverstein, Thomas Stewart, Patrick Sullivan, Kevin Tarrant, Susan Grow, and Michelle Yakovac.

Chapter 1

The Importance of Intellectual Capital and Speed, the Knowledge Transfer Race, and the Power of Benchmarking

apid knowledge *transfer* is the central theme of this book. The underlying topics addressed within this theme are the discovery—capture, creation, transfer, sharing—and reuse of knowledge that becomes *intellectual capital*. Simply put, the authors will make the case that making speedy knowledge transfers a core competency gives organizations remarkable advantages over competitors. Knowledge transfer is not synonymous with knowledge management (KM). KM is the discipline born in the 1990s that is generally defined today as a set of strategies and approaches to create, safeguard, and use knowledge assets to flow knowledge to the right people at the right time so they can apply those assets to create value for the enterprise.

The authors contend that KM is an incomplete concept and advocate the broader umbrella concept of rapid knowledge transfer, which includes KM and considerably more in an integrated framework that consists of a "knowledge-enabled culture" and the four phases of a knowledge transfer race: (1) search and import best practices; (2) learn, understand, and share; (3) create intellectual capital; and (4) convert knowledge (via use and reuse) into value and profits. A knowledge-enabled culture consists of a system of aligned human resource policies, tactics, processes, and practices that ensure that knowledge is captured, created, shared, used, and reused to achieve superior organizational results as a sustainable advantage.

Rapid knowledge transfer takes KM and adds to it five key concepts: (1) a knowledge-enabled culture just described in the last paragraph (including a process managed organization); (2) development of a rapid learning organization; (3) systematic use of knowledge transfer methods; (4) a focus on knowledge that is intellectual capital (defined as that knowledge that may be converted into value and profit) with emphasis on how human capital is needed for its ongoing creation; and (5) a "how to" emphasis on reusing existing best practice knowledge in the new and different contexts, applications and industries, i.e. the powerful concept of knowledge reuse. The authors contend that it is through reuse that the phenomenal paybacks of creating value and profits may be achieved and a competitive advantage sustained.

Between 1990 and 2005, four global phenomena have converged to make rapid knowledge transfer essential for nearly every organization:

1. Driven by the capabilities of high speed bandwidth, PC microchip improvements, digital technology, and growth of the Internet, speed has become critical to every facet of business, creating an edge to those who rapidly transfer knowledge. Just as Moore's Law has held true since 1965 insofar as Intel cofounder Gordon Moore predicted that the complexity of integrated circuits would double every 18 months, each new generation of microchips increases —transactional speed exponentially — and this speed gain is likewise—accelerating the pace of knowledge transfer, enough to turn it into a race to gain competitive advantage. Simply put, what used to take weeks takes days, what used to take days now takes hours, and what once took hours takes minutes.

2. Intellectual capital has become a prominent concept that now overshadows physical capital, bringing the realization that knowledge is its main ingredient and human capital (the tacit knowledge in the minds of employees) is the source of it all, including intellectual property, and needs to be nurtured and protected from loss. For example, when master jet engine technicians leave Gulfstream Aerospace of Savannah, Georgia, that company must protect itself against the loss of the expert tacit knowledge needed to maintain the BMW Rolls-Royce BR700 series engines. Since 1992 the BR700 series engine has been the sole source engine of the Gulfstream V, Gulfstream's large, ultra long range business jet. Many other examples exist in other industries where the knowledge loss risks are high, ranging from software design, architectural design, air traffic control, and hazardous materials handling, to just name a few.

3. Record retirements of the 77 million baby boomers and the transition to Generations X and Y workforces threaten organizations with huge losses of vital knowledge. The first of the boomers, born between 1946 and 1964, will turn age 65 in 2011. By 2030, the 65-year-old-plus segment will account for about 20 percent of the U.S. population, doubling the percent that segment held in 2000. When these workers retire they will take their tacit knowledge with them. This phenomenon is making rapid knowledge transfer all the more important.

4. There is a large and growing reservoir of proven, valuable, and profitable best practice business knowledge that is available for transfer compared to

anytime before in history and most of it is free for the asking. A worldwide improvement revolution has produced an array of business excellence models (Baldrige Awards, European Quality Awards, Shingo Prize, ISO9000, Lean Enterprise and Six Sigma) that achieve breakthrough performance successes in one location, so they may be replicated everywhere else. Knowledge transfer is the proven way to replicate successes within and between organizations. Why not take advantage of the excellent intellectual assets already captured through these models that are available for transfer and reuse?

Because of these four phenomena, every organization, whether management or employees realize it yet or not, needs to rapidly transfer knowledge to succeed.

This book's core concepts are presented and discussed in the context of winning a metaphoric *knowledge transfer race*. The metaphor works because repeated references to different phases of the race figuratively correspond to similar phases in the competitive real-world economy. It is also a fun way to study and learn about knowledge transfer. So readers should prepare for a four-phase race that has five rules:

  I. Contestants must master each phase before going on to the next phase.
 II. Pit stops can be taken as needed to master each phase of the race.
III. Speed and mastery of the concepts trump any other advantages.
 IV. Those who don't even start the race or who drop out are losers.
  V. Those who stay in the race and master every phase, overcome every obstacle, and use speed to their advantage are winners.

Oh, and also, this is a race that needs to be won by every enterprise, but it has no finish line.

Even though the race involves the transfer of every kind of intellectual capital, one type, *best practices*, will be featured throughout the book. One reason is that best practices usually need to be imported into enterprises through benchmarking, and few enterprises have the capability to do this well. Therefore, this is an area that is emphasized in this book. Readers will be shown how to incorporate very potent best practices benchmarking competency into their improvement strategy. This capability will enable enterprises to achieve ultimate levels of defect-free output.

Six Sigma is the Greek expression that is frequently used to describe that ultimate level of defect-free performance. In Chapter 6, the Six Sigma improvement strategy will be defined and described. Later, Chapter 8 will explore the Six Sigma approaches that Raytheon and Bank of America have adopted using benchmarking as a key ingredient.

The authors suggest that until Chapters 6 and 8 have been read, each time readers encounter a reference to Six Sigma, they consider it to be a defect elimination strategy targeting a spectacular 99.994 percent defect-free output (or 3.4 defects per million). By the end of Chapter 9, it will be clear how Six Sigma fits into and integrates with the knowledge transfer race. However, this is not intended to be another A to Z book about how to design and implement Six Sigma—or, for that matter, knowledge management. While the book does include a series of discussions about what knowledge management and Six Sigma are and aren't, the primary focus is always on leveraging knowledge in the form of intellectual capital to achieve extraordinary results.

Still, this book's focus dovetails with importing best practices knowledge to make Six Sigma implementations better, especially for small businesses. In fact, a target audience for this book is the often forgotten managers and professionals in small organizations. The "off-the-shelf" practices of large organizations just don't fit "as is" for them.

The book starts with introductory discussions of knowledge and intellectual capital. These set the stage for understanding how combinations of best practices, benchmarking, and knowledge sharing or management can be properly integrated into any enterprise's Six Sigma or performance excellence system. Next, the metaphoric knowledge transfer race will be introduced. Phase 1 of the race is to *search for and import best practices*. Here, compelling Bain & Company research will substantiate the claim that benchmarking is one of the top two management tools worldwide. This work will also show that the level of satisfaction with benchmarking as a tool is high and rising. Then, a benchmarking self-assessment tool will be provided to help enterprises determine how effectively they've integrated best practices benchmarking into their organization. Next, brief descriptions of phases 2 (*learn, understand, and share*), 3 (*create intellectual capital*), and 4 (*convert into value and profits*) will be provided. This leads to a discussion we give at the end of nearly every chapter, "The Bottom Line for People in Small Organizations." Finally, this chapter closes by discussing what's ahead in future chapters.

Knowledge as It Pertains to Business and Industry

The dictionary definition of the word *knowledge* is a noun meaning "the state of knowing" or "understanding that which is known." While such a definition helps, it is not enough to act on. Taking the definition a step further, to *know* is to apprehend with a conscious mind. Taking this one more step further, *know-how* is having a thorough knowledge of the theory and actual practice of a process or procedure. This last definition brings to life the meaning of *knowledge* and creates a context for it as being able to be acted on, leading practitioners to focus on using it to achieve process excellence.

Organizationally, knowledge is that information that is essential for transacting business in ways that improve employee performance and an organization's competitiveness. Indeed, this means that the type of knowledge under discussion is intellectual capital. This will be discussed in depth in Chapter 5. For organizations to compete successfully in the twenty-first-century global economy, they must treat particular knowledge that contributes to their core competencies as cherished *human capital* or *intellectual assets*. These competencies, although not well understood, set organizations apart from their competitors. Leveraging such intellectual capital into competitive advantage is a key focus of this book.

To illustrate, Ford Motor Company, General Motors, Toyota, Nissan, and the other leading automobile companies treat the knowledge they've gained about the design, manufacture, sales, distribution, and financing of their automobiles as sacred. Some of this knowledge may be trade secrets, proprietary, protected forms of *intellectual property*. The same is true for Microsoft, PeopleSoft, and Oracle regarding software; Coca-Cola and Pepsi regarding soft drinks; Dell Computer and Hewlett-Packard regarding personal computers, and so on. Some knowledge may be leveraged into competitive advantages.

A prime example, and one of the world's most famous trade secrets, is the formula for Coca-Cola. Had inventor John S. Pemberton patented his formula as a new compound in 1886 instead of making it a trade secret, after only 17 years, anyone could have manufactured his drink using his formula.[1] Instead, the only written copy of Pemberton's secret formula is locked up, protected to this day, in a SunTrust Bank vault in Atlanta, Georgia.[2]

Besides trade secrets and patents, there are many other valuable and unprotected forms of intellectual capital that are advantageous for organizations to import, share, and transfer through reuse into new adaptations. They can be as simple as a process and as complicated as an off-the-shelf software program. Many are simply best practices.

To safeguard such knowledge, organizations are being proactive. Companies have created internal classification systems to restrict the external release of sensitive information that contains proprietary knowledge such as pricing strategy, marketing plans, or manufacturing processes. They have required employees to sign restrictive agreements to protect unauthorized release of this sensitive knowledge. Alliances between companies often require both of the organizations involved to restrict sharing beyond that involved in the alliance by using signed nondisclosure agreements (NDAs) that indicate that violators may face serious consequences. Even benchmarking exchanges among organizations follow a code of conduct (provided in Chapter 2) that calls for approval before shared knowledge is transferred beyond the closed group of participating partners.

The fact is that the best practices of work-related knowledge are the Holy Grail of for-profit organizations. Sooner or later, such organizations need to search out, import, share, create, transfer, repurpose, or reuse their best practices knowledge, and convert it to profit whenever they can. Successful organizations probably perform most of these steps already, but, too often, they do them in an ad hoc manner and not as a systematic strategy. When they get serious and perform these process steps in a deliberate and systematic way, they'll be practicing a true form of knowledge management and recognize its value. This approach, which will be reviewed later in this chapter and in later chapters, is a systematic method of managing intellectual capital to achieve a competitive advantage. Table 1-1 illustrates the paybacks involved. In other words, managing knowledge is a means to a greater end; in business, this end is to convert knowledge into value and profits while winning customers and market share. Table 1-1 illustrates in the left column how gains in knowledge translate into the right column in terms of quantified improvement.

However, confusion about what constitutes knowledge can obscure and fog people's understanding of knowledge and how to manage it. As a result, organizations don't take the steps that lead to leveraging knowledge. They also don't realize the results listed in Table 1-1. To begin with, it's not easy to distinguish among data, benchmarks, information, best practices, and knowledge. All of these terms get jumbled together, and so, without clarity, one thing is often mistaken for another. If a concept is not understood, it is impossible for any organization to leverage that concept into any kind of competitive advantage. Fortunately, however, there are breakthrough-thinking approaches that remove the sources of confusion. One such approach has been developed by author Bryan Bergeron, who has built a hierarchy to clarify the relationship among data, information, metadata, knowledge, and understanding.[3]

Accordingly, Bergeron's hierarchy has been adapted into Figure 1-1. The figure uses the serious medical condition of a child with the flu as an effective way to picture the relationship among data, information, metadata, and knowledge.[4] These four concepts are displayed together to define knowledge in a hierarchical way that builds from data on the bottom up to knowledge at the top.[5] In the end,

Table 1-1   Competitive Advantages Enabled by Best Practices Knowledge

Improvement in	Drives Results in
Employee experience and training	Productivity, cost savings, employee satisfaction, and employee retention
Employee innovations	New products
Brand and reputation	Customer acquisition rate
Customer collaboration	Repeat purchases
Understanding customer needs	Customer retention
New products and services	Profit margins
Market leadership	Market share
Shareholder satisfaction	Corporate valuation

knowledge should be a clear and complete idea about the nature or significance of something and should be able to be acted upon. As displayed in Figure 1-1, knowledge has more meaning when it is in context with data, information, and metadata. The individual measurements of temperature, pulse, and patient age, when combined, form a healthcare diagnosis for treating the patient. Some may contend that this concept of knowledge is roughly equivalent to that of metadata.[6]

Metadata is described as data about information. It is information about the context in which information is used. In the Figure 1-1 example, it is combining the information about the presence of a fever and the presence of tachycardia with the age (if this person were over age 75, and thus elderly, the metadata finding would be "the condition is life threatening.") According to Bergeron, metadata includes high-level categorization of data and information and descriptive summaries.[7] Metadata can take advantage of the capability of computers or artificial intelligence to search for and sort the information. Metadata tags like age, geographical location, and date can help classify the information and make searches easier. Pure knowledge, on the other hand, also contains the human trait of "awareness," which is not always needed when organizations leverage knowledge for competitive advantage.

Knowledge Is the Key Ingredient of Intellectual Capital

In twenty-first-century capitalism, the concept of capital has been expanded to include ephemeral or short-lived *intellectual capital.* As the dominant worldwide

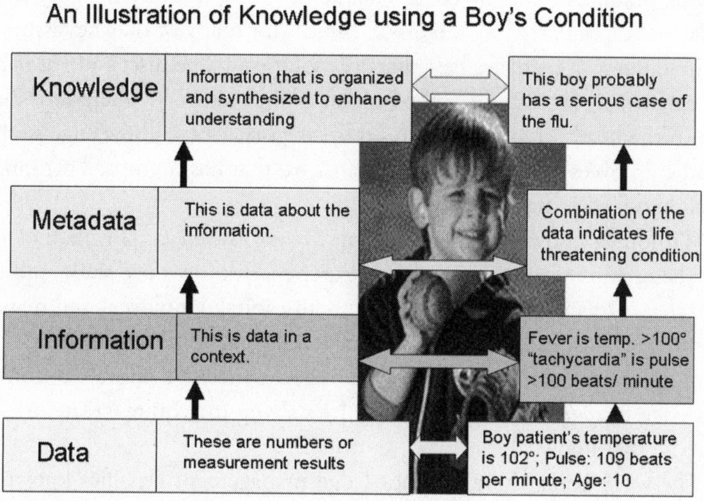

An Illustration of Knowledge using a Boy's Condition

Figure 1-1 Clarifying what constitutes knowledge.

economic system, capitalism relies on the investment of capital (in exchange for profit) into privately owned and operated means of production and distribution. Besides labor, the traditional factors involved in production and distribution are such capital items as equipment, land, and factories. Now, however, there's another form of capital that is growing in importance: intellectual capital. It consists of the three categories displayed in Table 1-2. Visually, this table helps readers picture and understand exactly what the intangible things are that make up intellectual capital. Each and every item will be reviewed at length in Chapter 5.

Unmistakably, knowledge is to intellectual capital what flour is to bread: each is the key ingredient. In fact, the knowledge that underlies the intellectual capital of several renowned enterprises is so crucial that it accounts for most of the value of their brand. Consider Microsoft, with a brand value of $64.1 billion in 2002, placing it second to Coca-Cola's $69.6 billion in *BusinessWeek* magazine's annual survey of the world's top one hundred brands. Yes, Microsoft beat out Apple and IBM as the dominant supplier of the operating systems for IBM-compatible personal computers. And in the 1990s, Microsoft's Windows operating system controlled 90 percent of the market. It is the copyright monopoly that Microsoft has on its software code (i.e., its intellectual property) that underlies the value of its brand and its shareholder value.

Above and beyond managing brand trademarks, there are key issues to manage for all the other categories of intellectual capital. Table 1-2 provides a list of these and, more important, displays in the left column all the categories and types of intellectual capital. Leveraging these categories and types of intellectual capital will be explored in detail in Chapter 5. Until then, think of intellectual capital as knowledge that may be converted into profit.

Best practices—the subject of Chapter 2—exist in every category and type of intellectual capital listed in Table 1-2. In fact, for many of the "key issues to manage" in Table 1-2, there are best practices solutions. The discussion at hand, however, narrows in focus to only the human capital category, where *tacit* knowledge exists in the heads of employees. It's this category, where knowledge is often fragile and employees too unpredictably transient, that has prompted organizations to launch knowledge management initiatives.

Without a knowledge management system, when employees and managers leave the organization, they take their experience, know-how, skills, and creativity with them. Organizations don't own human capital; employees and managers do. To protect against excessive loss and make best practices knowledge a competitive advantage, leading organizations have made concerted efforts to convert tacit knowledge to *codified* or *explicit* forms by striving to acquire, create, use, transfer, and reuse that knowledge.

The work being done on knowledge management classifies knowledge into three categories: it's tacit, implicit, or explicit (codified). *Tacit* knowledge is the

Table 1-2 Issues to Manage for Three Categories of Intellectual Capital

Categories of Intellectual Capital	Key Issues to Manage
Human Capital	(Tacit knowledge in the heads of employees and managers)
▪ Experience	Employee turnover
▪ Know-how	Competencies
▪ Skills	Education and training
▪ Creativity	Empowerment and recognition
Intellectual Assets	(Previously tacit knowledge that has been codified or documented)
▪ Programs	Specifications
▪ Inventions	Creativity
▪ Processes	Process management
▪ Databases	Information technology and database warehousing
▪ Methodologies	Systems and standards management
▪ Documents	Codification techniques
▪ Drawings	Document control
▪ Designs	Design centers and document control
Intellectual Property	(Legally protected subset of intellectual assets)
▪ Patents	Exclusive use and licensing
▪ Copyright	Content convertible to profits
▪ Trademarks	Brands
▪ Trade secrets	Recipes, codes

knowledge that resides inside the heads of individuals; it hasn't been written down or documented for others to learn, understand, and use. Indeed, tacit knowledge is difficult to learn because the people who possess it may have great difficulty instructing others in how to duplicate what they do, like the expert machinist who is so skilled at sheet metal riveting that it's become a subconscious activity. Bryon Bergeron has observed that there are even a number of professionals with tacit knowledge, such as radiologists, pathologists, and chess players, who "use one system and teach another."[8] Tacit knowledge is difficult to explain to others, and thus it's a big concern to people who are trying to improve the transfer of knowledge within their organizations. In simple terms, it's the know-how that has been accumulated over many cycles of learning, often by making mistakes and incorporating lessons learned in the new process.

Implicit knowledge, like tacit knowledge, resides in the heads of individuals. However, the difference is that implicit knowledge can be extracted or pulled out of the minds of the experts and easily and routinely documented as explicit knowledge for others to use. Managers need to specifically support and expect routine capturing of this type of knowledge. An example of implicit knowledge would be sales contact lists, results of sales calls, and sales plans for the next week.

Explicit or *codified* knowledge is the third type of knowledge, and its characteristic is that it's easier to transfer. This type of knowledge is usually documented in a practice, procedure, book, process specification, operating manual, or some other document. Recipes found in cookbooks are good examples of explicit or codified knowledge.

The Knowledge Transfer Race

Sooner or later, those who ponder everything involved with competitive advantages and achieving performance excellence reach a similar conclusion. While some describe it as a knowledge race and others call it a learning race, almost everyone thinks of their organization being in a race. Some picture a path of improvement over rivals. Others see the race as being decided by forward-thinking leadership. Yet others visualize a race toward market leadership, superior profitability, or Six Sigma product reliability. Yet others see the race as involving everything already discussed. The authors of this book see it as the knowledge transfer race because of their belief that the fast and effective transfer of knowledge is the only truly sustainable competitive advantage

As mentioned earlier, the authors' core concepts in this book are framed and presented in the context of winning a metaphoric knowledge transfer race. As shown in Figure 1-2, the race corresponds to the fast-paced global economy, where competitors' drivers are running with leaders using radios to the pit team. The drivers represent the front-line organizations. The drivers are trying to get everything out of their cars, which represent the products and services of the enterprise. The pit crews are the support people. There's no limit on pit stops. They're encouraged in order to create new capabilities or eliminate any deficiencies from keeping the car running fast from one phase of the race to the next. Obstacles exist in every phase, and the team must be flexible and learn fast during the race. The four phases of the race correspond, figuratively, to real phases of the global economy. Earlier, five rules were presented. They are repeated in Figure 1-2.

Those who manage a NASCAR—race team, like those overseeing knowledge transfer and performance excellence strategies, continually compare the performance of their car and their team against that of other race teams. They are constantly searching out and adapting best practices and doing whatever is necessary to keep running fast and staying in competition. Figure 1-2 depicts the race. In the center, a knowledge-enabled culture is needed to enter the race and must be enlarged throughout the race. Think of the white circle surrounding knowledge-based culture as the race car's fuel reservoir, which must be replenished regularly.

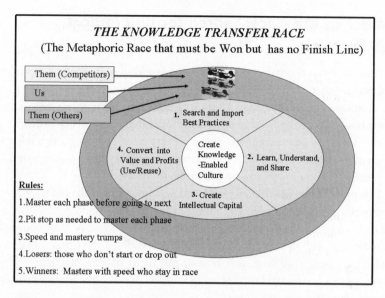

Figure I-2   The knowledge transfer race

Contestants should buckle themselves in for a journey, because this is a race without a finish line. Phase 1 of the race involves reaching out, finding hundreds of gold nuggets outside in the world's stockpile of knowledge, and importing them for reuse to achieve enormous value and profit. But there are many difficult obstacles to overcome. Phase 2 involves fast learning and sharing knowledge internally. To do well in this phase, teams need to take the knowledge acquired through individual experiences and transfer it to everyone on the team. Here again, there are obstacles to overcome. Phase 3 of the race is crucial, as it involves creating intellectual capital or knowledge with value (convertible to profit) as perceived by managers and employees. It will be the subject of Chapter 5.

It's in phase 4 that the big payoffs occur. This is where knowledge is converted to value and profits. This, too, will be discussed in detail in Chapter 5. The obstacles keep coming, and some may require pit stops before the organization can accelerate back to running at full speed. Breakdowns may occur, too. Leadership will be tested regarding its willingness to stay the long-term course. New leaders and CEOs tend to drive their own personal agendas when they come into power, so a pit stop may be warranted to educate them about the value and vital importance of rapid knowledge transfer. However, finishing phase 4 puts the car into phase 1 again because this race has a closed-loop racetrack with no finish line. Unlike the Indianapolis 500, which consists of 200 laps at 2.5 miles per lap, the knowledge transfer race continues indefinitely unless the organization or car breaks down and is forced to retire from the race.

Phase I of the Race: Search for and Import Best Practices

Even though the race involves the transfer of every kind of intellectual capital, one form, best practices, is often featured throughout the book. One reason is that this type of knowledge usually needs to be imported into most enterprises. Second, mining best practices knowledge using benchmarking has immediate benefits and payoff. Third, few enterprises have the capability to do it well. So this is an area that is emphasized in this book. Just the same, the primary focus is always on leveraging intellectual capital to achieve extraordinary results.

Best practices are intellectual assets, and benchmarking is the outreach process for importing such knowledge into an organization. To be sure, forms of human capital do constitute best practices, but because they consist of tacit knowledge, they're troublesome to transfer or import. When codified, best practices become transferable intellectual assets. Of course, the focus of best practices is always knowledge that is essential for transacting business in ways that improve performance and company competitiveness.

Best practices will be the subject of Chapter 2. Until then, readers are asked to think of a best practice as a process input, step, output, or enabling capability that fully satisfies customers, produces superior results in one or more locations, performs as reliably as any alternative elsewhere, and is adaptable by others. As earlier stated, best practices are the Holy Grail of organizations. And like the diagnosis of the boy with the flu, best practices knowledge enables organizations to perform better, faster, and cheaper.

The organizations that are most competitive will import (by way of benchmarking), share, create, use, transfer, repurpose, or reuse knowledge and convert it into value and profit. Best practices, like all knowledge, are more meaningful when they're used in a context with data (measurements and benchmarks), information, and metadata. The best practices for Accounts Payable, for example, are more powerful when they are applied in the context of data, information, metadata, and knowledge.

For Accounts Payable, for example, the data are measurement and benchmark results for percentage of electronic funds transfers (EFT), percentage of invoices processed within objective, EFT invoices paid as a percentage of total paid, cycle time, defects per million transactions, and dollars of unreconciled and unexplained differences greater than 90 days old. The results build up to information, metadata, and knowledge. Like pulse, temperature, and age in the example given earlier, when results and benchmarks are combined to form the context for metadata, the acquisition of best practices is powerful. Once best practices knowledge is created internally or imported through benchmarking, it needs to be used, archived, transferred, repurposed, or adapted as appropriate, and reused as needed. Until actual process changes are made, there is no value added or extra profit generated.

Benchmarking: A Truly Remarkable Worldwide Management Tool

During 2000, Bain & Company, a global management consulting firm one of whose specialties is the study of management tools, published the results of its seventh annual (1999) management tool research. Bain surveyed 475 companies. The purpose of its ongoing research is the identification (for Asia, Europe, North America, South America, and worldwide) of the most used management tools and satisfaction with them. In particular, one graph from that research is enlightening and surprising about the use of benchmarking in North America and the world.

Figure 1-3 shows graphically that in 1999, benchmarking achieved about 80 percent worldwide usage as a management tool. Its usage placed third, after strategic planning and mission and vision statements. However, more data were needed for the period from 2000 to 2002 in order to determine that usage remained high and is increasing, and to make the claim that benchmarking is a prominent management tool in North America, if not the entire world.

Therefore, in response to a request, Bain & Company provided the authors with the summarized results of its 2002 annual research, published during 2003. Respondents from four world regions completed 708 surveys. New tools were added for evaluation in the 2002 survey. With regard to benchmarking, one key table from the research (displayed in Table 1-3) is relevant and eye-opening.

Benchmarking, then, it can be concluded, is one of the two most-used management tools in the world. Because Table 1-3 covers nine years of Bain & Company's

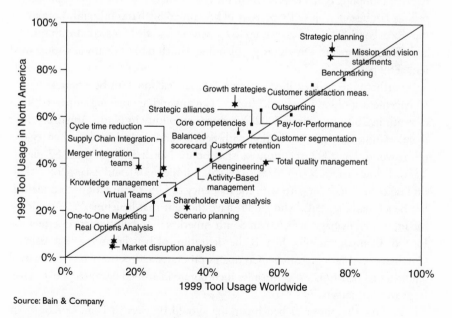

Source: Bain & Company

Figure 1-3 1999 tool usage worldwide.

Table 1-3 Top 10 Management Tools: Shifts in Usage between 1993 and 2002

First Year Management Tool	Capture Usage	2002 Usage	2002 Rank	2000 Rank
Strategic planning	83%	89%	1	1
Benchmarking	70%	84%	2 (Tied)	3
Mission and vision statements	88%	84%	2 (Tied)	2
Customer segmentation*	60%	79%	4	9
Outsourcing*	71%	78%	5	4
Customer surveys	86%	78%	6	5
CRM†	35%	78%	7	15
Corporate codes of ethics‡	78%	78%	8	-
Growth strategies§	55%	76%	9	6
Pay-for-performance	70%	76%	10	8

*Tool added in 1998.
†Tool added in 2000.
‡Tool added in 2002.
§Tool added in 1996.

Source: Bain & Company

research (sampling 6,323 respondents), the results are definitive and incredibly compelling. For instance, since 1993, usage of benchmarking has consistently been in the top three. For 2002, its usage was up to 84 percent and tied for second with mission and vision statements. Only strategic planning, which ranked first, was a more used tool at 89 percent.

Furthermore, as identified in Table 1-4, satisfaction with benchmarking as a management tool has increased.[9] In fact, benchmarking's ranking improved from eleventh in 2000 to sixth in 2002. Yet there's an oddity in North America, where there's significantly less satisfaction with benchmarking than in the other regions of the world. For 2002, the mean satisfaction for North America was 3.87, significantly below that for South America (4.15), Europe (4.02), and Asia (3.92).[10] This finding corresponds, in part, with the tendency of U.S. organizations to underutilize benchmarking. Plus, who would have thought that benchmarking would be the most used management tool in South America?[11] To help readers interpret the Bain & Company results, here is the definition of benchmarking that Bain & Company used in its research: "Compares processes and performance to internal and external benchmarks; companies incorporate identified best practices to meet improvement targets."[12]

By now the power of benchmarking should be clear. It is an extraordinary management tool for importing best practices. So beneficial is its use as a core com-

Table 1-4   Changes in Levels of Satisfaction with Management Tools Between 2000 and 2002

	2000 Mean	2002 Mean	2000 Rank	2002 Rank
Corporate codes of ethics	N/a	4.04	N/a	1
Core competencies	3.83	4.01	18	3
Customer surveys	3.91	3.99	10	5
Benchmarking	3.89	3.96	11	6
Pay-for-performance	4.09	3.90	1	7
Customer relationship management	3.67	3.81	22	13

Source: Bain & Company 2000 & 2002 Management Tool Usage Research.

petency that in the next subsection, the authors provide a self-assessment of an organization's maturity in the use of benchmarking. It provides readers with the macro-capability of scoring how effectively their organization is using the tool.

Benchmarking Self-Assessment Tool

One of this book's secondary themes is that, if it is sufficiently integrated into an organization, best practices benchmarking will dramatically improve that organization's business performance. The authors are convinced of it. Breakthroughs will be achieved that will create direct and speedy paths to excellent performance. Yet, too often, benchmarking has been left out or overlooked. For an organization to remedy this, the first thing that needs to be done is to establish a *baseline* of where the organization is today in the everyday use of benchmarking. This creates a *starting point* from which to build and grow competency in benchmarking.

To discover such a baseline, a self-assessment tool has proven to be successful when it is diagnostic in design and identifies root causes. Also, when such self-assessments identify any gaps (in this case, use gaps), it helps users develop action plans. Such plans are aimed at closing the use gaps that are identified.

Accordingly, Table 1-5 is presented as such a self-assessment tool. It contains five horizontal columns. The first four display four stages of any organization's performance orientation, anchored left by the stage *unconscious incompetence*. This is the earliest stage of the organization's survival, when it is reacting to problems but has only a general improvement orientation. Here, organizations are unconscious of how poorly they are operating. At stage 2, *conscious incompetence*, organizations understand that they have performance deficiencies and are beginning to do something about them. At stage 3, organizations have fully deployed a systematic approach to improvement and refined it to make it better. Such organizations have become very well run and they know it, but they still are driven by humility and are looking to improve more.

Table 1-5 The Four Stages of Importing Best Practices (Using Benchmarking Competency) Self-Assessment

Enter self-scored points using this formula: stage 1 = 0–25, stage 2 = 26–50, stage 3 = 51–75, stage 4 = 76–100.

Area	Stage 1 Unconscious Incompetence	Stage 2 Conscious Incompetence	Stage 3 Conscious Competence	Stage 4 Unconscious Competence	Self-Scored Points Entered
1. Management vision	Survival	Competitive advantage	Growth	Market leadership	+
2. Management focus	Solving problems, "firefighting"	Managing processes and change	Becoming customer-driven	Eliminating defects and errors	+
3. Improvement system	Ad hoc, employee involvement	Process/project management, ISO 9000	Baldrige, European criteria, Shingo, CRM	Lean Six Sigma strategy with culture change	+
4. Measurement system	Investor, SEC, or Wall Street financials	Key performance indicators for strategic plan and tactics	Customer satisfaction; products, services, and complaints	Balanced scorecards with performance targets via benchmarks	+
5. Benchmarks	Financial only	Ad hoc studies for strategic plan KPIs	Systematic to identify areas of strength and weakness	Targeting from gap analysis and to identify best-in-class	+
6. Performance goals	Arbitrary	Clearly identified and set with standards	Defined by best practices benchmarking, benchmarks	Six Sigma excellence at 3.4 defects per million	+
7. Benchmarking	Nonexistent; solutions are internally created	Start of systematic search for best practices	Memberships, databases, and all types employed	Everyday use for decisions, strategy, and improvement	+
8. Best practices	Foreign concept	Start of import and adaptation	Leveraged as organizational learning	Integrated with knowledge management	+
Total score	0 to 200	201 to 400	401 to 600	601 to 800	=

In stage 4, described as *unconscious competence*, organizations have become exceptionally high performing. This stage uses the adjective *unconscious* because employees no longer have to think about what they're doing; it's ingrained and automatic and part of what's expected in the organization's culture. It's like driving a vehicle without thinking about doing it. Everything has become second nature. The needed core competencies have been developed, are ingrained, and are continually reinforced. As a result, people are competent and automatically do what they've been trained and empowered to do.

Likewise, there are four stages of best practices benchmarking. Table 1-5 also contains vertical rows of competencies, including measurements, benchmarks, benchmarking, and best practices. As competency in each of these areas grows, it fuels organizations' progression from stages 1 and 2 to 3 and 4, achieving the ultimate stage of unconscious competence.

The fifth column is for readers to do a self-assessment. Practitioners are encouraged to enter a score for each row. At the end, total the score. If a threshold score of 401 is achieved, it's a good start. It indicates that the minimum level of best practices benchmarking integration has been achieved. However, to be a winner of the knowledge transfer race, organizations need to score between 601 and 800. The lower the score, the more valuable and helpful this book will be.

Of course, the value of this book goes well beyond benchmarking. The authors are of the opinion that a vibrant benchmarking capability is like a tachometer in a race car: it tells the driver (representing the front-line organization) how the engine is running and what capability there is for revving its performance at every phase of the race. Nonetheless, knowledge shared in this and future chapters will educate readers and help them to fully integrate best practices benchmarking into their organization and score between 601 and 800 on Table 1-5, the market leader level or best-in-class benchmark. As will be shown later, this will also help organizations achieve Six Sigma process excellence.

Phase 2 of the Race: Learn, Understand, and Share

After repeated searches to uncover best practices for their clients, in their book, *If Only We Knew What We Know*, Carla O'Dell and Jackson Grayson say that they kept turning up cases of unknown or unshared adaptable knowledge that already existed in the same organizations that were doing the benchmarking.[13] The masterful description they gave these cases was, "The grass was greener in their own backyard. And they didn't even know it."[14] What was paradoxical, too, is that each of the organizations involved was also exceptionally well run.

The truth is that, figuratively, inside these organizations the right hand didn't know what the left hand was doing. This paradox occurs frequently in large, siloed global organizations. Yet the condition also often occurs in small organizations and even family-owned businesses. To understand more about how easily this may occur, just consider the personal communication between husbands and wives. How often is either spouse surprised to learn after the fact that the other has made a commitment involving him or her, but without informing him or her of it? It may be an evening with another couple, babysitting grandchildren, making a donation to help a charity, attending a sporting event, and so on. Almost everyone can come up with three examples of "the left hand not knowing what the right hand is doing" in their personal lives. People try to check with one another before-hand, but circumstances just happen where checking or informing is overlooked, forgotten, neglected, or not possible.

The key business issue is to learn, understand, share, and transfer knowledge. Indeed, the necessity for doing this is what has given birth to the new discipline of knowledge management. And as O'Dell and Grayson state, the discipline seems to be "about how organizations can achieve excellence in their own backyards." That's because, despite all of the hype about the importance of knowledge management, it all seems to come down to the issue of how well the internal transfer of best practices knowledge gets done. Said another way, this is about transferring best practices from one part of an organization to the other parts to either increase revenues or improve speed, productivity, competitiveness, effectiveness, and/or efficiency. O'Dell and Grayson put it like this: "Knowledge management is therefore a conscious strategy of getting the right knowledge to the right people at the right time and helping people share and put information into action in ways that strive to improve organizational performance."[15] When all is said and done, there are many obstacles to overcome at this phase of the knowledge transfer race. At the end of the day, this is about the effective management of knowledge for reuse inside organizations.

The *water-cooler effect* illustrates how information sometimes gets shared or transferred in large organizations with many different locations and unique identi-ties. This age-old visual notion is that more knowledge transfer occurs around the water cooler than anywhere else in the organization. Consequently, those inside the water-cooler group are well informed, while those outside are not nearly as well informed. A study by William O'Connor entitled "Workplace of the New Millennium" concluded that there is a metaphoric *30-foot radius* that limits knowl-edge transfer to a close communication circle.[16] Thus, it is often difficult for employees to stay current on the latest happenings even in their chosen specialty if they are not within the 30-foot radius.

There is a segue between phases 1 and 2 of the knowledge transfer race. One enduring definition of best practices benchmarking that applies to phase 1 of the race is *the process of seeking out and studying the best internal and external practices that produce superior performance.*[17] Once such superior practices have been adapted, phase 2 of the race begins as the enterprise shares, spreads around, and reuses those intellectual assets inside and across its operations at various sites.

However, at every stretch of the way, there are potential roadblocks that can prevent learning or knowledge transfer.

So to keep running at full speed in the knowledge transfer race, in phase 2 there must be deliberate and systematic efforts to remove barriers. Just as weeds thrive in gardens and choke vegetable growth, in knowledge transfer such barriers prey on frailties in human nature and choke learning. Culprits on the list of these barriers include ignorance (not knowing what's not known), insufficient capacity to absorb (not enough time or resources) enough information, preexisting relationships, motivation, and trust. Also blocking progress is the ever-present "If it's not invented here, it can't be any good," or *Not Invented Here (NIH)* syndrome and the "We're different!" attitude. The good news is that the integration of best practices benchmarking better equips organizations to remove most of these barriers to learning. If the organization bases its decisions on facts rather than on intuition, history, or "We've always done it that way," then benchmarking is at the forefront of providing facts. The ways to knock down such barriers will be reviewed in greater detail in future chapters.

Once management meets employees' needs for understanding the competitive dilemma and gets every employee's mindset aligned with the company's needs, the willingness to embrace change becomes a tremendous enabler compared to other organizations that have ignored this step. In fact, the new mindset brings with it a newfound humility, seen everywhere in the organization, a recognition that "we aren't the best" and that "many things could be better." Indeed, this humility is the cornerstone of best practices benchmarking. Organizations must be willing to learn from others.

To illustrate the dramatic possibilities of such learning, consider an example involving General Electric (GE). During 1995, at one of GE's famous executive training classes at its Crotonville management-training center, executives reached the point in the class where they were expected to search for GE's next strategic opportunity. This had become part of the curriculum.

Using an abbreviated benchmarking exercise, students were expected to put together a proposal for what GE should be doing. As it turned out, after hearing one team's proposal, Jack Welch, the CEO at the time, sent that particular team of executive students out to conduct benchmarking of Six Sigma with the leaders at AlliedSignal and Texas Instruments. This team of senior-level GE managers was given the assignment of bringing back and reporting their analysis of the best practices they discovered. Then the team was given a weekend to craft a plan for how GE would adapt those practices to the GE environment. On the following Tuesday, to finish the assignment, the team presented its plan to Welch during a very short review meeting with him. The team was expected to sift through all the benchmarking data and present a very concise overview of the best practices and their possible impact, then present a deployment plan for GE.

From that benchmarking beginning, GE crafted what has become the most successful deployment of Six Sigma in the world today. This GE case also validated the Six Sigma design principles of initiating specific projects around elimination of non-value-adding activities and reducing variation until there is no waste or scrap generated by the system. Consequently, an enormous cost is saved in production and service operations. The often-used statement was born: "A Four Sigma company can't compete with a Six Sigma company" because of the far higher cost burden that the Four Sigma company must carry. Though Six Sigma and how to achieve it will be discussed in Chapters 6 and 8, it's clear that a defect elimination strategy may be improved upon by the kind of teamwork just described in the GE example. Through benchmarking, GE was able to gain management support and mobilize and energize the whole organization rapidly by leveraging the knowledge that AlliedSignal and Texas Instruments had shared. This step involves benchmarking to learn what other organizations around the world are doing and how individual performance results compare. Completing this step begins the knowledge transfer process.

The authors are convinced that the knowledge transfer and learning race is the present-day battlefield for competitive advantage. For years, organizations have thought of gaining competitive advantage in terms of superior products and technology, lower costs, and increased productivity. But that changed during the 1990s. Fast learning was discovered as a differentiating competency. Fast-learning organizations train employees quickly and effectively, adapt rapidly, leverage past successes and failures to continuously improve, and are fast and time-responsive.[18] Peter Senge, in his breakthrough book *The Fifth Discipline: The Art and Practice of the Learning Organization*, hit the nail on the head when he identified learning as the next frontier of competition.

For a company to become a learning organization, it's clear that managers and employees have to be involved and leverage the new knowledge they learn into weekly if not daily advantages or improvements. Intellectual capital has to be managed extraordinarily well. Learning takes place during every part of each day. Soon, speed is the emphasis in first creating new best practices knowledge. Before long, there are deliberate efforts to speed up the import (benchmarking), capture, use, transference, repurposing, and reuse of best practices knowledge. Advances in technology then speed up and equal the organization's ability to absorb and apply it. Suddenly, speed turns everything into a race. Like the virtual reality of a video game car race, the focus is on getting the lead and keeping it. The race is on, and it's those who learn the fastest who take the initial lead.

Phase 3 of the Race: Create Intellectual Capital

As defined and expanded upon in Chapter 5, intellectual capital is knowledge that can be converted into profit. It consists of human capital, or all the knowledge that employees have in their heads. It also consists of what the organization has codified into intellectual assets. And intellectual property is a subset of intellectual assets. How all of this may be leveraged is also a subject of Chapter 5.

Earlier, Table 1-1 displayed how improvements in employee experience and innovations, as examples, drive improvements in productivity and new products. To win the knowledge transfer race, enterprises must pay attention to creating an enterprise knowledge-driven culture that enables employees to create knowledge that is convertible into profits. In Table 1-2, key issues to manage were listed. To create the culture that is needed, such things as employee education and training, empowerment, rewards, competencies, creativity, and so on need to be managed properly.

Next, an *innovation process* may need to be designed and put in place. A pit stop during the knowledge transfer race may be necessary to address this. As an adjunct, a formal patent application policy may be necessary, along with other policies to round out a process for inventorying and managing formal intellectual assets. Such a process and policies can help reduce the effect of employee turnover (including baby boomer retirements) and positively influence employee satisfaction by adding recognition and rewards to prevent a knowledge drain. So a strategy and tactics with timetables may be needed to ensure that human capital (tacit) knowledge is converted into inventoried and managed intellectual assets. Once an effective innovation process has been put into place, contestants may reenter the knowledge transfer race for phase 4.

As an example of creating intellectual capital consider this: during December 2001, U.S. engineer Dean Kamen introduced the Segway Human Transporter, a scooterlike invention that can travel up to 15 mph. It probably won't be long before this invention and others like it transform how short-distance travel takes place while reducing traffic and pollution. Also known as "the people-mover," the two-wheeled, battery-powered Segway is self-balancing and contains aviation-grade gyroscopes. The result of introducing the Segway is still unclear, but the idea and the introduction of this unique approach using Kamen's intellectual asset clearly provided his company a lead in this new market—in fact, created the new market.

Phase 4 of the Race: Convert into Value and Profits

This is the payoff phase of the race. It's where human capital (experience, creativity, and so on), intellectual assets (inventions, processes, programs, methodologies, and so on), and intellectual property (patents, copyrights, and so on) are actually converted into profits. These profits can be in the form of licensing fees, monopoly rights with expirations, new products with revenue streams, increased market share, increased customer satisfaction, or reduced costs through combinations of productivity gains, defect elimination, or cost avoidance.

Actually, converting knowledge into profit is mandatory during this phase. Why? Because intellectual capital is too easily stolen, pirated, or infringed upon. Patents expire, too. It may be only such heavily guarded trade secrets as the recipes for Coca-Cola and Kentucky Fried Chicken that are safe. Even high-tech companies lose their intellectual capital through industrial espionage. And so profits are needed to grow the enterprise and to prevent revenue erosion to pirates and competitors. The Napster case is a prime example. The Napster and similar copyright infringement cases have exposed individuals and some organizations as being guilty of file-swapping copyrighted music, CD-ROM content, DVD films, and knowledge content that has value in an eBay Dutch auction. The Internet, intranets, extranets, and satellites are media that are here to stay, and they need to be factored into business models.

By January 2002, 58.5 percent of the U.S. population (165.14 million people) were using the Internet, and worldwide the number of users reached 544.2 million.[19] Also, software is available and regularly used for every conceivable purpose, including income tax preparation, antivirus protection, language, education, and every kind of game imaginable. These forms of intellectual capital are growing at an exponential rate, and so is their availability on the Internet, legally and illegally. Copyrights and patents are increasingly difficult to enforce. Production of pirated content is a major business in countries like China and Russia.

Knowledge also leaves organizations in several other ways. It leaves when people leave through transfers, retirements, or being hired away by competitors. For one thing, people don't stay employed with the same organization as long as they once did. Also, the demographics indicate that the risk of loss in the near future is higher because of the increase in the retirement-ready age groups (the baby boomers). Furthermore, 24-hour cable and satellite television and other broadband technologies have made more information available and usable, and it can be transmitted instantaneously to anywhere in the world. Speed improvements of a factor greater than 10 times have been achieved in nearly every facet of life.

Despite the aforementioned obstacles, roadblocks, or problems, enterprises must overcome them to keep running in the knowledge transfer race. Speedy knowledge reuse has big paybacks. Several examples will be provided in Chapters 5 and 9.

The Bottom Line for People in Small Organizations

This book pays particular attention in each chapter to the needs of people in small organizations as it delivers answers, insights, best practices, and tools. This is done in two ways. First, at the end of each chapter, there is a section entitled "The Bottom Line for People in Small Organizations." In these sections, the content of each chapter is translated or reinterpreted into suggested actions that are sensible and usable for small businesses. These reinterpretations consider that

1. There are fewer people with far less resources available in small organizations.
2. People tend to be generalists, wearing many hats because full-time specialists (such as "black belts", facilitators, or librarians) are unaffordable.
3. People tend not to have developed broad industry perspectives or to have the time to automatically follow technology trends.
4. The communication and relationships among the small number of employees is all the more crucial to building a culture of creating, sharing, transferring, and reusing knowledge.

So for a small organization to try to deploy certain types of actions that work in large organizations would be like trying to put a round peg in a square hole. It doesn't work.

The second way this book addresses the needs of people in small businesses is through "A Bottom-Line Summary of 55 Tips for People in Small Organizations," which is contained in Chapter 11. Purposely designed as concise knowledge, or gold nuggets of advice based on firsthand experiences, these tips are aimed at letting this book's content be acted upon by small businesses. To illustrate, there are ten tips from this chapter that are carried forward into the Chapter 11 summary of 55 tips. They are numbered 1 through 10 in Chapter 11. In capsule form, they are:

- Assign and rotate the responsibility for figuring out how to adapt the knowledge in this book among people as secondary focal-point roles [or as subject-matter experts (SMEs)] on top of their primary job responsibilities.
- Do not postpone action indefinitely, even though business coming in the door has priority. This would create a "know-do" gap, which will be discussed in Chapter 9 and must be avoided.
- Because a few key people have tacit critical knowledge in their heads that is not backed up, owners need to be proactive in vesting these people so that key skills, experience, know-how, and creativity are not lost.
- Use to advantage the ability to change on a dime when decisions justify it.
- Develop a plan to capture (codify) the essential knowledge of the business.
- Document the deliverables expected from employees, including the monthly schedules of knowledge capture and transfer.
- Deploy a systematic approach to rapid improvement, a balanced scorecard that includes knowledge transfer, sharing, and reuse, and use best practices benchmarking to create an agenda for future improvement.
- Keep the start-up mentality, so that speed of learning is emphasized.
- Concentrate knowledge use and reuse on innovating solutions for customers.
- Emphasize an "I can learn from anyone" attitude, so that people will have humility and the desire to learn.

Every one of the competitive advantages listed in Table 1-1 (improved productivity, products, savings, customer acquisition, market share, and so on) applies to small organizations. Small organizations must also deliberately import, create, share, use, and reuse best practices knowledge. The approach, however, must be scaled down to what's affordable and can be done in stages. Nonetheless, because of small companies' size, scant cross-training resources, and having key knowledge in the minds of a few crucial people, the human capital component of intellectual capital requires continual senior management attention.

Without a knowledge management system, there are steps that should be taken to protect against losing the knowledge, competencies, and skills if and when employees and managers leave the small organization. First, people who individually or in combination have tacit knowledge should be encouraged to identify and codify what is essential knowledge. In fact, an ongoing plan is needed for continually converting tacit knowledge into an explicit or codified form. Second, plain and simple job descriptions are needed, along with documented monthly schedules of knowledge capture. Documenting the deliverables expected for each employee position is recommended. Third, use of ISO 9000, an international quality standard that will be discussed in Chapter 6, is also recommended. Fourth, process steps should be documented on a "living document map" to help small companies align inputs, processing steps, and outputs with customer specifications and requirements [using inputs–process steps–outputs (IPO) charts, for example] for every key product or deliverable. These simple documents will go a long way to reduce the loss of knowledge as employee losses occur. To offset losses of knowledge, it is all the more important that small organizations make a commitment to importing best practices using simple and cost-effective forms of benchmarking.

With two minor changes, the self-assessment in Table 1-5 applies equally to small organizations. First, for area 2, "management focus," at stage 3, instead of "Baldrige, European criteria, Shingo, CRM," substitute "A systematic and fully deployed approach to improvement." Second, area 6, "performance goals," at stage 3, instead of "Defined by best practices benchmarking, benchmarks" substitute "Focused on closing key performance gaps." Otherwise, the scoring ranges remain the same. With these changes, the assessment will equally benefit those who work in small and large organizations.

Small organizations are, like it or not, in a knowledge transfer race along with large organizations. Speed of learning is a critical issue. Everyone is in a learning race. For smaller organizations, the first part of the race is for survival, and the later part is for growth. Fortunately, the start-up mentality of small organizations helps them to do more with less. By focusing on best practices that help them leverage market niches, people in small organizations can use their greater agility to grow horizontally as well as vertically.

It is the authors' opinion that it is crucial for small organizations to be able to capture, create, share, transfer, and reuse their organization's own best practices as they are innovating and launching products and services. With the anticipated future speed of innovation, the movement of people between organizations, and the knowledge of the best practices of the future to be gained, best practices benchmarking will need to be integrated into the few "jack of many trades" jobs that exist. Each person who is multitasking jobs must always carry with him or her the mentality of "How do we compare?" and "Who's the best at doing this today?" That way, with humility and the desire to learn, needed learning will occur every day, whether the best practice started out in sales, customer relationship management, new product development, or collecting on a receivable due.

One illustration of this principle is to highlight the current success of Google and its extremely good search engine capability on the Internet. Google has become the search engine benchmark, and other search engines are measured against Google's look, feel, user-friendliness, attractive colors, and performance. This comparison and expectation applies regardless of one's experience, market, or focus. Google is now the standard that all search engines are measured against, whether it's an Internet, an intranet, or an extranet application. Internal applications that the final customers never see are compared to Google because everyone's expectations have been elevated. Google, which is a relatively small organization, has become the standard for small and large organizations that operate in the same markets as Google and with similar technologies.

Actually, small organizations have a tremendous advantage, since they can change on a dime if they need to. There are not thousands of people at 50 or more sites to coordinate and communicate with to get their minds in the game. However, the critical few must be on the same page. The entrepreneur (or owner/leader) must be plugged into the marketplace, the shareholders' wishes, and the employees' expectations while keeping his or her eye on the ball to beat the competition.

The key is to manage growth while not losing the small-company entrepreneurial viewpoint and an aggressive "I can learn from anyone" mindset. As the organization grows, there will be those who will think that benchmarking is someone else's job because it's not in their job description. For a business to survive and thrive in today's world, benchmarking must actually be everyone's primary job! Part of this mindset is for employees to ask themselves the questions, "How do I compare?" and "Who is the best at what I do?" As time goes on, everyone can also discuss the answer to the forward-looking question, "What are we going to do about it?"

What's Ahead in Future Chapters

Following is a synopsis of each of the ten chapters that follow and how the content of each relates to the metaphoric knowledge transfer race. Readers are encouraged to continually reference back to Figure 1-2, which depicts the race.

Chapter 2: Defining, Searching for and Importing Best Practices: Mastering Phase 1 of the Knowledge Transfer Race

Definitions and distinctions for best practices, benchmarking, and knowledge management are provided. This book's authors contend that there are two types of "practices" and they will be presented. Type 1 *process practices* and type 2 *enabling capability practices*. A best practice will be defined as one that fully satisfies customers, produces superior results in one operation, performs as reliably as any alternative, and can be adapted elsewhere. The best practice criteria used by the QuEST Forum is reviewed, followed by a discussion of how best practices are misunderstood and misused. Learning and insights from Raytheon's advanced experiences, knowledge management and benchmarking will be shared. The authors put forth a straightforward and simple third generation benchmarking process that contains fourteen process steps within the five horizontal phases of *Initiate, Plan, Import, Formulate,* and *Act.* A strategic Raytheon case study involving the creation of *Raytheon Six Sigma* is presented to illustrate the benchmarking process along with the use of the Benchmarking Code of Conduct. Finally, there is a bottom-line discussion for small organizations. The knowledge in this chapter helps contestants in phase 1 of the knowledge transfer race.

Chapter 3: Learning, Understanding, and Sharing: Mastering Phase 2 of the Knowledge Transfer Race

The "I can learn from everyone" attitude and what's involved in becoming a learning organization, along with five knowledge transfer strategies, are featured subjects. The discussion identifies "learning" as the new frontier of competition and clarifies why the characteristics and advantages of being a learning organization are so compelling. Toyota's approach to learning is highlighted. Transformational learning is illustrated. Five types of knowledge transfer identified in author Nancy Dixon's research are presented with examples and use of them advocated. Examples of learning strategies and strategies from the American Productivity and Quality Center, Texas Instruments, and the Raytheon Company for recognizing and rewarding sharing and reusing knowledge are provided. Bottom line tips for small companies are provided that focus on doing more with less. The material presented in this chapter will help contestants excel in phase 2 of the knowledge transfer race.

Chapter 4: A Process Framework for Classifying Best Practices and Intellectual Capital: Building a Culture for Winning the Knowledge Transfer Race

The importance of processes and the concept of a process-centered and process-managed organization are presented, along with the APQC Process Classification Framework (PCF) created and updated through a team led by the American Productivity and Quality Center. Processes are shown to be the source of value creation and the mechanisms that convert ideas and innovation into products and services. The PCF or taxonomy system is a sort of Dewey Decimal System for process, an architecture for classifying measures, benchmarks, best practices, and any other intellectual capital. The product of an extraordinary worldwide collaboration, the PCF has proven to be an extremely valuable tool that is being continually refined and is free for the asking. Four considerations are also provided to make processes *explicit* so they may be managed and improved. Advice is simplified for small organizations. The content in this chapter helps enterprises build a knowledge-enabled culture.

Chapter 5: Leveraging Intellectual Capital into Competitive Advantages: Mastering Phase 3 of the Knowledge Transfer Race

The three types of intellectual capital (human capital, intellectual assets, and intellectual property) are presented and discussed in terms of how they are created and converted into value and profit. The authors contend that before long CEOs of prominent global enterprises will be using their annual reports to describe how they are managing their organizations' *intellectual capital* to accomplish more goals. The focus is on knowledge reuse to reap big paybacks. Reuse case studies involving Buckman Labs and Texas Instruments are provided. Insights are provided, too, about managing knowledge. The criteria and recipients of the Most Admired Knowledge Enterprise (MAKE) Awards are provided as illustrations of how to manage and leverage intellectual capital knowledge into competitive advantage. The importance of growing and nurturing human capital is illustrated. Tips are provided to people in small organizations. The content in this chapter is essential for competitors during phases 3 and 4 of the knowledge transfer race.

Chapter 6: Knowledge That Propels Improvement: The Baldrige Award Criteria, European Quality Award, Shingo Prize, ISO 9000, Six Sigma, and Lean Six Sigma

These are business excellence models that are valuable intellectual assets and examples of knowledge reuse insofar as they've been designed to transfer knowledge to those who want the help. This is a large and growing reservoir of proven, valuable and profitable best practice business knowledge and much of it is free for the asking to transfer and reuse. The characteristics of each are reviewed followed by a discussion about their purpose. Tips for scaling-down approaches are provided for small organizations. Contestants will profit from one or more of these models, and their use will pay dividends in phase 4 and catapult them into the lead of the knowledge transfer race.

Chapter 7: Worldwide Approaches to Leveraging Knowledge

This chapter surveys and shares noteworthy developments, examples, and trends for managing knowledge in Asia, Japan, Europe, and North America. The establishment of global benchmarking networks, the leveraging of knowledge by the Japanese automobile industry, international MAKE award recipients, and learning from the specific cases of Samsung, Siemens, and Sony are discussed. The content is targeted to an international audience. Still, attention is paid to people in small organizations through tips for leveraging the MAKE award criteria and international recipient experiences, communicating in several languages, and meeting the ISO 9000 quality standards. This content is helpful for performing in all four phases of the knowledge transfer race.

Chapter 8: Integrating and Leveraging Best Practices Knowledge into Six Sigma Strategies: Mastering Phase 4 of the Knowledge Transfer Race

The approaches of Raytheon, Bank of America, and others will be reviewed, focusing particularly on how they have incorporated benchmarking and intellectual capital knowledge into their system. A deeper definition and description of Six Sigma is provided. What makes Raytheon's approach so unique is discussed along with descriptions of how they use a benchmarking maturity matrix and a blitz mindset. Five key lessons are provided, one that illustrates the Bank of America approach. Pitfalls to avoid are provided along with key success factors for the long haul. An authors' process to achieve Six Sigma excellence is presented. Raytheon's experiencewill be featured, including a list of dos, don'ts, and lessons learned. People in small organizations are remembered, too. Tips are provided, one of which is to keep it simple for most small organizations, so that projects undertaken should recover 100 percent of their investment within six months.

Chapter 9: Converting Knowledge into Value and Profit: Part 2 of Mastering the Innovation and Change Involved in the Payoff Phase 4 of the Knowledge Transfer Race

The focus of this chapter is on what it means to convert knowledge into customer value and profit. It is shown how the reuse or re-purposing of knowledge that already exists has phenomenal payback possibilities. An *enterprise innovation pipeline* is advocated for obtaining a groundswell of ideas from the entire employee base for reusing proven knowledge in new and different contexts. Innovation reuse is the name of the game, a powerful lever for transforming intellectual capital. The authors provide a starting list of reuse ideas that illustrate reuse concepts in eleven of *Business Week's* twenty-three Best Products for 2004. Examples are provided from the Public Service Electric and Gas Corporation for reusing knowledge to create profits and from the Verizon Corporation for reducing time for product development. Customer Relationship Management (CRM) will be shown to reuse knowledge to broaden and deepen business with customers. Eight success factors are provided for avoiding a know-do gap. Knowledge reuse is also shown to identify best practices for managing change and the links to measurements and benchmarks to populate Balanced Scorecards. The content in this chapter is robust and helps contestants master phase 4 and become leaders of the knowledge transfer race.

Chapter 10: New Twenty-First-Century Tools, Techniques, and Methods for Importing and Leveraging Intellectual Capital, including Benchmarking

This is a review of new and promising developments involving knowledge that, if properly managed, will have positive impacts on strategic and tactical decision making, benchmarking, and the four phases of the knowledge transfer race. Pertinent concepts, networks, memberships, forums, or conferences are appraised including Communities of Practice (CoP), quick-turnaround benchmarking, fast-track searches, the Global Benchmarking Council, the KNOW Network, Quality Excellent Suppliers of Telecom (QuEST) Forum, the American Productivity and Quality Center (APQC) International Benchmarking Clearinghouse, *Industry Week* magazine's Best Plants Conference, and the available databases. Based on the firsthand experience of Raytheon, eight rules are provided for when and how to start a CoP. Beginning with the adoption of quick turnaround benchmarking, four tips are provided to people in small organizations. The good news is all the tools for large organizations can also benefit people in small organizations.

Chapter 11: The Conclusion: a Summary of 33 Key Points and Calls to Action, Along with 55 Tips for People in Small Organizations

The conclusion is that rapid knowledge transfer and reuse is a sustainable competitive advantage. This closing chapter reviews *why* and then summarizes 33 key points that call for many actions. The key is in the process to rapidly create, learn, share, transfer, use, and reuse intellectual capital in ways that produce more and better customer value and profitability than the competition. Finally, the authors deliver on their promise to pay particular attention to the needs of people in small organizations. 55 valuable tips are provided for people in small organizations to act on to gain competitive advantages considering they have fewer people and must do more with less. And so the knowledge transfer race is on, and the fundamental question is, what should the twenty-first century organization do about it? The answer is in the form of the 33 key points and 55 tips provided.

Endnotes

1. Shell, G. Richard Shell, *Make the Rules or Your Rivals Will,* (New York: Crown Business, New York, 2004), p. 152.
2. Ibid., p. 152.
3. Bryan Bergeron, Bryan, *Essentials of Knowledge Management,* (Hoboken, N.J.: John Wiley & Sons, Hoboken, NJ, 2003), p. 10.
4. Ibid., pp. 10–13.
5. Ibid., pp. 10–13. Bergeron actually uses five levels in his hierarchy, building up to Iinstrumental Uunderstanding, which has been omitted to simply the figure.
6. Ibid., p. 13.
7. Ibid., p. 10.
8. Ibid., p. 18.
9. "Management Tools and Trends 2003," slide presentation of Bain & Company dated June 2003, slide 28;, obtained from Dan Pinkney of Bain & and Company with permission for use on June 26, 2003.
10. Ibid., slide 33.
11. Ibid., slide 33.
12. Ibid., slide 36.
13. Carla O'Dell, and Carla, Grayson, C. Jackson, Grayson, Jr., *If Only We Knew What We Know,* (New York: The Free Press, New York, NY, 1998), p. x.
14. Ibid., p. x.
15. Ibid., p. 6.
16. William O'Connor, William, "Workplace of the New Millennium," White Paper, July 1, 1999., CEO G TECH.

17. Bogan, Christopher E., Bogan and English, Michael J. English, *Benchmarking for Best Practices: Winning through Innovative Adaptation*, (New York: McGraw-Hill, New York, NY, 1994), p. 5.
18. Senge, Peter M Senge, The Fifth Discipline: The Art and & Practice of The Learning Organization, (New York: Currency Doubleday, New York, 1990), pp. 139–233.
19. *Time Almanac 2003*, (Needham, Mass.: Time, Inc., 2003), ISBN 1-929049-87-0, p. 570.

Chapter 2

Defining, Searching for, and Importing Best Practices: Mastering Phase 1 of the Knowledge Transfer Race

Overview of Best Practices

One of the pioneers of organizational benchmarking, Bob Camp, originated the long-standing definition for it as *the search for industry best practices that lead to superior performance*.[1] The trouble, then and since, is that most people don't exactly understand what constitutes a *best practice*. So while a number of similar definitions for benchmarking have been floated and have stuck, that's not true for best practices. It's an elusive concept.

First, the word *best* is ambiguous. This adjective conjures up a range of images that include "most advantageous, largest, superior, winner, most, and get the better of." Then there's the noun, which means "anything that is the best," such as the greatest. Moreover, there's the adverb superlative of *well*, meaning "most" or "in the most excellent way." Thus, the authors will first define the word *practices*. Afterward, a complete and concise definition will be provided for *best practices*.

At first glance, the word *practice* seems synonymous with the words *process*, *method*, and *procedure*. Bob Camp didn't define *practices*, but he did contend that there are three major components of them: process practices, business practices, and operational structure.[2] Camp was savvy enough to have identified the importance of *enablers* early on, but he argued that they are not practices. Michael Spendolini, in his book on benchmarking, provided an excellent definition for benchmarking, but, like others in the benchmarking literature, he didn't define *practice* or *best practices*.[3]

The current authors, having pondered and debated this, are of the opinion that *practice*, in the context of performance improvement, is a noun and means "the established method of conducting and carrying on business." The word, however, is

33

usually associated with the exercise of a profession, especially law or medicine.[4] For example, lawyers have a law practice and doctors have a medical practice. Nonetheless, as displayed in Table 2-1, the authors contend that there are two types of practices: process practices and enabling capability practices.

Table 2-1 Two Types of Business Practices for any Enterprise

Process Practices (Type 1)	Enabling Capability–Practices (Type 2)
INPUTS	LEADERSHIP: creation and alignment of
▪ Received without defects	▪ Vision and values
▪ On time, every time	▪ Direction, short and long term
▪ Supplier performance managed	▪ Expectation of performance
CORE PROCESSES: Continually improved with value creation and removal of nonvalue steps:	▪ Process management system
	▪ Governance of organization
	▪ Empowerment and innovation
1. Develop vision and strategy	▪ Relationships with stakeholders
2. Design and develop products and services	▪ Ethical behavior and social responsibilities
3. Market and sell products and services	▪ Competencies for root cause analysis
4. Deliver products and services	▪ Education, learning, and training strategy
5. Manage customer service	▪ Resource allocation
SUPPORT PROCESSES: Continually improved with value added and nonvalue removed:	MEASUREMENT AND ANALYSIS
	▪ Management by fact
6. Develop and manage human capital	▪ Key performance indications (KPIs)
7. Manage information technology	▪ Customer relationship and satisfaction systems
8. Manage financial resources	▪ Benchmarks for KPIs
9. Acquire, construct, and manage property	STRATEGIC PLAN AND OBJECTIVES
10. Manage environmental health and safety	▪ Strategy developed with aligned action plans
11. Manage external relationships	▪ Targets established from KPIs/benchmarks
12. Manage knowledge, improvement and change	▪ Resources for current year aligned with plan
OUTPUTS	▪ Communications plans in place
Defect free to fully meet customer requirements	RAPID KNOWLEDGE TRANSFER
▪ Products	▪ Create, import, manage, and reuse intellectual capital

Table 2-1   Two Types of Business Practices for any Enterprise (*continued*)

Process Practices (Type 1)	Enabling Capability–Practices (Type 2)
OUTPUTS Defect free to fully meet customer requirements (Cont.) • Services • Documentation • Delivery on time, every time • Process management principles • Process managed to standards • Customer expectations understood by everyone • Customer requirements/expectations met Cycles of continuous improvement and alignment	• Identify, import, and transfer best practices • Ensure integrity, timeliness, reliability, security, accuracy, and so on of information POLICIES: aligned for • Cross-functional teams • Rewards and recognition

Process practices, type 1, include five core and seven support processes that, together, capture the essence of a process-centered or process-managed organization. These processes will be the subjects of Chapter 4, where they're presented as an APQC sponsored Process Classification Framework (PCF) or taxonomy for classifying, archiving, and accessing measurements, benchmarks, and best practices. The PCF that will be presented may be adapted to become the foundation of a knowledge management system. The authors subscribe to the view that what gets done and creates value in any organization is derived from its processes. Thus, to be successful, sooner or later, every organization must become process-centered and managed to achieve excellence in its core processes.

Type 2 practices are enabling capability practices. Type 2 includes everything of importance outside process practices, such as the enabling capability practices of visionary leaders, the values of customer-driven excellence, valuing employees and partners, data-driven management by fact, creating value through process management, intellectual capital, organizational and individual learning, managing innovation and knowledge, strategy, and policies. This second type of practice involves key capabilities or key activities that must be performed to support the process practices and make them viable. Enabling processes include such practices as aligning cross-functional teams, rewards and recognition, and so on. Thus, this type of practice includes what Camp called business practices which he excluded from his definition of practices and called enablers.[5]

Camp described these as enablers that make a difference but are not practices. However, the current authors disagree and contend that after the year 2000, enablers such as capabilities, policies, and strategies are enabling practices that can be compared to similar practices at other organizations to identify which are better or superior, similar, or inferior. Thus, such enablers as the communication of clear objectives; providing good feedback; mentoring programs; providing Six Sigma training and problem-solving skills to employees; and deployment of a teamwork strategy, a Lean Enterprise strategy or a Total Quality strategy—are type 2 practices.

These Type 2 kinds of practices apply across core and support processes and can involve methods for allocating resources to processes. Some could also be described as business policies, since they involve employment practices, skill levels, training, and similar activities. These enabling practices are also key to the overall effectiveness of the organization and enable the focus to be on the customer in a more effective manner. Having defined practices, it's time to return to the discussion of best practices.

Best Practices: What Are They?

The phrase *best practices* is even used in a passage from Webster's Dictionary. It reads, "The dictionary conforms to the *best practices* of those dictionaries . . . that do not puristically rule factual information out of lexicography, but treat word-information and thing-information as equally valid and equally deserving of space in a useful reference work." The phrase *best practices*, like *generally accepted accounting standards* for CPAs, has become a common way to describe the best ways of doing things. A better definition will create better understanding. Now that the word *practice* is better understood, a brief discussion of the word *best* is necessary before a complete definition of *best practices* can be reached.

O'Dell and Grayson observed that *best* is a moving target and is situation-specific; they preferred terms like *better, exemplary*, or *successful*.[6] They agree with critics who argue "that no one knows what's 'best,' and what's optimum in one place may not be even good for another."[7] Nonetheless, they continue to use the term *best practices* because "it has such common usage and because we do always want to strive for the best." Their definition, which is equivalent to that of the American Productivity and Quality Center, is "those practices that have produced outstanding results in another situation and that could be adapted for our situation."[8]

The closest Camp came to defining *best practices* was "the methods used in work processes whose outputs 'best' meet customer requirements."[9] But there's no certain way to tell which of several good practices is the best at satisfying customers, since every situation is unique. Still, everyone would agree that the first test of a practice to be considered "best" is that it must fully satisfy customers. Camp also added the following when trying to describe a best practice: "This probably means those methods that improve a process step by 10 to 15 percent or more." In his original work, Camp makes repeated references to industry best practices but stops short of defining what they are. He makes mention of *dantotsu*, the Japanese term that approximates striving to be the *best of the best*—in practice, best of class, or best of breed.[10] But instead of worrying about which practices are best, Camp focused on classes or *breeds* of performance benchmark comparisons.

Bogan and English later addressed this as a range of benchmarks, as shown in Table 2-2.[11] This, however, has confused people about best practices. Benchmarks are performance measurements that are used to identify gaps and help set target performance goals. Benchmarks do identify those organizations that achieve superior results for the processes or enabling capabilities being looked at. However, that discussion shifts the subject to best-in-class comparisons instead keeping the focus on best practices, which is one reason why people get confused and end up misunderstanding what best practices are.

Despite efforts to replace *best* with another, less almighty adjective, *best practices* is standard industry terminology, but with relaxed definitions. A few companies have gone to terms like *better practices*, *good practices*, or *most accepted practices* to avoid the notoriety of being called *best*. However, those efforts are usually temporary and counterproductive. The term *best practices* is so commonly used that it is the universal standard. Chevron uses four levels of best practices (good idea, good practice, local best practice, and industry best practice) and defines it as, "any practice, knowledge, know-how, or experience that has proven to be valuable or effective within one organization that may have applicability to other organizations."[12]

Chevron's definition requires only that a practice be proven valuable and have applicability to others. By including the word *knowledge* in its definition and having four levels of it, Chevron introduces the concept of knowledge management. Such knowledge needs to be transferred and shared among employees and teams. This is discussed in Chapter 3.

Table 2-2 Levels of Benchmark Comparisons

Class/Breed	Benchmark Level	Type of Comparison	Focus
Best-of-best	7	Process, outputs	Strategic
Best-in-country	6	Process, outputs	Strategic
Best-in-industry	5	Competitors	Advantage
Industry norm	4	Industry	Average
Industry standard	3	Industry	Minimum
Best-in-company	2	Internal	Improvement
Baseline	1	Internal	Starting point

Another successful approach is that of Raytheon, and it, similarly, involves the use of four levels of best practices. The authors have had firsthand experience debating about what best practices are and aren't while engaged with teams doing benchmarking at Verizon (formerly GTE) Directories, Texas Instruments, and Raytheon. In the case of Raytheon, its Benchmarking Core Team—of which Bill Baker was the founding member—decided, after considerable discussion and debate, to have four levels of best practices. First, the Raytheon team defined a best practice as a process, methodology, or technique "that works best for me in my situation," recognizing the fact that all customer situations may be different.

In the end, while the Raytheon team recognized that use of the term *best* does cause some confusion, they accepted it because it's such a universally used concept. However, several key points surfaced during their discussions. First, it's unlikely that there will ever be conclusive proof that there is only one best way or best method of doing things. Second, being a best practice is a temporary condition. Today's best practices replaced those of the past and will be replaced by those of the future. So the trade-off decided on by the Raytheon professionals, which is still practiced to this day, was to have four levels of best practices based on the *quality* of any given best practice.

Raytheon has four levels, with Level Four being the *highest quality* of a best practice. A Level One best practice is any *initial* best practice; it could be an idea that had just recently been developed but was not fully deployed. A Level Two best practice is one that has been deployed in one instance and has successfully improved output and key performance indicator results. A Level Three best practice is one that has been deployed across more than one location and has had good-to-excellent results in relevant key performance indicators. Finally, a Level Four best practice is one that has been recognized by an outside agency and has been identified externally as best-in-class. Using these four levels, Raytheon has been successful at identifying best practices and capturing them in its database, and part of the reason is that the *intimidation facto*r (the threshold to get over to qualify as a best practice) has been greatly reduced. Finally, Raytheon conducts an annual review of the best practices it's captured in its best practices repository to validate that those practices are up-to-date and still relevant.

It's time, finally, to agree on what best practice means. Earlier, one criterion identified was that such practices should fully satisfy customers. In addition, the following phrase captures the essence of the term *best*: "As reliably as anyone can presently do." Also, earlier we defined *practices*. Therefore, displayed in Table 2-3 is the working definition for *best practices* that the authors will use throughout the remainder of this book.

Misunderstandings and Misuses

Three years into implementing Six Sigma (6σ), GE's CEO, Jack Welch, realized that he had misunderstood what it was about. This realization came in 1998 when

Table 2-3   Best Practices Defined

Best	It fully satisfies customers, produces superior results in at least one operation, and performs as reliably as any alternative elsewhere.
Practice	Type 1 process practice and/or type 2 enabling capability practice
Best practice	A process input, step, output, or enabling capability that fully satisfies customers, produces superior results in at least one operation, performs as reliably as any alternative elsewhere, and is adaptable by others.
Concise definition	A practice that fully satisfies customers, produces superior results in one operation, performs as reliably as any alternative, and can be adapted elsewhere.

his staff, in a conversation with him about variation, offered a suggestion that GE make *span* a key performance indicator. *Span* measures the variance from the exact date when customers want delivery. Getting span to zero means that customers always get delivery when they want it.[13] Welch got it. He realized that span was what GE needed to focus on. It took the complexity out of 6σ, got more employees' minds into the game, and enabled GE to take 6σ project team results to all-time highs.

Despite the success of going from three thousand 6σ projects in 1996 to six thousand in 1997 and reaching $320 million in gains, after the span breakthrough, GE elevated the impact of 6σ, and customers noticed. GE reduced span in its plastics operation from 50 days to five, in aircraft engines from 80 days to five, and in mortgaging from 54 days to one.[14] GE also increased its operating margin from 14.8 percent in 1996 to 18.9 percent in 2000 and grew 6σ savings to $1.5 billion in 1999.[15] Misinterpretations such as Welch's also can occur with best practices.

One of the biggest misunderstandings about best practices is that, like Henry Ford's design of a moving assembly line in 1913, they must be extraordinary and unequaled anywhere in the world. This is a mistake because it aims expectations so high that they become intimidating, making the standard for what can be called a best practice almost unattainable. The fact is, there are literally thousands of things to learn about and adapt from the world's stockpile of knowledge. Such unrealistically high expectations also inhibit people from making suggestions because they hesitate to claim that their practice is one of the world's best. It is not a bad thing to be the best on the third floor or the best at the Atlanta plant site.

Instead, the authors contend that it's better to define, as done earlier, *best practices* as "those that fully satisfy customers, produce superior results in one operation, perform as reliably as any alternative, and can be adapted elsewhere." If another practice is superior to what's being done today and its adaptation adds enough value, the process owner should be obliged to implement it. The knowledge transfer race is a never-ending race, so the best on the third floor needs to be looking at the best on the other floors in order to be a leader in the race. Besides, very few best practices are 100 percent transferable and adaptable because of any number of differences (especially culture) between the two organizations. In short, a practice doesn't have to be the best in the world to be a best practice.

Another misconception is that a best practice is forever. Although this is sometimes difficult to accept, change is inevitable. Major advances in technology, business-cycle fluctuations, fierce competitor initiatives, changing governmental laws and regulations, mergers, shifts in customer expectations, and supplier-policy changes are bombarding the marketplace and altering the face of competition at an ever-increasing rate. Likewise, best practices have a life cycle. The need to navigate the turbulent and dangerous river of white-water change makes benchmarking a valuable management tool; it provides access and intelligence concerning what's going on elsewhere. In fact, such intelligence often shows pathways that lead to Six Sigma excellence. The point is that today's best practices replaced those of the past and will be outdated by those of the future. A benchmarking mindset anticipates and prepares people for the future by continually recycling three questions through everyone's mind: "How do we compare?" "Who's doing this the best now?" and "If it's not us, what are we doing about it?"

A common misuse of benchmarking is for managers to bring back to their organization a best practice to implement without first having done a reality check and getting buy-in from those who will have to implement the change. In such cases, the team that is given responsibility for the implementation lacks the first-hand experience of actually seeing the practice in operation. The managers also haven't validated whether that adaptation of the practice is possible and what the investment is in which enablers will be required. Without doubt, the firsthand experience of taking part in a benchmarking site visit is eye-opening. Seeing really is believing, and it creates buy-in, too. It creates an attitude of, "If they can, we can, too!" and helps eliminate excuses. Table 2-4 displays some other common misunderstandings and misuses of best practices benchmarking. Some are about best practices, and others are about benchmarks and benchmarking.

Best Practices Criteria Used by the QuEST Forum

During 1998, the QuEST Forum (Quality Excellent Suppliers of Telecommunications) was founded. Its mission is to create a telecommunications industry-leading quality system with standardized benchmarkable performance measurements and to share best practices through industry collaboration.[16] Its membership list looks like a Who's Who in telecommunications. As of June 2005, it consists of 25 of the world's best-known and largest providers, including Belgacom, Bell Canada, BellSouth, British Telecom, China Mobile Communications, Deutsche

Table 2-4   Best Practices Benchmarking Misconceptions

Misunderstanding/Misuse	Clarification
Benchmarking is a mature tool that is diminishing in use.	Untrue; benchmarking is now the second most used management tool in the world.
Best practices are just what somebody thinks are good.	Untrue; see Table 2-3 for the rigorous definition used in this book.
Benchmarking projects take too long (two to six months).	This used to be true, but not any more; now there are databases, memberships, and fast solutions.
Best-in-class means being superior in every process.	Not so; it means being superior in one or more but not all processes.
The "Not Invented Here" syndrome no longer lives.	Untrue; it lives, but benchmarking neutralizes it with a "we can learn from anyone" attitude.
People doing benchmarking need only common sense.	Generally yes, but they also need to follow a code of ethical conduct and be legal and rigorous. It's work to do it well.
Benchmarking doesn't apply to white-collar functions.	Benchmarking applies to any function, process, product, service, and so on.
Benchmarks are only mechanisms for making budget cuts or downsizing.	This happens, but benchmarks primarily identify positive and negative gaps to enable targeting of goals and best practices to lead the way to achievement.
Benchmarks and benchmarking are the same things.	The first are gap metrics, and the second, the ongoing search for best practices.

Telekom AG, France Telecom, Korea Telecom, Nippon Telegraph and Telephone, SBC Communications, Shanghai Mobile, Sprint, Telstra, Verizon Communications, and Zhejiang Mobile Communications. Also, over 60 other members are suppliers, including 3M, Alcatel, Cisco Systems, Corning Cable Systems, Fujitsu, Intel, Lucent Technologies, Motorola, Nokia, Nortel Networks, Siemens Carrier Networks, Solectron, and dozens of others.

Jack Pompeo, a distinguished quality management expert, former chairman of the Dallas Section of the American Society of Quality, member of the board of Quality Texas, and at the time Alcatel's vice president of quality, was a key figure in the formation of the QuEST Forum collaboration. According to Pompeo, "After the breakup of AT&T, Bellcore (which became Lucent), and the 'baby Bells,' a huge void existed in how industry standards could be established and if we hadn't banded together as industry, before long, suppliers would have had to complete, submit, and be evaluated by more than ten different performance report cards."[17] Adds Pompeo, "As we began to standardize performance measurements, it made sense to also standardize on TL 9000 and have the quality management audits performed by independent and accredited registrars such as the Bureau Veritas Quality International

(BVQI), Det Norske Veritas (DNV), SGS International, TUV Management Service, Underwriters' Laboratories (UL), and so on."

Aside from advocating and assisting its members in obtaining TL 9000 (discussed in Chapter 6 as the telecom version of ISO 9000) registration, the QuEST Forum puts particular importance on sharing best practices among its membership. In fact, since 2000, it has hosted an annual best practices conference. The purpose of these sharing events is "to enable attendees at the Best Practices Conference to learn techniques and methodologies that could have an immediate impact on their business results, and to enable the QuEST Forum to build a database of best practices for the telecom industry."[18]

Accordingly, each year, the QuEST Forum publicizes the *Best Practices* Conference and encourages people to submit abstracts regarding their breakthrough work. Each year, the QuEST Forum also makes a call for abstracts for presentation at the conference. Out of the 50 to 70 abstracts received each year, the QuEST Forum's panel of judges uses its own criteria to select approximately 20 abstracts to be presented during the general session and every year, the bar has been raised. The relevancy of the QuEST Forum's Annual Best Practices Conference is to make readers aware that this event exists and to review the judging criteria used by the QuEST Forum to select best practices abstracts to be presented and shared with its members and conference attendees. The authors consider these criteria to be strong and believe that they can be used by any organization.

Table 2-5 displays the criteria used during 2002–2003. The definition provided in Table 2-3 may be compared with the QuEST Forum criteria to validate the definition and strengthen readers' understanding of the concept. The concise definition provided earlier in Table 2-3 was, "a practice that fully satisfies customers, produces superior results in one operation, performs as reliably as any alternative, and can be adapted elsewhere." This definition embodies ten of the QuEST Forum's 17 criteria, excluding only the following: "3. Effectiveness of practice/improvements was determined"; "7. Used creative ideas to accelerate business performance"; "8. Demonstrated use of benchmarking"; "9. Practice stimulates/leads to new ideas or innovations"; "10. Practice considered all stakeholders"; "11. Practice addressed customer-supplier relation building"; and "12. Practice plans received strong support from management." None of these criteria require a revision of the best practices definition provided earlier to be made. Nonetheless, all of these QuEST Forum best practices criteria are important, and readers are encouraged to consider using them because they may be relevant when considering the adaptation of external best practices to improve performance in their organization.

Best Practices Benchmarking Redefined

According to Spendolini, best practices benchmarking is "a continuous, systematic process for evaluating the products, services, and work processes of organizations

Table 2-5 Best Practice Acceptance Criteria for QuEST Forum

To evaluate abstracts for its Best Practice Conference.

Criteria	Checkpoints	Score (1–5)
1. Impact	Demonstrated positive impact on business or process results.	
	1. Results met or exceeded business or process targets.	( )
	2. Problem statement addressed the gap between the current and targeted values.	( )
	3. Effectiveness of practice/improvements was determined (via cost or other measurable aspect).	( )
2. Reproducible	Able to be replicated in other areas through a clear methodology.	
	4. Specific areas for replication were considered.	( )
	5. Practice can be reproduced within the telecom industry.	( )
	6. Others have learnt or benefited from the practice.	( )
3. Innovation	Exhibited creativity in addressing the initiative.	
	7. Used creative ideas to accelerate business performance.	( )
	8. Demonstrated use of benchmarking.	( )
	9. Practice stimulates/leads to new ideas or innovations.	( )
4. Partners	Demonstrated effective use of partnership.	
	10. Practice considered all stakeholders.	( )
	11. Practice addressed customer-supplier relation building.	( )
	12. Practice plans received strong support from management.	( )
5. Customer satisfaction	Exceeds the expectation of customers.	
	13. The criteria for selection were customer-oriented.	( )
	14. Practice improved ability to meet identified customer requirements.	( )
	15. Practice has positively impacted business performance as perceived by customers.	( )
6. Challenge	Overcame obstacles in established programs.	
	16. Practice is fully implemented and part of daily work.	( )
	17. Includes on-going evaluation of practice (continuous improvement).	( )

Source: QuEST Forum

that are recognized as representing *best practices* for the purpose of organizational improvement."[19] Similarly, Camp's description is "the search for those *best practices* that will lead to superior performance of a company."[20] O'Dell and Grayson like simplicity with the definition, "benchmarking is the process of finding and adapting *best practices*."[21] Bogan and English describe it "as the process of seeking out and studying the best internal and external practices that produce superior performance."[22] It is safe to say that there's consensus agreement that it is the systematic process of discovering and adapting best practices.

However, it's time for the concept of best practices benchmarking as a management tool to be broadened by adding three other components to its definition. As Bogan and English contend, best practices benchmarking also "includes but isn't limited to the study of statistical benchmarks."[23] This is not controversial, as benchmarks, while separate, are included by everyone in the literature.

Furthermore, the time has come, finally, to include both internal best practices development and knowledge management. The rationale for including internal best practices development is to legitimize a new art form that is emerging in more and more high-performing organizations. With the emergence of process-centered or process-managed organizations along with Six Sigma strategies and *Lean* concepts (to be discussed in Chapters 6 and 8), expert change agents are being trained to add value to processes (and eliminate nonvalue). On occasion, the experts or teams involved also adapt best practices from outside the organization using benchmarking. But today, more than ever, they are designing or developing new internal best practices using the Six Sigma traditional statistical and Lean tools. Including this skill and work under the best practices benchmarking umbrella creates synergy. Benchmarking (or outreaches) benefits from the downstream skill (developing internal best practices) that makes upstream searches more focused on being adaptation-easy.

Also, since best practices management and knowledge management (so closely) focus on the transfer of best practices (imported and adapted via benchmarking or developed internally) from one part of an organization to another, it's a natural fit to have it be the fourth component in Table 2-6. After all, the purpose of all these transfers is to leverage particular intellectual assets of the organization in order to improve customer satisfaction, eliminate defects, reduce cycle time, improve productivity, promote innovation, and/or reduce cost faster. If there is concern that knowledge management has a much larger context within the organization (e.g., it includes all information management and networking processes), then this work may be labeled "best practices knowledge management." Including the four components displayed in Table 2-6 into best practices benchmarking creates a supercharged method of learning-how-to-learn practices, knowledge, know-how, and/or valuable experiences that will be systematically evaluated for transfer to other parts of the organization where their application can have a big impact and big paybacks. This sets the stage for discussing examples and paybacks.

Table 2-6 Reformulated Practical Definitions of the Four Components of Best Practices Benchmarking

Benchmarks	Measurements to quantify process performance excellence gaps and enable strategic performance targeting and goal setting.
Benchmarking	The systematic process of seeking out and adapting best practices and using benchmarks.
Best practices development	The systematic process of reusing knowledge with best practices adaptations to develop *new* internal best practices.
Best practices management	Transfer of the right knowledge (best practices) to the right people at the right time to improve performance and achieve excellence.

Practical Examples (with Big Paybacks) of Best Practices Benchmarking

When best practices are imported via benchmarking and then deployed within an organization along with a change process, improvements will occur through combinations of cost reduction or avoidance, productivity improvement, and revenue creation. Real-world examples serve as testimonies to how valuable the payback potential is when organizations make serious deployments. Indeed, competitive advantages can really be created, too. To illustrate, the following are three examples supplied by Best Practices, LLC, a research-based full-service consulting company based in Chapel Hill, North Carolina.[24]

The largest mortgage company in the United States, Norwest, quantified the following benefits from its implementation of a best practices benchmarking campaign:

- $430,000 in savings from a sales brochure consolidation.
- $1 million in savings from customer/direct mail consolidation.
- $20 million in added growth from opportunity lending.
- A 5 percent increase in teller referrals, creating more sales.
- Sales road maps that drove an increase in sales of up to 102 percent

The British unit of Xerox, named Rank Xerox, documented the benefits of adopting the best practices of its operating countries as follows:

- Sales improved from 152 percent to 328 percent for country units.
- Over $200 million in new revenue was developed.

Also, Lucent Technologies, a member of the QuEST Forum and one-time Global Benchmarking Council member, identified best individual engineering practices that boosted its productivity levels by 10 percent in eight months, paying for the program within one year and yielding an ROI of more than six times after two years.

Speed Has Turned Knowledge Transfer into a Race

The more businesspeople examine how to create new competitive advantages (many are listed in Table 1-1) over existing rivals and new marketplace entrants, invariably the issue of speed reemerges. Speed matters. It's a difference maker, and many times a key success factor. Accomplishments in speed have made possible 24-7 (24 hours a day, 7 days a week) quick access to every form of knowledge, which is enabling faster decisions based on facts. In fact, accomplishments in speed have hurried up twenty-first-century decision making so that it can be nearly instantaneous.

The need for speed in business and industry is an insatiable craving; more is always better, and there's never enough. And it's not just getting the same things faster, it's figuring out how to do hundreds of things in a flash, using microchips, software, and hardware, for example, to achieve a tenfold increase in speed every two to four years. Advances appear daily in such forms as electronic funds transfers (EFT), online banking and stock trades, automatic bill payment, e-mail document transfers, on-demand telephone entertainment programming, 911 emergency services, bar code scan checkout technology, fire and forced-entry alarm and security services, genealogical research—the list goes on and on. In fact, the need for speed has made telephone dial-up Internet access obsolete and replaced it with faster solutions such as DSL, ISDN, and cable modem services.

Things just can't be done fast enough. Like a desert thirst, the need for speed in business can't be quenched. Instead of fluids, the craving is for instantaneous solutions or rapid-response knowledge, answers, opinions, and decisions to win customers, shareholders, suppliers, and intellectual property. There is momentary gratification, too, in succeeding a step or two ahead of rivals. It's easy to see how this "never-enough" thirst for speed has turned into a phenomenon that's produced a race for knowledge. Ergo, this book's title is about *Winning the Knowledge Transfer Race*. It's acknowledged, too, that some people make compelling arguments that the race we're describing could just as easily be called *the learning race* or *the race for speed in business*. The authors prefer *the knowledge transfer race* because it defines value as being created when knowledge is successfully transferred and reused to meet customer needs. One thing is certain: both speed and best practices knowledge are involved in the race; achieving either one leads to the other.

Another reason for speed in searching for and locating knowledge is that because of the overall speed of learning, each organization's intellectual property is a short-lived advantage that will eventually evaporate. Patents are limited in scope and do expire. Copyrights have loopholes and may be circumvented. Because of the Internet, copyright infringements occur but are hard to prove, and enforcing copyrights is expensive. Intellectual property content (music, video, and so on) is being file-swapped or pirated. There's hardly any knowledge content that can't be eventually downloaded off the Internet. If it has value, it's eligible for download and reuse by competitors.

During 2002, the United States reached 160.7 million Internet users, which constituted 24.2 percent of the 665.9 million users worldwide.[25] Based on past growth, it's reasonable to forecast that by 2010, 75 percent of the adult population in the United States will be using the Internet, and there will be nearly a billion users worldwide. This dynamic will continue to drive more solutions that are fast. And because the percentage of U.S. households with a computer grew from 42.1 percent in 1998 to 56.5 percent in 2001,[26] it should easily reach 75 percent before 2010. Software advances will thus continue to grow, and so will the speed at which they perform.

Consider, too, that the list of speed-oriented sources of newly discovered breakthrough ideas and tips includes 24-hour cable and satellite television news and broadband broadcasts. Discoveries made every day in every part of the world are being reported all around the globe. Present-day humanity is seeing only the tip of the iceberg in terms of the information that's available. Yet in the knowledge transfer race, certain types of discoveries are breakthroughs in learning that trigger the active interest of knowledge gatherers. These are people with first-class research and investigation skills who are constantly scanning and mining new knowledge for import, use, transfer, and reuse. This has been the work of corporate librarians, but the need for speed has changed the expectations and nature of the work they've historically done. Such librarians are evolving into value-adding knowledge gatherers in organizations that are taking seriously the adage "knowledge is power." Such people have become information specialists or knowledge brokers, and they're key to any work involving knowledge.

At Raytheon, for example, former librarians now have the title of "information specialists" and, together, they've formed a Community of Practice (CoP) (a group that has knowledge gathering expertise in common with one another and that shares any pertinent new discovery to benefit one and all). They conduct research, educate teams, and share their knowledge about how to do effective searches, access rich databases, and provide a valuable list of follow-up key contacts. These specialists are leveraging their skills through their CoP to help them and improvement teams become more successful. For Raytheon, these information specialists form a learning community that is a resource for the organization because as individuals, and as a CoP, they're the experts to go to; they are quick to educate and assist others while keeping one another current about cutting-edge developments.

Figure 1-2 depicts the knowledge transfer race as a competition that occurs in four phases. With the exception of bottom-line information for people who work in small business, the remainder of this chapter explores in more detail how to do well in phase 1 of the race.

Some Thoughts about How to Search for and Import Best Practices

Just as was done in Chapter 1, the discussion returns to phase 1 of the metaphoric knowledge transfer race. Up to this point in Chapter 2, clear and explicit interpretations have been put forth to answer the questions, "What are business practices?" and "What are best practices, and why should anyone care about them?" Hopefully, misunderstandings have been dispelled, too.

Best practices aren't forever, and they don't have to be as extraordinary as the 1990 Hubble Space Telescope technology. Instead, they are simply practices that fully satisfy customers, produce superior results in at least one operation, perform as reliably as any alternative, and can be adapted elsewhere. Furthermore, it will become clear by Chapter 5 that when best practices are codified, they become an organization's intellectual assets. All of this and the discussion about benchmarking in Chapter 1 relate to phase 1 of the knowledge transfer race. Negotiating this phase of the race comes down to reaching out and importing intellectual capital that can be converted to value and profit. Indeed, a self-assessment tool was provided. Now, it's time to tie everything together, so that race contestants can master phase 1 and move on to phase 2.

Best practices are intellectual assets, and benchmarking is the outreach process for importing such knowledge into an organization. The Bain & Company research presented in Chapter 1 substantiates the value of benchmarking as a management tool. Also, types of human capital (e.g., creativity) do contribute to best practices, but since they involve tacit knowledge, they're very hard to transfer and replicate. On the other hand, codified best practices are much more transferable. It is always a challenge to capture or codify the know-how that is tacit knowledge, but it is the organization's responsibility to try. The Coca-Cola recipe was tacit knowledge until it was perfected and codified, thereby making the production capabilities reusable worldwide. In short, knowledge transfers will improve employee performance and company competitiveness.

To get to phase 2, organizations also need to experiment and settle on a portfolio of other legal intelligence-gathering methodologies. This requires searching for, locating, and mining all sorts of one-time and ongoing sources of rich, insightful, valuable, and recent best practices knowledge that can be acted on. This alone will save organizations hundreds of thousands of dollars just by avoiding the costly mistakes already made by others. It will also help managers weed out the theoretical high-risk opportunities from practical opportunities so that those with promise may be pursued.

This stage of the race involves memberships in industry associations such as the QuEST Forum for telecommunications or the YPPA (Yellow Page Publishing Association) for telephone directory publishers. In addition, it is desirable to have memberships in the top two U.S. based worldwide benchmarking associations: Best Practices, LLC's Global Benchmarking Council (GBC) and the American Productivity and Quality Center's (APQC's) International Benchmarking Clearinghouse. Both these organizations provide excellent networks and offer a full array of mechanisms ranging from access to best practices databases, sponsorship of partnerships to create new research that identifies existing and emerging best practices, access to best practices reports, networking meetings, and other customized services.

Speed is achieved at this beginning stage of the race by importing knowledge from elsewhere after there's cultural acceptance of the humility that more good ideas will come from outside the organization than will be created inside. This in itself creates speed because organizations can then bypass having to reinvent the wheel in hundreds of new and different areas or processes. Just as the Baldrige criteria contain a scoring methodology for assessing and distinguishing the difference between *early, matured, refined* approaches and deployments of Total Quality Management (TQM), the same applies to the knowledge search capability.

Well-developed approaches have become deliberate, systematic, and continually improved. Mature approaches include data mining, data warehousing, knowledge management repositories, and collaboration in the APQC's 2003–2005 work to update the Process Classification Framework (PCF) taxonomy system and to continuously experiment with new and better ways of sharing valuable knowledge. To illustrate, Raytheon's approach to searching for new knowledge with speed is based on the initial clear understanding of the scope of the knowledge search. The initial definitions that define the search must limit the scope and address exactly what is to be included and what excluded. When an information specialist (or librarian) is enlisted, time is invested up front to specifically define the search criteria. A key learning about what's delivered back from the specialist is, "less is more." This means that those initiating the search would rather have 20 pages of relevant material back from the specialist than to get 150 pages that have to be scanned to find the knowledge "nuggets." Like so many other successes derived from ideal teamwork, an effective partnership needs to be forged between managers and information specialists. This works best when both parties understand the needs of the other.

The adage "if you can't beat them, join them" is true and the advisable course of action. Besides, the critical issue is converting knowledge into action, which is a unique experience for each organization. So instead of consuming too many resources trying to protect the outflow of nonproprietary information, in the twenty-first century, the better way to go is to share the learning about what others outside are doing. After all, with the Internet and other media knowledge transfers, it's extremely difficult to block the outflow of nonproprietary information, considering all the information and data that are reported to investors, employees, and retirees. The notion of "join them" refers to getting back information in exchange for providing the same to other companies (e.g., benchmarking events with a "win-win" approach bound by a code of conduct). Occasionally, unsuccessful undertakings are more important learning experiences than successful projects; breakthrough learning is ideal, but it occurs less frequent.

A new breed of knowledge safeguards will be created during the next five years to block the outflow of certain types of knowledge more effectively when employees leave. The first will be to continue the focus on transferring tacit or implicit knowledge to explicit or codified knowledge. This protects the organization from employees taking all the knowledge with them. The second focus will be on limiting what any one employee knows about certain knowledge, so that what's exported elsewhere is restricted, much like classified (military or Defense Department secrets) security and a "need to know" criterion. Such safeguards will be effective at keeping too much knowledge in the mind or hands of any one individual and from being totally lost.

Raytheon's Experiences and Insights[27]

The network of Knowledge Management Champions at Raytheon forms an overarching network within the company that links people to data and people to people. The Knowledge Management Champions have been designated and trained to understand inquiries, link them to organized *Raytheon Six Sigma* projects that align with strategic corporate goals, and recommend tapping into current databases or Communities of Practice (referred to as CoPs inside Raytheon) or individual subject-matter experts (SMEs). Internal databases include the *Raytheon Six Sigma* Project Library, the Best Practice Knowledgebase, the Benchmarking Library, the Specialist Tracking System, Docushare repositories, and internal Web pages.

Because this information has been captured and is now considered explicit knowledge (it also has a shelf life and might become outdated), it's often appropriate to tap into the CoPs that are operating on the leading edge of the particular knowledge domain. The CoPs involve SMEs as well as new employees to forge and maintain links to the outside world in order to stay current and keep pushing the "knowledge envelope."

The experience of Raytheon (including the now merged Texas Instruments Defense Systems & Electronics Group, a 1992 Baldrige Award recipient) illustrates how a company knowledgeable in benchmarking uses information technology to enable its teams. "We utilize intranet Web pages and our Knowledge Management Portal to help all our managers and benchmarking teams," cites Barbara Newell, Raytheon's knowledge transfer and benchmarking coordinator.[28] Everyone in the company of about 74,000 has access to a wide range of useful information through the intranet Web pages and portal. Raytheon's Benchmarking Home Web page

Table 2-7   Raytheon's Knowledge and Benchmarking Home Web Page Menu

Menu
Benchmarking homepage
■ Knowledge Transfer & Benchmarking expectations
■ View Best Practices Knowledgebase
■ Search Best Practices Knowledgebase
■ "So You Need to Benchmark" Guide
■ Knowledge Management Overview
■ External Guru Quotes
Information
■ Benchmarking Core Team contacts
■ Benchmarking Process
■ Code of Conduct
■ Definitions
■ Communications—monthly Benchmarking Newsletter
■ Information Sources
Contacts
■ Name, address, and contact info for twenty-two members of the Core Team
Tools
■ Benchmarking Toolkit
■ Internal Consulting Guide
■ Metric Guide
Submit Best Practices
■ Online Best Practice submittal form
Top Ten Benchmarks
■ A listing of current "off the shelf" external Benchmarking studies of interest
Conference and Seminars
■ Upcoming information on leading conference and seminar learning opportunities

opening menu—which presents eight different tab top-level options and twenty-one second-tier options—is depicted in Table 2-7.

Raytheon's benchmarking Web pages, together, enable its benchmarking teams to be effective and successful. This is because they (1) make ongoing benchmarking orientation and training available, (2) keep teams in touch with the right people, (3) enable teams to learn about research contained in the Raytheon Benchmarking Library from the experience of past projects, (4) keep users informed of the latest Raytheon news and practices, and (5) orient teams with the Benchmarking Code of Conduct.

Raytheon has developed and uses an intranet site called *Raytheon's Knowledge and Benchmarking Web Page*. The home page menu is shown in Table 2-7. Some of the ways in which Raytheon achieves speed in the knowledge transfer race are by doing the following:

- Conducting a quick data search of internal databases.
- Completing a quick search of external databases.
- Doing a scan of CoPs that have been established on the knowledge domain of interest.
- Contacting the Knowledge Management Champion Network for "pockets" of knowledge by business unit.
- Commissioning a Fast Track Benchmarking Study, a phenomenon that caught on during 2000 and has added speed to benchmarking exchanges. It will be described in more detail in Chapter 10.

A Simple Framework for Benchmarking

Benchmarking tends to succeed when it's made simple. When it was first introduced in the late 1980s, approaches tended to be technical and perhaps too complicated. After 15 years of experience, refinement, technology change, and advances in speed, however, benchmarking can now be greatly simplified. Use of the Internet and intranets, as illustrated in Table 2-7, and the emergence of best-practice-sharing memberships and online databases makes it possible to remove or simplify previously complicated steps.

As a consequence, in Table 2-8, the authors put forth a straightforward and simple benchmarking process. Though it contains 14 process steps listed vertically, it's the five horizontal phases, Initiate, Plan, Import, Formulate, and Act, that simplify the process. Since 1988, the authors have experimented with, tested, and successfully used over 20 variations of this framework to complete hundreds of benchmarking projects. Nonetheless, Table 2-8 is being provided more as a tested tool than as the best approach for how to conduct benchmarking. Indeed, in the opinion of the authors, the methodology set forth in Chapter 8 is more significant in that it integrates best practices benchmarking into Six Sigma strategies and projects that reduce defects per million to world-class levels.

Nonetheless, the intellectual capital–oriented benchmarking framework presented in Table 2-8 is an effective and user-friendly template for organizations to

Table 2-8   Intellectual Capital–Oriented Benchmarking Framework

Description	Initiate	Plan	Import	Formulate	Act
1. Clarify the scope and focus of learning	√				
2. Research what knowledge exists	√				
3. Develop plan for reuse leverage		√			
4. Cost-justify sponsoring new research		√			
5. Import the knowledge needed		√			
6. Assimilate learning			√		
7. Make findings and recommendations				√	
8. Communicate and gain acceptance				√	
9. Establish goals ands action plan				√	
10. Fund and allocate resources				√	
11. Take action and manage change					√
12. Leverage intellectual capital					√
13. Attain leadership position					√
14. Perform and sustain improvement					√

use and develop as they conduct benchmarking. Over 30 years of experience—incorporating the learning from both successes and failures—has been drawn upon in developing it. And virtually any organization's benchmarking process can be mapped into its five phases. The 14 steps displayed vertically are based upon over 40 years of firsthand experience. Just the same, the authors are more concerned that organizations have an effective process that works for them than that the process use any specific approach in particular.

A Raytheon Case Study to Illustrate Use of the Intellectual Capital–Oriented Benchmarking Framework

As stated, Table 2-8 is a simplified five-phase framework that models how to start and successfully complete benchmarking projects. To illustrate use of the framework, a Raytheon benchmarking team's experience will be reviewed as it completed each of the five phases: Initiate, Plan, Import, Formulate, and Act. In the case study that follows, a Raytheon benchmarking team was given the goal of reaching outside its organization to learn, adapt, and implement a broad, state-of-the-art version of Six Sigma for Raytheon. In Chapter 3, this type of knowledge transfer will be called a strategic transfer. This is a true story, and what ended up as the solution is now described as *Raytheon Six Sigma* or *R6σ*.

The Initiate Phase

At the outset, managers must decide what improvement and growth opportunity areas have the greatest impact or potential for the organization. Such decisions, like turning the key in a car's ignition, start the process. For example, the decision may be a top-down edict following a senior manager operations review that identified a deficiency in the supply chain involving 15 suppliers. In this example, the decision was to overhaul and improve the supply-chain system because its vulnerability had been exposed and competitors were exploiting it. The organization was hemorrhaging because of it. An edict to fix the problem starts the initiate phase of a benchmarking project, and it may be stated something like, "We need improvement; what can we do fast?"

Any number of other circumstances can also trigger the beginning of the initiate phase. In many organizations this is called the *burning platform*, which generates a *case for action*. In truth, several types of catalysts, stimuli, or circumstances can initiate a benchmarking project. Deficient performance areas identified by Baldrige Award Criteria, European Quality Award, Shingo Prize, and other assessments; key performance indicator (KPI) performance not meeting goal; areas with unacceptably high customer complaints. The list goes on.

Consider the example of how an ISO 9000 (international quality standard) audit deficiency finding may trigger the start of a benchmarking project. The audit finding identifies customer invoicing as deficient in how accurately and timely customer payments are being applied. Given an organization's commitment to become and remain ISO 9000 certified, such an audit finding would trigger the initiate phase of a benchmarking project. Table 2-8 identifies two steps involved with the benchmarking initiate phase, which are "clarify the scope and focus of learning" and "research what knowledge exists." These steps identify what needs to be improved and the knowledge that will be needed to do it.

Whatever the source for initiating a benchmarking project, any project that is created will have to be calibrated so that it's focused neither too broadly nor too narrowly. If the project is too narrowly focused, the knowledge transfer possibility will be underutilized. On the other hand, if the project is too broadly scoped, like "solving world hunger" or "boiling the ocean," the project will usually try to accomplish more than is possible. Table 2-9 illustrates these distinctions for customer support services, human resource management, distribution and logistics, training, and employee development. Examples are provided of what is too narrow or too broad for each. The far right column displays what's called an appropriate focus for each.

The Raytheon Case Study—the Initiate Phase

The "new" Raytheon's strategic plan, for instance, articulated goals for combining and integrating each of the recently acquired legacy companies into a totally new company. This meant the "old" Raytheon, and the acquisition of Magnavox, CAE Link, E-Systems, General Dynamics Missiles, ST Systems {STX}, Hughes Aircraft, Chrysler Technologies, Texas Instruments Defense Systems & Electronics Group, and Allied Signal Communications Systems, had to be integrated into one "new" company. And yet the vocabulary, language, and level of employee empowerment were very different for each of the merged business units, and so was each unit's culture. The empowerment of employees, for example, was all over the map. The systems for performance evaluation, compensation, recognition, and even training

Table 2-9   Focusing a Benchmarking Project Properly

Process or Functional Area	Too Broad to Enable Success	Too Narrow to Enable Success	Appropriate Level of Detail
Customer support services	Best customer satisfaction process	Best phone greeting	Best call center management practices
Human resource management	Best empowerment process	Best refund policy below $20	Best values communication systems
Distribution and logistics	Best distribution process	Best materials receipt stamp	Best warehouse management practices
Training	Best training process	Best classroom configuration	Best needs assessment process
Employee development	Best development process	Best job transfer request form	Best orientation practices

were more dissimilar than alike. And yet, after convincing the U.S. Department of Defense that it was in the best interests of the United States for these acquisitions to take place, Raytheon's Board became committed to accomplishing the pre-merger goals for improvement and synergy to become better, faster, and cheaper.

Another catalytic factor was the Raytheon board's recruitment of Dan Burnham from AlliedSignal to become the CEO of the "new" Raytheon. Burnham, in addition to being vice chairman at AlliedSignal under Larry Bossidy, also carried the title of Six Sigma program manager. Bossidy later became the CEO of Honeywell when AlliedSignal and Honeywell merged. It was evident that Burnham believed in the power of a Six Sigma strategy. He also indicated that he was not totally happy with what he and his team had accomplished at AlliedSignal with Six Sigma. Consequently, Burnham created a *blue ribbon* benchmarking team to learn from the leaders of those using Six Sigma successfully how to design a bigger and better version of it. The result was the creation of *Raytheon Six Sigma*, which would become the unifying, umbrella strategy for the "new" Raytheon.

The Plan Phase

During the second benchmarking phase, managers design a plan that determines the boundaries of the project and the steps necessary to achieve targeted performance improvement. It's here that a clear project focus is established. During this time, senior-level managers identify important issues, weaknesses, and improvement opportunities; and they prioritize the specific processes, functions, or products to be studied. They also obtain the necessary support and approval of process owners and stakeholders. This is usually where resources are allocated to execute and fund part of the project or the entire project. In some challenging cases, the team is told that the funding for its work must come from savings that the team identifies. In any case, a team is formed to work the plan, and it is usually staffed with at least one and sometimes three people from the functions that normally perform work within the process being examined for improvement. It could be a first- or second-line supervisor who is assigned to the team. The team then prepares a benchmarking project plan.

Team Size

An important planning consideration is staffing benchmarking teams with enough of the right people but keeping the membership size within manageable limits. Three to eight team members is usually optimal, depending on the scope of the work and the time constraints. If this is the team's first benchmarking work, an experienced benchmarking facilitator or team leader should ideally be identified. This person will lead and facilitate the team's benchmarking project.

Usually, the team's first responsibility is to develop the benchmarking plan with everyone's input so the team takes ownership of it. The plan serves as a road map for the team's work. The benchmarking plan may include the following ingredients:

- Statement of purpose
- Justification for the study
- Statement of problem(s) or opportunities to be addressed
- Baseline survey or results data from those involved in the process or function
- Relationship of the project to company business priorities and goals
- Preliminary benchmark measures
- Quantification of benefits to be achieved by the benchmarking study
- Scope of where the project starts and stops
- Methodologies sketched out that the team would use
- A resource plan, identifying the time, people, equipment, and costs expected

The Raytheon Case Study—the Plan Phase

Raytheon named 15 senior leaders (nearly all vice presidents) to participate on the blue ribbon benchmarking team. Bill Baker, coauthor of this book and the long-time established Benchmarking Champion from the 1992 Baldrige Award–winning TI Defense Systems & Electronics Group, served on the team as the benchmarking process facilitator and arranged benchmarking exchanges with General Electric and AlliedSignal, CEO Dan Burnham's former company. The team soon formulated its project plan, including key priorities, a schedule, expected deliverables, and required resources. The scheduled expectation was that within a month, CEO Burnham would review the team's preliminary Six Sigma deployment plan for Raytheon.

The Import Phase

With a solid understanding of the process and how it works inside the organization, the team conducts this third phase of the benchmarking project. During this phase, the team reaches out to capture knowledge about how high-performing organizations elsewhere perform the same process. During the import phase, the team

- Specifies what the customer requirements and expectation for the process are.
- Documents the inputs-process-outputs (IPO) for the process under study.
- Captures related data and information pertinent to performing the process.
- Clarifies the key success factors and key performance indicators (KPIs) for the process.
- Identifies key knowledge to be gained via questionnaires, interviews, and so on.
- Arranges and/or conducts interviews and necessary knowledge capture.
- Arranges and conducts knowledge exchanges with benchmarking partners.
- Conducts on-site visits with the best-performing partners.

Understanding the Process

A priority for team members, shortly after forming the project, is to map the current process or practice to gain a thorough understanding of all the inputs, processing steps, outputs, and customer satisfaction levels for the end-to-end process. This also serves as a baseline for future improvements and allows the team to share a frame of reference with prospective benchmarking partners. It is essential that the team have a thorough operational understanding of the process under study.

Performing Research

Once the team thoroughly understands the process under examination, it will collect information about breakthroughs by others within and outside of the industry that are performing the same process. This usually identifies prospective benchmarking partners. This wave of research usually involves Internet and public domain searches. If the organization is savvy enough to belong to a benchmarking organization such as the Best Practices, LLC Global Benchmarking Council or the APQC, two preliminary searches may be performed: First, research reports for the previous three years may be reviewed to ascertain whether any research is pertinent and reusable. Second, a best practices database may be scanned and mined for use or reuse.

The resources residing within an organization mustn't be overlooked, either. Knowledge repositories such as corporate libraries, databases, competitive reports, past and current studies, customer satisfaction measurement research, Six Sigma project reports, and market research are often valuable sources of knowledge. Then again, subject-matter experts within the organization are great sources of rich knowledge.

More and more, public domain information is available through the Web sites of media giants CNN, MSNBC, AOL Prop News, Yahoo News, New York Times Digital, ABC News Digital, Knight Ridder Digital, BBC Sites, CBS Sites, FoxNews.com, Newsweek.com, and others. Librarians or information specialists may search for pertinent knowledge in journals and periodicals, position papers, business directories, conference proceedings, database subscriptions, and company publications such as prospectuses and annual reports. Other external sources of best practices information include trade and professional societies, consultants, industry experts, academics, trade journalists, Wall Street analysts, vendors and service bureaus, and public seminars. Many benchmark teams also conduct original research, including preliminary surveys and telephone interviews with prospective benchmarking partners; surveys mailed to experts, customers, and suppliers; personal interviews with subject-matter experts; third-party studies; reverse engineering; and, of course, onsite observation.

The first round of research enables the benchmarking team to narrow its sights to a few really good benchmark partners and to create a list of detailed site-visit questions for each performance area under study. A preliminary qualifying survey or questionnaire often proves invaluable as a screening device and a time saver when evaluating whether a prospective benchmarking partner warrants a site visit.

Conducting a Benchmarking Survey

Ten years ago, a lot of effort went into this; in the year 2005, this is simplified by belonging to an organization such as the Best Practices, LLC Global Benchmarking Council or the APQC International Benchmarking Clearinghouse. These organizations have experts that can help design surveys that can be distributed in a matter of hours, with responses being tabulated within five days. Before, this could take weeks. In 1994, the focus was on finding out which companies had achieved excellence in the process of being benchmarked. Now, over 10 years later, an inquiring organization just turns to its trusted network of 60 or so companies and asks for help with its survey or to identify key learning that any of them has already captured on the process under study. Speed has made the process instantaneous. Compared to the mid-1990s, benchmarking teams are the exception rather than the rule. Since the year 2000, a good deal more learning occurs using virtual mechanisms such as e-mail, team software, and conference calls. Team members do individual research or knowledge gathering, then assimilate it together as a team. Thereafter, small senior manager teams may go out to "see for themselves" so that they buy into adapting the innovations that have been found highly effective elsewhere.

Accessibility of Benchmarking Partners

Not all site visits require extensive travel. In fact, organizations that belong to such sharing groups as the Global Benchmarking Council or the International Benchmarking Clearinghouse of the American Productivity and Quality Center may request that a topic, subject, or issue be featured at a quarterly members' meeting. In this case, a highly skilled staff of research associates will design an agenda and recruit three to five of the world's best-performing enterprises on the featured topic. There's also a great deal of virtual networking done with partners in the same sharing groups or communities. Over a hundred of America's Fortune 500 belong to the sharing organizations already named. Whether benchmarking is done through one of these sharing organizations or through individual efforts, there are ethical standards to follow. Indeed, there is a Benchmarking Code of Conduct that codifies some general principles governing ethical behavior when benchmarking.

The Benchmarking Code of Conduct[29]

To contribute to efficient and ethical benchmarking, individuals agree for themselves and their organizations to abide by the following seven principles for benchmarking with other organizations:

1. *Principle of Legality.* Avoid discussions or actions that might lead to or imply an interest in restraint of trade: market or customer allocation schemes, price fixing, dealing arrangements, bid rigging,

bribery, or misappropriation. Do not discuss costs with competitors if costs are an element of pricing.

2. *Principle of Exchange.* Be willing to provide the same level of information that you request in any benchmarking exchange.

3. *Principle of Confidentiality.* Treat benchmarking interchange as something confidential to the individuals and organizations involved. Information obtained must not be communicated outside the partnering organizations without prior consent of participating benchmarking partners. An organization's participation in a study should not be communicated externally without their permission.

4. *Principle of Use.* Use information obtained through benchmarking partnering only for the purposes of improvement of operations within the partnering companies themselves. External use or communication of a benchmarking partner's name with their data or observed practices requires permission of that partner. Do not, as a consultant or client, provide the benchmarking study findings of an originating company to another organization without the permission of the originating company.

5. *Principle of First Party Contact.* Initiate contacts, whenever possible, through a benchmarking contact designated by the partner company. Obtain mutual agreement with the contact on any hand-off of communication or responsibility to other parties.

6. *Principle of Third Party Contact.* Obtain an individual's permission before providing their name in response to a contact request.

7. *Principle of Preparation.* Demonstrate commitment to the efficiency and effectiveness of the benchmarking process with adequate preparation at each process step, particularly at initial partnering contact.

After the benchmarking team plans and organizes completely, a smaller site-visit sub-team will call on a few select benchmarking partners to collect on-site information and view actual operations. Frequently, this detailed, on-site review helps the benchmarking team learn what specific practices and operating principles enable the partner to achieve its superior performance and validates the previously supplied data. When possible, key stakeholders should be members of the site visit teams, so they can *internalize* back in the operations the performance and best practices they witnessed firsthand. "Seeing is believing" is an energizing and contagious concept, which helps to create a desire for change.

Conducting Site Visits

Still, there are valid reasons to conduct site visits, just fewer of them. As the most interesting and credible method of gathering information, the site visit affords firsthand feedback. Site visits also often result in long-term relationships that foster an ongoing exchange of information between benchmarking partners. Site visits are also the most time-consuming and expensive method of gathering information because of the travel required. However, they produce the highest-quality information because companies view work processes, methods, and practices in action. The following guidelines may help site visits become more effective.

- *Do research on the benchmarking partner and share it with the team before the visit.* Advance research helps the team quickly become capable of getting the most out of visits. It's also good reading material on an airplane trip.

- *Prepare site-visit checklist to guide and structure the visit.* These tools will help the team stay focused on accomplishing its work within the time constraints. If prioritized, checklists will also ensure that the knowledge of greatest value is exchanged and that the greatest value is achieved from the visit. In addition to benefiting itself, a prepared benchmarking team demonstrates respect and courtesy for its partner's time. Partners can easily detect unprepared visitors. Though they may not show their disappointment during the visit, many host organizations will feel insulted that the visitors wasted everyone's time by not taking the time to learn rudimentary facts about the host company. Some companies will decline participation in future exchanges with a company if its benchmarking teams seem ill prepared and unprofessional. The visiting benchmarking team needs to assign three different people to fulfill three key roles. The first is the leader, who conducts the agenda items and leads discussion on the individual questions in the interview guide. The second is the scribe, who is the person who captures the answers to each question and publishes the findings for the team. The scribe frees up others on the team to be effective at probing. Finally, the observer is the one with the responsibility for observing all the nonverbal signals and meanings that occur during the visit. Those filling these three roles can participate in the discussions, but not to the detriment of fulfilling their primary role.

- *Prepare the benchmarking partner for your team's visit.* To ensure that the partner will be prepared and will have subject matter experts present, the visiting company should agree on the agenda and information-sharing packet before the visit takes place.

- *Use a structured interview guide and agenda for site visits and discussions.* Before any tours and in-depth discussions begin, start with a review of the code of conduct and then ask for flowcharts, diagrams, or other published materials that explain the process. A few flowcharts or diagrams can save hours of discussion about how a processing system works and is structured.

- *Travel in escorted groups during the site tour.* Traveling in small groups affords the team several advantages: one person can take notes while another converses; the group can split up to view different operations; group members can validate discussion points and observations.

■ *Arrange for follow-up actions to resolve open issues.* At the end of the site visit, review any open actions and/or open issues. This provides a resolution process for unresolved questions, uncertain answers, or open matters that surface during the site visit. In fact, this process can clear up questions that surface during debriefings after the site visit. In fact, some of the most experienced teams send summaries after visits to get confirmation that the knowledge that was exchanged has been correctly interpreted.

■ *Conduct a postsession debriefing to summarize the team's observations.* By debriefing immediately after a site visit, team members may more easily capture their thoughts and observations while they remain fresh and clear. Some companies have their teams stay over an extra night to review in a hotel. Other debriefing reviews have been done in the visited company's building, and still others have been done in the airport while waiting for the flight back home. The key learning here after numerous benchmarking visits over the past 15 years is that people hear and listen differently. Therefore, a common set of understandings and takeaways is very important before the site visit team separates with different understandings and learning.

■ *Prepare a trip report summarizing the site visit findings and conclusions.* This report codifies what knowledge was learned and exchanged. This can be done by the leader or by the scribe. This document helps the team to share and transfer the knowledge they've learned when they return home.

■ *Send a thank-you letter and confirm the accuracy of the key knowledge gained.* The thank-you note shows appreciation and encourages a continuation of knowledge sharing in the future. It also recognizes the people who made the visit successful. At the same time, this is a last opportunity to confirm the accuracy of something exchanged that has come into question.

The Raytheon Case Study—the Import Phase

During the import phase, Raytheon's blue ribbon benchmarking team set its critical performance variables, collected data, selected benchmarking partners, and, used a formal questionnaire to guide and focus in-person interviews, completed during site visits to the two companies. The first partner was AlliedSignal, which under Chairman and CEO Larry Bossidy and Vice Chairman Dan Burnham had refined Six Sigma with a fresh approach and very successful deployment. Bossidy, a devout believer in the capability of Six Sigma, had introduced it to Jack Welch, then CEO of General Electric (GE). The second company, GE, had, under Jack Welch, taken Six Sigma to another level and made it an integral part of the company's strategy and financial reporting. Raytheon also did significant literary research on others involved in Six Sigma, including Motorola, which was the originator and had sponsored the first consortium of companies to promote Six Sigma methodology in the early years.

"This was the most exciting and gratifying part of the study," recalls Bill Baker, who at that time was Raytheon's benchmarking champion. Adds Baker, "It opened the eyes of everyone on our team to the fantastic possibilities Six Sigma could open up for Raytheon. We saw firsthand how AlliedSignal added 'teeth' to Six Sigma by having it applied to engineering and established accountability for defect and waste elimination and involved high potential fast track managers as Black Belts. We also got to learn firsthand how GE used the concept on their aircraft jet engine business in Cincinnati. All of what we saw and learned enabled our team to add the concepts of Lean enterprise and change management and design Six Sigma so that it would touch every employee at Raytheon. Because what we designed was much broader in than Motorola's concept, we called it *Raytheon Six Sigma*."

The Formulate Phase

During the fourth phase, the benchmarking team assimilates the best practices information it has developed and prepares this information and corresponding improvement recommendations for senior management's review. During this phase, the team normalizes any measures that may still be in different reporting formats, studies and highlights performance gaps produced by different operating approaches, targets future performance goals, and develops change recommendations. The outcome of this phase is a best practices report.

Normalizing Data

To ensure that management can easily review benchmark data or metrics, the benchmarking team needs to normalize quantified results so that they are comparable across companies. This is accomplished by mathematically truing up common denominators for all performance indicators used. For instance, if a benchmarking partner measures billing productivity per week and the benchmarking team's company measures productivity per month, the measures should be normalized to daily, weekly, monthly, or some other common denominator. Once the measures are in a form that can be easily compared, the team charts its company's measures against the benchmarking partners' measures.

Prepare Recommendations as Part of a Benchmarking Report

After concluding the research, interviews, and exchanges of information, the benchmarking team completes its duties when it prepares and presents a team report that details findings and recommendations. This report consists of a mission statement describing the purpose and scope of the assignment. A description of the study process then follows and includes the people involved in the project, the departments and operating units represented, and the methods of gathering information. The sources of information need to be identified.

A key to the best practices summary report lies in the performance indicators and best practices findings. Performance indicators may include measures of productivity, quality, speed, yield, staffing levels, customer satisfaction, utilization rates, error rates, and cost. Key findings include best practices identified, process diagrams, critical success factors, and general observations.

To display performance measurement results, benchmarking teams can use several different graphical tools. Each tool has a unique function.

- A performance matrix has proven to be effective. It provides a summary and comparison of the performance of each partner's process according to key performance indicators.
- Another tool is a comparison matrix, which relates performance criteria (usually listed in the left-hand column) to a collection of benchmark partner companies (listed in the top row). For example, it might present the performance of organizations W, X, Y, and Z on profitability, defects per million, mean time to failure, and cycle time. Such a matrix enables, too, the use of descriptive text and metrics.
- A third tool is similar to the performance matrix but is known as a survey matrix. It lists the answers to survey questions for each best practices partner. This allows a summary of all the collected information to be viewed side by side.

The Raytheon Case Study—The Formulate Phase:

Upon completion of its fact finding and site visits, the Raytheon blue ribbon benchmarking team assimilated a large body of collected information and focused on the best practices of the site-visit partners. "This phase required more time than expected due to inconsistent measurements among our benchmarking partners," recalls Bill Baker. Baker adds, "We had to investigate further and normalize our data." The success of this phase is highly dependent upon how well focused and detailed is the question set that's developed during the import phase.

In Raytheon's case, the project results supported a host of proposed improvements and changes, including a best practices approach that made Six Sigma a pervasive change methodology, utilizing a common language, for the previously independent companies that together formed the new Raytheon. The team took the focus of eliminating waste and defects and added a refined adaptation of Lean enterprise thinking. In addition, the team also made effective change management a core concept. Using a term for making a good shot in tennis, it hit the sweet spot of the racket, too, by designing cultural change as every bit a part of the *Raytheon Six Sigma* process.

The Act Phase

Unless there is positive change resulting from the study, little of significance has occurred. Benchmarking just to collect data and to prove that "we are already better than them!" is a waste of time and effort. In fact, if the recommendations of benchmarking teams are not acted upon or a legitimate explanation is not provided for a drawn-out decision-making process, the people on the teams will become frustrated, and the process will have a negative impact throughout the organization. Therefore, this fifth and final benchmarking phase involves action. The team works with management and the affected process owners to prioritize recommendations (based on the findings) and to reach agreement on an implementation strategy, paying attention to managing the changes involved. Agreement leads to formalizing action plans, deployment schedules, measurement and tracking mechanisms, cycles of refinement and improvement, and management reviews. When the action plans are completed, ongoing responsibility for managing the improvement efforts usually is handed off to those in the organization who will be responsible for implementing the approved plans. This handoff can be enhanced if the stakeholders are part of the benchmarking team.

The Raytheon Case Study—the Act Phase

At Raytheon, the change recommendations prepared by the blue-ribbon benchmarking team were fully supported by the CEO and the company's board of directors. Dan Burnham reviewed the findings and recommendations and actually enhanced some of them based on his expert knowledge of Six Sigma. At year-end 2002, the fully deployed *Raytheon Six Sigma* strategy had increased Raytheon's gross benefit by $1.8 billion, increased net operating profit by $500 million, and improved cash flow by $865 million. Other key results by year-end 2002 included educating and training 7,500 leaders, certifying 20 Master Experts (similar to Master Black Belts), training 1,100 Experts (similar to Black Belts), and training 11,500 Specialists (similar to Green Belts).[30] Furthermore, *Raytheon Six Sigma* is considered one of the world's most successful best practices implementations of Six Sigma, and Raytheon is offering it to its key customers and suppliers

The Bottom Line for People in Small Organizations

There are five tips from this chapter that are carried forward into the summary of 55 tips for people in small businesses in Chapter 11. These five tips are numbered 11, through 15 in Chapter 11 and are given in capsule form as follows:

- To simply Six Sigma project work, a Black or Green Belt may be brought in quarterly and other strategies considered that may fit in the budget.

- To develop the needed Six Sigma mentality, have hats made with writing on them that reads "Benchmarking to Reduce Defects and Variation."
- Aim to resolve in days what Six Sigma teams in large organizations take weeks to accomplish. The focus is on the "here and now."
- When best practices are discovered, share them with everyone.
- As growth occurs, work to retain the "I can learn from anyone" mindset.

On the whole, it is the authors' opinion that it is crucial for small organizations to be able to capture, create, share, and reuse their organization's own best practices as they are innovating and launching products and services. With the anticipated future speed of innovation, the movement of people between organizations, and the knowledge of the best practices of the future to be gained, best practices benchmarking will need to be integrated into the few "jack of many trades" jobs that exist. Each person who is multitasking jobs must always carry with him or her the mentality of "How do we compare?" and "Who's the best at doing this today?" That way, with humility, needed learning will occur every day, whether the best practices started out in sales, customer relationship management, new product development, or collecting on a receivable due.

Because people in small organizations must wear multiple hats since the business cannot support specialists, each hat worn must have a hatband on it that reads, "Benchmarking to Reduce Defects and Variation." Accordingly, a shortcut version of the Six Sigma-DMBAIC (define, measure, benchmark, analyze, improve, and control) needs to be on forms that can be used as problem-solving tools for every significant problem as it occurs. Normally, what Six Sigma project teams in large organizations take weeks to accomplish must be resolved in a day or two in a small organization. The cycle time expectation is *here and now*. Then, once a quarter, the authors suggest that a contracted Black Belt or Green Belt be brought in to assist people in analyzing key core processes to identify root causes and plot the value stream to help prevent defects and reduce variation. However, the emphasis will have to be on multitasking as part of the coaching job rather than on a Six Sigma team. Likewise, best practices need to be shared regularly within the organization. The company culture needs to expect knowledge sharing and reuse. Some other ways in which sharing can be highlighted are through scheduled quarterly or semiannual sharing meetings, best practices benchmarking from the outside, or internal transfer of best practices.

The key is to manage growth while not losing the small-company entrepreneurial viewpoint and an aggressive "I can learn from anyone" mindset. As the organization grows, there will be those who will think that benchmarking, along with defect and variation elimination, is someone else's job because it's not specifically in his or her job description. For a business to survive and thrive in today's world, benchmarking must actually be everyone's primary job! Part of this needed mindset is for employees to continually ask themselves the questions "How do I compare?" and "Who is the best at what I do?" As time goes on, everyone can also discuss the answer to the question "What are we going to do about it?"

Endnotes

1. Robert C. Camp, *Benchmarking: The Search for Industry Best Practices That Lead to Superior Performance* (Milwaukee: Quality Press, 1989), p. xi.
2. Ibid., p. 141.
3. Michael J. Spendolini, *The Benchmarking Book* (New York: AMACOM, 1992), pp. 1–123.
4. Definition of practice, *New Webster's Dictionary and Thesaurus of the English Language* (Danbury, Conn.: Lexicon Publications,)p. 787.
5. Camp, *Benchmarking*, p. 142. Note: Camp also includes operational structure as enablers because it "is not a practice in and of itself." What he says is important about it is the geographic location of facilities and operations located at a site, whether they're centralized or decentralized, near or far from customers, and so on. The authors include these same things in type 2 practices as part of leadership, strategic plan, or policies.
6. Carla O'Dell and C. Jackson Grayson, Jr., *If Only We Knew What We Know* (New York: Free Press, 1998), pp. 12–13.
7. Ibid.
8. Ibid., p. 13.
9. Camp, *Benchmarking*, p. 252.
10. Ibid., pp. xi, 129.
11. Christopher E. Bogan and Michael J. English, *Best Practices Benchmarking: Winning through Innovative Innovation* (New York: McGraw-Hill, 1994), p. 42.
12. O'Dell and Grayson, *If Only We Knew*, pp. 13–14.
13. Jack Welch, *Jack: Straight from the Gut* (New York: Warner Books, 2001), p. 337.
16. Information obtained from QuEST Forum's Web site, www.questforum.org.
17. Interview of Jack Pompeo by Mike English on Jan. 21, 2005.
18. Information obtained from QuEST Forum's Web site, www.questforum.org, and online brochure.
19. Spendolini, *Benchmarking Book*, pp. 9–10.
20. Camp, *Benchmarking*, p. xi.
21. O'Dell and Grayson, *If Only We Knew*, p. xiv.
22. Bogan and English, *Benchmarking for Best Practices*, p. 5.
23. Ibid.
24. The source for these examples is http://www.best-in-class.com/site_tools/faq.htm as of Nov. 22, 2003.
25. Brunner, Borgna (ed),, *Time Almanac 2004* (Needham, Mass.: Time, Inc., 2005), p. 560.
26. Ibid.

27. Unless otherwise specified, the source for the Raytheon case study information and references is Bill Baker, former knowledge management and benchmarking champion for Raytheon. He had firsthand experience with the studies cited, and he relies on his presentations, calendars, notes, and memory.

28. Barbara Newell, Raytheon's knowledge transfer and benchmarking coordinator, was interviewed by Bill Baker during October 2004.

29. The Benchmarking Code of Conduct was originally produced through a collaboration between the American Productivity and Quality Center and the Strategic Planning Institute Council on Benchmarking during the early 1990s. What's presented comes from the original work.

30. Raytheon materials presented in the public domain at the 2003–2004 Lean Aerospace Initiative (LAI) Plenary Conferences.

Chapter 3

Learning, Understanding, and Sharing: Mastering Phase 2 of the Knowledge Transfer Race

Introduction

Despite an ancestry that dates back between two and three million years, it's just in the last 4,500 years that humans have started to become proficient at creating, learning, understanding, and sharing knowledge. In fact, everything that occurred before 2500 BC, when humans began codifying knowledge by writing, is considered prehistoric. Thus, the recorded history of humanity begins around 2500 BC.

And yet, despite advances in civilization through the Classical Age (2000 BC to AD 500), the Middle Ages (500 to 1350), and the Renaissance period (1350 to 1600), it was not until the seventeenth century that humanity truly began to learn, understand, and share on a wide scale. Yes, the ancient Egyptians, Romans, Greeks (Plato, 428–347 BC; Aristotle, 384–322 BC), and Chinese (Confucius, 551–479 BC) did make remarkable advances. Catholic clergy became influential as a central core group that was literate and knowledgeable. Their devotion to capturing and transferring knowledge was evident in their manuscripts, which were works of art but were not available to the general population. Books began to spread knowledge after Gutenberg built the first printing press using movable type in 1440. And then, in the seventeenth century, the so-called Age of Reason, a flurry of intellectual and scientific activity occurred on a grand scale.[1] It was during that time that great minds advanced science and mathematics to discover the laws of nature and begin to understand the universe. Tools like the microscope, slide rule, sextant, thermometer, and telescope were invented to test hypotheses. It was during this age, too, that universities and schools began to spread around the world, in Italy, Greece, France, Spain, Portugal, England, and in the new Americas.

Galileo Galilei (1564–1642) stands out as a genius during the Age of Reason for his astonishing achievements in the areas of learning, understanding, and sharing knowledge. Galileo is prominent because of his contributions to the modern method of learning through experimentation. He advocated and designed tests to prove or disprove hypotheses and then objectively observed the results. Before Galileo, so-called scientific theory was mostly hypothesis and conjecture. Equally impressive is Galileo's incredible list of discoveries and inventions, which makes him second only to Thomas Edison in the history of learning. To conduct accurate tests and make precise observations, Galileo invented the hydrostatic balance (a device designed to measure the density of objects) in 1593. He was the first to construct an astronomical telescope (1608) to study the skies, leading him to discover, in 1610, that the moon shines with reflected light, that the surface of the moon is mountainous, that the Milky Way is made up of countless stars, that Jupiter has four large satellites; and that the dark spots that appear from time to time on the sun's surface are sunspots.[2] It was Galileo who, in 1613, advocated the controversial Copernican system of the universe, proposing that the earth revolves around the sun. In 1589, at the age of 25, he even published a treatise on the center of gravity in solids. From 1602 to 1609, Galileo studied the motion of pendulums and other objects along arcs and inclines and concluded that falling objects accelerate at a constant rate, which later helped Sir Isaac Newton (1642–1727) derive the law of gravity.[3]

After Galileo, humanity's learning quickened and expanded exponentially over the next three centuries, transforming civilization, trade, and commerce. There was a new-found prosperity, and trade with the New World generated many possibilities. Spices and raw materials revolutionized commerce. Institutions were formed and reshaped. Humanity stumbled, yet advanced through the exploration, colonization, revolutions, the wars of the 1700s, and the Industrial Revolution of the 1800s. During the centuries that followed Galileo, the merchants of his time were slowly replaced by larger enterprises. The new enterprises—at first family merchants or artisans, then partnerships, and eventually the corporation—at first made use of indentured servants. Over time, indentured servitude disappeared, and these enterprises were staffed by first laborers and then employees as labor laws and unions took hold to protect workers from abuses. The new enterprises relied upon Galileo-like knowledge gains so that employees could convert their learning and knowledge of trades or industry into profits. Through the decades, all of this knowledge-infused progress elevated human prosperity and reduced disease, famine, and poverty. In the wrong hands, however, the new knowledge also led to the production of more devastating weapons that were used in deadly world wars.

In the eighteenth through twentieth centuries, a knowledge explosion occurred that transformed business and industry. Advances in agriculture, transportation, manufacturing, medicine, and technology were stimulated by competitive markets that determined prices through the dynamics of supply and demand, which drives market equilibrium between buyers and sellers. Key inventions of the nineteenth and early twentieth centuries were built upon to create new markets: the steam engine led to fast travel by train, the cotton gin led to mass market textiles, gas-powered automobiles replaced horses for transporting individuals and families, the Wright Brothers' invention eventually created even faster travel by air, the telegraph and telephone revolutionized communications, Edison's harnessing of electricity opened unlimited possibilities, and Henry Ford's assembly-line methods transformed manufacturing. Capitalism flourished, with private ownership (for profit) of the means of production and distribution. Firms or enterprises openly competed with one another, seeking economic gain or advantage. Creating knowledge and the capacity of employees to learn and transfer that knowledge became an engine that generated enterprise business preeminence.

Today, to adapt, thrive, and win in the twenty-first century, enterprises have come to realize that they must institute a second level of learning, on top of the knowledge that employees are already acquiring, in order to convert employees' knowledge into value and profit. This second level, as strange as it may sound, is learning new and better ways of learning. Just as Galileo advanced a method of learning and, at a second level, created the tools he needed to support that method, so enterprises must create both methods by which employees can adapt new know-how for their changing competitive environment and, on a second level, methods that expand their capability to learn in the future. This means that enterprises must enable the capacity in their employees to build on the past and move forward successively, rather than having to continually reinvent the wheel. This is the crux of phase 2 of the knowledge transfer race: to learn, understand, and share knowledge, all at a rapid pace.

Becoming a Learning Organization

The second part of the knowledge transfer race is to create an "I can learn from everyone" attitude and to become a learning organization. The winners will be those organizations that never stop expanding their people's capability and capacity to learn while they're producing incredible results and focusing on a common vision for the organization. Such organizations consist of people at all levels, individually, in teams, and collectively, who are incessantly increasing their skills, experience, know-how, and creativity so that they produce remarkable results and win the knowledge transfer race. Organizations that already have such a culture have a tremendous advantage.

Indeed, learning, understanding, and sharing are present-day battlefields for competitive advantage. Up until the mid-1990s, just a handful of approaches were thought to be the keys to competitive advantage: superior technologies, new patent creation and protections, superior value-chain creation, and lowest-cost methods.

But then the concept of intellectual property began to emerge. Consider, for example, the storied creation of 3M's famous *Post-it Notes™*. The glue used on this product was originally considered a failure because it performed poorly as an adhesive. But because 3M encouraged its employees to think, learn, experiment, and innovate, the "poor glue" became a breakthrough for a newly invented product. This Post-it Notes example is just one of many that began to surface that showed how an organization's use of its intellectual property could create new product lines and profits.

And so in the mid-1990s, organizational and personal learning were discovered to be differentiating competencies. Organizations such as 1988 and 1989 Baldrige Award recipients Motorola and Milliken & Company rallied their employees around themes like "stealing [knowledge] shamelessly" to achieve continuous improvement. Benchmarking, adapting best practices, and opportunistic (and legal) borrowing of great ideas, structures, strategies, procedures, and systems came to be seen as healthy and good things to do.[4] The identification and borrowing of best practices legitimized plagiarism in business learning like never before. Just a few years earlier, people like Arie De Geus, then head of planning for Royal Dutch/Shell, were saying, "The ability to learn faster than your competitors may be the only sustainable competitive advantage."[5]

Ever since, *learning* has become accepted by many as the new frontier of competition. Learning organizations train their employees quickly and effectively, genuinely learn from past successes and failures, and adapt innovations quickly, and the speed at which they do this spills over into almost everything they do. In fact, by the early 2000s, the importance of organizational and personal learning became so universally recognized that it became one of the 11 core values and concepts of the U.S. Malcolm Baldrige National Quality Award criteria.[6] The discussion of the Baldrige criteria in Table 3-1 is specific, if not complete, in its description of organizational and personal learning. It includes a well-developed approach, is adaptable to change, is continually improved, and has five listed conditions. Four of the conditions are about what organizational and personal learning is, and one is about what it results in. To clarify those conditions, they've been diagrammed in Figure 3-1 and visually depicted to aid reader understanding.

The five conditions are listed vertically in Figure 3-1 against horizontal headings of "personal," "work," and "organization" to show how learning is part of daily work, is practiced on every level, results in solving problems at their root causes, and so on. To add more meaning to the Baldrige description, however, more has been added to the "sources of learning are" entries in Figure 3-1. Rather than only "customers' input," the word *stakeholders* is substituted to provide for input from teammates, supervisors, suppliers, and any others with a vested interest. Also, best practices are listed as a source on every level, which is meant to equate to the Baldrige terminology of "best practice sharing."

Table 3-1   Organizational and Personal Learning According to the Baldrige Criteria

Achieving the highest levels of business performance requires a well-executed approach to organizational and personal learning. Organizational learning includes both continuous improvements of existing approaches and adaptation to change, leading to new goals and/or approaches. Learning needs to be embedded in the way your organization operates. This means that learning:

1. Is a regular part of daily work;

2. Is practiced at personal, work unit, and organizational levels;

3. Results in solving problems at their source (i.e., at the "root cause");

4. Is focused on sharing knowledge throughout your organization; and

5. Is driven by opportunities to effect significant change and to do better.

Sources for learning include employees' ideas, research and development (R&D), customers' input, best practice sharing, and benchmarking.[7]

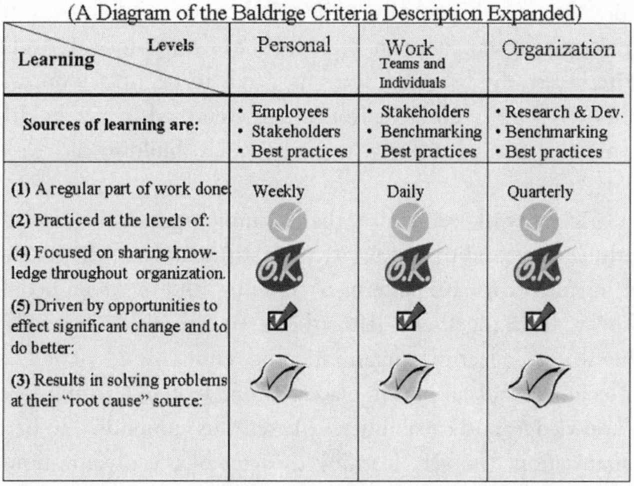

(A Diagram of the Baldrige Criteria Description Expanded)

Learning Levels	Personal	Work Teams and Individuals	Organization
Sources of learning are:	• Employees • Stakeholders • Best practices	• Stakeholders • Benchmarking • Best practices	• Research & Dev. • Benchmarking • Best practices
(1) A regular part of work done;	Weekly	Daily	Quarterly
(2) Practiced at the levels of:	✓	✓	✓
(4) Focused on sharing knowledge throughout organization.	O.K.	O.K.	O.K.
(5) Driven by opportunities to effect significant change and to do better:	☑	☑	☑
(3) Results in solving problems at their "root cause" source:	〰	〰	〰

Figure 3-1   Organizational and personal learning depicted.

The authors believe that such sharing results from one form or another of benchmarking, and thus we believe that sharing and benchmarking are interchangeable concepts. What's key is noticing and understanding how best practices benchmarking is a source of learning for every level. Second, to create a better understanding of organizational learning, it should be clear that root cause analysis is essential for the proper identification and creation of solutions or countermeasures for problems, defects, or errors. Toyota, one of the world's best manufacturers, refers to this in its revered Toyota Production System (TPS) as "asking why five times," which helps Toyota be a learning organization and is discussed later in this chapter.[8] Also, "Team" has been added to the "Work" column. A key concept pictured in Figure 3-1 is that learning must occur on several levels.

Peter Senge, author of *The Fifth Discipline: The Art and Practice of the Learning Organization*, collaborated in a more recent book, *The Fifth Discipline Fieldbook*, which provides a detailed list of characteristics that are defined as making up a learning organization. The list is displayed in Table 3-2.[9] Interestingly enough, rather than define what a learning organization is to everyone, the authors instead suggest that readers take characteristics from Table 3-2 and add their own to form a definition that they own. Then, in a workbook format, Senge and his coauthors suggest narrowing down the items noted in Table 3-2 to a top five list. Thereafter, participants who want their enterprise to become a learning organization are asked to identify the barriers standing in the way of achieving these top five characteristics. Logically, then, participants must identify how they will know if their organization is making progress. Steps are provided for how to proceed. And as with the Baldrige criteria already discussed, learning needs to take place on several levels, although they are slightly different from those identified by the Baldrige criteria: systems thinking, personal mastery, mental models, building shared vision, and team learning.[10]

Senge's original work emphasizes that learning organizations are places where people continually expand their capacity (to learn) to achieve the results they truly desire, that nurture expansive patterns of thinking, and in which people continually learn how to learn together.[11] Jeffrey Liker, author of *The Toyota Way*, suggests that, in other words, "a learning organization does not only adopt and develop new business or technical skills; it puts in place a second level of learning—how to learn new skills, knowledge, and capabilities."[12] Liker thus contends, "To become a true learning organization, the very learning capacity of the organization should be developing and growing over time."[13] So the question is, how does an organization develop and grow a learning capacity?

Developing capacity is based on building people's mental ability, individually and together, to acquire knowledge or understanding quickly—usually of skills or more effective ways of conducting oneself (behavior). And to establish a mental ability in employees or teams, organizations must build intellectual exercises or learning into jobs—just as exercising the body develops muscle for brawn strength, exercising the mind develops cerebral strength and the capacity to contribute. As the organization invests in its employees' personal learning through education, training, and experiences, employees expand their cerebral strength and add skill through practice so that they're quickly able to grasp concepts and to synthesize and translate knowledge, experiences, and information into new and better ways of doing things.

Table 3-2 Characteristics of Learning Organizations

---

1. People feel they're doing something that matters—to them personally and to the larger world.

2. Every individual in the organization is somehow stretching, growing, or enhancing his or her capacity to create.

3. People are more intelligent together than they are apart. If you want something really creative done, you ask a team to do it—instead of sending one person off to do it on his or her own.

4. The organization continually becomes more aware of its underlying knowledge base—particularly the store of tacit, unarticulated knowledge in the hearts and minds of employees.

5. Visions of the direction of the enterprise emerge from all levels. The responsibility of top management is to manage the process whereby new emerging visions become shared visions.

6. Employees are invited to learn what is going on at every level of the organization, so they can understand how their actions influence others.

7. People feel free to inquire about each other's (and their own) assumptions and biases. There are few (if any) sacred cows or undiscussable subjects.

8. People treat each other as colleagues. There's a mutual respect and trust in the way they talk to each other, and work together, no matter what their positions may be.

9. People feel free to try experiments, take risks, and openly assess the results. No one is killed for making a mistake.

Source: Peter M. Senge, et al., *The Fifth Discipline Fieldbook* (New York: Currency Doubleday, 1994), p. 51.

For business enterprises, it's about employees converting their experience and the knowledge they gain (learning) into better processes, productivity, products, and profitability. But to accomplish this, going back to Figure 3-1, the organization must build such learning exercises and expectations into the daily work of individuals and teams. A key is what Liker describes as putting in place a second level of learning, where employees and teams regularly do mental exercises that help them become better at learning. The payback is enormous and often results in (1) increased value to customers through new and improved products and services; (2) improved responsiveness and cycle time performance; (3) reduced errors, defects, waste, and associated costs; (4) increased productivity and effective use of resources; and (5) developed innovative future business opportunities.

Consider Figure 3-2, Peter Senge's concept of a learning organization. The figure shows the authors' interpretation of Senge's ensemble of five learning disciplines working in harmony.[14] The fifth discipline, *systems thinking*, is at the heart of a learning organization. It enables people to grasp and improve the complex business and industry systems of the twenty-first century. It causes individuals to envision how all the subparts work together and minimize the stovepipe thinking that leads to the suboptimization that is so prevalent in today's organizations. This fifth discipline is the conceptual cornerstone that underlies all five disciplines.

The discipline of *personal mastery* is the journeyman-like competency that each employee can achieve if he or she is assigned jobs by the organization that enable him or her to do so, resulting in the people in these jobs pursuing a lifetime of learning to become and remain expert. Organizations need to ensure that these people are encouraged to grow their knowledge. Next, *building a shared vision* is the discipline that makes employees want to bring the vision to life as they perform their jobs. They don't strive for excellence because they're told to; instead, they do so because they want to achieve results and make a contribution. Next, the discipline of *mental models* is about organizations creating the correct pictures for employees of what the organization is, what it stands for, what markets it competes in, what rivals it competes against, and so on. It's about making sure that employees picture the world correctly. Finally, *team learning* is the discipline of creating synergy so that the intelligence of the team is greater than the sum of its individuals. The combination of all five disciplines creates the comprehension of a learning organization. And with practice and mastery, people and teams quickly absorb, simulate, and convert knowledge into improvements. Hence, before long they're described as fast-learning organizations.

This discussion emphasizes that the learning organization itself must be centered on a culture consisting of the five disciplines as values, which is a foundation for the organization. To use a harvesting metaphor, like grapes in a vineyard that yields superb wine, trust and reinforcement of each discipline's value must be

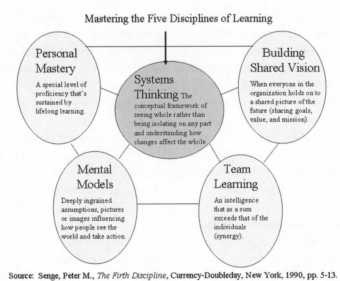

Source: Senge, Peter M., *The Fifth Discipline*, Currency-Doubleday, New York, 1990, pp. 5-13.

Figure 3-2 Peter Senge's concept of a learning organization

planned, cultivated, planted, watered, fertilized, pampered, trimmed, and watched before they can be successfully harvested. Because the disciplines are fragile, just as grapes are, they must be protected from diseases, pests, weather, and other dangers. Yet when they're leveraged in the competitive market, just as well-protected grapes may be turned into exquisite wine, the disciplines turn ordinary products into grade A crops that are very valuable in the marketplace.

The Toyota Way of Being a Learning Organization

According to author Jeffrey Liker, Toyota is one of the best learning organizations. The reason Liker gives is that Toyota sees standard work and innovation as two sides of the same coin, melding them in a way that creates great continuity.[15] It uses standardization and stability to transfer individual and team innovation into organization-wide learning. But as Liker points out, "It is one thing for individual employees to come up with innovative ways to do things." It is another thing for innovation to be transferred to organizational learning. For that to happen, the new way must be standardized and practiced across the organization until a better way is created. This demonstrates what the authors call knowledge transfer. Standardization punctuated by innovation is the Toyota way of learning.

Liker contends that to be a learning organization, it's necessary to have stability of personnel, slow promotion, and very careful succession systems to protect the organizational knowledge base. "To 'learn,'" says Liker, "means having the capacity to build on your past and move forward incrementally, rather than starting over and reinventing the wheel with new personnel with each new project."[16] But Liker may pass too quickly over what it takes for organizations to protect their knowledge base. Several questions come to mind: First, are best practices in use for managing employee turnover to the lowest levels necessary? This includes best practices for succession systems, career planning, and promotions. Second, do organizations have a strategy with priorities for converting tacit to explicit or codified knowledge? Thus, benchmarking helps those organizations that want to become learning organizations.

Returning to the Toyota case, a key to learning from Toyota is to understand how the company uses the "five whys" root cause solutions technique along with *kaizen* and *hansei* to be a learning organization. *Kaizen* is the Japanese equivalent of continuous improvement, which works best for Toyota when the process involved is stable (within variation limits) and standardized. *Hansei*, on the other hand, is the deeply rooted Japanese cultural concept involving self-reflection. It is a key part of Toyota's organizational learning. It is an adult version of the American *time-out* that parents use to discipline their children. The Japanese, who carefully introduced *hansei* into Toyota's U.S. operations during 1994, take this concept seriously, as individuals who create future plans to solve their problems do so in the belief that they will prevent these problems from ever happening again.[17] One big difference, however, is that the focus is not on blame, but on correcting root causes. It's not the people, it's the processes that are the source of problems.

To relate these Japanese techniques to winning the knowledge transfer race, the authors again introduce the concept of speed. For instance, in their book *The Kaizen Blitz*, authors Laraia, Moody, and Hall make a strong case for instigating *kaizen* change using a short, rapid-fire process. A major step-function change in a process can be accomplished within five days by performing two steps. First, the value-creation stream needs to be analyzed and all waste eliminated, particularly unnecessary work, travel, and space. Second, improvement will result from challenging every one of the assumptions that have, historically, bound the way work is performed within the process.[18]

At the heart of what makes Toyota a learning organization, however, is how the company gets to root causes by asking "why?" five times. Figure 3-3 shows an illustration of this technique, which creates widespread learning in Toyota. In fact, its use is central to the company's *kaizen* process. Figure 3-3, borrowed from Liker [who borrowed it from Peter Scholts's *The Leader's Handbook* (McGraw-Hill, 1998)], is an illustration of the type of analysis that Toyota uses in its problem-solving training and expects its employees to use in their daily work (a point made earlier in Figure 3-1). Like peeling the onion back five times, countermeasures are developed that go deeper to correct the root cause.

In this example, six levels of problems that can be fixed are revealed, and in the end, a performance review policy in the human resources department has to be changed because it is rewarding the wrong behavior by the purchasing agent. By correcting these six levels of problems, future problems resulting from these causes will be eliminated, or at least minimized. This is a systematic and planned understanding of the whole system, not just a departmental stovepipe solution. Use of the five whys question-set illustrations—more than anything else that is said about Toyota—is why the company is a learning organization. It has become part of Toyota's daily work, expectations, and standard problem-solving techniques. Toyota is also a recipient several times over of the annual MAKE (Most Admired Knowledge Enterprise) Awards.

Thoughts Regarding Transformational Learning

There is a school of thought that contends that learning is optimized though a system of double-loop learning. As pictured in Figure 3-4, the focus is on how the brain and mind work best for optimal learning to occur. The concern is that the typical, everyday single-loop type of learning (displayed in the left circle in Figure 3-4) is too limiting for those in learning organizations. In this single loop, incoming information is processed through the mind in four stages: observe, reflect, decide, and do.

The "5-Why" Investigation Questions to Solve Root Causes

	Level of Problem	Corresponding Level of Countermeasure
Why?	There is a puddle of oil on the shop floor.	Clean up the oil.
Why?	Because the machine is leaking oil.	Fix the Machine.
Why?	Because the gasket has deteriorated.	Replace the gasket.
Why?	Because we bought gaskets made of inferior material.	Change gasket specs.
Why?	Because we got a good deal (price) on those gaskets.	Change purchasing policies.
	Because purchasing agent gets evaluated on short-term cost savings.	Change the evaluation policy for purchasing agents.

Sources: Liker, Jeffrey K., *The Toyota Way*, McGraw-Hill, NY, 2004,
p. 253 & Scholtes, Peter, The Leader's Handbook, McGraw-Hill, 1998

Figure 3-3 The five why investigation questions to solve root causes

"However," says Marilynn Brennan, an advocate for developing minds for learning organizations, "80–85-percent of our learning is based on our past. So as new incoming information arrives at the mind—through the five senses of sight, sound, touch, taste, and/or smell—it is initially processed by the mind against a scan of short-term and long-term memory banks to find any matches in our past experiences, our *mental models*. That's too limiting. Instead, double-loop learning enables better and faster learning with big payoffs for learning organizations."[19]

Like Peter Senge, with his mental models discipline, Brennan contends that each person's mental models, because they consist of deeply ingrained assumptions, pictures, or images, trap that person into interpreting new information through paradigms formed from past experiences. For example, when fifty people of Native American background are shown a picture of an animal's tracks in the snow, sixteen of them tend to believe—based on their mental models—that these are coyote tracks. Fifteen others in the same group, on the other hand, have vivid memories of playing with pets in the snow, and so they believe that what they are seeing are dog tracks. The others, because they have vastly different experiences, all believe that the tracks are of an animal, but their conclusions also differ; some say wolf, others say mountain lion, one says fox terrier, and one even thinks it's a bear cub.

There are two points to be made here. First, when something new is to be learned, mental models have to be accounted for; otherwise they may prejudice what's being perceived and, thus, be barriers to fast learning. Second, teamwork helps overcome individual preconceptions (acting as barriers) by broadening each individual's mental models to the sum of the team's knowledge. This is a strong argument for using teams to grasp and apply certain types of knowledge.

Returning to the double-loop learning argument, again referring to Figure 3-4, it's at the reflect stage that there's an opportunity to go into a second loop involving *reconsider, reconnect, reframe*, and back to *reflect*. By doing this, individuals may escape the trap of mental models. To transform learning in this way, it is necessary to understand long-term and working memory. The way the brain stores long-term memory is in pairs, categories, procedures, processes, systems, patterns, and rules. Memory tests of people in a number of settings tend to confirm this phenomenon. Why not, then, teach new knowledge in such ways?

More important, *working memory* (a combination of short- and long-term memory that is displayed in Figure 3-4) is a series of building blocks that assembles into *synthesis* and, finally, *value/meaning*. It starts with rote recall, which is rumor and often water-cooler talk. The next step is comprehension, which means that the individual can converse about it. Application, the next step, is when people can perform it. Analysis is when people are able to break down something complex into its parts. Then, when synthesis is achieved, the parts or bits of knowledge are being combined to create something new, sometimes called *human capital*. This is creativity. Finally, there's the stage called value/meaning, where the big payoff exists. This is what's described in Chapter 5 as creating knowledge that may be converted into profit. This is the creation of *intellectual capital*.

Another finding from transformational learning has to do with making the mind feel safe enough for learning to be able to occur. For a nanosecond, the argu-

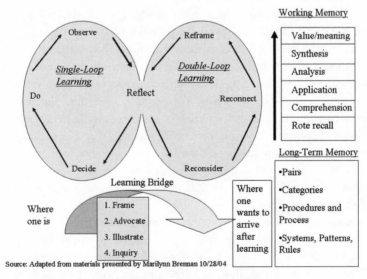

Figure 3-4 Transformational learning illustrated

ment goes, new information passes through the emotional side of the brain to ascertain whether the information is safe or unsafe. If it's unsafe, an emotional response occurs and forms a barrier to any learning. On the other hand, if the person feels safe, he or she is comfortable, willing to take risks and participate. This sets the stage for learning. Such a finding pertaining to the mind's receptivity for learning both coincides with and validates Senge's characteristics of learning organizations, listed in Table 3-2.

The bottom line for advocates of transformational learning—using double-loop learning as their mantra—is that a bridge needs to be built to close the gap between where people are before learning and where they want to be after learning. The bridge needs to consist of the four keys to learning new knowledge, which may be thought of as principles. They are

- *Frame.* Create a context for what's being presented. This is weaving knowledge into a bigger picture where it has more meaning. For example, a discussion of the knowledge transfer race throws light on why becoming a learning organization is essential in phase 2 of the race. As discussed earlier, pairs, categories, processes, patterns, and rules are also contexts for learning.

- *Advocate.* When presenting new knowledge regarding the science of stem cell research to medical students, advocating its use to save lives will help the students grasp the new knowledge. Suggesting, with moral guidelines, how the knowledge may benefit humanity through eventual cures for Parkinson's disease, spinal cord injuries, cancer, and even AIDS will make minds more receptive to learning.

- *Illustrate.* This involves telling a story, using a picture or diagram, a case study, or an analogy to bring the concept or knowledge to life. Later in this chapter, the authors tell a story about two medieval knights who are too busy sharpening their spears to listen to the bow-and-arrow salesman. This cartoonlike story illustrates that if you're in a competitive situation that has win-lose implications, it's important to take the time to learn about new innovations.

- *Inquiry or demonstration.* This is to demonstrate or show how the knowledge may be used or applied for benefit or payback. For knowledge reuse, this is powerful because demonstrations show an application of the knowledge. An effective way to learn a recipe, for example, is to watch someone use it. The learner of the knowledge gets to witness the stand-alone ingredients before the tacit knowledge of the recipe is applied.

The authors' perspective on transformational learning is that learning organizations need to consider it because, by definition, they must continually learn how to learn, too. Brennan contends that it's the mind that has to be changed first, not behavior.[20] There is logic to the argument that when the mind changes, learned behavior will follow. To close the discussion of transformational learning, because it opens conversations that need to take place about the role that the mind plays in learning and the limitations that mental images present, transformational learning does validate the use of teamwork for many forms of learning.

Types of Successful Knowledge Transfer

In addition to learning, in order to win phase 2 of the knowledge transfer race, organizations must become proficient at sharing knowledge. As teams and individuals perform the tasks of their organization, they become that organization's source of new knowledge. The ongoing process of performing produces learning and experience, or a know-how that is the source of knowledge—which originates through knowledge source teams or individuals.

The challenge is that the knowledge created by source teams needs to be transferred to and received by everyone in the organization who can use that knowledge to perform their tasks in ways that make their output better, quicker, cheaper, and superior to competitors'. There are cases in which the receiving team needs to be the same team that originates the knowledge. For example, a team of large telecommunication system (voice, data, and video) installers is working at a Texas university, replacing an inadequate system that supplies all of the communications services to the faculty, support staff, and student dormitories. Despite a one-day overrun against the budgeted schedule, the installation team not only succeeds but also solves 15 problems that were not anticipated. The same team uses the knowledge from the Texas assignment to install a similar voice-data-video telecom system for a Delaware university. The knowledge that the team gained in one context is applied to another. The name for this is a *serial transfer* because it occurs in a succession or series of experiences. There are, however, many other cases in which the teams that need to receive and use knowledge aren't the same people who originated it.

In her relevant book *Common Knowledge*, author Nancy Dixon documents her research and findings about how ten prominent organizations transfer internal knowledge to their teams of people who need to receive and apply the wisdom.[21] Dixon looked at leaders in knowledge management. The list consisted of Bechtel, British Petroleum (BP), Buckman Labs, Chevron, Ernst & Young, Ford, Lockheed Martin, Texas Instruments (TI), the World Bank, and the U.S. Army.[22] For months Dixon observed what she called "lessons learnt," "mistakes," "best practices," "better ways," "naturally occurring work products," "peer assists," and "virtual team networks." The linking of knowledge to action distinguishes it from information. In the end, Dixon found five types of team knowledge transfers, which she called *serial transfer, near transfer, far transfer, strategic transfer,* and *expert transfer*.

The five types of knowledge transfer that Dixon found are listed in Table 3-3, which includes definitions and examples.[23] Dixon borrowed the labels *near* and

Table 3-3 Five Types of Knowledge Transfer

	Serial Transfer	Near Transfer	Far Transfer	Strategic Transfer	Expert Transfer
Definition	The knowledge that a team has gained from doing its task in one setting is transferred to the next time that team does that task in a different setting.	Explicit knowledge that a team has gained from doing a frequent and repeated task is reused by other teams doing very similar work.	Tacit knowledge that a team has gained from doing a nonroutine task is made available to other teams doing similar work in another part of the organization.	The collective knowledge of the organization is needed to accomplish a strategic task that occurs infrequently but is critical to the whole organization.	A team facing a technical question beyond the scope of its own knowledge seeks the expertise of others in the organization.
Example	U.S. Army squadron engages in Iraq battle and uses after action review (AAR) knowledge when engaging in future combat.	A team in a Detroit auto plant figures out how to install brakes in 10 minutes. A team in Dallas uses that knowledge to reduce its time by one minute.	Peers travel to assist a team dealing with a unique oil exploration site. The collaboration provides new approaches.	GE uses know-ledge from AlliedSignal to develop a Six Sigma system. Two years later, Raytheon uses what was learned from GE to design its *Raytheon Six Sigma* system.	A technician e-mails the network asking how to increase the brightness on out-of-date monitors. Seven experts provide answers.
Type of knowledge	Tacit and explicit	Explicit	Tacit	Tacit and explicit	Explicit
Nature of task	Frequent and nonroutine	Frequent and routine	Infrequent and nonroutine	Infrequent and nonroutine	Infrequent and routine
Similarity of task and context	The receiving team (which is also the source team) does a similar task in a new context.	The receiving team does a task similar to that of the source team and in a similar context.	The receiving team does a task similar to that of the source team, but in a different context.	The receiving team does a task that affects the whole organization in a context different from that of the source team.	The receiving team does a different task from that of the source team, but in a similar context.

(continued)

Table 3-3 Five Types of Knowledge Transfer (continued)

	Serial Transfer	Near Transfer	Far Transfer	Strategic Transfer	Expert Transfer
Design guidelines	■ Meetings are held regularly and are brief. ■ Everyone involved in the action participates in the meetings. ■ There is no punishment for speaking out, and reports are not forwarded. ■ Meetings are facilitated locally.	■ Knowledge is spread electronically, supplemented with personal interaction. ■ Knowledge is "pushed." ■ There is compliance with choice. ■ Usage and business goals are monitored. ■ Brief descriptions are adequate. ■ The database is targeted.	■ Exchange is reciprocal. ■ Source team knowledge is translated. ■ People carry the knowledge across the organization. ■ Process is given a recognizable name.	■ Knowledge needed is identified by senior-level managers. ■ Knowledge specialists collect and interpret the knowledge. ■ Collection occurs in real time rather than after the fact. ■ Focus is on the end user. ■ Multiple voices are synthesized.	■ Electronic forums are segmented by topic. ■ Electronic forum are monitored and supported. ■ Differing levels of participation are encouraged. ■ Knowledge is "pulled."

Source: Adapted from Nancy M. Dixon, *Common Knowledge: How Companies Thrive by Sharing What They Know* (Boston: Harvard Business School Press, 2000), Table 8-1, pp. 144–145.

far from learning theorists. The details involved in each transfer method are masterfully documented in Dixon's book, *Common Knowledge: How Companies Thrive by Sharing What They Know.* Serial transfer is summarized in the first column of Table 3-3. The telecom installation in Texas and Delaware is an illustration. So is the U.S. Army's use of after action reviews (AARs) to make the same team more effective by analyzing what it has learned from former engagements. An example of near transfer occurs when an automotive plant in Dallas uses a knowledge breakthrough from Detroit to shave one minute off the time it takes to install brakes. Dixon's example from British Petroleum of a peer assist is an example of a far transfer. The example provided in Chapter 2 of Raytheon's leveraging of GE's learning from AlliedSignal to design *Raytheon Six Sigma* is an example of strategic transfer. Finally, expert transfers involve networks of, say, technicians sharing troubleshooting fixes or similar tacit knowledge on nonroutine and infrequent tasks.

The issue is when to use any particular method. All five types of knowledge transfers are needed in different circumstances. Indeed, Dixon makes a compelling case for use of a decision tree to make decisions about which of the five methods to use in a given situation. Use of any one method depends on the answers to several questions. Dixon configured the key questions into a decision tree, which has been adapted as Figure 3-5.

To illustrate the use of the decision tree, consider the *Raytheon Six Sigma* benchmarking team example from Chapter 2. What the team was asked to do was to study the best deployments of Six Sigma up to that point in time, take the best of what the leading companies had done, and design a better and broader version of Six Sigma for Raytheon. This new *Raytheon Six Sigma* would go way beyond the

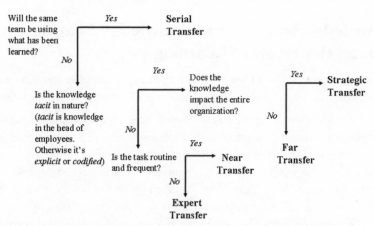

Source: Adapted from Dixon, Nancy M., *Common Knowledge*, Harvard Business School Press, Boston, 2000, p. 147.

Figure 3-5   The Dixon decision tree for applying five types of knowledge transfer

use of the benchmarking team. So the answer to the first decision-tree question is no, which excludes serial transfer. The answer to the next question, "Is the knowledge tacit?" is yes. The reason is that the desired knowledge resided in the heads of executives at AlliedSignal, GE, Motorola, and the leaders of a Six Sigma strategy. This answer excludes both expert transfer and new transfer, which involve explicit knowledge. The answer to the third question, "Does the knowledge affect the whole organization?" is also yes. The vision of CEO Dan Burnham was that *Raytheon Six Sigma* would touch every employee. This answer points to strategic transfer as the preferred knowledge transfer solution, at the same time eliminating far transfer.

Looking across all five types of transfer, Dixon made three observations. First, everyone engaged in work tasks (not just experts) has knowledge that someone else in the organization can use to advantage. Second, knowledge is just as much embedded in communities (e.g., Communities of Practice, or CoPs) as it is in individuals. There is a synergy between colleagues that makes it more appropriate to say that a team or community originated something new than to try to figure out which member of the team or community was most responsible when they can't figure it out either. Third, knowledge is dynamic and ever-changing. The picturesque metaphor that Dixon uses is *water flowing*. It is powerful, and little can stand in its way.[24]

In phase 2 of the knowledge transfer race, what Dixon's work points to is the need for organizations to be deliberate and systematic in how they share knowledge. They may need to create an organizational structure, conduct knowledge-sharing assessments, and create a framework, or design processes, methods, and tools, for knowledge transfer. Use of all five knowledge-sharing methods needs to be part of the system. It's not optional; it's a necessity for winning the knowledge transfer race.

Knowledge Transfer and Knowledge Sharing Are on the Heels of Learning

The authors' "how to" list of key proven and practical things that organizations can do to become faster at organizational and individual learning contains the following:

1. An organization's culture has to support rapid and continuous learning. It needs to have the expectation that everyone's job is to continuously learn. Phrases such as "We've always done it this way" or "We're different" need to be treated as words to fight over, more for the attitudes they represent than for the words alone. Culture involves the kind and level of performance that is expected of individuals and teams and how they are evaluated and rewarded. To "walk the talk," organizations need systems that reward the right behavior. Managing employee performance includes the way individual and team objectives are set and aligned with organizational goals

2. The training provided for new tools and job performance techniques needs to be robust. People need to know where to learn within their organization. A college education is just the beginning. For people to learn aggressively after college, many of the principles are the same, but the approach has to be adapted to the culture of the organization. Developing a knowledge network on the job is the choice of each individual employee. Belonging to a knowledge network will not be prescribed in the typical college curriculum of required courses. Yet the authors contend it's a very effective way to learn once on the job. Also, once on the job, education, experiences, and training need to be designed by type of employee and aligned to employees' competency and development needs.

3. Establish knowledge-sharing symposiums and internal meetings to elevate, highlight, and share knowledge. Benchmarking will identify several very successful approaches to doing this that may be adapted to particular organizations. Several MAKE (Most Admired Knowledge Enterprise) Award recipients have an established record of doing this very effectively and have gone through several cycles of refinement and improvement. Use CoPs to concentrate rapid learning among core technology groups.

4. Provide recognition and rewards for sharing and reusing knowledge. While achieving reuse is not easy, getting people to share knowledge regularly is even harder. Thus, addressing "What's in it for me?" right up front is advised. Once again, several MAKE recipient organizations serve as excellent role models and benchmarks.

5. Obtain access to several of the splendid knowledge databases and use document-friendly software packages. These tools are necessities for searches and learning, and they enable organizations to quickly document and update explicit knowledge content for training. Engage corporate librarians and information specialists to expand the knowledge network capabilities.

The American Productivity and Quality Center (APQC), in existence since 1977 and an internationally recognized resource for benchmarking and knowledge management since 1992, identifies three themes that resonate with it regarding successful learning, knowledge transfer, and benchmarking. The three themes are identified in Table 3-4. The gist of these themes underscores the importance of relationships, a passion for learning, and learning something new every day.

Texas Instruments' NIHBIDIA Awards and ShareFair

One innovative approach to sharing knowledge was started in 1996 by Texas Instruments (TI) as a sharing day with awards. TI launched its "Not Invented Here

Table 3-4 Three Themes Regarding Learning, Transfer, and Benchmarking Observed by the APQC[25]

Transfer is a people-to-people process; meaningful relationships precede sharing and transfer.
Learning and transfer is an interactive, ongoing, and dynamic process that cannot rest on a static body of knowledge. Employees are inventing, improvising, and learning something new every day.
Benchmarking stems from a personal and organizational willingness to learn. A vibrant sense of curiosity and a deep respect and desire for learning may be the real keys.

Source: www.apqc.org/portal/apqc/site/generic.

But I Did It Anyway," or NIHBIDIA, awards. The purpose was to encourage best practices sharing (BPS). It was called ShareFair. Best practices teams manned booths to publicize those practices and engaged in Q&A with fellow TI employees. The name of the awards reinforced TI's desire that its teams and individuals go outside; tap into the world's stockpile of rich knowledge; and import, adapt, and innovate upon best practices knowledge that already existed. This event got TI people actively talking about ways in which they could reuse valuable knowledge. To the extent that TI wanted to encourage sharing, ShareFair did just that. Individuals and teams were recognized for the most successfully shared best practices and knowledge, including those that produced great results. Senior managers presented the awards, which further encouraged others to share and reinforced the idea of sharing.

The first year, the event attracted 500. Besides booths, seminars were held on how to share effectively. Two leading-edge thought leaders were speakers: Tom Davenport of the University of Texas and Carla O'Dell, president of the APQC. They energized the attendees with perspectives on knowledge sharing and reuse. Overall, 52 nominations were submitted for the NIHBIDIA Awards, which resulted in the recognition of 450 team members who, combined, generated over $1 billion in annual savings.

During the second year, 1997, the focus of ShareFair was on the use of Internet technologies to share best practices and company intranet and extranet capabilities. The important effect of teams was recognized. That year, 51 nominations were received involving the work of 480 TI employees. TI's Dallas Wafer Fabrications Operations and Silicon Systems, Inc., received awards. TI's Defense Systems and Electronics Group, which had just been sold to Raytheon and renamed Raytheon TI Systems (RTIS), also participated jointly. Five winners from RTIS were recognized, with acknowledgments to both the teams that shared and those that reused knowledge.

All in all, the TI approach was innovative and changed the compensation systems so that knowledge sharing and reuse were recognized, rewarded, and encouraged. This was but one of many steps that TI took to make best practices sharing an integral part of individual, unit, and overall company performance reviews.

Raytheon's New *Raytheon Six Sigma* Celebration

As the *Raytheon Six Sigma*™ (*R6σ*) process was beginning in 1998, it became evident that face-to-face learning and recognition would be an important part of sustaining the momentum of *R6σ* teams. Several business units had begun business-unit recognition events as well as participating in the corporate-level event. As each unit held a little better event than the last, a healthy rivalry began regarding the team accomplishments in one unit compared to the team accomplishments in others.

Senior leaders decided to hold an annual gala Raytheon recognition event, and they named it *R6σ* Celebration. The winners from each business unit were invited and recognized at this annual event. Before the planning had gone very far, it was evident that five hundred employees needed to be invited. To produce a conference of this size effectively, one of the business units needed to host the event and assign resources to handle the detailed planning and logistics involved. And so the event would rotate from one business unit to another year after year. At each event, booths were allocated to each winning team. For publicity, internal one-page press releases were written and distributed to the attendees to share knowledge about each team's project, including the problems they encountered and the results they achieved.

The Raytheon CEO toured the booths and discussed the projects with each team. Later, the CEO also recognized the teams onstage, presented them with trophies, and had group photos taken with him. The Raytheon Knowledge Transfer Champions sponsored a KM Passport game that educated and trained attendees on Raytheon's knowledge sharing and reuse process. Completed Passports had to be validated by a KM champion before they were made part of the KM winners drawing, which was for free airplane tickets for two people to go anywhere in the United States, including Alaska and Hawaii. Winners were recognized on the stage in front of all attendees.

In the 2003 and 2004 *R6σ* Celebrations, the Knowledge Management (KM) Champions also sponsored a KM track of five knowledge management success stories that were presented by the participants. In 2004, the KM champions created the Knowledge Sharing and Reuse Award (KSARA) for the top five teams that met the defined criteria. In addition to the crystal trophy and recognition that each team member received, each winning team also presented its case studies to the open forum. This illustrates the kind of high-level support and culture change that organizations are encouraged to undertake if they are to win the knowledge transfer race.

Learning Is a Here and Now Frontier of Competition and One of the Keys to Creating and Leveraging Intellectual Capital

Consider the effects of being a learning organization, particularly one that is fast at it. It is like fresh rain pouring down on and revitalizing a desert. Learning, like the rain, has the effect of revitalizing people. Learning quickly turns organizations into vibrant greenhouses that nurture and multiply innovations like a hive of bees does honey. Such greenhouses grow the capabilities of any organization. It experiments and becomes capable of market leadership. Such organizations also have the persistence of a business and industry version of Darwin's survival of the fittest because leading (and learning) organizations create migrations inside their markets, create new markets, and all the while are in lockstep with their customers. Consider some of the outcomes of learning organizations, particularly those that have become fast at it:

- Employees are knowledgeable, up-to-date, hopeful, and systems thinkers who can take enterprises into new markets and achieve unheard-of results. Such a highly competent and engaged workforce takes swift action to implement better practices for the situation at hand. Because of the systems thinking behind the actions, error and defect rates shrink quickly. Also, new initiatives are rolled out quickly and modified quickly to meet the needs of customers. As a result, learning organizations tend to be good at managing change. They are agile organizations. Consider the example of Amazon.com, the 2003 Global MAKE winner. Based in Seattle, Washington, it started a Web business during July 1995. Its employees have contributed to making Amazon.com one of the most customer-centric companies ever, where customers can find almost everything they might want to buy online at very low prices. Amazon.com is a learning organization that delivers value based on customer knowledge and maximizes the value of its intellectual capital.

- Learning organizations have happier employees who feel free to learn, play, and achieve mastery. The nine characteristics described earlier are testimony to how invigorated employees feel when they are working inside a learning organization. For most, it's an approach that not only increases joy in work, but also increases what is commonly called quality of life. Part of the joy comes from feeling that each person's private aspirations are being respected and legitimized; part of it is the acceptance of being in a community of shared values that is more versatile and contributes to an improved environment for innovation. Such employees tend to be more open-minded about change, more agile when responding to changing priorities, and more open to helping others succeed. They are more apt to accept job redefinition, workflow redesign, and more new responsibilities because they've provided as much input as anyone into the decision-making process. Consider the World Bank, the only nonprofit recipient of a 2003 Global MAKE award. It was recognized for developing strong knowledge-based workers and a culture of mutual collaboration. Now, leaders of the World Bank see themselves as knowledge brokers who help underdeveloped countries learn and grow as rapidly as possible. Everything from improving a country's infrastructure to planting and harvesting crops to fighting diseases is within their scope. It was a big mental model change when World Bank employees realized that they were not bankers but knowledge brokers. Once their leaders confronted this new concept and accepted the model, then they began building the knowledge management processes to achieve the excellence recognized by the MAKE award.

■ People in learning organizations tend to make them knowledge-based organizations that excel at the fast delivery of knowledge-based solutions and products. Such people tend to be system thinkers who have the rare capability of translating technologies into customer solutions. Because they pay close attention to customers and listen to how their needs are changing, they innovate on the fly. Consider the four knowledge-intensive leaders in information technology, all 2003 MAKE award recipients: Hewlett-Packard, Infosys Technologies, IBM, and Microsoft. Each in its own way uses a strong base of knowledge and knowledge workers to deliver knowledge-based products. These companies are time responsive. They are also learning organizations that are known for creating value based on customer knowledge. Most of their company capital value is based on their intellectual capital, as they have very few assets in the form of plants, machinery, or bricks and mortar—the old accounting method of valuing companies. They also pay attention to speed by removing waste, streamlining their processes, and striving for productivity gains. Speed, as is mentioned throughout this book, is something learning organizations achieve that tends to make them leaders in the knowledge transfer race.

Becoming a learning organization is not a be-all and end-all, either; it is also the wherewithal for greater profitability. Because of their capacity to learn and to convert knowledge into improvements, employees of learning organizations also create, reuse, and share more intellectual capital than their contemporaries. In Chapter 5, the authors review intellectual capital. For now, one type of intellectual capital is human capital, which consists of employee experience, know-how, skills, and creativity—all tacit or implicit knowledge that's in the minds of and owned by employees. What is key is that it may be converted into value or profit.

Employees of learning organizations (often called knowledge worker employees) create more, share more, and reuse more intellectual capital. This will be demonstrated in Chapter 5. What all this means is that learning organizations have a greater prospect of being profitable, and, all other things being equal, probably more profitable. Better employees are also attracted to learning organizations, where, together, they have a greater prospect of achieving their own personal aspirations and are better aligned with bringing the organization's vision, values, strategies, and tactics to life.

Referring back to Senge's list of nine characteristics of learning organizations, it's clear that employees flourish in these environments. They feel that they're doing something that matters, that they're stretched, that teams do intelligent work, that their visions are shared, that they're invited to learn, that people are respected, and that they can experiment and innovate. People jump at the opportunity to be a part of such an organization. And that is one of the reasons it behooves contestants in the knowledge transfer race to become learning organizations: it enables them to win the knowledge transfer race. It's recommended that as many pit stops as necessary be taken to do so. The knowledge transfer race vehicle will need tune-ups, tire changes, fluid checks, and an occasional reality check on the original race strategy. On the other hand, those that don't do this now will be at a disadvantage later.

Once the fundamentals of learning as a core competency are in place, the speed of learning becomes the emphasis. Before long, there are deliberate efforts to speed up the import (benchmarking), capture, use, transference, and reuse of best practices knowledge. Advances in technology then speed up and equal the organization's ability to absorb and apply them. Suddenly, speed turns everything into a race. Like the virtual reality of a video game car race, the focus is on getting the lead and keeping it. The race is on, and it's those who learn the fastest and excel at sharing knowledge what are in the lead heading into phase 3 of the race. Indeed, Art Kleiner, coauthor with Peter Senge of *The Fifth Discipline Fieldbook*, when asked the question, "Why bother?" (to become a learning organization), provided the ideas listed in Table 3-5 as his answers.[26] Taken together, they make a compelling argument for why organizations should bother.

Mastering Phase 2 of the Knowledge Transfer Race

In many respects, phase 2 of the race requires that contestants become learning organizations. This is no easy task, considering that doing it requires a commitment by senior management along with many cultural human resource systems that, together, create a learning environment. Understanding follows. Once the organization accepts a learning organization strategy, the more difficult part of phase 2 has been completed. The challenge of mastering the remainder of phase 2 is the actual

Table 3-5   Why Bother Creating a Learning Organization?

- Because we want superior performance and competitive advantage.
- For customer relations.
- To avoid decline.
- To understand risks and diversity more deeply.
- For innovation.
- For our personal and spiritual well-being.
- To increase our ability to manage change.
- For understanding.
- For an energized, committed workforce.
- To expand boundaries.
- To engage in community.
- For independence and liberty.
- For awareness of the critical nature of interdependence.
- Because the times demand it.

Source: Art Kleiner, coauthor, *The Fifth Discipline Fieldbook*, from http://world.std.com/.

deployment process, spreading knowledge around by sharing it with the right people at the right locations. There are, however, many potential roadblocks to understanding and sharing. A key success factor is how well internal transfers of best practices knowledge are accomplished. Figuratively, it's the right hand knowing what the left hand is doing.

The authors are convinced that the knowledge transfer and learning race is the present-day battlefield for competitive advantage. For years, organizations have thought of gaining competitive advantage in terms of having superior products and technology, lower costs, and increased productivity. But that changed during the 1990s. It's an information age, and business and industry are fueled by knowledge. Fast learning has become a differentiating competency, a competitive advantage. In the twenty-first century, enterprises need a deliberate strategy of getting the right knowledge to the right people at the right time and helping people share information and put that information into action in ways that strive to improve organizational performance.

To be at top speed in the race coming out of the second turn (phase 2), contestants must be deliberate and systematic at removing barriers to learning, understanding, and sharing. Issues have to be faced head on, such as ignorance (not knowing what's known); insufficient capacity to absorb (not enough time or resources); inadequate cooperation, teamwork, and relationships; too little motivation; a lack of will; and mistrust. Attitudes have to be faced, too, like "If it's not invented here, it can't be any good" or "We're different; it won't work here" or "I'm too busy." There is a cartoon about two medieval knights that is relevant. They are sharpening their spears and saying that they're too busy to talk to the crossbow salesman. This cute story demonstrates that learning about new weapons just might be more important than sharpening old weapons. The point is, a new mindset is needed, one of profound humility. A knowledge-age mindset, on the other hand, is one that declares, "We aren't the best," "Many things could be better," and "We can learn from anyone." Such humility is the cornerstone to becoming a learning organization and winning the knowledge transfer race.

The Bottom Line for People in Small Organizations

While large organizations have many barriers to organizational learning, surprisingly, small organizations face many of the same barriers. However, small companies usually benefit from still having a start-up mentality of doing more with less. Also, they're usually more agile and always on the lookout for a market niche from which to position themselves for greater success. Indeed, an important driving force for small organizations is settling on a niche geographic market to enter, survive, and thrive in by the delivery of a product or service that is not currently being provided and for which there is or will be sufficient demand.

Bear in mind that when Starbucks began offering high-quality gourmet coffee and tea drinks in 1971, demand estimates initially completely overlooked the ambiance and social factors involved with specialty coffee drinks, along with the value of partnerships with Barnes & Noble bookstores, Nordstroms, and other such organizations. By 2005, Frappuccino™, now available in grocery stores, has become one of the favorite beverages of a growing segment of the consuming public. Frappuccino is a registered trademark of Starbucks. Also, Starbucks, with over 8,000 locations, is no longer small. In any case, the small-business focus—like what Starbucks did when it was small—is on producing and delivering products and services that are of value to customers, staying viable, and growing and sustaining the business case rather than the usual emphasis of large organizations on being more efficient and effective.

There are six tips from this chapter that are included in the list of 55 tips for people in small organizations in Chapter 11. These six tips are numbered 16 through 21 in Chapter 11. In an abbreviated form, they are:

- The learning organization concept needs to be integrated into small businesses because it's just as valid for small as it is for large businesses.
- Of the five types of knowledge transfers discussed, serial and expert transfers should be implemented immediately.
- The transformational learning principles of frame, advocate, illustrate, and demonstrate can be simplified to one-page handout formats.

- An organized water-cooler effect may be a very effective method of communicating with people at any given location.
- Encourage people to reuse best practices knowledge, and recognize those who do so.
- Make it a company value to ask for help and to give suggestions.

Commenting on a few of these tips, an organized yet informal water-cooler effect may be a very effective method of sharing information in a bullpen manner. Perhaps there are regular times that people can gather for a planned Q&A. Then, impromptu gatherings may be called when there's time-sensitive information to share. Piggyback work-group meetings may follow to take action on matters that were discussed. Besides, if the usual water-cooler effect results in those insiders being well informed compared to those who are not insiders, why not be inclusive and have company management bring everyone into one insider group?

Regarding other tips, small organizations can effectively create a learning organization culture by making it a company value to ask for and give suggestions and to recognize those who learn, share, and reuse best practices knowledge. The point here is that employees in small organizations usually have broad responsibilities and tend to be more receptive to continuous learning. Encourage it. The departmental stovepipes haven't been built yet or aren't so strong that they're difficult to overcome. Small learning and sharing meetings can be arranged to support this strategy. Each person can speak about what he or she has learned and the knowledge he or she has reused. If these meetings are expected and fun, they can be a real bonding occasion, and people will look forward to sharing with others what they've learned. Management will have to continually facilitate and support the meetings. Remember, though, that trust, like confidence, is fragile and must be built and continually reinforced. All in all, to master phase 2 of the knowledge transfer race, a learning organization is needed so that knowledge is learned, created, shared, and transferred.

Endnotes

1. Rebecca N. Ferguson, *The Handy History Answer Book* (Canton, Mich.: Visible Ink Press, 2000), pp. 1–26.
2. Ibid., p. 417.
3. Ibid., pp. 417–418.
4. Christopher E. Bogan and Michael J. English, *Benchmarking for Best Practices: Winning through Innovative Adaptation* (New York: McGraw-Hill, 1994), p. 17.
5. Peter M. Senge, *The Fifth Discipline: The Art and Practice of the Learning Organization* (New York: Currency Doubleday, 1990), p. 4.

6. Baldrige National Quality Program, "2003 Criteria for Performance Excellence," published by the National Institute of Standards and Technology (NIST), U.S. Department of Commerce, pp.1–2; www.quality.nist.gov.

7. Ibid., p. 2.

8. Jeffrey K. Liker, *The Toyota Way* (New York: McGraw-Hill, 2004), pp. 252–259.

9. Peter M. Senge, Art Kleiner, Charlotte Roberts, Richard B. Ross, and Bryan J. Smith, *The Fifth Discipline Fieldbook: Strategies and Tools for Building a Learning Organization* (New York: Currency, 1994), p. 51.

10. Ibid., pp. 13–444.

11. Senge, *The Fifth Discipline.*

12. Liker, *The Toyota Way*, p. 251.

13. Ibid.

14. Senge, *The Fifth Discipline*, pp. 5–13.

15. Liker, *The Toyota Way*, p. 251.

16. Ibid., p. 252.

17. Ibid., pp. 252–258.

18. Anthony Laraia, Patricia E. Moody, and Robert W. Hall, *The Kaizen Blitz: Accelerating Breakthroughs in Productivity and Performance* (New York: John Wiley & Sons, 1999).

19. Marilynn Brennan's presentation at the American Society of Quality, Dallas Section 1410, on Oct. 28, 2004, which included two handouts and flipchart content.

20. Ibid.

21. Nancy M. Dixon, *Common Knowledge: How Companies Thrive by Sharing What They Know* (Boston: Harvard Business School Press, 2000), pp. 17–20.

22. Ibid., pp. 14–15.

23. Ibid., pp. 17–147.

24. Ibid., pp. 148–159.

25. Information obtained from the APQC's Web site at www.apqc.org/portal/apqc/site/generic on Nov. 24, 2003.

26. Information obtained from http://world.std.com/-lo/WhyLO.html. This is input that Art Kleiner provided to a Web site created by Richard Karash addressing the question, "Why a learning organization?" According to Karash, Kleimer had originally planned to include a section in the book *The Fifth Discipline Fieldbook* entitled "Why Bother?" and it was to have been organized around the 15 themes listed in Table 3-5.

Chapter 4

A Process Framework for Classifying Best Practices and Intellectual Capital: Building a Culture for Winning the Knowledge Transfer Race

Introduction

At the center of the knowledge transfer racetrack, Figure 1-2, is a circle described as "Create Knowledge-Enabled Culture." In the context of a civilization, culture consists of the customs, beliefs, social norms, and behaviors that institutions (families, communities, and governments) pass on from one generation to the next; they include education, aesthetics, morals, and religion or spiritual enlightenment. This includes knowledge such as Galileo's modern scientific method in use today. However, in the knowledge transfer race, a knowledge-enabled culture is something altogether different.

In business and industry and this race, a knowledge-enabled culture consists of a unique combination of human resource systems that together determine what people in an enterprise accomplish. Starting with a vision and a business strategy, culture is supported by a system of aligned human resource policies, tactics, processes, and practices that together ensure accountability and that

- Jobs are designed properly, with clear descriptions and qualifications.
- The best people are recruited to fill the jobs.
- Appropriate performance measurements are created for each position.
- Challenging goals are established for the people occupying each job.
- Education, training, and developmental experiences are designed for each job to correspond with the way the jobs have been designed and the goals expected.

- Performance is properly evaluated in terms of what was achieved versus goals and how the performance (ethics and behavior) was accomplished.
- Rewards (compensation) and recognition are administered effectively to reward the right behavior and to enable the enterprise to achieve its strategy and vision.
- Promotions, reassignments, and dismissals are handled as required, enabling the cycle to be repeated as a closed-loop system.
- Innovation and risk taking are promoted and fear of failure is not rampant.

In other words, culture has to do with modeling, structuring, empowering, training, and rewarding people to do the hard work of bringing life to the organization's vision and strategy. In the metaphoric knowledge transfer race, the vision is to win the race, and the strategy is to master all four phases of the race. To overcome obstacles or create needed capability, as many pit stops as necessary may be taken to put in place the necessary policies, systems, or processes. But as in the race, the pit stops need to be preplanned and to be as speedy and efficient as possible.

This chapter is about making one or more pit stops to install a knowledge-enabled culture. This means making *knowledge* the center of every one of the cultural human resource bullets previously listed. In other words, learning and knowledge become the focal point of job design, performance measures, goals, compensation systems, and so on.

What should be clear, too, is that what was just discussed in Chapter 3 (becoming a learning organization) is an essential component of creating a knowledge-enabled culture. Chapter 3 concentrated on mastering phase 2 of the race, *learn, understand, and share*. But to master that phase of the race, it is necessary to become a learning organization, which is the foundation of the knowledge-enabled culture. In this chapter, a process-centered architecture is introduced that, like pillars that hold up a ceiling, supports, enables, and brings to life a knowledge-enabled culture.

Processes: The Source of Value Creation

The fundamental difference between those organizations that win and those that lose is that with few exceptions, winning organizations have superior processes. The winners acquire and transfer more of the best knowledge into processes that transform inputs into better, cheaper, and quicker outputs that fully meet customer requirements and expectations. In other words, the processes of winning organizations contain more value-adding work and less unnecessary work. In this context, the definition of *unnecessary* is work that either is wasted or is something that the customer will not pay for (or non-value-adding work). Therefore, because the mission of any business is to create customer value, not only do organizations have to focus on creating high-value processes, but they also have to continually improve those processes and build more capability into them. Most business processes crisscross departmental lines and become entangled in territorial priorities and suboptimized decisions that do not focus on the process from the customers' viewpoint.

The underlying and fundamental concept involved here is that any and all value created by an organization comes from its processes. In other words, as illustrated by Figure 4-1, processes are the mechanisms that organizations use to produce products and services that have value to customers. Superior processes create superior value. Therefore, it also makes sense to base the design of a best practices and knowledge repository system around a business process taxonomy or classification framework. What a breakthrough it is to catalog metrics, benchmarks, best practices, and knowledge according to an easy-to-understand common process taxonomy. It's as though all the businesspeople on the planet could talk with one another in one common language. It is the language of process.

An effective business process is an integrated grouping of activities that together transform inputs (simultaneously creating customer value) into outputs (with minimal variation) that fully meet customers' needs and deliver on their expectations. Yet processes are intangible and are not easily identifiable or understood by the human mind. They are invisible. So processes have to be made explicit, fully revealed without vagueness. It is an arduous but necessary task to make processes explicit so that they can be given the attention required for organizations to become high performing.

There are four considerations involved in making processes explicit. First, each category—process, major process, subprocess, and activity—needs to be given a

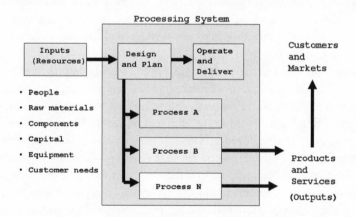

Processes are Mechanisms that convert Ideas
and Innovation into Products and Services

Figure 4-1 Processes are mechanisms that convert ideas and innovation into products and services

unique and corresponding name. For example, "1.0 Develop Vision and Strategy" would be a process category; "1.1 Define the business concept and long-term vision" would be a process group; "1.1.1 Assess the external environment" would be a process; and "1.1.1.1 Analyze and understand competition" would be an activity. Second, a process architecture that uses a common vocabulary is needed. In the example just given, the architecture includes a hierarchy of 1.0, 1.1, 1.1.1, and 1.1.1.1. A framework is needed so that all processes that are common to almost every organization are identified and defined in precise language. This way, any organization will be able to map a given process under a different name to corresponding activities, subprocesses, and processes as defined in a master architecture so that people can be certain that they're describing the very same value stream when they're discussing, sharing, and transferring knowledge. Think of the framework as the Dewey Decimal System for processes with a common set of definitions.

Third, an end-to-end value stream needs to be mapped for each process to make that process visible and explicit. Inputs, processing steps, outputs, and customers need to be identified, with definitions for each. Input-processing-output (IPO) maps enable people to wrap their minds around a process and grasp what it means. Next, measurements for inputs, processing, outputs, and customer satisfaction need to be specified. Benchmarks are advisable, too, for key performance indicators. Measurements enable goal setting to manage beginning-to-end performance so that the process can be continually improved. The mapping begins with the timely receipt of the proper inputs. The stream continues through processing steps that transform the inputs into outputs, adding value along the way. The stream ends with receipt by customers. The products received should be delivered on time, without defects, and should completely satisfy customers. The fourth consideration is how to eliminate the root cause sources of variations in output that occur in the value stream as the processing steps are performed. Reducing variation will be reviewed in Chapter 6.

These four considerations open up possibilities for improvement using a DMBAIC (define, measure, benchmark, analyze, improve, and control) mindset. In Chapters 6 and 8, Six Sigma tools and techniques will be shown, along with how they may be used to reduce or eliminate variation. Design for Six Sigma, (DFSS), or process reengineering focuses on expanding process capability and understanding the available process capability within which the organization is operating. Sooner or later, emphasis on reducing variation and expanding capability leads most improvement practitioners to conclude that the adequacy of process design is the source of most performance problems (or opportunities). In most cases it is the process that is at fault, not individuals' performancess that fail and cause variation.

For now, the essential point is that every organization must create and manage its processes in order to produce value for its customers. This notion regarding processes is easier to understand by thinking of a process as a value chain, where each step is designed and managed to add value to the preceding step and, taken all together, the steps create a valuable product or service for customers. Thus, managing processes is crucial. Whether the criteria are the European Quality Awards criteria, the Shingo Prize, ISO 9000, or the U.S. Baldrige National Quality Award criteria—each of which will be reviewed in Chapter 6—process management is universally recognized as the foundation for creating value for any organization. Indeed, the Baldrige criteria are clear and specific:

> Your key value creation processes are those most important to "running your business" and maintaining or achieving a sustainable competitive advantage. They are the processes that involve the majority of your organization's employees and produce customer, stockholder, and other key stakeholder value. They include the processes through which your organization adds greatest value to its products and services. They also include the business processes most critical to adding value to the business itself, resulting in success and growth.[1]

Business processes are therefore absolutely essential value-adding activities that span functional boundaries and silos, linking together human resources, management proficiencies, technologies, and capital to enable any organization to bring to life its strategy for creating value for its stakeholders and especially its customers. Of course, business processes also transcend individual sites and geospatial locations. Inevitably, separating people—even though originally deemed necessary by the organizations involved—makes it very difficult for them to communicate and accomplish the kind of cross-functional teamwork needed to optimize end-to-end process performance.

At this juncture, it's fitting to make a distinction between business processes and work processes. Work processes are those activities that are performed entirely within the control of a single function, such as finance or human resources. When the word *process* is used hereafter, it is meant to describe a business process. A business process (e.g., "develop marketing, distribution, and channel strategy") is performed through steps involving at least two and usually three or more functions (e.g., sales, marketing, and operations), making it cross-functional.

A process-based management system focuses on a core set of processes, explicitly mapping the work flow of those processes from beginning to end through the organization. Once process measurements for the inputs, processing steps, outputs, and customer satisfaction are in place, methods are used to optimize the end-to-end performance. The work begins with customer requirements and ends with a completely satisfied and delighted customer who receives what he or she required on time. Value-stream maps show how work is accomplished across internal functional areas and identify the relationships of the supplier and customer to the business process. The focus is on customer value, so that those steps that do not add value can be identified and eliminated. The question that needs to be asked over and over again is, "If the customer doesn't perceive that he or she is receiving value from a given step and therefore doesn't want to pay for it, why are we doing it?" A well-designed process-based management system also includes recurring cycles of continuous improvement to address performance gaps and changing customer needs. In fact, rather than being caused by people, defects usually stem from management's adoption and use of defective (incapable, flawed, poorly designed, and so on) processes.

The Achilles heel of traditional command-and-control organizations is, if unchecked, the everyday performance of individual functions will be optimized, resulting in disconnects and breakdowns (or suboptimization) of end-to-end value-stream business process performance. Necessary functions such as marketing, sales, business planning, manufacturing, operations, human resources, information management, and finance inherently provide specific skills and competencies and a governance structure for those functions. The pervasive shortcoming of these organizations, however, is that they tend to suboptimize cross-functional business processes, disrupt supply-chain performance, and deliver low value to customers.

The Concept of a Process-Centered Organization

The concept of a process-centered organization was developed to counterbalance this shortcoming of functional organizations. It came about through the process reengineering work of Michael Hammer and Associates during the middle 1990s.[2] The process management notion is centered on dominant functions. It focuses otherwise functional organizations on customer value, like counterbalancing navigation of a sailboat blown off course by weather, to recenter operations around processes into order to create the greatest customer value. During this migration, the strengths of the previously dominant functions evolve into "centers of excellence." Figure 4-2 illustrates the phases this evolution goes through before the organization is centered and the business processes are truly operated and managed as processes.

Such centered organizations assign process owners, who are charged to operate across the functional boundaries to achieve process excellence. "The true test of organizational process effectiveness is to challenge each step in the value chain with the question, 'Would the customer pay for this activity?'" says Michelle Yakovac, vice president of client services for Symmetrics Marketing Corporation, a company specializing in lasting customer relationships.[3] Yakovac, who is also a passionate advocate of process management, adds,

> There may be instances that legal or social drivers require some processing steps, but, nonetheless, each step must be challenged. The old adage, "We've always done it this way," is no longer good enough, and is, indeed, often a call for challenging the status quo in the interest of what's best for customers.[4]

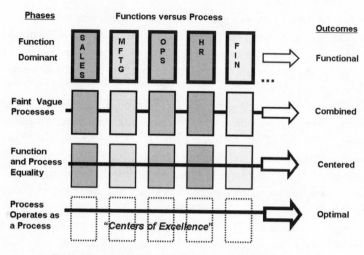

Evolution to a Process Centered Organization

Figure 4-2 Evolution to a process-centered organization

Process owners focus on end-to-end process performance to ensure that what is delivered to customers meets or exceeds expectations, is defect-free, and is on-time, every time.

As pictured in Figure 4-2, the evolution to becoming a process-centered organization involves a successful shift and a de-emphasis of functional dominance while key processes are being identified and managed effectively. A mindset shift must take place. Inflexible mindsets can be a major barrier, since functional managers do resist changes that erode their power and authority. In many such cases, change management techniques will need to be employed to create "win-win" situations for all stakeholders. Previously successful functional managers tend to be the biggest barriers to change.

After major processes have been made explicit and mapped, process measurements need to be established and process-based tools and methods (activity-based costing and management, value-stream analysis, input/output mapping, service-level agreements, and so on) need to be introduced. Also, before long, an infrastructure of process owners, executives, and teams and a realigned individual and team recognition and reward system need to be established to optimize process performance.

As core business processes are operated and managed as processes, the functions fade into the background and become *centers of excellence*. These centers are organizational pockets of functional expertise that recruit, train, develop, certify, equip, and supply competent performers who can accomplish the functional activities of the processes. For example, finance is a center of excellence for the "invoice customers" process (process 8.2.2 in the process classification framework presented later in this chapter). In this example, the Finance Department recruits, trains, and develops the specialists who perform the accounts receivable steps involved in the process. But it's the process owner for the "invoice customer" process who is responsible for the performance of the end-to-end process on both a day-to-day and a long-term basis.

Likewise, the marketing department is a *center of excellence* for the "Market and Sell Products and Services" core process category (3.0 in the Process Classification Framework, PCF, soon to be presented). In this example, the Marketing Department recruits, trains, and develops the specialists who perform the advertising strategy and deployment steps involved in the process. Again, the transition to a process-centered organization is pictured in Figure 4-2. Benchmarking should be done to identify the best practices and benchmarks for the core processes, and also for the centers of excellence. The people managing need to both be aware of how they compare and to take aggressive steps to continually improve.

Table 4-1 has also been provided to clarify even further the difference between functional or hierarchical organizations versus those that are process-centered. What readers need to understand is that these are two significantly different orientations. The idea of the process-centered organization is to retain the advantages of functional expertise, yet enable true process management. The creation of cross-functional process teams with sufficient empowerment and authority is a key to successful process management. It is extremely difficult, if not impossible, to optimize end-to-end process performance when empowerment, decisions, and controls for process performance are entirely vested in each function's managers, and they are only rewarded for optimizing their department's performance.

Knowledge, Best Practices, and Intellectual Capital Process-Based Taxonomy for Any Enterprise

Earlier in this chapter, the point was made that using a business process framework or Dewey Decimal classification system for processes makes a lot of sense in terms of making continuous improvement. "Such a process classification system would also enable the capture, cataloging, sharing, transfer and reuse of best practice knowledge pertaining to each process," says Kay Hunn, senior manager for process assurance for Lockheed Martin's Missile and Fire Control operations in Dallas, Texas.[5] "However," adds Hunn, "such an endeavor would require a great deal of collaboration and agreement. And if it's to be universally accepted and used, the collaboration must be worldwide."[6]

And that's exactly what happened in 1992 when the American Productivity and Quality Center (APQC), in collaboration with a total of 80 worldwide organ-

Table 4-1 Differences in Emphasis: Functional vs. Process-Centered Organization

Dimension	Functional (Hierarchical)	Process-Centered
Leadership hierarchy	Vice president–led functional heads of sales, marketing, manufacturing, operations, finance, HR, etc.	Process owners, cross-functional teams, and function heads manage, but process is managed separately.
Measurement	Functions' performance measured independently of one another.	Each function's contribution to key processes is measured.
Budget (resources)	Allocated/controlled by functions.	Resources allocated to address needs of process owners, who have "sign-off" authority.
Management scope	Processes managed and optimized within functions, not end-to-end.	Processes managed end-to-end to optimize output/customer value and satisfaction.
Optimization goal	Functional performance at the cost of end-to-end process performance.	End-to-end; functional performance is evaluated by process owners.
Executive performance evaluation	On the performance of the function within the process.	On both functional and end-to-end process performance.
Improvement focus	Functional achievement, including use of tools, recognition, and rewards.	Process performance to end customers; map, tools, rewards, and plans.

izations, issued the first version of the Process Classification Framework (PCF). For 12 years an increasing number of active benchmarking enterprises, although still a minority overall, have used the PCF. Its power lies in organizations seeing how process activities compare across industries. The PCF is "a high-level, industry-neutral enterprise model that allows organizations to see their activities from a cross-industry process viewpoint."[7] It creates a common language and a common set of references for organizations that want to research benchmarking and quick learning in the knowledge transfer race. It's the Dewey Decimal System for business processes.

During 2004, an updated version of PCF was released by the APQC as a result of collaboration to reflect the latest thinking. Though many companies were involved, those that the APQC gave special mention to were Raytheon, the Boeing Company, Boehringer Ingelheim GmbH, BT Group plc, Ensco International Inc., Ford Motor Co., IBM Corp., Schlumberger Ltd., Solvay S.A., and the U.S. Navy.

Then, in June 2005, Version 3 of the PCF was issued. Figure 4-3 shows the processes categories that make up the PCF.[8] Of a total of twelve business process categories, the first five are the core business processes of any enterprise, be it large, medium, or small; a manufacturing, service, or public service organization or a combination. The PCF uses a process decomposition scheme in descending order of "category" (e.g. 1.0 and 5.0), "process group" (e.g. 2.1 and 4.1 are process areas), "process" (e.g. 2.1.1 and 5.1.1, "and activity" (e.g. 4.1.1.1.)

The remainder of this chapter is devoted to presenting and explaining this framework of the 12 PCF process categories, and then includes some closing comments to help people in small organizations. The purpose is to enable those in the knowledge transfer race to create a knowledge-enabled culture. This architecture adds to a learning organization the kind of framework needed to become knowledge-enabled.

Imagine how the PCF can benefit organizations, large and small.

■ It forms a universally accepted (because of the more than 20 organizations that collaborated to produce it) framework of the essential processes that an enterprise might perform to identify and achieve its vision and mission. It thus is an instrument—much as a species classification system is for anthropology—that models everything that an enterprise might do to achieve its purpose for existing. While it does not list every process within any given organization, and not every subprocess listed is present in every organization, it forms enough of an architecture to permit comparisons between different types of organizations on a process basis.

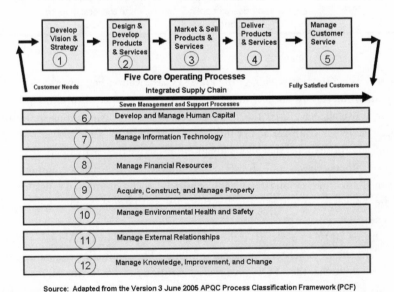

Source: Adapted from the Version 3 June 2005 APQC Process Classification Framework (PCF)

Figure 4-3 The process classification framework illustrated

- It enables benchmarking exchanges of knowledge to be precise because it is an industry-neutral (generic) framework that enables pinpoint agreements about specific categories, process groups, processes, and activities. Before the PCF, a great deal of attention had to be given to normalizing data during benchmarking exchanges in order to ensure that valid "apples to apples" comparisons were being made. Language differences were also barriers. Now, the PCF has precise process definitions and pinpoint-accurate scope and focus. It eliminates previous sources of confusion, ambiguity, and misunderstanding.

- It provides organizations with a classification to capture and populate knowledge-sharing systems on a forward-going basis, knowing that the descriptions fit a commonly accepted framework for conducting future benchmarking exchanges. The PCF is a high-level, open standard from which those giving may receive information, metadata, or knowledge resembling the same operation.

- It reflects business models that exist in 2005 and will be continually refined and updated over time. The APQC ensures that the PCF is supported by the Open Standards Benchmarking Collaborative (OSBC) and the collaborative's advisory council of global industry leaders as an open standard. The PCF will be continually refined as the Open Standards Benchmarking Collaborative further develops corresponding definitions, processes, and measures related to process improvement. One need only visit www.apqc.org and seek the pages in the APQC's Knowledge Sharing Network (KSN) where the current version of the PCF may be accessed and downloaded free of charge. This is a "living document." The version 3 update has been issued in June 2005 and the APQC expects to make refinements annually as required.

- In its previous form, it was found valuable enough to warrant updating and continued use. In its previous form, the PCF was used hundreds of times between 1992 and 2004 and was found to be valuable for knowledge transfers, and its value justified the updating and the resources required from the 20 enterprises that participated in the updating work. It has proven to be an effective tool for communications, negotiation, and sharing.

- The PCF represents a series of interrelated processes that, in combination, represent the major dimensions of business and industry. In its simplest form, Figure 4-3, the PCF is a categorical system of 12 high-level processes that are necessary to conduct business and industry in the twenty-first century. In its most complex form, the PCF is a system [from category (e.g., 2.0 Design and Develop Products and Services) to process group (e.g., 2.1 Design products and services) to process (e.g., 2.1.1 Develop strategy and concepts for new products and services) to activity (e.g. 2.1.1.1 Research customer and market needs)]. Category is the highest level, indicated by whole numbers (e.g., 3.0 and 10.00). Process groups are all the items with one decimal number (e.g., 3.1 and 10.1). Processes are all PCF items with two decimal numbers (e.g., 3.1.1. and 10.1.1). Activities are the items with three decimal numbers (e.g., 3.1.1.1 and 10.1.1.1) and are activities within a process. As a system, each process has inputs (knowledge, labor, resources, capital, equipment, tools, and so on) that are transformed through the processing steps into outputs that become products and services or become inputs to other processes, which, ultimately, are delivered to the end customer.

■ Though an intellectual asset of the APQC, the PCF is available and applicable to all industries at no charge. No matter what the size of an organization, whether it is a manufacturing or service company, not-for-profit or for-profit, public or private sector, the PCF has been designed to enhance and enlarge sharing. Its one clear intent is to help organizations make process improvement through the use of a common understanding and language of processes.

The Five Core Business Processes

These are the five fundamental business processes that start and end with customers. The input of customer needs begins an integrated value chain that involves developing a vision and strategy, designing and developing products and services, marketing and selling products and services, delivering products and services, and, finally, managing customer service. Each of these major processes has inputs, processing steps, and outputs, many of which are inputs to other major processes. The first process category is "Develop Vision and Strategy." Every category, process group, process, and activity, incidentally, has performance measurements and benchmarks, and best practices are therefore involved with winning the knowledge transfer race.

1.0 Develop Vision and Strategy
    Define the business concept and long-term vision.
       1.1.1 Assess the external environment.
            1.1.1.1 Analyze and evaluate competition.
            1.1.1.2 Identify economic trends.
            1.1.1.3 Identify political and regulatory issues.
            1.1.1.4 Assess new technology innovations.
            1.1.1.5 Understand demographics.
            1.1.1.6 Identify social and cultural changes.
            1.1.1.7 Identify ecological concerns.

1.1.2 Survey market and determine customer needs and wants.
    1.1.2.1 Conduct qualitative/quantitative assessments.
    1.1.2.2 Capture and assess customer needs.
1.1.3 Select relevant markets.
1.1.4 Perform internal analysis.
    1.1.4.1 Analyze organizational characteristics.
    1.1.4.2 Create baselines for current processes.
    1.1.4.3 Analyze systems and technology.
    1.1.4.4 Analyze financial positions.
    1.1.4.5 Identify enterprise core competencies.
1.1.5 Establish strategic vision.
    1.1.5.1 Align stakeholders around strategic vision.
    1.1.5.2 Communicate strategic vision to stakeholders.
1.2 Develop business strategy.
  1.2.1 Develop overall mission statement.
  1.2.2 Evaluate strategic options.
  1.2.3 Select long-term business strategy.
  1.2.4 Coordinate and align functional and process strategies.
  1.2.5 Design the organizational structure and relationships between organizational units.
  1.2.6 Develop and set organizational goals.
  1.2.7 Formulate business unit strategies.
1.3 Manage strategic initiatives.
  1.3.1 Develop strategic initiatives.
  1.3.2 Evaluate strategic initiatives.
  1.3.3 Select strategic initiatives.
  1.3.4 Establish high-level measures.

2.0 Design and Develop Products and Services
2.1 Design products and services.
  2.1.1 Develop strategy and concepts for new products and services.
    2.1.1.1 Research customer and market needs.
    2.1.1.2 Plan and develop cost and quality targets.
    2.1.1.3 Develop product life cycle and development timing targets.
    2.1.1.4 Research leading technology components and development requirements.
    2.1.1.5 Integrate leading technology into product/service concept and components.
  2.1.2 Produce new products and services, and evaluate and refine existing products and services.
    2.1.2.1 Translate customer wants and needs into product/service ideas.

2.1.2.2 Generate new product/service ideas.

2.1.2.3 Evaluate existing products based on NPD strategy.

2.1.2.4 Identify enhancements/extensions to existing product and services.

2.1.2.5 Define product and service functionality.

2.1.2.6 Retire outdated products/services.

2.1.2.7 Identify and refine performance indicators.

2.1.3 Design, build, and evaluate products and services.

2.1.3.1 Assign resources to product/service project.

2.1.3.2 Prepare high-level business case and technical assessment.

2.1.3.3 Develop product/service design specifications.

2.1.3.4 Document design specifications.

2.1.3.5 Build prototypes.

2.1.3.6 Eliminate quality and reliability problems.

2.1.3.7 Conduct in-house product/service testing and evaluate feasibility.

2.1.3.8 Identify design/development performance indicators.

2.1.3.9 Collaborate design with suppliers and contract manufacturers.

2.1.4 Test market for new or revised products and services.

2.1.4.1 Prepare detailed market study.

2.1.4.2 Conduct customer tests and interviews.

2.1.4.3 Finalize product/service characteristics and business cases.

2.1.4.4 Finalize technical requirements.

2.1.4.5 Identify requirements for changes to manufacturing/ delivery processes.

2.1.5 Prepare for production and marketplace introduction.

2.1.5.1 Develop and test prototype production and/or service delivery process.

2.1.5.2 Design and obtain necessary materials and equipment.

2.1.5.3 Install and validate production process or methodology.

2.1.5.4 Introduce new product and/or service commercially.

2.1.6 Support and implement changes to product manufacturing and service delivery process.

2.1.6.1 Monitor production runs.

2.1.6.2 Identify product/service design and configuration changes.

2.1.6.3 Capture feedback to "refine existing products and services" process.

2.1.6.4 Identify manufacturing/service delivery process performance indicators.

3.0 Market and Sell Products and Services
3.1 Develop marketing, distribution, and channel strategy.
   3.1.1 Understand consumer needs and predict customer purchasing behavior.
      3.1.1.1 Develop and manage customer profiles.
   3.1.2 Identify market segments and target customers.
      3.1.2.1 Determine market share gain/loss.
   3.1.3 Define offering and positioning.
   3.1.4 Define and manage channel strategy.
3.2 Develop and manage customer strategy.
   3.2.1 Develop customer management strategies.
   3.2.2 Establish customer management goals.
   3.2.3 Develop sales forecast.
   3.2.4 Establish overall sales budgets.
   3.2.5 Establish customer management metrics.
      3.2.5.1 Determine customer loyalty/lifetime value.
      3.2.5.2 Analyze customer attrition and retention rates.
   3.2.6 Prepare/analyze/evaluate customer management results.
3.3 Manage advertising, pricing, and promotional activities.
   3.3.1 Develop and manage advertising.
      3.3.1.1 Define advertising objectives and strategy.
      3.3.1.2 Define target audience.
      3.3.1.3 Engage third-party advertising agency.
      3.3.1.4 Develop advertising.
   3.3.2 Develop and manage external communication.
      3.3.2.1 Develop media budget.
      3.3.2.2 Develop media plan.
      3.3.2.3 Execute media plan.
   3.3.3 Develop and manage placement and campaign management.
   3.3.4 Develop and manage pricing.
      3.3.4.1 Develop volume/unit forecast and set price.
      3.3.4.2 Execute pricing plan.
      3.3.4.3 Evaluate pricing performance.
      3.3.4.4 Refine pricing as needed.
   3.3.5 Develop and manage promotional activities.
      3.3.5.1 Define direct-to-consumer promotional concepts.
      3.3.5.2 Plan and test direct-to-consumer activities.
      3.3.5.3 Execute direct-to-consumer promotional activities.
      3.3.5.4 Prepare/analyze/evaluate direct to consumer promotional performance metrics.
      3.3.5.5 Refine direct to consumer promotional performance metrics.

3.3.5.6 Define trade to consumer promotional concepts.

3.3.5.7 Plan and test trade to consumer activities.

3.3.5.8 Execute trade to consumer promotional activities.

3.3.5.9 Prepare/analyze/evaluate trade to consumer promotional performance metrics.

3.3.5.10 Refine trade to consumer promotional performance metrics.

3.3.6 Develop and manage packaging strategy.

3.3.6.1 Plan packaging strategy.

3.3.6.2 Test packaging options.

3.3.6.3 Execute packaging strategy.

3.3.6.4 Refine packaging.

3.4 Manage sales partners and alliances.

3.5 Manage sales opportunity and sales pipeline.

3.5.1 Identify and manage key customers and accounts.

3.5.1.1 Develop key customer plans.

3.5.1.2 Identify priority customers.

3.5.1.3 Establish budgets.

3.5.1.4 Develop sales/key account plan.

3.5.1.5 Schedule calls to customers.

3.5.1.6 Execute agreed-to sales plan.

3.5.1.7 Prepare/analyze/evaluate sales results.

3.6 Sales order management.

3.6.1 Manage inbound sales orders.

3.6.1.1 Accept and validate sales orders.

3.6.1.2 Collect and maintain customer account information.

3.6.1.3 Determine stock availability.

3.6.1.4 Determine logistics and transportation.

3.6.1.5 Enter orders into system and identify/perform cross-sell/up-sell activity.

3.6.1.6 Process back orders and updates.

3.6.1.7 Handle order inquiries including post-order fulfillment transactions.

3.6.2 Manage outbound sales and campaign calls.

4.0 Deliver Products and Services

4.1 Plan for and acquire necessary resources (Supply-Chain Planning).

4.1.1 Manage demand for products and services.

4.1.1.1 Develop baseline forecasts.

4.1.1.2 Collaborate with customers.

4.1.1.3 Develop consensus forecast.

4.1.1.4 Allocate available to promise

4.1.2 Create materials plan.
    4.1.2.1 Create unconstrained plan.
    4.1.2.2 Collaborate with supplier and contract manufacturers.
    4.1.2.3 Identify critical materials and supplier capacity.
    4.1.2.4 Generate constrained plan.
4.1.3 Schedule production.
    4.1.3.1 Generate site-level plan.
    4.1.3.2 Manage work-in-progress inventory.
    4.1.3.3 Collaborate with suppliers.
    4.1.3.4 Generate and execute detail schedule.
4.2 Procure materials and services.
  4.2.1 Develop sourcing strategies.
    4.2.1.1 Develop procurement plan.
    4.2.1.2 Clarify purchasing requirements.
    4.2.1.3 Match needs to supply capabilities.
    4.2.1.4 Analyze company's spend profile.
    4.2.1.5 Seek opportunities to improve efficiency and value.
  4.2.2 Select suppliers and develop/maintain contracts.
    4.2.2.1 Identify suppliers.
    4.2.2.2 Certify and validate suppliers.
    4.2.2.3 Negotiate contracts.
    4.2.2.4 Manage contracts.
  4.2.3 Order materials and services.
    4.2.3.1 Process/review requisitions.
    4.2.3.2 Approve requisitions.
    4.2.3.3 Solicit/track vendor quotes.
    4.2.3.4 Create/distribute purchase orders.
    4.2.3.5 Expedite orders and satisfy inquiries.
    4.2.3.6 Record receipt of goods.
    4.2.3.7 Research/resolve exceptions.
  4.2.4 Appraise and develop suppliers.
    4.2.4.1 Monitor/manage supplier information.
    4.2.4.2 Prepare/analyze spending and vendor performance.
    4.2.4.3 Support inventory and production processes.
4.3 Produce/manufacture/deliver product.
  4.3.1 Schedule production.
  4.3.2 Produce product.
  4.3.3 Schedule and perform maintenance.
4.4 Deliver product service to customer.
  4.4.1 Confirm specific service requirements for individual customers.

4.4.2 Identify and schedule resources to meet service requirements.

4.4.3 Provide the service to specific customers.

4.4.4 Ensure quality of service.

4.5 Manage logistics and warehousing.

    4.5.1 Define logistics strategy.

        4.5.1.1 Translate customer service requirements into logistics requirements.

        4.5.1.2 Design logistics network.

        4.5.1.3 Communicate outsourcing needs.

        4.5.1.4 Develop and maintain delivery service policy.

        4.5.1.5 Optimize transportation schedules and costs.

        4.5.1.6 Define key performance measures.

    4.5.2 Plan inbound material flow.

        4.5.2.1 Plan inbound material receipts.

        4.5.2.2 Manage inbound material flow.

        4.5.2.3 Monitor inbound delivery performance.

        4.5.2.4 Manage flow of returned products.

    4.5.3 Operate warehousing.

        4.5.3.1 Track inventory deployment.

        4.5.3.2 Receive, inspect, and store inbound deliveries.

        4.5.3.3 Track product availability.

        4.5.3.4 Pick, pack, and ship product for delivery.

        4.5.3.5 Track inventory accuracy.

        4.5.3.6 Track third-party logistics storage and shipping performance.

    4.5.4 Operate outbound transportation.

        4.5.4.1 Plan, transport, and deliver outbound product.

        4.5.4.2 Track carrier delivery performance.

        4.5.4.3 Manage transportation fleet.

        4.5.4.4 Process and audit carrier invoices and documents.

    4.5.5 Manage returns; manage reverse logistics.

        4.5.5.1 Authorize and process returns.

        4.5.5.2 Perform reverse logistics.

        4.5.5.3 Perform salvage activities.

        4.5.5.4 Manage and process warranty claims.

5.0 Manage Customer Service

5.1 Develop customer care/customer service strategy.

    5.1.1 Develop customer segmentation/prioritization (e.g. tiers).

    5.1.2 Define customer service policies and procedures.

    5.1.3 Establish service levels for customers.

5.2 Manage customer service.

    5.2.1 Manage customer service requests.

        5.2.1.1 Receive customer requests/inquires.

        5.2.1.2 Route customer requests/inquires.

        5.2.1.3 Respond to customer requests/inquiries.

    5.2.2 Manage customer complaints.

        5.2.2.1 Enter customer complaints.

        5.2.2.2 Route customer complaints.

        5.2.2.3 Resolve customer complaints.

5.3 Perform after sales installations and repairs

5.4 Measure and evaluate customer satisfaction.

    5.4.1 Measure customer satisfaction level for customer requests/inquiries.

        5.4.1.1 Solicit customer feedback on customer service experience.

        5.4.1.2 Analyze customer service data and identify improvement opportunites.

    5.4.2 Measure customer satisfaction of customer-complaint handling and resolution.

        5.4.2.1 Solicit customer feedback on complaint handling and resolution.

        5.4.2.2 Analyze customer complaint data and identify improvement opportunities.

    5.4.3 Measure customer satisfaction with products and services.

        5.4.3.1 Solicit post-sale customer feedback on products and services.

        5.4.3.2 Collect warranty data and product return reasons.

        5.4.3.3 Analyze product and service satisfaction data and identify improvement opportunities.

5.5 Manage customer service work force.

    5.5.1 Develop work force requirements and schedule work force.

        5.5.1.1 Forecast volume of customer service contracts.

        5.5.1.2 Forecast volume of inbound sales contacts

        5.5.1.3 Schedule customer service work force.

        5.5.1.4 Track work force utilization.

    5.5.2 Evaluate quality of customer interaction with customer service representatives.

        5.5.2.1 Monitor and evaluate agent calls with customers.

        5.5.2.2 Monitor and evaluate agent correspondence with customers.

In the search to identify the processes that are most *core* in terms of creating value and contributing to the success of any organization, the authors discovered that there are some organizations that deem some of the processes in the preceding list to be *not core*. For example, Cisco Systems outsources much of the "Deliver Products and Services" process to key suppliers. These suppliers thus act as *centers of excellence* for Cisco. This allows Cisco to conserve its resources and use them to stay abreast of the technology, capital, and innovations in other processes where the company believes its resources can produce a competitive advantage.

The Seven Support and Management Processes

While not in the organization's primary value-creation chain for customers, these processes directly support those that are. They usually involve direct (and functional) support for the core processes, such as with "6.0 Develop and Manage Human Capital," an outcome of which is the creation of intellectual capital (tacit and implicit knowledge) as the sum of employee experience, skill, know-how, and creativity. The discussion in Chapter 5 will clarify what intellectual capital is and how important human capital is as a component of it. It is there that phase 3 of the knowledge transfer race must be mastered.

Another support process category is "7.0 Manage Information Technology." While this includes the historically important process of "manage the business of information technology," it also includes "manage the information technology portfolio." The ever-important process category of "8.0 Manage Financial Resources" is next. In all these instances, the concept of *centers of excellence* applies. The other support process categories are "9.0 Acquire, Construct, and Manage Property," "10.0 "Manage Environmental Health and Safety," "11.0 Manage External Relationships," and "12.0 Manage Knowledge, Improvement, and Change." This last category includes the establishment of all types of performance metrics: knowledge management assessments, benchmarking, change management, and continuous improvement.

To a large extent, support processes support the daily operations of an organization and its product and service delivery. The design requirements for these processes depend on internal handoffs and the deliverables that are inputs for core processes, and they must be coordinated and integrated to ensure efficient, effective linkage and performance. Certainly they may not add direct labor to the products or services, but they are necessary as the glue that holds them together. Because they operate as *centers of excellence* and are not core processes, they are continually evaluated for value added and in today's world are candidates for outsourcing. Savvy support managers are continually benchmarking, for they know that they must be competitive and prove it year after year. In fact, most of the professional seminars and conferences cater to these support processes and the competition; i.e., the knowledge transfer race is fierce.

What follows is a listing of the PCF support process categories, process groups, and processes but not the fourth level activities. The specific activities and performance management structures and procedures for the most current version of the PCF may be accessed, downloaded, and used free of charge by visiting the Web site www.apqc.org, providing users make a proper copyright acknowledgement to the APQC. The PCF is ©2005 APQC and all rights are reserved.

6.0 Develop and Manage Human Capital

6.1 Create and manage human resource (HR) planning, policy, and strategies.

    6.1.1 Manage/align/deliver human resources strategy.

    6.1.2 Develop and implement HR plans.

    6.1.3 Monitor and update plans.

6.2 Recruit, source, and select employees.

    6.2.1 Create and develop employee requisitions.

    6.2.2 Recruit candidates.

    6.2.3 Screen and select candidates.

    6.2.4 Manage pre-placement verification.

    6.2.5 Manage new hire/rehire.

    6.2.6 Track candidates.

6.3 Develop and counsel employees.

    6.3.1 Manage employee orientation and deployment.

    6.3.2 Manage employee performance.

    6.3.3 Manage employee relations.

    6.3.4 Manage employee development.

    6.3.5 Develop and train employees.

    6.3.6 Manage employee talent.

6.4 Reward and retain employees.

    6.4.1 Develop and manage reward, recognition, and motivation programs.

    6.4.2 Manage and administer benefits.

    6.4.3 Manage employee assistance and retention.

    6.4.4 Payroll administration

6.5 Redeploy and retire employees.

    6.5.1 Manage promotion and demotion process.

    6.5.2 Manage separation.

    6.5.3 Manage retirement.

    6.5.4 Manage leave of absence.

    6.5.5 Develop and implement employee outplacement.

    6.5.6 Manage deployment of personnel.

    6.5.7 Relocate employees and manage assignments.

    6.5.8 Manage employment reduction and retirement.

6.5.9 Manage expatriates.

6.5.10 Manage employee relocation process.

6.6 Manage employee information.

6.6.1 Manage reporting processes.

6.6.2 Manage employee inquiry process.

6.6.3 Manage and maintain employee data.

6.6.4 Manage human resource information systems (HRIS).

6.6.5 Develop and manage employee metrics.

6.6.6 Develop and manage time and attendance.

6.6.7 Manage employee communication.

7.0 Manage Information Technology

7.1 Manage the business of information technology (IT).

7.1.1 Develop the enterprise IT strategy.

7.1.2 Define the enterprise architecture.

7.1.3 Manage the IT portfolio.

7.1.4 Perform IT research and innovation.

7.1.5 Perform IT financial management.

7.1.6 Evaluate and communicate IT business value and performance.

7.1.7 Perform IT staff management.

7.1.8 Manage IT suppliers and contracts.

7.2 Develop and manage IT customer relationships.

7.2.1 Develop IT services and solutions strategy

7.2.2 Develop and manage IT service levels.

7.2.3 Perform demand side management (DSM) for IT services.

7.2.4 Manage IT customer satisfaction.

7.2.5 Market IT services and solutions.

7.3 Manage business resiliency and risk.

7.3.1 Develop and manage business resilience.

7.3.2 Develop and manage regulatory compliance.

7.3.3 Perform integrated risk management.

7.3.4 Develop and implement security, privacy, and data protection controls.

7.4 Manage enterprise information.

7.4.1 Develop information and content management strategies.

7.4.2 Define the enterprise information architecture.

7.4.3 Manage information resources.

7.4.4 Perform enterprise data and content management.

7.5 Develop and maintain information technology solutions.

7.5.1 Develop the IT development strategy.

7.5.2 Perform IT services and solutions life cycle planning.

7.5.3 Develop and maintain IT services and solutions architecture.

7.5.4 Create IT services and solutions.

7.5.5 Maintain IT services and solutions

7.6 Deploy information technology solutions.

    7.6.1 Develop the IT deployment strategy.

    7.6.2 Plan and implement changes.

    7.6.3 Plan and manage releases.

7.7 Deliver and support information technology services

    7.7.1 Develop IT services and solution delivery strategy.

    7.7.2 Develop IT support strategy.

    7.7.3 Manage IT infrastructure resources.

    7.7.4 Manage IT infrastructure operations.

    7.7.5 Support IT services and solutions.

7.8 Manage IT knowledge.

    7.8.1 Develop the IT knowledge management strategy.

    7.8.2 Develop and maintain IT knowledge map.

    7.8.3 Manage IT knowledge life cycle.

8.0 Manage Financial Resources

8.1 Perform planning and management accounting.

    8.1.1 Perform planning/budgeting/forecasting.

    8.1.2 Perform cost accounting and control.

    8.1.3 Perform cost management.

    8.1.4 Evaluate and manage financial performance.

8.2 Perform revenue accounting.

    8.2.1 Process customer credit.

    8.2.2 Invoice customer.

    8.2.3 Process accounts receivable (AR).

    8.2.4 Manage and process collections.

    8.2.5 Manage and process adjustments/deductions.

8.3 Perform general accounting and reporting.

    8.3.1 Manage policies and procedures.

    8.3.2 Perform general accounting.

    8.3.3 Perform fixed-asset accounting.

    8.3.4 Perform financial reporting.

8.4 Manage fixed assets.

    8.4.1 Perform capital planning and project approval.

    8.4.2 Perform capital project accounting.

8.5 Process payroll.

    8.5.1 Report time.

    8.5.2 Manage pay.

    8.5.3 Process taxes.

8.6 Process accounts payable and expense reimbursements.

8.6.1 Process accounts payable (AP).

8.6.2 Process expense reimbursements.

8.7 Manage treasury operations.

8.7.1 Manage treasury policies, and procedures.

8.7.2 Manage cash.

8.7.3 Manage in-house bank accounts.

8.7.4 Manage debt and investment.

8.7.5 Manage financial risks.

8.8 Manage internal controls.

8.8.1 Establish internal controls, governance and policies.

8.8.2 Design and implement internal controls.

8.8.3 Manage and monitor compliance function.

8.8.4 Report on internal controls compliance.

8.9 Manage taxes.

8.9.1 Develop tax strategy and plan.

8.9.2 Process taxes.

8.9.3 Manage international funds/consolidation.

9.0 Acquire, Construct, and Manage Property

9.1 Property design and construction.

9.1.1 Develop facility strategy.

9.1.2 Develop and construct sites.

9.1.3 Plan facility.

9.1.4 Provide workspace and assets.

9.2 Maintain workplace and assets.

9.2.1 Move people and assets.

9.2.2 Repair workplace and assets.

9.2.3 Provide preventive maintenance for workplace and assets.

9.2.4 Manage security.

9.3 Dispose of workspace and assets.

9.3.1 Dispose of equipment.

9.3.2 Dispose of workspace.

9.4 Manage physical risk.

9.5 Manage capital assets.

10.0 Manage Environmental Health and Safety

10.1 Determine health, safety, and environmental impacts.

10.1.1 Evaluate environmental impact of products, services, and operations.

10.1.2 Conduct health and safety and environmental audits.

10.2 Develop and execute health, safety, and environmental program.

10.2.1 Identify regulatory and stakeholder requirements.

10.2.2 Assess future risks and opportunities.

10.2.3 Create EHS policy.

10.2.4 Record and manage EHS events.

10.3 Train and educate employees.

10.3.1 Communicate EHS issues to stakeholders and provide support.

10.4 Monitor and manage health, safety, and environmental management program.

10.4.1 Manage EHS costs and benefits.

10.4.2 Measure and report EHS performance.

10.4.3 Provide employees with EHS support.

10.5 Ensure compliance with regulations.

10.5.1 Monitor compliance.

10.5.2 Perform compliance audit.

10.5.3 Comply with regulatory stakeholders requirements.

10.6 Manage remediation efforts.

10.6.1 Create remediation plans.

10.6.2 Contact and confer with experts.

10.6.3 Identify/dedicate resources.

10.6.4 Investigate legal aspects.

10.6.5 Investigate damage cause.

10.6.6 Amend or create policy.

11.0 Manage External Relationships

11.1 Build investor relationships.

11.1.1 Plan, build, and manage lender relations.

11.1.2 Plan, build, and manage analyst relations.

11.1.3 Communicate with shareholders.

11.2 Manage government and industry relationships.

11.2.1 Manage industry relations with government.

11.2.2 Manage relations with quasi-government bodies.

11.2.3 Manage relations with trade or industry groups.

11.2.4 Manage lobby activities.

11.3 Manage relations with board of directors.

11.3.1 Report results.

11.3.2 Report audit findings.

11.4 Manage legal and ethical issues.

11.4.1 Create ethics policies.

11.4.2 Manage corporate governance policies.

11.4.3 Develop and perform preventative law programs.

11.4.4 Ensure compliance.

11.4.5 Manage outside counsel.

11.4.6 Protect intellectual property.

11.4.7 Resolve disputes and litigations.

11.4.8 Provide legal advice/counseling.

11.4.9 Negotiate and document agreements/contracts.

11.5 Manage public relations program.

11.5.1 Manage relations with global customers.

11.5.2 Manage relations with trade and industry groups.

11.5.3 Manage relations with global strategic suppliers.

11.5.4 Manage community relations.

11.5.5 Manage media relations.

11.5.6 Promote political stability.

11.5.7 Create press releases.

12.0 Manage Knowledge, Improvement, and Change

12.1 Create and manage organizational performance strategy.

12.1.1 Create enterprise measurement systems model.

12.1.2 Measure process productivity.

12.1.3 Measure cost effectiveness.

12.1.4 Measure staff efficiency.

12.1.5 Measure cycle time.

12.2 Benchmark performance.

12.2.1 Conduct performance assessments.

12.2.2 Conduct benchmarking capabilities.

12.2.3 Conduct process benchmarking.

12.2.4 Conduct competitive benchmarking.

12.2.5 Conduct gap analysis to understand the need for and the degree of change needed.

12.2.6 Establish need for change.

12.3 Develop enterprise-wide knowledge management (KM) capability.

12.3.1 Develop KM strategy.

12.3.2 Identify and plan KM projects.

12.3.3 Design and launch KM projects.

12.3.4 Manage the KM project life cycle.

12.4 Manage change.

12.4.1 Plan for change.

12.4.2 Design the change.

12.4.3 Implement change.

12.4.4 Sustain improvement.

Illustrating Supporting Process 8.6.1 of PCF Taxonomy, Process Accounts Payable, Using Verizon's Best Practices

Understanding the PCF taxonomy is essential for organizations so that they can use it to define, measure, and improve their processes to create greater value for their customers. To this end, Verizon's accounts payable practices—which as a group constitute a best practices portfolio—help to illustrate the value of using the taxonomy. The reference is to Supporting Process 8.6.1, Process accounts payable. The mission statement for this part of Verizon is

Verizon Accounts Payable Services will be the customers' first choice for providing accounts payable services. We will become world class by constantly pursuing all opportunities to become the low cost provider using state of the art technology and highly trained professional employees.[9]

Annually, Verizon processes 5.3 million invoices, 262,000 employee payments, and 1.5 million checks.[10] And because of its best practice use of technology, Verizon uses electronic funds transfers (EFT) to make 34 percent of its payments to vendors and 91 percent of its payments to employees. In addition, duplicate payment software (another best practices approach) enables Verizon to now avoid $8.9 million in duplicate payments.

Software paves the road to excellent performance in accounts payable. During 1998, Verizon implemented PeopleSoft's financial suite software package, which includes accounts payable. The company also implemented A/PEX *i*Inquire during January 2002, which allows vendors and employees to check the status of their invoices and payments over the Internet. In addition, Verizon implemented eiStream during July 2003, which eliminates all paper receipts, envelopes, and filing because it electronically links all receipts/bills to the PeopleSoft accounts payable online transactions. All these tried and proven technology applications would populate the repository for process 8.6.1. Other processes populating 8.6.1 would include such practices as "mechanized treasury file for check reconciliation;" "standardized method for booking and reporting wire payments with Treasury;" software that calculates tax liability; electronic filing of Tax Form 1099s; "direct pay to corporate credit card supplier with netting credits and debits to create one single monthly payment;" and so on.[11] This is just an illustration of the kind of best practices and benchmark entries that could be found in Section 8.6.1.

Moreover, Section 8.6.1 would contain the "best" benchmark measurements in use for accounts payable by other organizations for the same activities or process steps. To illustrate, consider the following sample of the measurements that Verizon uses.[12]

Total Supplier Invoice Processing

- Total number of vendors
- Total number of vendors paid in current month
- Total of invoices processed ($000)
- Number of invoices processed
- Number of invoices processed within objective

Supplier EFT Invoice Processing

- Number of EFT vendors
- Number of EFT vendors paid in current month
- Total of EFT invoices processed ($000)
- Number of EFT invoices processed
- EFT invoices as a percentage of total invoices
- Vendors as a percentage of total

On the other hand, the employee expense reimbursement process measurements would pertain to PCF process 8.6.2, process expense reimbursements. Following are measurements used by Verizon for process 8.6.2:

Employee Payments

- Total number of employee payments
- Number of EFT employee payments
- EFT payments as a percentage of total
- Reconciliation
- Number of accounts to be reconciled
- Number of accounts reconciled
- Percentage within objective
- Unexplained differences > 90 days ($000)
- Explained and uncleared differences > 90 days ($000)
- Liability ending balance for AP reconciled accounts ($000)

IBM's Approach to Managing Enterprise Processes, Creating One IBM Image, and Balancing Value Chains

After organizations focus and center their operations on processes and process management, depending on the number and type of their lines of business and researched customer expectations by market segment, value chains still have to be balanced. By then, organizations will have the equivalent "enterprise process trans-formation model," which is their customized adaptation of the 12 categories of processes (five core processes and seven support processes) that were presented ear-lier in this chapter. As discussed, processes for a homogeneous set of products and/or services drive such work. However, if an organization has several lines of business, it may find that it needs to create unique value chains for each line of business. Consider the example of IBM's transformation between 1997 and 2002.

Former CEO Lou Gerstner led IBM through a transformation that initially used process reengineering to make the company a smarter and faster organization. Early phases of process reengineering were directed at eliminating inefficient cost structures, slow development cycles, bureaucracy, redundancy, and inflexibility. The focus was on achieving three strategies.[13] First, transformation efforts put emphasis on the company's going to market as one IBM organization, an integrated, global organization. Customer dissatisfaction identified this as a problem. A second strategy was to make it easier for customers to do business with IBM. Finally, the charter was to transform IBM into a smarter, faster organization.[14] Initially, the transformation work focused on process commonality. To this end, IBM identified nine core processes: (1) market planning, (2) integrated product development, (3) integrated supply chain, (4) procurement, (5) production, (6) fulfillment, (7) customer relationship management, (8) human resources, and (9) finance.

Six of these processes are pictured in Figure 4-4. There were complications, however, as processes were reengineered outside IBM's personal computing line of business. IBM began to simplify and integrate employee-facing processes using its intranet as the foundation. This led IBM to shift to what the company calls a "more balanced approach between value chain end-to-end integration and ensuring *One IBM* for key constituents."[15] What IBM found was that it had multiple value chains that transcended traditional siloed "business unit" ways of thinking. To put emphasis on the value delivered to its customers, besides core processes, the company had to include business policies, rules, applications, and data that deliver value to its customers, partners, and suppliers. To enable "One IBM," collaboration was required to address all customer and partner-facing processes that are common across the value chains.

As a result, IBM's Enterprise Process Transformation Model has evolved into a "Value Chain Transformation Model," which is pictured in Figure 4-4. Horizontally, IBM has seven value chains: (1) high-volume, easily configured products, (2) complex, configured hardware, (3) OEM (original equipment manufacturer) hardware, (4) distributed software, (5) entitled software, (6) services, and (7) financing. IBM contends that this transformation model (as pictured in Figure 4-4), aligns its business strategies and value-chain transformation objectives.[16] It provides a balanced approach, focuses on the highest-priority "value-added" parts of value chains, provides for value-chain uniqueness and for leveraging commonalties, is a closed-loop process, and identifies specific points of responsibility and auditability.[17]

IBM people are quick to say that a governance structure is required for this approach to transformation. IBM's chief information officer governs the transformation of core processes and is responsible for connecting business strategy and the various IT agendas. Its value-chain governance model is build on top of the existing organizational structure and includes business transformation executives, collaboration executives, a senior vice president transformation steering committee, and a business transformation strategic council. In summary, the IBM approach,

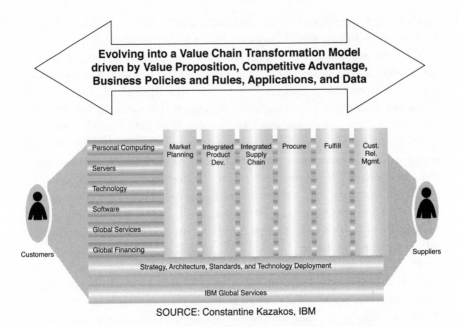

SOURCE: Constantine Kazakos, IBM

IBM's Work at Balancing Value Chains and Being One IBM

Figure 4-4   IBM's enterprise process transformation model

which may be a best practice in the making, takes the management of process and change to new levels of deployment.

The Bottom Line for People in Small Organizations

Up to now, this chapter has focused on four essential points. The first point is that any and all value that's created by any organization is through its processes. In fact, the argument has been made that what accounts for one competitor organization winning over another is that winners have processes that contain more value-adding work and less unnecessary non-value-added work. Second, to effectively identify, manage, and continuously improve major processes, it has been suggested that functional hierarchies make the transition to process-centered organizations. This involves defining processes and making them explicit; putting process measurements in place; establishing a process infrastructure of owners, teams, and so on; and adopting a wide variety of process-based management methods and tools, including value-stream maps.

Third, using the Process Classification Framework when creating a best practices and knowledge management repository makes a lot of sense. Fourth, an updated version of the PCF was presented, which entails 12 major process categories, five core and seven support. This PCF enables organizations to catalog and keep the best or ideal metrics, measurements or key performance indicators, benchmarks, best practices, and lessons learned and other categories of knowledge in an easily retrievable repository that transcends differing company jargon and language.

What Does This Mean for Owners of Small Businesses?

Eleven of the 55 tips for small businesses summarized in Chapter 11 are from this chapter. They are numbered 22 through 32 in Chapter 11, where some detail is provided. They are given here in capsule form:

- All the value of a small organization also comes from its processes. These processes need to be made explicit, so that they can be managed and improved. Begin with the top three to five to keep it simple.
- Implement process management for everyone by making the investment in employees' education, training, and practice.
- Simplify process management by using one to three measurements and benchmarks for the inputs, processing, outputs, and customer satisfaction.
- Reuse portions of the PCF for the three to five processes to be made explicit. This is reuse of a valuable best practices intellectual asset.
- Grow into adoption of all 12 process categories of the PCF provided in Figure 4-3 and discussed earlier in the chapter. The PCF helps people in small businesses think about their business in process terms.
- Off-the-shelf software is suggested for helping to manage processes.
- Instead of trying to create a best practices repository, people are encouraged to visit commercial Web sites such as http://www/bmpcoe.com and http://bestpracticedatabase.com to reuse what already exists at far less cost.
- Carefully consider outsourcing portions of major processes or subprocesses when that is a more effective and efficient alternative.
- Leverage "social networking" through contacts at local chambers of commerce, neighbors, old friends, professional associations, and industry leadership groups.
- Don't underestimate what's involved with "normalizing" data comparisons. Be very specific with metric definitions. "The devil is in the details!"
- Devote time to cultivating networked contacts because they're more apt to help a friend in need in exchange for a favor down the road.

The focus here at the end of Chapter 4 is on simplifying for small business the concept of managing by process. The question for people in small organizations is: what can they do to simplify, combine, shortcut, or abbreviate what's been advocated to get the greatest payback from the limited resources they have available to devote to this? First, small organizations can organize themselves around the processes, which is a key to success. But, just as with large organizations, people in small businesses must decide which processes are crucial to survival and growth. These are the processes that must be honed to a sharp edge to create competitive advantage and create more value for customers.

Using the PCF taxonomy approach often makes it simple and easier for people to identify what the specific problem areas are in their organization so that they can obtain and leverage the correct knowledge and make quick improvements. In the past, interpretation difficulties kept people from being on the same page. Use of the PCF taxonomy enables the involved parties to agree on already defined, generic, and universally common process categories, groups, and processes. This is knowledge management in its most useful form; it is reusing knowledge according to a common vocabulary and definitions so that the organization can leverage this knowledge better and faster than competitors. This is particularly useful for a small organization with limited assets and time. Indeed, just by avoiding the creation of functional departments and their inherent inefficiencies, small organizations can position themselves to better optimize the performance of their key processes.

To this end, it is suggested that small organizations adopt, with minor customization, the 12 categories of the PCF shown in Figure 4-3 and listed in detail earlier in this chapter. This action alone will leverage learning and provide savings in excess of $30,000 in equivalent value of outside consulting work. One good example to illustrate the point involves the term *revenue*. This term means different things to different companies and to difference industries. Some consider revenue to be the "sales" made in a defined time period; others interpret it to be actual "dollarized" (billed) deliveries or shipments. Without a standard language or taxonomy, misinterpretations are too frequent, and comparisons are often inappropriate.

To illustrate this further, consider process 3.5.1, identify and manage key customers and accounts. The PCF makes it quite clear that this is the process of selling, while process 3.6.1 (accept and validate sales orders) is the process for logging in or recording those sales and process 8.2.2 (Invoice customers) is the process for billing the customer. Thus, it should be clear that the PCF helps people in small businesses think about their business in process terms and in ways that help them define, limit, and refine their knowledge searches in order to maximum the benefit.

Second, small organizations may obtain off-the-shelf software to help them manage their processes. Such software enables them to define and map their processes, including inputs, processing steps, outputs, customers, and customer evaluation results. One good source for software and other off-the-shelf materials is the online bookstore at http://qualitypress.asq.org, which is operated by the American Society of Quality. In addition, organizations may visit such organizations as Best Practices, LLC online at http://www.benchmarkingreports.com or the American Productivity and Quality Center International Benchmarking Consortium at http://www.apqc.org to purchase and benefit from researched off-the-shelf best practices.

Third, rather than create their own best practices and knowledge repository, people at small organizations may visit such commercial Web sites as http://bestpractice-database.com. Once there, inexpensive memberships may be obtained, and the knowledge gained can be leveraged rapidly to create and continuously improve the business's processes. This is a cost-effective alternative to what large organizations spend and invest in gaining and transferring knowledge across their organizations.

Fourth, small organizations need to take a careful look at outsourcing any number of the PCF processes. At the early stages of business enterprise, when small organizations are growing, there are points in time when they must contemplate whether to take the leap and add dedicated human resource people rather than continuing to add service delivery people. One fear is the marbling of levels of bureaucracy, which works against agility.

At these decision points, it is recommended that small organizations carefully consider outsourcing such subprocesses as "manage human resource information systems (HRIS)," "manage and administer employee benefits," and "create and manage employee orientation program," to mention just a few. As part of any outsourcing plan, the supplier may be requested to provide quarterly or semiannual reports regarding the preexisting best practices in measurements, benchmarking standings, and evolving methods being tested. Thus, small organizations can obtain the advantages of importing centers of excellence while being regularly updated on competencies and practices in which no one in their small organization is obtaining firsthand experience. To a lesser extent, the benefits of outsourcing also apply to some finance and information technology resource subprocesses and "deliver products and services" processes that are not considered core competencies that provide a competitive advantage.

Fifth, small organizations can leverage to the hilt the age-old and still-thriving approach called social networking. It is still one of the best ways to benchmark and collect best practices data and performance metrics. This can be done through contacts at local chambers of commerce, industrial cooperation groups, neighbors, professional associations, and industry leadership groups. When forming networks, it's important that the beginner supply valuable information to others in order to cultivate the relationships.

The key to success here, as in all forms of benchmarking, is having common terms that are defined and used and normalization steps to ensure that performance metrics contain identical factors in the numerators and denominators and confirm that the data used in calculations are valid. For example, "revenue per month" hinges on what is revenue and what is a month. They must be the same if the business is to have a legitimate comparison with the benchmark measurement. Social networking activities create lists of contacts from which relationships may be forged. Such networked contacts are more apt to be willing to help a struggling friend than an unknown outsider.

Accordingly, contacts among these networks involve richer levels of trust than could ever be obtained via cold calls. Since people in small organizations are trying to identify quick and effective solutions, it's important that they trust the knowledge they gain and use to be reliable enough to base large investments that lead to the desired improvements. Thus, most experienced benchmarkers will agree that, with rare exception, the reliable solution is one (best practice) that is low risk and has been proven or tested under fire and produced superior results in at least one location. To this end, it is crucial for people in small organizations to develop trust in both the people they work with outside their organization (their counterparts elsewhere) and the knowledge gained through benchmarking exchanges. This is more easily achieved through such organizations as the Global Benchmaking Council seen at http://globalbenchmarkingcouncil.com.

Endnotes

1. Baldrige National Quality Program, "2003 Criteria for Performance Excellence," published by the National Institute of Standards and Technology (NIST), U.S. Department of Commerce, p. 24, para. N1; Web site www.quality.nist.gov.
2. After several publications [Michael Hammer, "Re-engineering Work: Don't Automate, Obliterate," Harvard Business Review, July–August 1990; Michael Hammer and James Champy, Reengineering the Corporation: A Manifesto for Business Revolution (New York: HarperCollins, 1993)], during 1995–1996 Hammer and Associates launched a process reengineering research forum that came to be known as the Phoenix Project with training including modules on process-centered organizations; Hammer and Associates is credited with doing original work underlying the discussion here, which has been adapted and refined.
3. Interview of Michelle Yakovac by Mike English, Feb. 16, 2005.
4. Ibid.
5. Interview of Kay Hunn by Mike English, Feb. 18, 2005.
6. Ibid.

7. Process Classification Framework (PCF), Version 3 dated June 2005, a brochure received from the APQC's Web site http://www.apqc.org on June 28, 2005 with permission of President Carla O'Dell and with the assistance of Kelly Butler of the APQC staff, pp. 1-16.
8. Ibid., pp. 1–16.
9. Marsha Krashoc, "Practical Best Practices in Accounts Payable," a presentation to the American Society of Quality (Dallas Section) Fall Conference, Oct. 1, 2003, p. 3.
10. Ibid., p. 6.
11. Ibid., pp. 13–18.
12. Ibid., pp. 19–22.
13. Constantine Kazakos, "e-business@IBM: Fusion of Business and IT: IBM's Transformation Story," slide presentation made to the Global Benchmarking Council, Palm Beach, Florida, Aug. 29, 2002, pp. 2–7.
14. Ibid., pp. 8–10.
15. Ibid., p. 25.
16. Ibid., p. 24.
17. Ibid., p. 32.

Chapter 5

Leveraging Intellectual Capital into Competitive Advantages: Mastering Phase 3 of the Knowledge Transfer Race

"Knowledge has become the key economic resource and the dominant and perhaps even the only source of comparative advantage."
—Peter Drucker, Managing in a Time of Great Change

Introduction

Before long, CEOs of prominent global enterprises will use their annual reports to describe how they are managing their organization's intellectual capital to accomplish their goals. Because knowledge is the fundamental ingredient of intellectual capital, CEOs will also soon report on how they are acquiring new knowledge and converting it into useful innovations that have commercial value. In fact, before long Balanced Scorecards will likewise contain ROI performance measurement results for investments in human capital and intellectual assets. Shareholders, themselves knowledge-enabled, will expect senior managers to provide such results regularly, along with the outlook for future performance.

In the twenty-first century, there's good reason for all this. Now more than ever, success depends on how organizations create and use intellectual capital to keep the pipeline full of new innovations that are convertible into profitable growth. Those who are deliberate, systematic, and quick to discover, learn, and translate knowledge into moneymaking actions will be leaders in the knowledge transfer race. And while the advantages of traditional plant and equipment capital are usually considered ephemeral or short-lived, the advantages of intellectual capital may be sustained indefinitely.

If a company is to be a leader, organizational learning needs to expand the capacity of employees to do more in the future. As Peter Senge and his colleagues have observed, "If you strike it rich by winning the lottery, you have achieved something extraordinary, but you have not expanded your capacity to win future lotteries."[1] Thus, for an enterprise to change for the better, the people in that enterprise must have learned enough to extend their capacity for doing more in the future. As this occurs, these people will think and interact differently, too. They will continually test their experiences against their sacred cows, individually producing relevant knowledge so that each and every person develops capabilities that he or she didn't have before, and each will be better at sharing knowledge so that it's accessible to everyone, regardless of geographical location or time zone.[2] When people think and interact in these ways, they will become the principal leverage of their organization's learning and, thus, will become the source that creates advantages over competitors.

After all, every enterprise needs to develop, distribute, and service products quickly, all the while shrinking its cycle times in order to meet and exceed its customers' expectations. Enterprises also need to acquire more new customers more quickly and retain existing customers longer. All the while, they also need to provide their employees and partners with the expertise needed to work smarter and faster. Knowledge solutions bring together an organization's information, which is often stored in its intranets, portals, databases, content management systems, customer relationship management (CRM) systems, and other internal systems. Today, most organizations have too much information from these sources, but not enough knowledge. Software solutions, however, are now available to capture the knowledge of employees, customers, and partners, regardless of where they are or what language they do business in, managing intellectual capital securely, automatically, and in real time. Yet the organizational cultures and personal work styles needed to complement these advanced software solutions are lagging behind. The software solutions must be part of the everyday work life of people doing their jobs.

Management of Intellectual Capital

Just as best practices and knowledge management have emerged as consequential concepts during the past ten years, the age of intellectual capital and its management has arrived. This new concept is integrating the appropriate discoveries in learning, content design, and information architecture for any particular business objective. It's more than implementing stand-alone search solutions. Intellectual capital systems want to increase the return on existing and future investments in intellectual capital. Intellectual capital, made up of intangible knowledge (human capital and intellectual assets, including properties such as patents and trade secrets), has quickly become a mainstream tool to increase competitiveness. Indeed, one Columbia University study estimates that spending on intangible assets like research and development and employee education produces a return eight times that of the same investment in new plant and equipment.[3] Why? New machinery generates only incremental improvements, while R&D coupled with education generates innovations that are revolutionary advances and breakthroughs. The recent positive trends in U.S. national productivity suggest that intellectual capital is being leveraged with great success.

Indeed, measuring intellectual capital, managing it, and putting it to use has quickly become one of the top priorities of worldwide enterprises. In fact, since 1998, the KNOW Network, a global community of knowledge-driven organizations, and the consulting firm of Teleos have conducted studies of the Most Admired Knowledge Enterprises (MAKE) and use judging criteria to annually recognize winners in the Asian, European, Japanese, North American, and Global Enterprises categories.[4] To illustrate who these leaders in the knowledge transfer race are, Table 5-1 lists the top 13 North American 2005 MAKE winners. These winners are judged against eight nominating criteria, which are identified in Table 5-2. The fourth criterion on the list in Table 5-2 explicitly addresses the success that the enterprise has in maximizing the value of its intellectual capital. Overall, the emphasis is on how the enterprise creates, shares, and uses knowledge to gain a competitive edge. In other words, enterprises that score well on the MAKE award criteria are also front-runners in the knowledge transfer race.

Table 5-1   Winners of the 2005 MAKE Awards for North America

Enterprise (listed alphabetically)	Industry
▪ Buckman Laboratories	▪ Chemicals
▪ Dell Computer.	▪ Computers/office equipment
▪ Fluor	▪ Construction
▪ General Electric	▪ Electronics
▪ Google	▪ Web search engines
▪ Hewlett-Packard	▪ Computers/office equipment
▪ IBM	▪ Computers/office equipment
▪ McKinsey & Company	▪ Consulting
▪ Microsoft	▪ Computer software
▪ Raytheon	▪ Aerospace/defense
▪ SAIC	▪ Research/engineering
▪ Southwest Airlines	▪ Air transportation
▪ 3M	▪ Diversified technologies

Source: The KNOW Network Web site, www.knowledgebusiness.com.

What's becoming clear is that to have the capacity to successfully and consistently produce innovations of remarkable commercial value, the enterprise must become knowledge-based. But what is a knowledge-based enterprise? Scoring a 7 or higher (on a scale of 1 to 10) on each of the eight MAKE criteria in Table 5-2 is the consensus answer. After all, MAKE is an acronym for Most Admired Knowledge Enterprise. As with other "total" or holistic principles such as the Baldrige criteria, enterprises must make a total commitment to transforming their complete organizational character and how they conduct business. As a metaphor, this is akin to redesigning (remodeling) a three-story home over five years while a family of six is living in it. Everything is in flux as conflict (the need to manage change) and learning become daily occurrences until, just as driving an automobile becomes automatic and without thought, it becomes "natural" for nearly everyone to create, share, use, and reuse knowledge. By then, the enterprise has been forever changed. As it transforms its leadership culture (to recognize and reward knowledge sharing and learning) and its systems (to be knowledge-based) and deploys initiatives that add value for customers, suddenly, the enterprise is metamorphosed.

The transformation also instantly makes the enterprise a contestant in the knowledge transfer race, except that this is a different type of competition. There

Table 5-2 Criteria for the Most Admired Knowledge Enterprise (MAKE) Awards

Criteria to Judge	Self-Assessment Score, 1 (Poor) to 10 (Excellent)
1. Success in establishing an enterprise knowledge culture	_____
2. Top management support for managing knowledge	_____
3. Ability to develop and deliver knowledge-based goods/services	_____
4. Success in maximizing the value of intellectual capital	_____
5. Effectiveness in creating an environment of knowledge sharing	_____
6. Success in establishing an environment of continuous learning	_____
7. Effectiveness in managing customer knowledge to increase loyalty and value	_____
8. Ability to manage knowledge to generate shareholder value	_____

Source: The KNOW Network—MAKE Questionnaire at Web site, www.knowledgebusiness.com/knowledgebusiness/nonmembers/makesm.asp.

isn't a finish line. This is a marathon journey with twists and turns (or phases) and pit stops, but no one final destination. Therefore, to be a winner, all the obstacles in the road to effective knowledge transfer must be overcome and all the challenges met. Once an organization realizes that it is in a race, its objective is to get into the lead. Those who never realize that they are in a race or who drop out are losing the race, and they may not even know it. This book aims to get enterprises into the race and help them conquer the challenges and obstacles so that they're competitive and can become winners.

At the end of the day, the one key measure of success is how successful an enterprise is at managing customer knowledge to increase customer loyalty and value. This can involve the use of enterprise intranets, portals, and intellectual property research—for example, in health care, matching knowledge pertaining to patients with doctors and clinical trials. Other examples include recruiting by matching job postings with résumés, law enforcement crime solving via criminal profiling, and an increasing number of customer relationship management (CRM) approaches. In fact, there is much to be learned from a deeper discussion of CRM approaches.

Knowledge-Enabled Customer Relationship Management

Successful twenty-first-century enterprises knowledge-enable how they manage customer relationships so that those relationships produce enormous added value. Some reputable research indicates that a 5 percent increase in customer retention may increase an organization's profitability by as much as 40 to 100 percent.[5] That's because happy customers perceive that they're receiving higher value and make repeated purchases. When an enterprise has a track record of on-time, defect-free performance, customers develop loyalty to that better-performing supplier. It's no surprise that customer loyalty is a tremendous competitive advantage and is strategic to the success of many organizations. And at the heart of it, strategic pre- and postsale support play a bigger role in shaping it. Customer loyalty is paramount.

The good news is that most organizations already have all the information they need to achieve superior customer loyalty. What's missing is the capability to put all the information they already have to work. In other words, enterprises need to translate their information into knowledge that they can act upon. What's key is bringing together the knowledge from across the organization in ways that make it quick and easy for customer-contact people to access and use it to solve customers' needs or develop answers to their questions.

To this end, a new breed of software enterprise solution suppliers has emerged to match applications to the needs of CRM process owners, with a focus on customer value. Their niche is furnishing software solutions that help organizations manage knowledge. Intelligence is used to redesign processes so that customers are connected with subject experts who are best able to help them. To illustrate what's possible, here is a partial list of the kinds of changes that are being made:

- Call avoidance. Customers are being provided with the ability to self-service their need, which lowers inbound calls and avoids the cost that would have otherwise been required to satisfy customers' needs and expectations.
- Shortened call times. As problems and questions are resolved faster, the length of calls drops, along with cost, while customer satisfaction climbs.
- Fewer repeat calls. Resolution of problems and questions on the first call climbs, which drives up satisfaction while driving down repeat calls and cost.
- Problem avoidance. As proactive process steps are added, notifications regarding recalls, glitches, fixes, workarounds, scheduled software releases, and other such events may be triggered, heading off problems (including bad publicity hits or even litigation) before they happen.
- Lower information technology costs. Well-designed and well-managed data warehousing, retrieval, and proactive out-of-limit notifications have been shown to hold down demands upon and costs of databases, systems, and networks.

The CRM process owner is a key figure because the CRM process has to be managed actively to anticipate where customers perceive value to exist in the relationship. It is a closed-loop, ongoing, and ever-changing cycle. The most successful companies seem to operate with knowledge as though they're functioning inside their customers' heads, understanding their needs, wants, and expectations. Executives of such companies reach out via benchmarking to learn about competitors' core best practices and related trends as they emerge.

One such successful trend is a focus on "customer intimacy." One convincing example is the Ritz-Carlton Hotel Company, a two-time Baldrige Award recipient.[6] This luxury, high-service hotel chain has become expert at capturing and personalizing customers' preferences. In fact, when customers return to this hotel they find their room customized with their individual favorite touches, such as their first-choice newspaper, desired bedding, favorite pillow, especially-liked flowers, and preferred music, soap, shampoo, and room service menu.[7] Applying this personal knowledge makes customers feel special and makes them want to come back again and again.

Intellectual Capital: What Is It, Anyway?

Until a series of global intellectual capital management (ICM) gatherings took place between 1995 and 1999, there were many definitions for intellectual capital.[8] It's a relatively new concept. Initially, the ICM gathering agreed to the definition of "knowledge that can be converted into profits."[9] Because of its brevity, this concise definition continues to be used to this day to describe the bottom line. Then, over time, as the group grew to 30 members (the original members were Dow, DuPont, Hoffman LaRoche, Skandia, Hewlett-Packard, Hughes Space Systems, and Law and Economics Consulting Group), its members created a graphical depiction of intellectual capital and its components and their relationships to one another.

This breakthrough work of the ICM gatherings, shown in Figure 5-1, clarifies what the components of intellectual capital are and how they relate to one another. The first component is human capital, which consists of the tacit knowledge that people or employees possess, identified generally as experience, know-how, skills, and creativity. To the extent that humans codify or document knowledge that is of value, it becomes an enterprise's intellectual assets, which generally consist of programs, methodologies, inventions, documents, processes, drawings, databases, and designs. Intellectual property, on the other hand, is a subset of intellectual assets and consists of those assets that are legally protected (patents, copyrights, trademarks, trade secrets), hence the term *property*.[10]

What makes the graphic framework in Figure 5-1 so powerful is the way it identifies all the relationships and, figuratively, connects the dots. Most important, this graphical depiction represents the painstaking collaboration and consensus thinking of 30 of the world's leading knowledge-based enterprises. Those enterprises were among the first to enter and lead the knowledge transfer race. For these reasons, the authors of this book are using the Figure 5-1 graphic throughout the book to define and describe how to leverage intellectual capital.

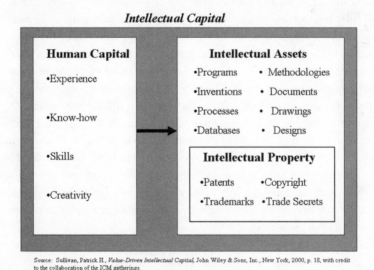

Intellectual Capital

Source: Sullivan, Patrick H., *Value-Driven Intellectual Capital,* John Wiley & Sons, Inc., New York, 2000, p. 18, with credit to the collaboration of the ICM gatherings.

Figure 5-1 Intellectual capital and its major components and relationships

Leveraging Human Capital into Competitive Advantage

The goal is to provide the right knowledge to the right person at the right time in order to enable more informed decisions and to ensure customer success.

—*Raytheon's Leadership Team*

As identified in Figure 5-1, human capital is one of the key components of intellectual capital and consists of employees' experience, know-how, skills, and creativity. Human capital is the source and repository of all of the enterprise's tacit (nondocumented) knowledge. However, while an enterprise owns its intellectual assets, it doesn't "own" its human capital; its employees and managers do. So whatever knowledge employees bring with them when they're hired or whatever they learn while they are employed, that human capital leaves with the employee when they depart. On the other hand, whatever bits of knowledge employees help to codify (or document) remain behind and become the intellectual assets of the enterprise.[11] Knowledge management professionals typically describe this process as taking tacit knowledge and converting it to explicit knowledge.

Thus, a great deal more attention needs to be given to managing human capital in order to anticipate and initiate contingency strategies for employee resignations, layoffs, retirements, and terminations. In this day and age, managing human capital is further compounded by the aging of the worldwide workforce and the record baby boomer retirements that are occurring. In fact, enterprises face major workforce upheavals because of these population age shifts from the baby boom generation to Generation X and Generation Y. These shifts threaten enterprises with huge losses of employees and the sometimes-indispensable knowledge (human capital) that they possess. The answer comes from having a vision, a strategy, and systematic tactical approaches for managing intellectual capital.

Ever mindful that the focus should be on managing the particular knowledge that can be converted into profit, enterprises need to establish an innovation process that includes the appropriate systemic processes to manage their explicit intellectual asset portfolio, just as they manage their investment portfolio. Over time, this systematic approach will identify what knowledge in the enterprise needs to be codified into programs, inventions, processes, databases, methodologies, documents, drawings, and designs.

As the system is refined, it will also produce the policies the enterprise needs for creating or investing in intellectual property (patents, copyrights, trademarks, and trade secrets). As a result of this work, a determination concerning how much of which particular knowledge needs to be codified will be made. And for all the approaches or processes just discussed, there are best practices that may be learned via benchmarking and then leveraged across the organization to achieve superior performance.

To illustrate the vulnerability of human capital and the need to manage it with an innovation process, consider the example of Raytheon's knowledge management strategy. In the year 2000, Raytheon accepted the common belief that about 80 percent of a typical company's knowledge is undocumented or unshared. This is portrayed in Figure 5-2. With a vision and process and a strategy that integrated knowledge management and benchmarking into *Raytheon Six Sigma* (*R6σ*), the company set specific goals for documenting essential knowledge from company projects. Because of this cultural shift and the results obtained, indeed, Raytheon was selected as one of the winners of the 2004 and 2005 North American MAKE Awards (the MAKE Award criteria were given in Table 5-2). Raytheon, with annual sales of $18.1 billion and 78,000 employees worldwide, was commended for how it transforms enterprise knowledge into shareholder value. Raytheon manages its intellectual capital to achieve its stated goals of "leveraging our strengths in technology, integration and services to deliver superior customer solutions."[12]

Indeed, the Raytheon intellectual capital paradigm calls for

1. A common vision or strategy that everyone can support
2. An encouraging culture that's free from micromanaging, provides employees with meaningful and challenging work, and enables employees to grow their competencies
3. Open communication
4. Sharing of the gains

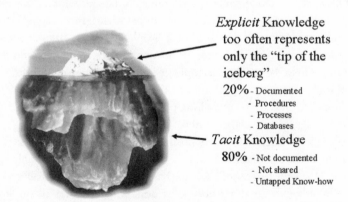

Explicit Knowledge too often represents only the "tip of the iceberg"

20% - Documented
  - Procedures
  - Processes
  - Databases

Tacit Knowledge

80% - Not documented
  - Not shared
  - Untapped Know-how

Source: Bill Baker's presentation to the QuEST Forum Third Annual Best Practices Conference in Richardson, Texas during September 2002.

Figure 5-2   Raytheon's explicit versus tacit knowledge graphic

Human Capital Strategies

Human capital competencies, whether they are technical or managerial, must first support the business strategy. To do this, most managers use some combination of the following:

1. Replace the less-qualified performers with people who are more qualified. This is not easy, especially when the labor market is tight, but it is the objective.
2. Invest in the current workforce to make it stronger by concentrating on activities that will help employees learn new technical and management skills that will increase the organization's intellectual capital. This emphasizes the importance of being a learning organization, as the process of transferring explicit or documented information from a printed piece of paper or database via a PC monitor into one's head is called learning.
3. Outsource what cannot be done efficiently or effectively in-house or use a consultant who has the competencies required. Many enterprises, especially those in high-tech businesses, tend to focus almost entirely on the competence dimension in an effort to increase their intellectual capital. They tend to ignore tools for the creation and maintenance of employee commitment. They relegate this to the category of "soft stuff," which they believe contributes little to a hard-hitting, fast-moving organization. However, today's businesses need committed employees who are involved emotionally as well as intellectually if the business is to continue to be successful.

Before leaving the discussion of human capital, its importance to intellectual capital and a few related closing points need to be emphasized. Displayed in Figure 5-3 is a diagram that pictures how human capital is the source for any organization's new knowledge creation. To describe in a nutshell what human capital is, an argument can be made that it's the capacity of people to provide customers with solutions.[13] Merely converting data into information in a research report and then into tacit information in the mind of an employee is not the creation of knowledge. When the employee transfers the explicit information in the research report into his or her head, it is called learning. Yet as Sullivan points out, "information acquired this way is not knowledge."[14] It's only when those bits of learned information are used that they become knowledge. So, for example, when an employee uses the same bits of information to create a new methodology for serving customers, not only has he or she created new knowledge, but he or she has created an intellectual asset.

Finally, although the differences aren't dealt with here, not all employees are equal when it comes to creating new knowledge. Even though the term *human capital* has been used to refer to all the employees of an enterprise, sooner or later most knowledge-based enterprises have to differentiate sets of employees by their contributions. The creativity of employees will vary depending on the type of enterprise

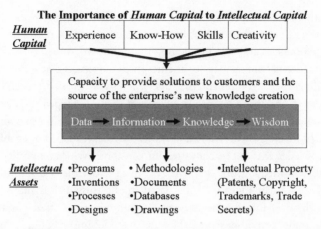

Figure 5-3 The importance of human capital to intellectual capital.

involved. Sullivan makes distinctions between product companies, process companies, 24-hour service companies, and discrete service companies.[15] Thus, human resource policies need to treat employees differently rather than treating them all equally. Such an approach conflicts with the American egalitarian philosophy, which posits that, except for individual compensation, all employees should be treated exactly the same.[16] However, viewed through the lens of intellectual capital management, employees are not all the same. There are often special classifications of creative employees who, literally, have the enterprise's future in their hands. Invariably, these people need to be treated, compensated, and managed differently.

Two Keys to Success: (1) A Knowledge-Enabled Culture That Appreciates, Grows, and Nurtures Human Capital and (2) Leadership

The bigger issue is the need for enterprises to completely overhaul their cultures and management systems to ensure that managers pay enough attention to the creation of intellectual capital. This begins by educating managers and providing them with systems and tools that encourage the creation of new intellectual capital, especially knowledge that can be converted into profits. Few organizations truly "walk the talk" about committed employees being an enterprise's most important asset for achieving its business goals. A focus on intellectual capital has been missing from the never-ending debates about what managers should focus their attention upon. Yet there are compelling reasons to change how managers and employees think about and do work as well as how the enterprise supports (rather than discourages), via policies and systems, getting the right work done.

First, intellectual capital may be the enterprise's only assets that appreciate. Other assets (buildings, plant, equipment, machinery, and so on) begin depreciating the day they're acquired, and many have short lives until they're scrapped. Besides, without exception, intellectual capital must grow if an enterprise is to prosper and it is an investment in future growth. More and more, a manager's job is to enable the creation of knowledge that can be converted into customer value and profit.

Second, knowledge work is on the rise, not the decline. Dartmouth College Professor James Brian Quinn substantiated in the early 1990s that the service industries (finance, information services, communications, transportation, real estate, retail trade, and other services like travel and leisure) account for more than 77 percent of all U.S. employment and 75 percent of the Gross National Product (GNP) of the United States and are growing by far more than the combination of agriculture, mining, and the traditional manufacturing industries of autos, durable goods, and equipment.[17] As service industries grow, so does the need for human capital knowledge, as it is an essential prerequisite to effective customer relationships and competence in solving customer problems.

Third, the employees who are best at creating intellectual capital are, essentially, free-agent volunteers because they choose to be where they are despite having the option of going elsewhere. They're talented and heavily recruited, and it's not mandatory that they keep the job they have. *Voluntary* means that they're doing their current job because they like it, not because they're donating their time free of charge. This may be because they feel emotionally connected to their team of coworkers and/or because they feel a commitment to the enterprise. Such people are frequently not totally focused on their economic return (after a certain threshold has been crossed); they are also focused on the "meaning and significance of their work" or on their lifestyle, especially if young children are involved. If they or members of their team are mistreated, these talented people can easily leave for a more supportive environment elsewhere, which could be with a competitor.

Fourth, unless educated otherwise, most managers ignore or discount the importance of intellectual capital. In the face of recurring cycles of downsizing or rightsizing, squeezed budgets, edicts to "do more with less," increasing customer requirements, and pressures of every kind, managers aren't paying attention to intellectual capital. Institutionally, their performance isn't being measured on how well they manage their intellectual capital, nor does their compensation reflect it. They don't have simple tools, either. Senior managers must provide leadership if progress is to be made. In the meantime, the work lives of employees and managers rarely change for the better.

In a recent workshop with 60 high-potential managers from a successful global company, careers were discussed. Of these managers, most of whom were in their thirties or early forties, 50 percent did not think that they would stay with their current company long enough to retire, not because of lack of opportunity, but because of the enormous stress and high demands. Within this group, 90 percent had personal knowledge of someone who had voluntarily left the company in the past six months because of the increased workload. When one member of the group shared these concerns with one of the enterprise's executives, it fell on insensitive ears. The group member was told that the jobs at the company were good ones, that there were backups for anyone who did not want to work hard, and that discussions of work-life balance were not useful for improving business results. This attitude on the part of some senior managers is caused, in part, by organizations' strong push to achieve productivity increases. Added technology tools also tend to keep people involved with their work more hours of each day. Cell phones, networked personal computers, personal data assistants (PDAs), and pagers have added demands to jobs.

Fifth, those employees who possess the most human capital are often the least appreciated. Study results indicate that the attitudes of front-line employees often correspond to those of customers of the same enterprise. As examples, peoples' opinions of McDonald's restaurants, Sears, or Ford closely correspond to their opinions about the service they receive from each of those organizations' local franchise, store, or dealership. Yet while enterprises like McDonald's are investing millions in training their franchise executives to think strategically and act globally, their customers' impressions are more likely to be formed by the employees who serve them their food. Employees put into these jobs often are ill trained, are paid minimum wage, are transient, and, thus, lack the competence or commitment to fully answer customers' questions and completely meet their needs. Consequently, the overall image of enterprises fails at its weakest link, the purchase point where personal moments of truth occur.

From these five key points about the importance of human capital in twenty-first-century business, it is crystal clear that it is leadership that's responsible for establishing the proper emphasis on creating, capturing, sharing, and reusing knowledge in enterprises. The payback is in both the short and the long term, but it is the result of strategic priority and being high on priority lists. Thus, it is the authors' opinion that knowledge transfer and reuse need to be integrated into managers' annual plans and performance reviews.

How effectively managers actually make knowledge transfers occur needs to be evaluated and weighted to determine annual merit compensation, including bonuses. This will bring about the cultural change needed, but it requires years of persistence. It's a change in focus that takes coaching, practice, and repetition to bring about the changes needed in managers' behavior. It's cultural change because it has to do with what gets done and doesn't get done in the organization. So, recognition, rewards, and reinforcement are involved. And senior managers must "walk the talk" as well.

Leveraging Intellectual Assets into Competitive Advantage

The focus now turns to generating gains from codified knowledge (or intellectual assets) and the transfer (import and sharing) of such knowledge. The central theme of this chapter continues to be creating knowledge that can be converted into profits, but now, instead of human capital (with tacit knowledge), the subject is documented (or codified) knowledge that can be transferred. Carrying on the use of the intellectual capital framework in Figure 5-1, documented (or codified) knowledge is referred to as the enterprise's intellectual assets.

As tacit knowledge is transferred from the mind of human employees into a document, be it on paper, software, canvas, or any other medium, as shown in Figure 5-4, the document thus created becomes a codified asset of the enterprise and becomes part of the firm's intellectual assets.[18] Even though Figure 5-4 shows only eight types of intellectual assets (programs, methodologies, inventions, processes, drawings, databases, designs, and documents), for all practical purposes, any document created by an employee is an intellectual asset. And whereas employees own the tacit knowledge they possess in their mind, the enterprise owns the intellectual assets.

Source: Sullivan, Patrick H., *Value-Driven Intellectual Capital*, John Wiley & Sons, Inc., New York, 2000, p. 8, with credit to the collaboration of the ICM gatherings.

Figure 5-4 How human capital in the source for intellectual assets and intellectual property.

A subset of intellectual assets is a special category of codified knowledge that is legally named intellectual property. This consists of patents, copyrights, trademarks, and trade secrets. Sometimes referred to as legally protected intellectual assets, patents, copyrights, trademarks, and trade secrets need to be created and managed according to an enterprise's vision and strategies. Obviously, the creation of intellectual property and its conversion into new value for customers and, ultimately, new profits is an imperative, and for knowledge-based enterprises, it's vital.

This book's central theme comes into action when intellectual capital is created, captured (imported), shared, or reused, especially when it's intellectual property. This is, then, a key juncture in the authors' work, as the content being presented is tied directly to the theme and is relevant to the book's metaphoric knowledge transfer race. After all, this book is about designing, creating, integrating, and leveraging knowledge, particularly best practices imported via benchmarking. The primary focus has always been on leveraging (or taking advantage of) knowledge to achieve extraordinary results, including profits. Also at play is the compulsion for speed, driven by the growth and capabilities of the Internet. Indeed, the insatiable thirst that enterprises have for more speed has turned their pursuit of knowledge into a race.

So the race is on, and it's got four phases beginning with the "search for and import best practices" phase. This is where best practices are sought out and imported. Next is phase 2, which is named "learn, understand, and share." In this phase, organizations explore the relationship between employee and team actions and outcomes, and the knowledge extracted from experiences and knowledge transfer systems is put to use. Phase 3 is named "create intellectual capital," and it involves the creation of human capital, intellectual assets, and intellectual property. Here, too, with a vision and strategy, protected intellectual property is created and managed. Finally, there's the money phase of the race, named "convert into value and profits," where intellectual capital generates profits as it is applied to new and better reuses of the knowledge, but in a different context. It's in phase 4 that intellectual capital is leveraged to the hilt and converted into added value for customers or commercial profits. Enabling performance in all four phases is the knowledge-enabled culture consideration, which builds a learning organization that manages by process. The culture includes use of a process classification framework.

Still, there isn't a finish line for the race. This is a key point: the race is without an end. Once enterprises get into the race, they've got a chance to win, but they must stay in the race or they're out. If they're out, they're on the sidelines, which dooms their long-term future. In the twenty-first-century knowledge age, enterprises that aren't knowledge-enabled will fail. On the other hand, it's okay for enterprises to make as many pit stops as they need in this race.

For example, consider the example of a pit stop to redesign and deploy a process that afterwards gets the contestant back into the race, competing far better than it was before. During benchmarking studies, for instance, it's not uncommon to uncover a new best practice for product development, and every once in a while it may even be a radical breakthrough, as was the case with "design for Six Sigma." In such an instance, it may be better to stop and completely redesign the current process to include a new best practice that makes the enterprise more competitive.

That's fine, but the contestant has to get back into the race. Staying in the race for the long haul will automatically turn contestants into race leaders. When they overcome all the obstacles they'll face and meet every challenge along the way, they will be winners, too. With linkage to the metaphoric knowledge race in mind, the discussion reverts to leveraging intellectual assets, something that is essential in the race.

Reiterating content that was presented in Chapter 2, best practices, when documented or codified, by definition are intellectual assets. Table 5-3 contains the same definitions for *best*, *practices*, and *best practices* that were provided in Table 2-3, except that the words "is documented (codified)" have been added. Yes, undocumented forms of human capital (tacit knowledge) have intellectual capital importance. For example, there are many techniques in the heads of service representatives that are translated into value by those representatives to solve problems for customers. These so-called moments of truth occur hourly, day in and out, when highly skilled and charming telephone service representatives use information regarding customers and their own skills and experiences to develop the right solutions to resolve customer needs and problems. However, if the human capital (tacit knowledge) is extraordinarily special, it should be documented or codified.

The bottom line is that enterprises need to have a vision, strategy, and tactics for converting their most valuable human capital into documented or codified intellectual assets. For one thing, as previously discussed, people who leave (including baby boomers who retire) take with them the tacit knowledge that they possess. After all, they own it. Just as important, too, when the knowledge is documented or recorded, it's usually made all the more valuable because once it has been captured (creatively or imported), learned, shared, used, and reused time and

Table 5-3   Best Practices Redefined

Best	It fully satisfies customers, produces superior results in at least one operation, and performs as reliably as any alternative elsewhere.
Practice	Type 1 process practices and/or type 2 enabling capability practice.
Best practice	A process input, step, output, or enabling capability that fully satisfies customers, produces superior results in at least one operation, performs as reliably as any alternative elsewhere, is documented (codified), and is adaptable by others.
Concise definition	A practice that fully satisfies customers, produces superior results in one operation, performs as reliably as any alternative, is documented (codified), and can be adapted elsewhere.

time again, it may be truly understood. Therefore, all best practices are valuable intellectual assets. However, the reverse is not true. Not every intellectual asset is a best practice. Yet because the enterprise needs to concentrate on deciding which intellectual assets to transfer across the entire enterprise, beginning with best practices is a good start.

As mentioned earlier, intellectual assets are categorized into eight general classifications: programs, methodologies, inventions, processes, drawings, databases, designs, and documents. These are broad, all-encompassing categories. The category *processes* is broad enough to include everything that was discussed about processes in Chapter 4. This includes the five core business processes ("Develop Vision and Strategy," "Design and Develop Products and Services," "Market and Sell Products and Services," "Deliver Products and Services," and "Manage Customer Service") and the seven support and management processes. Another category, *methodologies*, includes all the methods, procedures, and product and service delivery systems. *Programs* comprises software programs, improvement initiatives, and financial and human resource systems and such. *Databases* includes all the data residing in any electronic systems. The *drawings* category includes ideas or concepts that are still in handwritten or brainstorming form. And, finally, *documents* seems to be the catchall for anything that has been codified that is not covered elsewhere. It's safe to say that any knowledge that employees transfer from their head into a document becomes an intellectual asset of the enterprise.

It should be evident by now that to effectively create, import, share, and truly manage intellectual assets so that they're converted into the maximum value and profits, enterprises require a tailored version of a best practices intellectual asset inventory and management system. As has been alluded to earlier, enterprises need to have a vision and strategy for converting the most valuable human capital into documented or codified intellectual assets. A system is needed to support this work as well as to keep inventory and track what qualifies for the protection or offensive action of patents, copyrights, trademarks, or trade secrets. The work of managing all this—including policies, procedures, and systems—is the work of staying in the knowledge transfer race.

Sooner or later, enterprises must determine which of their intellectual assets are commercializable, meaning that they can be sold or licensed to produce revenue and profit. As depicted in Figures 5-1 and 5-4, intellectual property is an important subset of intellectual assets. Actually, the term *intellectual property* is a legal name for protected intellectual assets. This includes patents, copyright, trademarks, and trade secrets, which are described in Table 5-4.

Depending on an enterprise's vision and strategies, it is absolutely essential that the enterprise, especially one that is truly knowledge-based, carefully manage, inventory, and properly harvest, commercially, its intellectual assets. Enterprises must have policies, strategies, and processes that cover obtaining, licensing, and

Table 5-4   Intellectual Property Definitions

■ A patent is a right granted by government that allows the holder to exclude others from making, using, or selling the invention that the patent pertains to. Patents may cover any new machine, article, composition of matter, process, use, or improvement.	■ A copyright protects "original works of authorship," whether they've been published or not. The copyright holder has the sole right to make copies, write derivative works, and perform or display the work publicly.
■ A trademark is a means of branding a that product that both identifies it and distinguishes it from the goods of others. Trademarks can take the form of words,names, symbols, sounds, or combinations of these. They are registered and protected for as long as they are in use.	■ A trade secret is valuable information that is kept from being known outside a particular business. It is such information as recipes, (e.g., Coca-Cola or Kentucky Fried Chicken), techniques, methods, designs, or formulas that are valuable to a business.

protecting patents, trademarks, copyrights, and trade secrets. This includes when and how to be offensive and defensive, from a legal point of view. Managing intellectual assets is imperative if an organization is to be able to convert knowledge effectively and efficiently into customer value and profits. Being competent at managing intellectual property is absolutely necessary if an organization is to be a leader in the knowledge transfer race.

To synthesize, in Chapter 2, best practices were defined and characterized as improvement knowledge that fuels for-profit enterprises. In this chapter, it has been clarified that best practices are intellectual assets, which need to be managed so that human capital is codified or documented. While winning the metaphoric knowledge transfer race is the central theme, the focus has always been on the creation, capture, sharing, use, and reuse of knowledge, converting it into value and profits, and leveraging all this into competitive advantages. Ultimately, winning the knowledge transfer race is synonymous with winning market share and being an industry market leader. Progress, however, comes beforehand in the form of payoffs that eventually lead to winning market share and leadership. The biggest payoff comes from the reuse of knowledge.

The Big Payoff: Breakthroughs in Reusing Knowledge

Besides the creation of knowledge that's convertible from intellectual capital into profit, reuse of knowledge that has already been learned and codified is a key to future success in the knowledge transfer race. This occurs naturally over time, but the natural process is not systematic enough to be advantageous. Indeed, winners of the MAKE awards are leading the way on this. But first, a story is shared to convey an understanding of how civilization would be affected if the use and reuse of knowledge were suspended for tens of decades.

Imagine a civilization that was so isolated that up until 20 years ago, it had been trapped in a time capsule since the year 1850. Its people had access to only the knowledge that existed over 150 years before. This was the case for a remote tribe of aborigines in the island state of Tasmania (Australia). For decades these people lived in a village with a life that resembled that of ancient times. This aboriginal civilization was cut off from the learning, sharing, and reuse of knowledge that had been going on around the world for over ten decades. It is thus no surprise that these people were primitive when it came to modern medicine, agriculture, communication, technology, transportation, and industry.

Until modern-day knowledge was shared and reused by the aborigines, they were literally reinventing the wheel every day, re-creating discoveries that had been made long ago in virtually every other part of the world. Like civilizations, enterprises also grow when they create, capture, share, and reuse knowledge.

More and more examples are surfacing of instances in which enterprises reused knowledge to unmistakably benefit their customers and other stakeholders. Two common characteristics that seem pervasive across these enterprises—which are also leaders in the knowledge transfer race—is the ability to have defeated the knowledge-hoarding tendency that is prevalent in most organizations and to have also conquered the infamous not invented here (or NIH) factor or syndrome. The NIH factor is the long-standing arrogant attitude that translates into "no one anywhere else could be creating anything better than us." On the contrary, the ideal knowledge-worker role model instead displays an attitude of "we can learn from anyone."

Next are case studies of two MAKE Award recipients—Buckman Labs and Texas Instruments—that demonstrate different but equally compelling approaches taken by leaders in the reuse of existing knowledge. Besides best practices portrayals of leadership, these two examples convey the importance of learning, collaborative knowledge sharing and reuse, and delivering value based on customer knowledge. The examples also illustrate how organizations can survive, thrive, grow, and prosper in the twenty-first century.

Buckman Laboratories[19]

One poster child for knowledge sharing and reuse is Buckman Labs, a private specialty chemical company located in Memphis, Tennessee. It is a 2003, 2004, and 2005 winner of the North American MAKE Awards, which singled out Buckman

Labs for its (1) strong corporate knowledge-driven culture, (2) knowledge leadership, (3) ability to deliver knowledge-based products and solutions, and (4) creation of value based on customer knowledge.

As the story goes, Chairman Bob Buckman came to the realization years ago that his salespeople were scattered all around the globe trying to sell chemical solutions mainly to the leather processing industry. The challenge resembled other situations where American technology, ingenuity, and resourcefulness needed to be shared with customers who could really benefit from that knowledge. There are plenty of previously formulated or engineered solutions to recurring problems that are on the shelf ready to be reused. Buckman realized this and saw and seized the opportunity to become an early adopter of knowledge sharing. Buckman's idea was to delivers value to customers by quickly sharing knowledge among sales representatives to benefit customers. Buckman realized that his sales force already had excessive demands on its time and that the behavior of the people in the group, by design, was almost totally commission-driven. Nonetheless, Buckman developed a concept that added some effort to the sales force's workload—at least in the short run—but overall was of impressive benefit to the enterprise.

Given the obstacles within a sales culture that was disinclined to share knowledge, Buckman decided to make knowledge sharing an initiative and a cultural norm. Hence, he designed and launched a system that would make it easy to share knowledge, created incentives to encourage sharing, and chided those in sales who didn't share. All the while, he recognized those who did share and reused proven solutions.

In the end, Bob Buckman dealt with a corporate problem that hadn't been solved any other way in his small company. Buckman's leadership was action-biased and was initiated with the understanding of what it would take to implement a change in the way the company conducted business. In addition to winning the already mentioned North American MAKE Award, Buckman's "leadership from the top" model was recognized when the company won the prestigious 2003 Global MAKE Award and was admitted to the MAKE Hall of Fame for continuous excellence.

A huge benefit of the Buckman business model is the extraordinary speed that Buckman brings to bear in solving customers' problems. Also, a particular efficiency is prevalent in Buckman's customers' operations that they attribute to the equivalent best practices knowledge received from Buckman. There is an ever-present emphasis on knowledge reuse. This practice leverages Buckman's intellectual capital. Salespeople now log into the Buckman system and ask for help getting best practices knowledge that would be of value to customers to those customers for their reuse. Often, responses come in within minutes or hours from experienced people all around the world. Respondents share experiences, best practices, lessons learned, and a variety of knowledge insights. The salesperson then assimilates the best practices and lessons learned knowledge and tailors it to address the customer's unique issue, problem, or concern. This is collaborative knowledge sharing, and it is adding to the competitive strength of Buckman Labs.

Texas Instruments (TI)[20]

During early 1994, the late Jerry Junkins, former chairman and CEO of Texas Instruments, TI, made one of his customary trips to visit worldwide TI locations. Junkins made a habit of paying these visits, both in the United States and worldwide. A typical trip had a threefold purpose. First, he toured the operations so that he could understand local performance and how it was linked and tied to TI's vision and strategies. Second, these were opportunities to familiarize himself with the people at each location and vice versa, so that faces were connected to names, including his own. Junkins was the kind of leader who believed that CEOs need to come out from behind their desk often and mix with employees, i.e., "management by walking around" and "walking the talk." That way he could connect with managers, and he would give them a sense of how they fit in and where they belonged in the vision he had for TI. So he often spoke with groups of employees. Last, Junkins also tried to size up the unique opportunities and challenges that existed at each location, especially any that might affect the ability to achieve that year's key objectives. This particular trip took Junkins to Southeast Asia.

On this trip, he stopped in Malaysia to visit a TI plant. While in conversation during the tour of the operation, Junkins recognized that a production yield problem that the Malaysian plant was having was almost exactly the same as a problem that had previously occurred and been solved at the TI plant back in Dallas. To Junkins, this brought to the surface a systemic, across the board problem that existed throughout TI.

Junkins concluded that TI's worldwide production plants were operating as independent geographical silos. Yes, when faced with problems, managers might occasionally check with their friends and colleagues within their particular TI site. However, these checks were hit and miss, and they certainly were not systematic. Also, site managers were unaware of the larger inventory of TI intellectual assets that was available to them.

As a result, when Junkins returned to the United States and to TI's Dallas headquarters, he developed a requirement that knowledge sharing take place across the company. Weeks later, at a 1994 TI leadership conference, he proclaimed, "We cannot tolerate having world-class performance right next to mediocre performance simply because we don't have a method to implement best practices." Junkins then gave his chief lieutenant at the time, Dean Clubb, prior president of the 1992

Baldrige Award recipient TI Defense Systems and Electronics Group and the TI Quality Leadership Team, the task of developing an enterprisewide solution or initiative. Clubb formulated and became the executive sponsor of a TI corporate-wide Best Practice Sharing Team, led by Cynthia Johnson, that was charged with designing a knowledge-sharing system.

Clubb, a senior executive who was accustomed to finding ways to get quick results, made it known that he was impatient to have a solution by year-end 1994. However, after the Best Practice Sharing Team evaluated all the requirements involved and determined what would be necessary for worldwide implementation, the team was able to convince Clubb that March 31, 1995, was both aggressive and realistic as a deployment date. In fact, to emphasize this date, the team set up a group e-mail address and named itself the "0331 Team." The formal name given the team in those days was the Best Practice Sharing Design Team, and the initiative was often described inside TI as "best practice sharing (BPS)."

The 0331 Team now had a deadline, and its members soon realized that they had to take a broad and sweeping approach if they were to effect the breath and depth of changes necessary to make a sufficient impact on a company with 50,000 employees at the time. Before long, they defined the data fields necessary to provide basic metadata and contact information to transfer knowledge. The team realized that in the fast-changing TI technical world, knowledge usually has a short half-life, so they wisely did not plan to capture large documents codifying particular best practices. By metadata, the team clarified that they meant entries such as

- Prime contact name
- Address
- Business location
- Telephone number
- E-mail address
- Breadth of best practices deployment
- Performance measurement
- Best practices summary (card catalog version)

So instead, the 0331 Team captured "card catalog" versions of best practices. This was so that searchers using the TI Best Practice Sharing System would be able to decipher and understand basic snapshot aspects of a basic best practice or process, while also obtaining a prime contact to call for more current detailed information, discussion, and collaboration.

The TI 0331 Team also learned from the American Productivity & Quality Center's (APQC) leaders C. Jackson Grayson and Carla O'Dell whose research identified *facilitated sharing* as the most effective method of promoting corporatewide knowledge sharing. Therefore, the team called for a position in each TI business unit with the title of best practice sharing facilitator. The training of 138 of these facilitators became part of the worldwide training plan, to be done before the March 31 rollout. The standard model called for between 10 and 50 percent of a facilitator's time to be devoted to best practices sharing activities. The team also designed a metrics reporting system so that it could collect the activity levels of each business searching for best practices, along with the ongoing value that the system provided TI as a company.

In the end, the Best Practice Sharing System was deployed worldwide on March 31, 1995, with great fanfare and expectations. Not only did it include internal company culture changes, it addressed the sharing issues among the geographical cultures in Europe, Asia, Australia, and Americas.

After the 0331 Team deployed the system, monthly follow-up meetings were held between the 0331 Team members and the business best practice facilitators. TI senior leaders determined that the company had already shared enough know-how for the enterprise to avoid investing in a new chip fabrication plant. At the time, the investment was valued at $500 million. This was a dramatic payback.

Later, the 0331 Team's work led TI to conduct a best practices ShareFair, which publicly and specifically encouraged TI employees to share and reuse best practices knowledge. This took place with the full support of TI's Baldrige recipient (manufacturing) defense business, Defense Systems & Electronics Group (TI/DSEG). The culture that was established by using the Baldrige criteria had preconditioned people in this TI unit to learn fast, collaborate, and share. TI/DSEG also had the benefit of Dean Clubb's support as the immediate prior president of the division, which itself had 15,000 people, mostly engineers and technical people. Bill Baker, coauthor of this book, led that effort. The recognition provided was noteworthy and included the ShareFair sponsored by the Best Practice Sharing Team, featuring two keynote speakers who have continued to be on the cutting edge of knowledge sharing today. These speakers were Carla O'Dell, now president of APQC, and Tom Davenport, a leading guru and author of knowledge and strategic thinking books and articles, now at Babson College, just outside of Boston.

Dean Clubb presented awards and recognition to winners of TI's Not Invented Here But We Did It Anyway (NIHBWDIA) Award. Winners included both those who shared and those who reused knowledge, thus emphasizing at a high level the kind of collaboration and teamwork that are required to successfully reuse best practices knowledge that already exists.

As in the Buckman Labs case, TI's leadership from the top strategic approach proved to be successful and put TI on a course toward achieving excellence by leveraging the reuse of best practices knowledge. The center of TI's success was its focus on overhauling its culture, realigning human resource systems, including recognition and rewards, to drive the needed behavior. Two of its other approaches warrant mention, too: First, the company developed a very professional communications subplan that met the need to get employee understanding and buy-in to make the changes work. Second, TI's trial of shared facilitation (a trained and motivated professional team of best practices facilitators) proved essential to making knowledge reuse a way of life at TI and an overwhelming success.

The TI case study on how to share and reuse best practices knowledge is a timeless model because all enterprises, regardless of industry, large or small, struggle to do better at it. Indeed, this TI/DSEG model was reused and modified by Raytheon to bring its knowledge management strategy to life, which enabled Raytheon to win a North America MAKE Award for 2004 and 2005..

By now, it should be clear to everyone reading this book that reuse of best practices knowledge has enormous paybacks. When an enterprise becomes highly proficient at reusing knowledge, just as a supercharger provides a big edge to race cars, reuse can be the supercharger to propel contestants in the knowledge transfer race. Because of paybacks, there are bound to be readers who are craving for more examples of knowledge reuse. It is suggested that they study the practices of the 2003 recipients of the Global MAKE Awards. Alphabetically, those winners are Accenture, Amazon.com, British Petroleum, Buckman Laboratories, Canon, Ernst & Young, General Electric, Hewlett-Packard, Infosys Technologies, IBM, McKinsey & Company, Microsoft, Nokia, PricewaterhouseCoopers, Royal Dutch/Shell, Siemens, 3M, Toyota Motor, World Bank, and Xerox.

Who Wants to Manage Knowledge, Anyway?

For some readers, a personal question may be lurking in the back of their mind: how smart is a career move into a position that's responsible for managing knowledge? The answer lies in the often-used quote "you'll get what is measured." This tidbit of wisdom also pertains to sharing and reusing knowledge. Nearly every leadership and manager compensation system is based on evaluating each individual's performance results relative to specific target ranges for preestablished measurements. There is little regard, if any, for how those results are achieved. It's about the measured results.

To illustrate, if a recently hired MBA has to ask many people in an enterprise for help or information, that MBA may feel that he or she is showing a weakness or a lack of knowledge. In this example, the natural tendency is for the new MBA not to ask for help, but instead to rely on what he or she has learned in graduate school as a way to demonstrate his or her knowledge and abilities. The point is that this natural tendency also exists in everyone to varying degrees; asking for help is not a natural act in most cultures.

So the answer to the earlier career question is yes, if one understands and accepts that he or she will be judged on the bottom-line results achieved by everyone. On the other hand, the answer is no, if the individual wants to be judged only on how effectively knowledge is shared and reused.

The uncomplicated process of managing knowledge has two dimensions to it: performance on an individual basis and the overall performance of the enterprise. A big barrier to overcome to achieve successful knowledge transfer is making managers become advocates and then "walk the talk," actually using, reusing, and leveraging knowledge inside their part of the enterprise. There aren't sufficient rewards and recognition for doing so. In other words, the dreaded middle managers may become the weak link because they don't see how emphasizing the things that are involved with knowledge reuse will do anything to get them ahead. And because middle managers tend to be pulled and pushed in many different directions, trade-offs occur, some of which are not ideal for knowledge sharing and reuse.

And yet middle line managers are the ones who can make or break success because, together, what they do is plan, organize, direct, and control people, priorities, use of resources, budgets, daily assignments, and so on to align them with the enterprise's vision and strategies and fulfill customer needs. In short, managing knowledge sharing and reuse is a continuous series of well-intended and positive clashes with middle managers to encourage and help them to do the right things that bring alive the behaviors needed to succeed. It's a struggle to change the culture when everyone is already very busy and conflicted about daily and weekly priorities.

This is why the "leadership from the top" model is so powerful. The attention, behaviors, and resources are brought to bear in a powerful way when the entire senior leadership team is committed and by its words and actions energizes the middle managers. Leaders are hands-on, doing performance reviews in which knowledge sharing and reuse are emphasized and reinforced.

Insights of a Benchmarking and Knowledge Management Champion

One of the most intriguing aspects of intellectual capital management is the insight that in any large enterprise, a good many people have only a partial picture of the whole operation. People see the enterprise through the close-up lens of their particular job or work group. Some describe this as operating in a silo. It's a narrow perspective, yet all employees have is what they're told by their boss, learn at the water cooler, or take in from what they see, hear, or touch. Company Web sites, newspapers, cross training, reassignments, and such do broaden, educate, and enlighten. For most employees, however, it's enough of a challenge just keeping up with what's happening in their own department. Besides, just when some employees begin to understand what's going on in other parts of the enterprise, some initiative or reorganization changes everything. In the end, the perspective of most employees is far too narrow.

One of the reasons small start-up companies can expand and grow so astronomically is that their entrepreneur founders have the organization's intellectual capital in their head, making it easy for the small number of employees to have a broad, complete perspective. The "invention" is human capital. Indeed, in the beginning, most of the key intellectual capital of the organization resides in the minds of the founders. And because start-ups begin small, it is easier to share knowledge and communicate informally around the water cooler or the coffeepot.

The systematic, yet informal, and exciting approach of a small start-up is nearly impossible to replicate in large enterprises, especially those with operations in many geographical locations in different time zones. Modern knowledge management approaches can compensate for and even overcome this obstacle by focusing on the four key result areas that are characteristic of start-ups:

- *People.* There need to be informal social networks that mentor and support sharing and rapid reuse and learning. People make it happen!
- *Process.* The process for sharing knowledge needs to be simple and well understood by all. Process makes it easy.
- *Tools.* While tools are absolutely necessary, they need to be useful and valuable at the lowest common denominator of work and be simple enough to use as a part of everyday life. Databases, subject-matter expert (SME) locators, collaboration tools, Web pages, portals, and search tools all play a part in making it easy at the personal level. Tools make it easy.
- *Culture.* The organization's culture, which collectively determines what gets done (and doesn't get done), is what's key here. Is knowledge sharing recognized and rewarded at the personal level and the middle manager level? Is sharing and reusing knowledge a good thing, or instead is knowledge power, i.e., something not to be shared? Culture keeps it going.

The Bottom Line for People in Small Organizations

There are five key points in this chapter that are carried forward into Chapter 11's list of 55 tips for people in small organizations. They appear in Chapter 11 as tips 33, through 37. Briefly, these five points are:

- The MAKE Award criteria are just as applicable to small companies, so learn them and use them.
- Small businesses need to have human capital strategies that focus on increasing intellectual capital and preventing its loss.
- Small companies must collect and learn knowledge about the characteristics of rival products and services, so that it can be shared and become common knowledge that enables better new product and service launches.
- The owner must make a personal commitment to being knowledge-enabled.
- The primary goal should be to reuse best practices that already exist.

Small organizations have several advantages and disadvantages when compared to large organizations, but the same principles apply. It is important that customers see the organization as one effective, efficient enterprise that's focused on their particular needs. This means that the needs of customers must be understood by everyone, that order status must be contained in a universally accessible system that is available to everyone, and that an effective product/service delivery process has been replicated. It's important to know, too, how the enterprise compares to the competition in key areas. Thus, a commonly shared knowledge system is needed for a new product launch so that a successful focus can be put on forming competitive advantages. To do this, people must learn and collect knowledge regarding the characteristics of those products that the enterprise's products are competing against head to head.

In a very small business, the owner/manager acts as the focal point of all relevant competitive knowledge, but he or she must also transfer that knowledge to employees as the organization grows and expands. This is one of the very critical phases of small business growth, as many owners do not do this effectively. The owner/manager also must promote and build a culture of continuous learning so that everyone comes to feel that he or she is adding to the business's collective brain trust, or human capital.

Small Business Advantages
1. There is one central location where employees work.
2. Everyone knows everyone.
3. Only broad jobs exist, so people aren't easily siloed.
4. Everyone identifies with how the business is going

Small Business Disadvantages
1. People may still not have a broad industry perspective.
2. People don't automatically follow technology trends.
3. The business can't afford full-time knowledge-sharing facilitators.
4. Any bad personal relationships can have bigger impacts.

The processes are the same for people in small organizations; they're just on a smaller scale.

- People still need to understand why and how knowledge sharing is important.
- This means, too, that people must be involved in and recognized and rewarded for sharing and fast learning.
- There also needs to be a process for knowledge sharing; this can be through weekly meetings or at the water cooler or coffee bar.
- Tools are still essential, but they need to be made very simple—such as a poster board or question board—and the key is that they be easily available to everyone.
- The culture needs to support learning, sharing, and knowledge reuse.
- And one rule to always try to follow is, whatever is done, make it easy and fun!

Endnotes

1   Peter Senge, Art Kleiner, Charlotte Roberts, Richard B. Ross, and Bryan J. Smith, *The Fifth Discipline Fieldbook: Strategies and Tools for Building a Learning Organization* (New York: Currency Doubleday, 1994), p. 48.

2   Ibid, pp. 48–49.

3   Information from Columbia University's Web site, http://www.columbia.edu/research/index.

4   See www.knowledgebusiness.com. The KNOW Network is a global community of knowledge-driven organizations dedicated to networking, benchmarking, and sharing best practices leading to superior performance.

5   The research that substantiates that a 5 percent increase in customer retention may increase profitability by as much as 40 to 100 percent is from the first-hand research experience of Mike English as director of quality and customer service for GTE Telephone Operations and GTE Directories and undertaking customer loyalty and relationship management research by Total Research Corporation (Princeton, NJ) and Walker Research (Indianapolis, IN) during the period of 1986 through 1997. The precise finding is that profitability increases as much as 40 to 100 percent when 5 percent of the customer base is retained (that would otherwise be lost) over three consecutive years. This results from compounding the preserved revenue streams and avoidance of costs otherwise required reacquiring or replacing lost customers. Of course, bottom line profitability is a function of several other independent variables as well.

6   See www.quality.nist.gov/award_recip.htm and www.quality.nist.gov/contacts_profiles.htm, two Web sites for the Baldrige National Quality Program. The Ritz-Carlton Hotel Company, LLC, was a recipient of awards in the service category during 1992 and 1999. Other information was received from Ritz-Carlton management presentations at the 2000 Quest for Excellence Conference in Washington, D.C., which highlighted several of the company's award-winning strategies leading up to its 1999 award.

7   Ibid.

8   Patrick H. Sullivan, *Value-Driven Intellectual Capital: How to Convert Intangible Corporate Assets into Market Value* (New York: John Wiley & Sons, 2000), pp. 16–17.

9   Ibid, p. 17.

10   Ibid, pp. 17–18.

11   Ibid, p. 158.

12   2005 North American Most Admired Knowledge Enterprises Study Executive Summary, a 10-page document prepared by Teleos and the KNOW Network, p. 9, obtained at www.knowledgebusiness.com/.

13   Sullivan, *Value-Driven Intellectual Capital*, p. 177.

14   Ibid, p. 176.

15   Ibid, pp. 193–194.

16   Ibid, pp. 191–194.

17   James Brian Quinn, *Intelligent Enterprise: A Knowledge and Service Based Paradigm for a New Era* (New York: The Free Press, 1992), pp. xi, 3-22.-

18   Sullivan, *Value-Driven Intellectual Capital*, p. 17.

19   The source for the Buckman Labs example came from several interviews, conducted by Bill Baker, of Dr. Melissie Rumizen, then assistant to the chairman for knowledge sharing at Buckman Labs.

20   The source for the Texas Instruments case study regarding knowledge reuse came directly from the notes and diary of Bill Baker from his firsthand experience as the key TI/DSEG 0331 Team member and his other TI career management assignments.

Chapter 6

Knowledge That Propels Improvement: The Baldrige Award Criteria, European Quality Award, Shingo Prize, ISO 9000, Six Sigma, and *Lean* Six Sigma

A poster child category of knowledge transfers that has delivered phenomenal success is the grouping labeled business performance acceleration mod-els. *Included are the Baldrige Award, the European Quality Award, the Shingo Prize, ISO 9000, and others that have codified, transferred, and shared (for reuse) many of the world's best practices and have put the enterprises using them onto a fast-track path that leads to superior performance results. Such banner knowledge transfers accelerate the participants to the front of the knowledge transfer race.*

—Mike English and Bill Baker

The prestige of American industry took a big hit in 1980 when Chrysler Motors narrowly avoided bankruptcy, but for Lee Iacocca's plea to the U.S. Congress for a bailout loan.[1] This was the beginning of a tidal wave of other humbling experiences and setbacks by icons of corporate America in the evolving 1980s global marketplace. These were also jolting experiences for many American managers under the age of 50, because, during their entire lifespan, not only was America the world's most technologically advanced country, but it dominated manufacturing technology. During the 40 years following World War II, especially during and just after NASA's spectacular 1960s Apollo program, which put a man on the moon, the growth of America's gross national product (GNP) fueled the economies of over a third of the developed nations around the world.

And the vision at the time was that automation would be the key to increased pro-ductivity in the U.S. economy. In fact, as America moved out of the sluggish 1970s, its GNP was still growing, so there was no reason for panic yet.

Then the wake-up calls came. And while the United States still had the world's most productive and prosperous economy, it was becoming less dominant. Figuratively speaking, as corporate America did battle in one market after another in the global economy, more and more chinks were showing in its armor. And like the USA's Olympic basketball Dream Team's experience in the 2004 Athens Olympics, for every seven or eight wins, there were three losses. During the late 1970s and early 1980s, Japanese industry embarrassed its American counterpart. First, there were setbacks in American shipbuilding. Then came steel. Then, as evidenced by the Chrysler bailout during 1980, it was happening in automobile manufacturing. It also happened in semiconductors.

In the 1980s, foreign companies with strange names like Toyota, Honda, Nissan, and Volkswagen began to capture, together, the lion's share of the new and fast-growing U.S. economy car market. More than ever, Americans were consider-ing fuel economy in their car purchases after experiencing the painful shortages at the pump and higher prices of the 1974 OPEC oil embargo. Still, the situation in the automobile industry in the early 1980s had become far more serious than just how poorly the miles-per-gallon performance of American cars compared to that of the foreign alternatives.

Sadly, American automakers had lost touch with their customers. Chrysler, Ford, American Motors, and General Motors also neglected, unfortunately, to understand what the deficiencies and flaws in their own designs and manufactur-ing processes were. Instead, their foreign competitors did it for them. Soon it became clear that American automakers had allowed themselves to fall into the "if we make it, they'll buy it" syndrome. In other words, they had become compla-cent. However, in the United States, conceit and a false sense of security weren't limited to the automobile industry.

American manufacturers were also having serious problems competing with Japanese manufacturers in electronics, telecommunications equipment, industrial machinery, and the exploding area of computer equipment. Table 6-1 highlights the categories of manufacturing in which the Japanese became fiercely competitive. However, American companies were also having problems surviving in other industries besides manufacturing.

To be sure, during the first half of the 1980s, the U.S. economy didn't help. Unemployment reached double digits, its highest levels since the Great Depression of the 1930s. Inflation exceeded 10 percent. And the economic indicator that was as disturbing as any was interest rates that exceeded 20 percent.

Once-almighty American companies like Braniff Airlines (which went bankrupt), Caterpillar (competing with Komatsu), DuPont (competing with

Table 6-1   U.S. Manufacturing Sectors Hit Hard by Foreign Competition

Major SIC Group	Description
35	Industrial & Commercial Machinery & Computer Equipment
36	Electronic & Other Electrical Equipment & Components
37	Transportation Equipment
38	Measuring, Analyzing, and Controlling Instruments; Photographic, Medical Goods; Watches and Clocks.
39	Miscellaneous Manufacturing

Source: U.S. Department of Labor, Standard Industrial Code (SIC), Division Structure.

Hoechst), Chase Manhattan (competing with Barclays), Kodak (competing with Fuji), RCA (competing with Sony), Xerox (competing with Canon), Westinghouse (competing with Hitachi), Upjohn (competing with Glaxo), Pratt & Whitney (competing with Honda), and many others fell on hard times as they fought for their survival. In fact, driven by a flourishing microchip technology, as new electronic markets involving products such as the Walkman, stereo equipment, big-screen television, VCRs, and cellular phones sprang up, Japanese companies such as Sony, Mitsubishi, NEC, Toshiba, Fujitsu, and Panasonic dominated from the beginning. While remaining strong in many other industries, American companies showed vulnerability and expressed real concern that something was missing.

Companies from Japan, Germany, and other countries in Europe that had previously been thought to be inferior in management techniques, technology, ingenuity, and skilled labor were now leaders. In fact, leading American journalists began criticizing and attacking American corporate boards. This was about the time that *Fortune* magazine and other publications like the *Harvard Business Review* began attacking corporate America with articles such as, "Europe Outgrows American Management Style," which accused senior American business leaders of being shortsighted and not growing their businesses while too often reassigning middle managers.[2] American businessmen were also criticized for not caring about their customers and not paying enough attention to all the details involved with meeting customers' requirements.[3]

Against this backdrop, at about the same time, America's leading quality management organizations—the American Society of Quality (ASQ) and the American Productivity and Quality Center (APQC)—began collaborating and together formulating what would come to be called a Total Quality Management (TQM) framework consisting of seven broad categories, described as the criteria. The goal was to create a tool from the best thinking in America (from practitioners, academics, manufacturing, service, and small businesses) and from the learning from around the world. The intent, then, was to enable any American enterprise to conduct a self-assessment of how well it was doing against the criteria or to have an independent, qualified third party conduct a professional examination. As a result, enterprises would receive professional feedback that identified their relative strengths and opportunities for improvement. From a continuous improvement perspective, this would provide the enterprise with a continuously replenished list of 20 or so improvement opportunities that it could work on to improve its competitiveness and achieve business performance excellence. By conducting annual assessments, businesses could set annual operating plans to make major competitive improvements.

The Malcolm Baldrige Quality Award and Criteria[4]

Enacted as U.S. Public Law 100-107 on August 20, 1987, the criteria, which have been continually improved every year since, are now the heart of the Malcolm Baldrige National Quality Awards (MBNQA). Named after the former secretary of commerce, who served from 1981 until his death in 1987, the law established a public- and private-sector partnership. Specifically, it said, "The leadership of the United States in product and process quality has been challenged strongly (and sometimes successfully) by foreign competition, and our Nation's productivity growth has improved less than our competitors' over the last two decades."[5]

Thus, as displayed in Figure 6-1, the Baldrige criteria were created as a business performance excellence model or framework consisting of a self-assessment

Source: Adapted from Pages 1-5 of the 2005 Baldrige National Quality Criteria for Performance Excellence.

Figure 6-1   The Malcolm Baldrige Quality Award criteria and framework.

methodology (or examination) that identifies strengths and opportunities for improvement within the approaches, deployment, and results for the seven Baldrige categories identified in Figure 6-1. The criteria universally apply to manufacturing, service, and small enterprises. With needed senior management leadership and taking action through recurring cycles of refinement and improvement, the criteria create an agenda that leads any organization to achieve excellence and better its competitive position.

The collective learning of expert researchers and practitioners in different enterprise sectors (manufacturing, service, small business, and the recently added sectors health care, education, and not-for-profit) is captured and codified, updated, and integrated into the criteria, which turn the knowledge it embodies into priceless intellectual assets. By the act of the U.S. Congress, all the intellectual assets produced in the process (the criteria, application materials, Web site, case study, training content, feedback reports, Quest for Excellence conference materials, and so on) are knowledge that is designed to be shared. The MBNQA evolved in 1988 into an annual formal application process utilizing independent examiners and gaining international prominence for those that scored high enough and were good knowledge transfer models. The "winners" were committed to openly sharing their best practices and lessons learned for one full year after winning. Many companies set up special departments to coordinate this knowledge sharing and to answer the outside inquiries that are generated. The transfer of all this knowledge is aimed at promoting the attainment of excellence within the United States. So the transfers produce learning and sharing of successful performance practices, principles, and strategies.

Relevance of Baldrige to the Knowledge Transfer Race

The entire concept of the Baldrige National Quality Awards embodies the concepts of knowledge transfer and reuse, which is an ongoing testimony to being proactive in the knowledge transfer race. After all, Baldrige is a codified road map to achieve excellence. And ever since the Baldrige criteria came into existence in 1988, they have, in a sense, contributed to making knowledge transfer a race.

Specifically, there are two important ways in which knowledge and knowledge transfer correspond to the use of the intellectual assets involved with the Baldrige Award materials. First, experts (from industry, academia, and not-for-profit organizations) have formed an extraordinary reservoir of human capital and converted it into the Baldrige criteria themselves, and they've continually improved it ever since. Besides the criteria, knowledge is formed from case studies, core values, concepts, glossaries, training materials, applications for the awards, examiner and judge scoring books and experiences, feedback reports, takeaways from the annual Quest for Excellence winners' presentations, and so on. All told, there's a fortune in knowledge. And by design, this is routinely shared with Americans, especially business managers and owners, who want to learn, reuse, and otherwise benefit from it. A lot has been learned and shared regarding the award-winning strategies and tactics dating back to 1988. And because the most important parts of this learning have been codified, Baldrige knowledge has become intellectual assets expressly created for easy and quick transfer and reuse. The purpose is to help organizations achieve business performance excellence and improve their capability to compete.

Second, expert knowledge translates the Baldrige criteria into a continuously improved and systematic framework that expressly spells out nonprescriptive action items. As shown in Figure 6-1, knowledge transfer occurs in the seven categories of (1) leadership, (2) strategic planning, (3) customer and market focus, (4) measurement, analysis, and knowledge management, (5) human resource focus, (6) process management, and (7) business results. Knowledge transfer is the core concept underlying the Baldrige National Quality Program (i.e., what it takes to achieve performance excellence).

European Quality Award[6]

Displayed in Figure 6-2, the European Model for Business Excellence—now called the EFQM Excellence Model—was introduced in 1991 as the European approach to quality improvement. Founded in 1988 by the presidents of 14 major European companies (Bosch, British Telecom, Bull, Ciba-Geigy, Dassault, Electrolux, Fiat,

Figure 6-2   EFQM Excellence Model

KLM, Nestlé, Olivetti, Philips, Renault, Sulzer, and Volkswagen), the European Quality Award was first given in 1992, four years after the Baldrige. In fact, the Baldrige Award from the United States and the Deming Prize from Japan were the models used to design the European approach, referred to as the European Framework for Quality Improvement. The EFQM is a not-for-profit membership foundation. Its purpose is to help European businesses make better products and deliver improved services through the effective use of leading-edge management practices. Like the U.S. National Institute of Standards and Technology (NIST), which administers the Baldrige processes, the EFQM manages and directs the European Quality Awards. This includes the design and conduct of training courses and workshops on the key business improvement disciplines, tools, and techniques.

The EFQM Excellence Model, portrayed in Figure 6-2, is a nonprescriptive framework based on nine criteria. Five of these criteria are *enablers* (leadership, people, policy and strategy, partnerships and resources, and processes) and four are *results*. The enablers address what an organization actually does through its leadership and how it develops and deploys people, policies, strategies, partnerships, and resources. The results criteria examine the known facts or outcomes in terms of what an organization actually achieves. Results are caused by enablers, and feedback from results helps to improve enablers. The model is based on the premise that "excellent results with respect to performance, customers, people and society are achieved through leadership driving policy and strategy, which is delivered through people, partnerships and resources, and processes." The arrows emphasize the dynamic nature of the model. Innovation and learning, then, strengthen the enablers, which in turn heads organizations down the path to improved results.

With a valid basis for doing so, the authors have made one slight extrapolation to the EFQM Model, adding "knowledge" to form "innovation, learning, and knowledge." This change makes knowledge explicit rather than implicit in the model and emphasizes the key role of knowledge and knowledge transfer in the success of the enterprise. Society benefits by leadership driving policy and strategy, which is delivered through people, partnerships and resources, and processes. The arrows in Figure 6-2 emphasize the dynamic nature of the model. They show that "innovation, learning, and knowledge" galvanize the enablers, which, in turn and in combination, produce improved results.

Relevance of the European Quality Award to the Knowledge Transfer Race

The short answer is, it's enormously relevant. Just as with the Baldrige criteria, the transfer of knowledge occurs in two ways. First, the model, criteria, definitions, and knowledge embodied by the entire process are codified knowledge (representing everything that's been learned) that is expressly intended for transfer as a form of knowledge reuse. The expressed purpose of the transfer and knowledge reuse is to help European businesses improve. Second, knowledge is a prerequisite for the model's working properly. In other words, just as oxygen provides vitality to the human body, rather than just filling lungs, knowledge is the source of life for the enablers (leadership, people, policies, strategies, and partnerships) of the European model, so, in combination, they make possible the achievement of excellent results.

The Shingo Prize for Excellence in Manufacturing[7]

Established in 1988, the same year as the Baldrige Award, the Shingo Prize model and framework promote awareness and knowledge sharing regarding lean manufacturing concepts and recognize enterprises in North America, specifically Canada, the United States, and Mexico. Named for Japanese industrial engineer Shigeo Shingo, the Shingo Prize recognizes two types of achievement: (1) the Business Prize promotes the use of world-class manufacturing strategies and practices to achieve world-class results, and (2) the Research Prize promotes research and writing regarding new knowledge and understanding of manufacturing processes.

Graphically displayed as a framework in Figure 6-3, according to the Shingo Prize Web site, the Shingo Prize is referred to as the "Nobel Prize of manufactur-

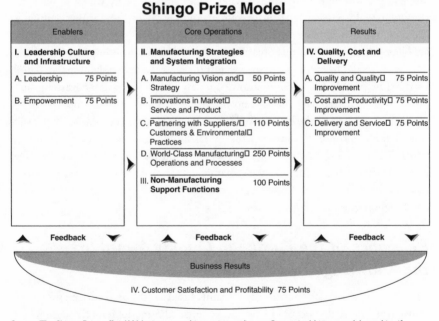

Shingo Prize Model

Enablers	Core Operations	Results
I. Leadership Culture and Infrastructure	**II. Manufacturing Strategies and System Integration**	**IV. Quality, Cost and Delivery**
A. Leadership 75 Points	A. Manufacturing Vision and 50 Points Strategy	A. Quality and Quality 75 Points Improvement
B. Empowerment 75 Points	B. Innovations in Market 50 Points Service and Product	B. Cost and Productivity 75 Points Improvement
	C. Partnering with Suppliers/ 110 Points Customers & Environmental Practices	C. Delivery and Service 75 Points Improvement
	D. World-Class Manufacturing 250 Points Operations and Processes	
	III. Non-Manufacturing 100 Points Support Functions	

▲ Feedback ▼   ▲ Feedback ▼   ▲ Feedback ▼

Business Results

IV. Customer Satisfaction and Profitability 75 Points

Source: The Shingo Prize official Web site, www.shingoprize.org/images/bus_prize/shingo_model_graphic.gif.

Figure 6-3   Shingo Prize model

ing" because it establishes a standard for world-class excellence. Like the Baldrige Award and the European Quality Awards, the Shingo Prize has a board of directors, sponsors, and a support structure including independent examiners.

Similarly, the mission of the Shingo Prize is threefold: (1) to facilitate awareness of excellent world-class practices and techniques that improve competitiveness, (2) to foster an understanding and sharing of successful core manufacturing and business improvement methodologies, and (3) to encourage research in all aspects of manufacturing by both academic and business practitioners. And as depicted in Figure 6-3, the Shingo Prize scoring criteria are organized in five principal sections: leadership culture and infrastructure; manufacturing strategies and system integration; nonmanufacturing support functions; quality, cost, and delivery; and customer satisfaction and profitability.

Relevance of the Shingo Prize to the Knowledge Transfer Race

Like the Baldrige Award and the European Quality Award, the Shingo Prize is very relevant to the knowledge transfer race. With a focus on manufacturing excellence, the Shingo Prize criteria, definitions, and all the other knowledge embodied by the entire self-assessment and application process have been codified with the express intent of transferring knowledge to those North American manufacturers that are targeting excellence. Also, the Shingo Prize has a specific focus on knowledge transfer, reuse, and sharing in the way it designs and conducts its annual conference, application feedback, training events, plant tours, state awards, and winner profiles. Knowledge transfer is at the heart of the Shingo Prize processes. Manufacturers who take advantage of the Shingo Prize learning experiences will propel their performance into a position of leadership in the knowledge transfer race. And as with the Baldrige and EFQM criteria, winning and being recognized as a Shingo Prize winner is secondary to the primary goal and real value of pursuing a continuous improvement journey that, like the knowledge transfer race, is never-ending and without a finish line.

ISO 9000 International Quality Management Standards[8]

The use of standards is every bit a part of the knowledge transfer race. Adopting standards boosts the performance of race contestants. While the Baldrige, European, and Shingo approaches are excellent knowledge transfer mechanisms that use assessments to identify strengths and opportunities for improvement, the ISO 9000 standards are designed to transfer knowledge through conformance to a set of international quality management standards. Because the standards involved are codified, validated, reusable, and certifiable, they, too, are shared intellectual assets that have been expressly created to benefit organizations wanting certification. Therefore, those who achieve a registered ISO 9001 Quality Management System are also leaders in the knowledge transfer race.

ISO is the acronym for International Organization for Standardization, which is headquartered in Geneva, Switzerland, and was established in 1947 to become the world's developer of standards. Given the number of manufactured products that are exported around the world, standards for reliability, safety and health, interchangeability, electrical interfaces, environmental protection, quality, and other such areas became necessary to safeguard consumers. Thus, guided by a Central Secretariat located in Geneva, one delegate from the national standards institute of each of the 146 member nations form the governing body of the ISO, which is a nongovernmental body. Depending on the country, delegates may come either from government or the public sector or from private enterprise.

The ISO's name was derived from the Greek word *isos*, which means "equal." Thus, whatever the language, the abbreviated name for the organization is always ISO. In brief, the ISO's primary purpose is to facilitate international trade by providing a single common set of standards that people everywhere can recognize, respect, and trust.

The term *ISO 9000* refers to a specific set of quality management standards. ISO 9000 currently includes three quality standards: ISO 9001:2000 presents requirements, while ISO 9000:2000 and ISO 9004:2000 present guidelines. All of these are process standards, not product standards. The ISO first published its quality standards in the 9000 series in 1987, revised them in 1994, and then republished an updated version in 2000. The new standards are referred to as the ISO 9000:2000 Standards.

ISO 9000 works somewhat like Baldrige and the other accelerated improvement models do, as it is up to each organization to decide to use them, since they're voluntary. The first step is for the organization to develop, if it hasn't done so already, a quality management system that meets the standard. The system comprises what the organization does to ensure that its products and services involved satisfy customers' quality requirements and to comply with any government regulations applicable to those products and services. Indeed, to a large extent, ISO 9000 is concerned with the enterprise's "quality management."

Figure 6-4 depicts this quality management focus in terms of ISO 9000 management clauses and how they translate into a quality manual, operating practices, procedures, interface agreements, contracts, and records or documentation about how effectively performance complies with the system. One of the most critical steps in any quality management system is the identification and reduction of nonconforming product through root cause analysis that prevents recurrences. To

Figure 6-4 ISO 9000 international quality management standard

summarize, ISO 9000 requires the enterprise to create a quality management system that specifies, through practices, procedures, contracts, and interface agreements, the detailed process steps that the enterprise will follow to ensure that downstream outputs deliver on and satisfy customer requirements. Another way to summarize this is to say that ISO 9000 requires the enterprise to say what it is going to do, do what it says it is going to do, and, finally, prove it. Some of this description is also contained in Figure 6-4.

Once an enterprise's quality management system has been fully developed and deployed, the second step is to perform internal audits to confirm that every one of the ISO 9000 standard clause requirements is being met. Then, when internal audits validate that the operations conform to the system and all identified defects have been or are being corrected, the third step is to retain an independent, third-party ISO 9000 registrar to conduct a formal audit of the quality management system.

When the registrar's audit has been completed and any discrepancies it identifies have been cleared, it issues an official certificate to the enterprise. Thereafter, the enterprise may publicize to its customers, suppliers, and other stakeholders that the quality of its involved products and services is being managed, controlled, and assured by a registered ISO 9001 quality management system. And because ISO 9000 is an international certification, prospective customers in countries around the world have the assurance, despite differences in language, labor force competencies, and applied technologies, that the product they're purchasing was produced using a system meeting the ISO 9000 quality standard. This doesn't mean that the product involved is the very best made; it only means that the system involved in manufacturing it conforms to the standard. Just the same, as codified knowledge, the ISO 9000 standard facilitates an exchange of knowledge that, like a recipe that keeps on generating award-winning fried chicken, keeps on replicating a proven quality management system for enterprises that want it.

Variations of ISO 9000, Such as TL 9000 and AS 9000

While ISO 9000 applies (generically) to any enterprise and has become the world's most recognized and respected quality standard, a few nuances have been needed to induce entire industries to adopt the standard. The big need was for industry-specific requirements and measurements. The ISO accommodation has produced variations of ISO 9000 for industries with exceptionally proactive associations that are making the standard the centerpiece of an all-out effort to elevate the industry's quality and reliability. Accordingly, AG 9000 has emerged for agriculture, AS 9000 for the international aerospace industry, FS 9000 for financial services, and QS 9000 for the international automotive sector, and others are in the works for other industries, all variations of ISO 9000.

Another such variation is TL 9000, the telecommunications adaptation of ISO 9000 and the nucleus of the QuEST (Quality Excellence for Suppliers of Telecommunications) Forum's standardization work, from which it's driving improvements in telecommunications services around the world.[9] Discussed briefly in Chapter 2, the QuEST Forum, which was established during 1996, maintains a measurement repository system (MRS) and uses four work groups to extend its global footprint, update the standard's requirements and measurements, give oversight, and drive improvement through the Telecommunications Business Excellence (TBE) work group. The TBE conducts annual best practices sharing conferences and assists its members in reusing the knowledge from the other business excellence acceleration models (Baldrige Award, European Quality Award, and so on) that have already been presented in this chapter.

Accordingly, the QuEST Forum is helping many companies in its industry win the knowledge transfer race. Its mission is to create a telecommunications industry leading quality system (TL 9000) with standardized performance measurements and to share best practices through industry collaboration.[10] Figure 6-5 depicts this. And with over two hundred TL 9000 certifications in place, knowledge transfer is taking hold. What's remarkable is that its membership consists of over 60 of the industry's most prominent enterprises, including Belgacom, Bell Canada, British Telecom, Deutsche Telekom, France Telecom, Nippon Telegraph & Telephone, SBC, Sprint, Telska, Verizon, and Zhejiang Mobile.

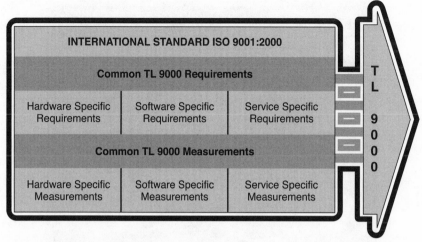

Source: From QuEST Forum's Web site, www.questforum.asq.org/.

Figure 6-5 TL 9000 Release 3.0, to be aligned with ISO 9000:2000

According to Rachel Buckley, director of quality programs for SBC Communications and vice chair of the QuEST Forum's TBE work group, "It is so valuable and beneficial for us at SBC to have standardized TL 9000 measurements and results from the QuEST Forum's Measurements Repository System (MRS). Don't get me wrong, it did take a lot of effort for all of us members to get up and running."[11] Buckley adds,

At SBC, it's enabled us to implement a world-class process for measuring, tracking, and reporting supplier performance. And as for the Telecom Business Excellence work group, having the standardized measurements and results has allowed us to concentrate on best practices offerings. What we're doing is sharing and transferring best practices knowledge. As a consequence, I see our work with the QuEST Forum driving improvements in telecommunications everywhere in the world, and certainly in the United States.[12]

Indeed, displayed in Figure 6-6 is SBC's picture of how the QuEST Forum's work, including TL 9000, integrates with SBC's in-house work to synergistically enable that company to continually improve the performance of its supply chain. In this context, TL 9000 delivers what SBC Communications describes as "robust reporting." Also, benchmarks are generated as part of the system, so that individual suppliers' performance can be compared against the low, average, and high performance levels for a given time period.

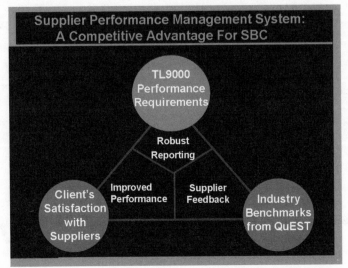

Source: Rachel Buckley's 9/22/04 presentation to the Dallas TL9000 Special Interest Group.

Figure 6-6 Supplier performance management system: a competitive advantage for SBC

Relevance of ISO 9000 to the Knowledge Transfer Race

Like the Baldrige Award, the Shingo Prize, and the European Quality Award, ISO 9000 is a codified collection of intellectual assets designed for transfer to and reuse by those seeking an "off-the-shelf" tested and refined quality management system. What's different about ISO 9000, however, is that it's also an internationally accepted standard. An official registrar attests (via the ISO 9000 emblem) to prospective customers that the product they are purchasing from a certified enterprise—regardless of language and country—has been produced by a company using an approved and systematic quality management system.

The applicant reuses knowledge that has been codified into the standard management clauses, and, after all discrepancies have been cleared, the system is certified as an effective and systematic approach that has been fully deployed. The idea of knowledge transfer is a central concept, and certifications signifying achievement of the standard encourage other enterprises to also enter the knowledge transfer race. If Baldrige is a codified road map to achieve excellence, ISO 9000 is a codified road map to achieve proven quality conformance.

As with Baldrige and the rest, there are two ways in which the transfer of ISO 9000 intellectual assets is related to winning the knowledge transfer race. First, experts from 146 countries have collaborated to create an enormous pool of human capital, and they have converted that pool into the codified ISO 9000 quality management standard, an intellectual asset. In addition to the clauses in the standard, the ISO governing body has also created knowledge in the form of printed concepts, glossaries, training materials, registrar registries, external audits, and takeaways from annual ISO 9000 conferences. In total, there is a mint of knowledge that has been created.

Second, the minted ISO 9000 intellectual assets (codified materials) are designed and used to expressly transfer the embodied knowledge through sharing and reuse. As the knowledge is continually updated year after year, what is learned is shared and reused. The intention is for ISO 9000 learned concepts to become ingrained into the way people work and become a part of the everyday life of business and industry. In this way, the measurements involved come to life as they are used as the basis of strategic and tactical decisions. Through each cycle of refinement, transfer and reuse become easier and quicker. In the specific case of ISO 9000, there are two considerations. First, the standards safeguard consumers. Second, the knowledge transfer helps organizations convert the learning of others into a fail-safe way of creating their quality management system. This exemplifies the knowledge reuse principle. Also, the expert knowledge embodied in the standard's clauses is a formula for an enterprise to continually improve its system. It should be clear that knowledge transfer and reuse are core concepts underlying ISO 9000.

Six Sigma and Lean Six Sigma

In brief, Six Sigma (6σ) is the strategic focus that an enterprise puts on eliminating defects to the level of 3.4 per million opportunities. *Lean Six Sigma* adds a focus on the elimination of waste. Both of these concepts are important enough to discuss at greater length.

The Evolving Six Sigma Definition, from Motorola to the Present

The dictionary definition of *sigma* is that it is the eighteenth letter (Σ or σ) of the Greek alphabet. Outside Greece, σ or Σ is a letter used in the Greek-lettered names of college fraternities or sororities. However, when the English adjective *six* precedes Sigma to forms Six Sigma or 6σ, the phrase takes on altogether different meanings. Two meanings of concern are the statistical and the strategic meanings.

First, σ, and therefore 6σ, has a statistical meaning. The lowercase Greek letter σ is the symbol that represents the statistical standard deviation of a specific population of data. It represents the amount of variation, or inconsistency, that exists in any process. Consider, for example, how hot and delicious pizza is when it's delivered from a local pizza parlor. If it's hot and delicious on Mondays, but only room temperature and bland on Fridays, that's variation. Similarly, if one of four new automobile tires purchased has ¼ inch less nylon tread, that's a defective type of variation. Actually, there's some variation in just about everything, including the weather.

However, it's only those variations that don't meet the critical requirements of customers, such as the tire tread, that are defined as defects. Therefore, using the earlier example involving delivered pizzas, the statistical σ measures the variation in temperature and taste in well-defined populations of pizza deliveries. Such statistical measurement produces a *process yield*, or *output without defect* results, for every million opportunities.

Furthermore, σ is applicable to the production of food or candy bars, on-time airplane flights, banking transactions, a litany of other manufactured goods, health-care services, or anything else, including all other services. In ascending order, higher coefficients of σ indicate geometrically higher levels of defect-free output. To illustrate, Table 6-2 shows the difference in defects per million opportunities (DPMO) and yield between the range of 2σ and 6σ.

As can be seen, there's an enormous difference between 2σ and 6σ statistical performance. It's a difference of 308,534 defects per million opportunities. At 2σ, output is 30.8 percent defective. At 3σ, output is 6.68 percent defective. Indeed, many worldwide organizations regularly operate at between 3σ and 4σ, which is 0.62 percent defective. While 4σ performance is an order of magnitude better than 3σ, there is still a lot of room for improvement in attaining 5σ and striving for 6σ, or 99.99966 percent defect-free output. Even then, it's for just a few processes. Thus, 6σ is more of an end game or strategic goal. It is reminiscent of an earlier approach used in the 1960s and 1970s by the U.S. Air Force called "zero defects" (ZD).

Table 6-2 The Sigma Measurement of Reducing Process Variation

The cause of defects not meeting customer requirements.

Sigma Level	Defects PMO*	Output Yield Without Defect (%)
6	3.4	99.99966
5	233	99.98
4	6,210	99.38
3	66,807	93.32
2	308,537	69.20

*PMO: per million opportunities.

The whole idea of ZD was to eliminate defects or errors so that quality would be extremely high. This was very important in the high-technology operations that the Air Force was addressing in its efforts to put a man into outer space and to build and operate high-speed jet aircraft. While no one expected that "no defects ever" would be achieved, the Air Force did realize that defects have life-threatening consequences and should be reduced to zero as far as possible. It's hard to convince people that a 99 percent process yield is bad and needs improving; in fact, 99 percent sounds pretty good. However, in highly technical and serial processing, where there are many steps that are linked together, a 99 percent yield at each step rapidly reduces the overall yield to unacceptable levels of waste and cost.

From looking at Table 6-2, it is evident that a 90 percent process yield corresponds to about 4σ performance, or 6,210 defects per million opportunities. That's an excessive number of defects for critical and serial processes. For example, adults expecting children would be appalled to learn that 6,210 babies were dropped in the hospital during the delivery process. This would be tantamount to a national health-care crisis! So instead of talking yields, which sound pretty good as percentages, there is much more immediacy and concern conveyed if the hospital delivery room is described as performing at 4σ. Each sigma level of improvement is also a step function or major change effort and signifies that there is a long way to go from 4σ to get to 6σ. Obviously, going from 2σ to 6σ is like, figuratively speaking, going from the Wright Brothers' invention of an airplane to the successful Apollo landing on the moon in 1969.

This leads to another aspect of 6σ and definition. Targeting 6σ levels of defect-free output has become a popular strategy. This is a business performance excellence strategy that is synonymous with revolutionary culture change focused on eliminating variation and defects. Originated by Motorola in the late 1980s, refined by Texas Instruments and AlliedSignal in the early 1990s, and adapted by many others, 6σ, like a deeply felt religious experience, has become a passionate, leader-driven movement that transforms and alters the DNA fabric of organizations.

This is true of former CEO Larry Bossidy's transformation of AlliedSignal (the predecessor organization to Honeywell). Senior managers there boldly included goals to achieve 6 percent annual gains in productivity "forever" in their 6σ plans.[13] Likewise, at General Electric (GE) in 1995, former CEO Jack Welch gave 6σ the highest strategic importance.[14] Similar transformations have occurred at the Bank of America, Citibank, DuPont, Dow Chemical, American Express, Raytheon, and many other global organizations. Because these organizations have a relentless focus on driving out wasteful rework, 6σ approaches have been successful at eliminating unnecessary costs, which directly improves bottom-line profitability. Accordingly, 6σ has become the predominant worldwide approach for achieving strategic performance excellence. Thus, this newly formed strategic approach to improvement needs to be defined, too (see Table 6-3).

Table 6-3 Six Sigma Defined as a Strategic Approach to Improvement

Six Sigma is a high-performance, data-driven approach to analyzing the root causes of production or processing problems that enables people everywhere in the organization to solve them. First, outputs, or the products of all enterprise processes, are linked to and measured in terms of delivering the requirements of end customers. A failure to meet a critical customer requirement is called a defect. Root cause analysis of these defects looks at reducing the variation in the process output to permanently eliminate the source of defects.

To achieve 6σ excellence, more understanding of it is needed than comes from a definition. For one thing, practitioners need to understand 6σ's characteristics. To that end, a summary comes next. Comprehending 6σ's features brings into focus a picture of what this business performance excellence system is and why it has such appeal.

Key Characteristics of Strategic Six Sigma

Strategic 6σ has four key characteristics. First, 6σ organizations give strategic importance to reducing defects by targeting 3.4 defects for each million opportunities of output. This strategy meets the needs of employees for understanding, so that "everyone's mind will be on the game." Second, to successfully "walk the talk," senior managers must be emotionally and personally involved and be passionately committed in their behavior and actions to staying the course. This is the high standard set by such former CEOs as Larry Bossidy of AlliedSignal, Jack Welch of GE, Dan Burnham of Raytheon, and current CEO Glen Barton of Caterpillar. Third, sooner rather than later, enterprises adopting this path tend to become process-centered or managed organizations. At the least, they make a strong commitment to managing by process. This requires culture change to provide enough infrastructure to ensure that everyone in the organization is trained, equipped, and empowered to solve and prevent variations in process output. Process management crosses boundaries between departments and shops, which previously operated in silos that allowed process suboptimization and outputs that did not meet customer expectations. Table 6-4 provides a summary of the characteristics of 6σ systems.

Lean Six Sigma Defined and Why to Care About It

Lean has become a widely used new term in the vocabulary of improvement practitioners within manufacturing in recent years. Depending on who's asked, *Lean* is a manufacturing philosophy that shortens the lead time between customer orders and shipments, or it's a systematic approach to eliminating waste.[15] But

Table 6-4 The Characteristics of 6σ Systems

- The ultimate goal is 3.4 defects per million opportunities.
  - Thus, 99.9966 percent defect-free output is the target.
  - The sine qua non of 6σ is eliminating defects.
- The CEO and senior leaders need to be passionate and committed.
  - A most senior official must be the "program manager."
  - It must meet employees' needs for training, understanding, and involvement.
  - "Staying the course" with culture and DNA change is necessary; this is not a short-term fix.
- It involves enterprise process management and redesign.
  - Process champions are accountable for end-to-end performance.
  - "Facilitators" or a Black and Green Belt infrastructure is needed to drive change.
    - Investments are made in education and certification.
    - Assignments are made by priority to achieve improvement targets.
    - Rewards and recognition make 6σ part of career plan.
  - A project team framework and infrastructure are needed.
    - Assignments and a rotation scheme are involved.
    - An education, training, and certification plan is needed.
    - It requires a reward and recognition process.
- A "data-driven" DMBAIC is a fundamental approach to improvement.
  - The principle is to define, measure, benchmark, analyze, improve, and control or DMBAIC.
  - Key processes are defined, mapped, measured, and benchmarked, enabling fact-based decisions.
    - Suppliers–inputs–process steps–outputs are identified.
    - Relationships (e.g., outputs that are inputs to other processes) are clarified.
  - Key performance indicators (KPIs) (measures) are set up for inputs, processing steps, outputs, and customer satisfaction.
  - Benchmarks set up stretch goals for KPIs to close negative gaps.
  - Analysis identifies variation and cause of defects.
    - Data (known results) quantify number and type of defects.
    - Statistical techniques help mine and analyze data.
    - Root cause analysis identifies causes and effects.
  - Data and techniques generate solutions for improving.
    - Brainstorming and cost-benefit analysis are done.
    - Action and effect diagrams (reverse fishbone) are prepared.
    - Knowledge is mined (inside) for best practices.
    - Benchmarking is done (externally) for best practices.
    - Project/change management plans are approved and integrated.
  - Controls to hold gains once actions are implemented.
    - Results are monitored to achieve defect reductions.
    - Process maps, KPIs, and so on are updated.
    - The process repeats itself

wait: others contend that Lean is merely focusing on the value-added expenditure of resources from customers' viewpoints. These two interpretations, however, seem too vague to understand what it means to be *Lean* in a context other than thin. A definition that's more helpful is: "Lean is a systematic approach to identifying and eliminating waste (non-value-added activities) through continuous improvement by flowing the product only when the customer needs it (called 'pull') in pursuit of perfection."[16]

The concept has roots that go back to the 1950s. Japanese auto maker Toyota is credited with first introducing it in its manufacturing system, called the Toyota Production System (TPS), which concentrated on reducing or eliminating non-value-added tasks. The concept eventually became popularized in the United States under the umbrella name of *Lean* manufacturing. The central concept is that customers should not be required to pay for the costs of any wasteful activities that do not add value to the manufacturing process. Therefore, such waste should be identified and eliminated. Over time, these *Lean* concepts have been broadened and found to be applicable far beyond the manufacturing shop floor and are known today as "*Lean enterprise concepts.*"[17] Today, *Lean enterprise concepts* apply to marketing, order receipt, operations, finance, quality, human resources, and strategy. From start to finish, processes are streamlined (bottlenecks removed) and non-value-steps purged, all to make the customer experience the best possible.

A key to achieving 6σ excellence is integrating and deploying *Lean enterprise concepts* and 6σ together to complement each other as a "one-two punch."[18] In fact, as author Bonnie Smith observes, "By looking at projects through both the *Lean* and Six Sigma lenses, you have the precision, actionable tools needed to find hidden problems while making sure you don't overlook the obvious."[19] The argument is that while Six Sigma is effective, its projects often take too long (months) to complete. Another drawback is that the expert Black and Green Belt team facilitators could be reducing variation in a process step that is non-value-added. To compensate for these two shortcomings, it is argued, *Lean* initiatives are well suited for quick action, attacking "low-hanging fruit" with *kaizen* events. In fact, the Association of Manufacturing Excellence (AME) has trademarked the term *Kaizen Blitz* to explain the quick-hit process of making immediate process changes to reduce waste such as travel distance, space utilization, inventory, and so on in a short period of time. The idea is to get both initiatives working together to achieve results that are consistently superior to what either system could achieve alone.[20]

To illustrate, consider Raytheon, which has adopted both 6σ and *Lean* as part of a corporate strategy that the company calls *Raytheon Six Sigma* (*R6σ*).[21] Its strategy integrates the tools of *Lean* along with the tools of Six Sigma so that its experts (similar to Black Belts) and specialists (Green Belts) have a wide array of tools available based on their analysis of the process and its performance. In Raytheon's case, R6σ value-stream analysis requires an examination of every task being performed to produce delivery of products to customers in the shortest possible time. The premise of this cycle-time analysis is that the shortest value-added cycle time that meets customer needs and expectations will be more efficient and, thus, less costly and more flexible.

The Raytheon argument became, "If you eliminate defects à la Six Sigma, it also helps reduce non-value efforts such as rework and repair and cycle time." Accordingly, the organization has a double-barreled approach to achieving excellence. In many cases, organizations will be able to make initial *Lean* cycle-time improvements and then follow up with Six Sigma variability reduction efforts to drive the overall project results to new levels. Thus, by combining *Lean* tools and 6σ tools, the Raytheon experts have an array of options to draw upon when developing a plan for a project.[22] One group of tools that needs to be in the Black Belt toolkit is those pertaining to best practices benchmarking and knowledge transfer across other Six Sigma projects. Reuse of already proven solutions can add tremendously to the productive output of an enterprise. Reuse is a tremendous accelerator that is a key to winning the knowledge transfer race and is the primary subject of Chapter 9.

Relevance of 6σ and Lean 6σ to the Knowledge Transfer Race

If 6σ is an enterprise's strategic focus on eliminating defects to the level of 3.4 per million and Lean 6σ overlays an emphasis on eliminating waste, the Baldrige Award, the Shingo Prize, and the European Quality Award are codified business performance acceleration models (intellectual assets). ISO 9000 and variations of it are intellectual assets called international standards. All serve as forms or formulas to aid intellectual asset transfers.

If the Baldrige criteria are a codified road map to achieve excellence and ISO 9000 is a codified road map to proven quality conformance, then 6σ is the codified path to driving out defects. Indeed, the sine qua non of 6σ is eliminating defects. Adding *Lean enterprise concepts* into the equation simultaneously and systematically brings a focus on eliminating waste. And like the business performance acceleration models, there are two ways in which the transfer of intellectual assets involved in 6σ and *Lean* 6σ relates to winning the knowledge transfer race. First, experts from leaders like Motorola, Honeywell, GE, Raytheon, and other such companies have collaborated on the various versions and adaptations of 6σ and have created a huge pool of human capital regarding Six Sigma projects. With refinement, enterprises like Raytheon have reused the concept so that it encompasses knowledge sharing and reuse in new and evolving 6σ projects. These enterprises are codifying their 6σ knowledge into printed newsletters, bulletins, training materials, process steps, best practices databases, project repositories, and knowledge management systems.

All in all, there's a king's ransom of knowledge that has been created, and its very existence leads to the second way in which 6σ and *Lean* 6σ relate to the knowledge transfer race. This same king's ransom of knowledge is being shared and reused so that others can benefit from the experience of those before them and each new implementation or project does not start from scratch. In fact, those benefiting from this growing stockpile of world knowledge about 6σ projects are running fast in the knowledge transfer race.

What's the Point of Doing Any of These Things, Anyway?

The short answer is to improve, build, and accelerate the capacity to excel or compete. But there's usually more than one reason. Part of the answer is to take advantage of the excellent intellectual assets that have already been developed and are available for transfer and shared reuse. In other words, why try to reinvent the wheel when it's already been created and improved upon many times over? Yet another factor is to adapt something that has already been created, but take it beyond its first creation to meet new and different needs in a new age. Still another factor is to continue the never-ending process of learning to see new possible approaches. To stand on what has already been accomplished is to become complacent and stagnant and ignore the knowledge transfer race.

Remembering the earlier example of Chrysler and the U.S. automakers, attitudes such as "if we make it, they'll buy it" or "we're already the leader" trap managers in unrealistic and overstated assumptions about their enterprise's performance. This is conceit, and it is a huge barrier to making improvements. Experienced practitioners know better than to think that they've become the best. That invites complacency, which can become a death sentence. Thus, such statements or serious thoughts as, "we're already in the top 10 percent," "we're the leader," and "we've always been successful in the past" are misconceptions that become barriers to achieving improved performance. These types of judgments are about temporary conditions and should be made by others outside the competitive struggle. The preferred attitude is one of enjoying moments when successes occur, but with the conscious humility of someone who has just won only two laps of a race without a finish and knows that there's no end to what can be learned from people in other organizations around the world. Some may see this attitude as a weakness, but it is a genuine strength because it causes the holder to aggressively search out best practices wherever they may be found. This is the attitude of someone who is leading in the knowledge transfer race.

Another damaging statement representing a arrogant attitude that has been widely verbalized and too often accepted is the classic saying, "If it ain't broke, don't fix it!" This misguided belief and the behavior it generates cause widespread damage within an enterprise. What is harmed is the cultural attitude toward progress and continuous improvement. In such settings, too often, progressive changes or improvements are postponed, stalled, abandoned, or never funded. What makes eminently more sense is, "If there's a way to do it better, improve it." The road leading to competitive advantage and industry leadership is paved with strong bricks consisting of (1) a fact-based and systematic evaluation and improvement process, (2) broad organizational learning, and (3) knowledge sharing. Together, these are key management tools. Therefore, the compelling argument for doing a Baldrige criteria self-assessment, undertaking ISO 9000, or looking at any one of the other business excellence acceleration models is to drive continuous improvement. And within the process of making continuous improvement, knowledge transfers inevitably occur.

One of the authors of this book actually conducted a nonscientific study at the Association of Manufacturing Excellence (AME) Conference held in Chicago in 2000. The nearly 50 executives in the audience were asked for a show of hands of those who believed that their organization was in the top 25 percent of their particular industry. More than 75 percent of the executives raised their hand, signifying their belief that their organization was in the top quadrant. While AME members are probably better than average, it's unreasonable to accept that three-fourths of them or any random audience actually are in the top quadrant of the industries they operate.

This type of unscientific result (the unrealistic belief in the level of one's performance) is a testament to the need to have universal benchmarks that enable one to compare one's current performance to past trends and to the top 10 percent. To fill the void left by the absence of such benchmarks, it's no surprise that consulting enterprises specializing in benchmarking have tried to create and standardize measurements and benchmarks. However, the drawbacks are enough to cloud or make invalid comparisons.

Hence applying for a Baldrige Award, a European Quality Award, a Shingo Prize, or ISO 9000, which can provide an external overarching evaluation, comparison, or benchmark of how the organization is performing, is in itself a form of knowledge transfer. In the case of using benchmarks, the required level of future performance may be successfully targeted. So, using one of the business performance excellence models helps by identifying weaknesses and a "top five areas to address" checklist during the next time frame.

Many managers who are not prone to make major changes on their own find that prodding by an external assessment process is needed to get them to schedule and get commitment to the needed improvements to better the entire organization. When an independent recommendation is made based on facts, there's no place to hide. Besides, independent and objective examiners are normally trained to have a keen eye for validating the deployment of well-developed approaches based on objective criteria rather than being concerned with the work group's history or internal politics. Furthermore, the application fees and site-visit expenses for these business performance excellence assessments usually deliver a high value for the money spent. In other words, instead of an expense, they're a great investment. Because the enterprise comes out of these assessments with an agenda (a prioritized list of improvement opportunities) for becoming a leader in its industry, the payback exceeds the investment many times over.

As far as Six Sigma or *Lean Six Sigma* are concerned, the basic approach is to aggressively reduce defects and waste, thereby creating customer value in the form of low-cost and high-quality products and services. Contrary to what some believe, every business process can be evaluated on this basis, and virtually every one has some opportunity for downstream improvement. *Lean Six Sigma* adds another dimension by focusing on the elimination of non-valued-added activities in addition to the basic Six Sigma defect reductions. The cadre of trained process improvement specialists called Six Sigma Black Belts or Green Belts has added a new mindset to process improvements by embedding the spirit and philosophy of improvement into the DNA of the organization.

Links between Best Practices, Knowledge Management, and Transfers

All of the aforementioned award criteria, performance acceleration models, and standards are based on becoming better than the competition on the things that are most important to customers and delivering them without error, on time, every time. The linchpins for delivering better, error-free, on-time performance every time are the fast-learning and knowledge-sharing capability of organizations. Best practices and learning lessons from new endeavors create the "knowledge nuggets" that are transferred from one person to five others, from one unit to three others, or from one business to ten others. The Baldrige Award, European Quality Award, Shingo Prize, and ISO 9000 criteria help people to identify and take action on weak spots (opportunities for improvement) in the organization's performance so that the following two questions are continually addressed:

I. "How do we compare?"
II. "What are we going to do about it?"

All the knowledge nuggets that are continually identified and transferred are the spearhead to step-function or leapfrog improvements. While incremental improvements are positive, they may not be sufficient to achieve a rapid catch-up for a company that is several laps behind in the knowledge transfer race.

Similarities, Differences, and What Matters

At the beginning of this chapter, business performance excellence models were singled out as "poster child" examples of phenomenally successful knowledge transfers. This includes codified knowledge—qualifying the knowledge as intellectual assets, but of the kind that are made public and specifically designed to be transferred to and shared by and within organizations that have the wisdom to take advantage of them.

As a summary, Table 6-5 compares these four systems. Indeed, it is the authors' opinion that those enterprises that quickly take advantage of one or more of these knowledge transfer opportunities will automatically accelerate their organizations to the front of the knowledge transfer race. As discussed in this chapter, these

Table 6-5   Characteristics of Key Improvement Approaches

	Baldrige Criteria	European Quality Award	Shingo Prize	ISO 9000
Emphasis	Criteria for performance excellence	Criteria for performance excellence	Manufacturing excellence	International quality standard
Scope	United States	Europe	North America	Worldwide
Purpose 1	Improve everything	Recognize excellence	Facilitate increased awareness	Standardization
Purpose 2	*Share best practices*	*Identify role models*	*Foster understanding and sharing*	Conformity with quality system
Purpose 3	Tool to manage and *learn*	*Share successes*	*Encourage research*	World trade
Value for applicant	Assessment; opportunities to improve	Opportunity for recognition and learning	*Learning* and recognition	Certification with ISO logo
Emphasis on knowledge transfer	*High*	*Low to medium*	*Medium to high*	*Low to medium*
Emphasis on knowledge sharing	*High*	*High*	*High*	*High*
Emphasis on knowledge reuse	*High*	*High*	*High*	*High*

Source: Info from Web sites for Baldrige, European Quality Award, Shingo Prize, and ISO 9000

include the Baldrige criteria, European Quality Award, Shingo Prize, and ISO 9000, where the key knowledge of many of the world's best practices has been codified, is transferred, and is shared (for reuse). Comparing and contrasting these improvement systems identifies similarities and differences. Highlighted in italics in Table 6-5 are characteristics that explicitly involve the transferring, sharing, learning, and reusing of what is typically described as best practices knowledge. Table 6-5 also invites comparisons to enable readers to pick and choose the approach or approaches that work best for their enterprise. Any choice and dedicated change management approach will pay immediate dividends and propel applicants into the metaphoric knowledge transfer race.

The Bottom Line for People in Small Organizations

There are three points from this chapter that are included as Tips 38, 39, and 40 in Chapter 11's 55 tips for people in small businesses. Briefly, they are

- Take advantage of published business excellence models.
- The self-assessment criteria of these models are excellent for identifying and prioritizing the highest-priority improvement opportunities.
- Along the way, identify what the enterprise's core competencies need to be for the future.

In small organizations, someone must have an eye on the outside world—particularly the business environment, including the products and services of competitors—both on a global market basis and for local markets. Usually, the person responsible for this is the owner or the operating manager. This difficult job is just one of a long list of many duties for this person, which probably includes customer relations, making payroll, negotiating contracts, and so on.

Unfortunately, while every duty on the list is important in the short term, the outward focus is what contributes most to enhanced performance, long-term growth, competitive advantage, and survivability. Thus, there is an answer when that person asks the question, "What should I do?" Experience suggests that using self-assessment criteria is an excellent barometer for discovering the top priorities and where to allocate the limited resources to improve. Certainly, the owner/manager should consider using one of the business performance excellence models (criteria) and objectively evaluating to what extent the organization is or isn't doing what is called for by the criteria involved. This is an exceptional opportunity to focus and deploy the limited resources available in a very effective way.

In larger enterprises, this work may be called "identifying the enterprise's core competencies." Once these are identified, the organization's performance on those core competencies may be compared to that of leaders in the industry or key competitors. Core competencies may involve unique processes and/or emerging technologies that may be radically affected by future developments. The owner/manager must also look at industry best practices, technologies, and opportunities, so that he or she can chart the future course of the enterprise.

Without scanning the environment in these ways, managers will not keep pace in the knowledge transfer race, and the organizations they lead will become competitively disadvantaged. It must be remembered that the criteria for these performance excellence models are continually updated and improved. Also, involving key people in the work of evaluating the organization's approaches, deployments, and results against what's called for by these expert criteria will help to create an enlightened and motivated learning organization.

Endnotes

1. Iacooca, who left Ford and joined Chrysler in 1978 as its CEO, inherited at Chrysler a huge inventory of low-mileage cars at a time of rising fuel prices. In 1980, the U.S. Congress agreed to guarantee $1.5 billion in loans to Chrysler if the company could raise $2 billion on its their own, which it did.

2. Ball, Robert, "Europe Outgrows Management American Style," *Fortune*, October 20, 1980, pp. 147–48.

3. Peters, Thomas J. and Waterman, Robert H. Jr., In Search of Excellence: Lessons from America's Best-Run Companies, (New York: Harper & Row: New York, 1982), pp. 33–35.

4. There are two sources for the information used to describe the Baldrige National Program; the Web site www.quality.nist.gov/eBaldrige/Sep_One.htm and copies (1988-2005) of the Criteria for Performance Excellence, an annually produced document by the National Institute of Standards and Technology. The "Criteria," as this document is referred to, contains over 60 sixty pages long and includes the history, purposes, core values, and concepts underlying the program.

5. U.S. Public Law 100-107 adopted on August 20, 1987 as documented in the 2005 Baldrige Criteria for Performance Excellence, the document published annually by the Baldrige National Quality Program, National Institute of Standards and Technology.

6. The source for the information used to describe the European Quality Awards is its official Web site, at www.efqm.org/model_awards/eqa/intro.asp, especially the sections with the headings "Introduction," "EFQM Excellence Model," and "History and past winners."

7. The source for the information used to describe the Shingo Prize is its

official Web site, at http://www.shingoprize.org/.

8. There are two sources for the information used to describe ISO 9000. The first is the official Web site of the International Organization for Standardization (ISO), which is http://www.iso.org/iso/9000-1400/. The second source is Mike English's notes and presentation materials from when he successfully led a team effort during 1994-1995 to ISO 9002 certify GTE Telephone Operations Special Services in Tampa, Florida.

9. Information obtained from the QuEST Forum's Web site, http://www.quest forum.asq.org/.

10. Ibid.

11. Remarks from Rachel Buckley's presentation to the Dallas TL9000 Special Interest Group on September 22, 2004, at the University of Texas, Dallas.

12. Ibid.

13. Honeywell's 1998 Annual Report.

14. Welch, Jack. *Jack: Straight from the Gut*, (New York: Warner Books, 2001), New York, NY, pp. 331–335.

15. George Alukal, George, "Create a Lean, Mean Machine," *Quality Progress*, Vol. 36, no. 4, April 2003, p. 29.

16. Ibid., p. 29. Alukal credits this definition as having come from the National Institute of Standards and Technology Manufacturing Extension Partnership, or NIST/MEP.

17. Ibid., p. 34.

18. Bonnie Smith, Bonnie, "Lean and Six Sigma—A One-Two Punch," *Quality Progress*, Vol. 36, no. 4, April 2003, pp. 37–41.

19. Ibid., p. 37.

20. Ibid., p. 37.

21. Interview between Bill Baker and Mike English on June 13, 2003.

22. Ibid.

Chapter 7

Worldwide Approaches to Leveraging Knowledge

The importance of visionary leaders who shape and expand the cultures of their global companies cannot be overstated; following are inspiring quotes from two highly respected executives of Most Admired Knowledge Enterprise (MAKE) Award recipient organizations and members of the MAKE Hall of Fame:

> The principles of knowledge sharing, collaborative working and best practice sharing are fundamental to the development of our people and the success of our global business.
>
> —*Walter van de Vijver, CEO, Shell International Exploration and Production*

> We need to focus on the importance of harnessing the minds that are in our organizations to meet our needs anytime/anywhere. It is the most powerful weapon that we have in the competitive arena today.
>
> —*Robert H. Buckman, former chairman, Executive Committee, Buckman Laboratories*

Overview of Worldwide Trends

On a global scale, the transfer of knowledge from one corner of the earth to the other is faster than ever. While achieving business excellence is the final end game, business and industry approaches vary, those used in Asia, Europe, Japan, and North America differ. Tendencies and trends are as diverse as the countries they occur in. "North American enterprises tend to rely more on information technology," according to Rory Chase, executive director of Teleos, the consulting sponsor of the KNOW Network, a Web-based community of leading knowledge-based organizations dedicated to benchmarking and sharing best knowledge practices that lead to superior business performance.[1] Rory Chase benefits from the unique perspective that comes from coordinating every aspect of Teleos's sponsorship of all five worldwide MAKE Award processes. Chase adds, "North American enterprises use databases, search engines, and other forms of IT more often, whereas Europeans and Asians tend to concentrate more on the people-to-people aspects."[2]

Chase voices concern that as an aggressive group, software companies in the North American sector have been trying to "hijack the knowledge management movement" through the proliferation of "automatic tools" that they've dumped into the market. This overabundance of knowledge management software tools gives beginners and some executives the false impression that these automatic tools are the sum total of what makes up knowledge management. "That's false," contends Chase, "and it leads managers to ignore the years of hard work it takes to create an enterprise knowledge-driven culture, develop knowledge workers, deliver knowledge-based solutions, maximize intellectual capital, create a learning organization, and transform enterprise knowledge into shareholder value."[3]

Melissie Clemmons Rumizen, author of *The Complete Idiot's Guide to Knowledge Management*, puts it this way: "Untold software vendors slap the label of knowledge management on their packages and tout miraculous cures for all our knowledge failings. Yet, behind all the jargon and the hype, we find companies engaged in serious efforts to manage their most precious asset—their working knowledge."[4]

The point is, knowledge management is about the people, not about IT. The IT software vendors may be giving knowledge management a bad name by overbuilding and promising software solutions to problems that actually require people solutions.

In Europe, promising work on creating knowledge-enabled cultures is underway. Leading European knowledge-enabled enterprises like British Petroleum and Siemens are focusing on mastering change management considerations and are doing pioneering work on embedding into cultures more and better ways of transferring, sharing, and reusing knowledge. The initial efforts at transforming cultures actually took place in North America during the early 1990s. By 1996–1997, however, it was European enterprises that began to leapfrog to the forefront of embedding knowledge considerations into the cultural fabric of how organizations conduct business.

High technology and oil appear to be two of the "hot" industry sectors that are proactive in knowledge creation, transfer, sharing, and reuse. This is partly due to rapid changes in technology and the requirements of customers. In telecommunications, for example, voice, data, and video technologies have not only geometrically multiplied, but also converged with information technology. In the oil industry, the never-ending need to discover, renew, and extract oil reserves or develop alternative energy sources has produced new technologies and know-how. Consequently, knowledge, too, has grown in these sectors, along with the need for transferring, sharing, and reusing it.

Since the year 2000, organizations in Asia have become very interested in managing their intellectual assets, and this seems to have started with a focus on the research and development process. This interest has been growing dramatically in Asia, and Rory Chase suggests that the Asians may be moving so swiftly that they will soon overtake European and North American efforts.

What's the Perceived Value of Being Knowledge-Enabled?

Peter Senge made a good point: "The entire global business community is learning how to learn together, becoming a learning community."[5]

What this chapter demonstrates through examples is that the drive to become the best depends on using all the valuable knowledge available and then fully leveraging, sharing, and reusing it across the global enterprise. International organizations are now becoming leaders in the race.

Asian and European companies seem to put value on transforming the culture of their organizations and supporting the growth of their intellectual capital. This corresponds with what the authors describe as taking the strategic long-range view. It is contrary to the predominant view taken by North American firms, which tend to look at metrics to prove cost savings and payback on the revenue invested in the process. None of these generalizations are 100 percent valid, of course; they are given simply to highlight some basic differences in their worldviews. In effect, the Asian view is that cultural and people-centered change pays off tremendously over the long haul, and that knowledge-enabled investments are not costs but investments that pay back handsomely, not only in innovations in products and services, cost savings, and customer satisfaction, but also in reduced turnover, increased employee satisfaction, and management education and enlightenment. The real question about value is how to build intellectual capital and sustain the free flow of ideas and knowledge. The authors contend that the knowledge transfer race is a long-term race with no end and that all four phases must be mastered if a company is to be a leader.

Global companies have determined that using "community knowledge," that knowledge held uniquely within their company, is essential to their leadership and survival. Asian companies have a built-in humility that enables them to master phase 1 as part of their everyday work process. Phase 2, "learning, understanding, and sharing," also requires a culture that emphasizes the value of this work process. While individual companies vary in their understanding, an important awakening to the concept that knowledge transfer and reuse are very beneficial is now underway in some North American companies.

In fact, the companies mentioned in this book, many of them MAKE Award recipients, are on the leading edge and true early adopters. As an example of phase 3, some companies have formed design teams that span the world and are given the task of product design efforts on selected high-priority projects. For example, a chip manufacturer used three design centers to perform chip design around the clock. The U.S. design center would kick off the workday, work for its eight-hour shift, and then hand off its work, including all its results and everything it had learned, to a team in the Philippines. The Philippine design team would pick up where the U.S. team left off and continue with the next stage of the design. At the end of its shift, it would hand off its work to a design team in Italy. The handoff process was important, for it included the knowledge transfer element: current status, problems encountered, results achieved, and problems not yet resolved. When the Italian design team completed its shift, a 24-hour day had passed, and three shifts of work had been done on the project. This exemplifies a design team that is really involved in the knowledge transfer race. The organization used the global team to speed the design by transferring knowledge around the clock and beat the competition in this part of the race, since it eliminates the need for pit stops to sleep!

It's like the Le Mans 24-hour race: the drivers are changed out to minimize fatigue, but the car continues in the race. The winning team has pit crew members, sponsors, and drivers. They all win. These design teams have to be finely aligned, be attuned to overall team goals, have interchangeable tools, operate to the same customer requirements, have a common language, and share extensively during handoffs. This knowledge work example is typical of what must also happen in one plant in face-to-face handoffs; the design team example is just doing it on a virtual basis. This is a prime example of mastering phase 4 of the knowledge transfer race by creating value in the form of a completed effective and efficient design that meets the customer's expectations.

While there are many language barriers in leveraging knowledge between countries, English is the business language of choice. Except for dealings in France, English is the accepted norm. To develop trust, there's no substitute for face-to-face meetings to overcome the many differences in culture, customs, labor and commerce laws, economies, and so on that exist. These meetings should be repeated with sufficient frequency to reinforce friendships within the network, open dialogue, identify collaboration possibilities, and create action plans of mutual benefit. A minimum of once or twice a year is suggested. This is a best practices approach to building networks that are effective. Cultural differences between plants, regions, and countries do exist, but they can be overcome by leadership traits such as defining the goals, outlining expectations, sharing tools, and recognizing behaviors that serve as role models.

The 1994 International Conference in Trondheim, Norway That Built Acceptance of Benchmarking throughout Europe

In contrast to the United States, where practitioners were the pioneers, in Europe it was the academics who were the trailblazers in the early efforts to carry out benchmarking exchanges and prepare the ground for managing knowledge transfers. In the early days of benchmarking, the International Federation for Information Processing (IFIP), which was formed in 1960 by the United Nations, and one of its components, the Working Group for Computer Aided Production Management, hosted a July 1994 conference in Trondheim, Norway to explore the process of benchmarking. Representatives from most European countries attended, including Bulgaria, Denmark, France, Germany, Greece, Italy, Poland, Norway, and Sweden. Also attending were representatives from Australia and the United States, including coauthor Bill Baker, who represented Texas Instruments. The IFIP was formed as an apolitical international organization to encourage and assist nations in developing, exploiting, and applying information technology to benefit people. Its roots trace back to 1959, when it held its first conference in Paris, on the topic of computers and computing.

This technique of drawing experts and researchers together in a face-to-face meeting proved particularly effective at creating acceptance for benchmarking and encouraging greater use of the procedure because of the concentrated knowledge exchange that took place. It actually was conducted like a *kaizen* event in manufacturing. After three days, the theory and practices of benchmarking had been thoroughly discussed by linking best practices, lessons learned, performance measures, tools, and enabling practices.

At the time, many of the European academic attendees were very apprehensive and considered benchmarking to be a modern-day "buzzword." The cynics were investigating, much like their counterparts in the United States, whether this new buzzword tool would be a passing fancy "flavor of the month" or a genuine and valuable tool that would have lasting worldwide application. Over ten years later, the outcome is (as the authors have indicated in Chapters 1 through 3) that benchmarking has become the second most used management tool in the world.

Not only has its usage increased by a factor of greater than 10, as evidenced by the research of Bain & Company presented in Chapter 1, but benchmarking has been on the top 10 list of management tools for over ten years, and for 2002, at 84 percent usage, it's second only to strategic planning. For 2002, it also ranked sixth in management satisfaction with the tool.

The leading industry companies that presented position papers at the Trondheim conference were Rank Xerox, Texas Instruments, and Bang & Olufsen. Rank Xerox claimed to have been involved in benchmarking in Europe for ten years before Robert Camp's original work for Xerox U.S.A. Texas Instruments had just received the Malcolm Baldrige National Quality Award in 1992, and benchmarking had been identified as a strength in the examiners' feedback report. Bang & Olufsen was a leading practitioner of benchmarking in Europe.

One thing that was particularly evident was that most of the attendees were academics rather than company practitioners. The academics were taking the lead and trying to analyze the tacit insights and knowledge nuggets concerning the practice of benchmarking and capture them as explicit knowledge in the form of a published book.[6] This is a distinct contrast to the U.S. situation, where benchmarking has been pioneered by practitioners, consortiums, and consultants. Several industrialist practitioners, including this book's coauthor, and academic research leaders presented position papers, which became the basis for the following workshop discussions. There was a lead facilitator for each work group who directed the discussion to develop a consensus on universal learnings that would subsequently be presented to the conference in summary form and then published. To the participants' surprise and relief, the official language of the conference was English. All discussions, lectures, and working groups during the three-day event were conducted in English. After selected papers were presented, several working groups held detailed discussions with the goal of capturing the knowledge and opinions for later publication in the form of a proceedings book to be provided to attendees.

Setting up Benchmarking Networks: The Global Benchmarking Exchange Founded by Robert Camp

Upon his retirement from Xerox Corporation, Dr. Robert C. Camp, author of the first complete industry book on benchmarking, published in 1989,[7] became involved in setting up benchmarking centers all around the world, especially in Asia and Europe. In 2005 Camp continues to head the Best Practice Institute and previously led the Global Benchmarking Network. It's important to note that the Best Practice Institute has three main foci on best practices and their time-frame relevance. All are based on current and future time frames as the competition gets tougher and more mature.[8]

1. *Today's focus* is on searching for, developing interest in, and understanding best practices.
2. *Tomorrow's focus* is on getting value from best practices through the use of three action verbs and their subheading elements:
   Capture—identify, collect, create, inventory, and archive
   Share—structure, process, transfer, and exchange
   Adopt—search, access, synthesize, reuse, and apply
3. *Future focus* is on fast organizational learning through best practices exchange.

This book takes into account the current focus and tomorrow's focus, but the goal is to prepare the reader for Camp's *future focus*. Camp sees a knowledge life cycle very similar to the one that the authors discussed in Chapter 3: create, capture, share, and reuse. Relative to Camp's outline, the current authors have elevated "create" because it is so important and is representative of the innovation process. "Reuse" has been elevated to a top level to make the whole transfer more action-oriented and to emphasize the importance of not reinventing. Camp recognizes the knowledge transfer race through the Best Practice Institute's emphasis on "fast organizational learning."

Also, Camp's latest book, *Global Cases in Benchmarking: Best Practices from Organizations Around the World*,[9] makes the point that the fervor for benchmarking and learning best practices in order to improve performance quickly is extremely high in both Europe and the Asia-Pacific region. Camp has helped to create the capability around the world to focus on the exchange of knowledge through best practices through the Best Practice Institute and his mentoring of others.

The Global Benchmarking Network

In 1993, discussions were held between the UK Benchmarking Centre, the Strategic Planning Institute (United States), the SIQ (Sweden), the IZB (Germany), and the Benchmarking Club of Italy to evaluate the possibility of a cooperative network. In 1994, after debate and agreement, the Global Benchmarking Network (GBN) was officially established by these founding members as a community of legally independent benchmarking centers, with the objective of achieving a consistent understanding of benchmarking as a management method and promoting its worldwide spread and utilization. Camp, whom some call the "father of benchmarking," came from the Best Practice Institute of the United States and was appointed the first head of the network.[10]

Since the GBN's founding, its members have held at least one meeting per year to discuss GBN matters and to exchange and share information on their respective activities. In 1998, the members agreed to annual affiliation fees when they approved a GBN logo and launched a Web site (www.globalbenchmarking.org) to facilitate communication among members and promote marketing. The network has been successful since at least 1996, facilitating the worldwide exchange of benchmarking activities among centers and companies as well as public institutions. GBN affiliates now respond to requests for benchmarking expertise from governments, including those of Germany and the U.K., and government ministries, like the Department of Trade and Commerce of the Slovak Republic, including such actions as the creation of national benchmarking centers. GBN affiliates also support several international organizations, such as the Benchmarking Competitiveness Group of the EU in Brussels and the International Trade Centre (ITC) of the World Trade Organization in Geneva. Current members represent 20 countries: Czech Republic, Denmark, France, Germany, Hungary, India, Ireland, Italy, Malaysia, Mauritius, Moldavia, New Zealand, Poland, Russia, Slovakia, South Africa, Sweden, Switzerland, the U.K., and the United States. They serve as focal points and operate benchmarking centers in their countries as well as serve as delegates to the network.

Table 7-1 displays the GBN's vision, mission, and values as summarized from the organization's Web site.

Examples of International Leveraging of Knowledge by the Japanese Auto Industry

Many people do not realize that the Japanese auto industry was based on Henry Ford's model. Many Japanese managers made several benchmarking trips to Ford's huge River Rouge operation in Detroit. Ford had laid out the "greenfield" operation and plant site to be able to handle the large volumes of cars he intended to produce. Ford was operating under the "product excellence" approach, as defined by Treacy and Wiersema.[11] There was no pressure to focus on customer intimacy; the customers needed the Model T's and Model A's. There was limited competition. Quality had not yet become an expectation; people were willing to put up with relative unreliability just because the cars gave them so much more mobility, so "operational excellence" and reducing costs did not take the main stage. Customers were willing to pay for Ford's inefficiencies; it was the only game in town. They assumed that Ford's price was the price one had to pay for this new technology. The huge inventories and inefficiencies of the Ford operations were taken for granted and had not yet been subjected to *Lean* thinking and the "five whys" investigation technique to determine root causes and challenge assumptions.

But when the Japanese returned home, they were faced with limited resources—money, land, buildings, and capital equipment. Toyota had limited resources, so the Toyota Production System had to be based on the operational excellence approach.

Table 7-1   Global Benchmarking Network (GBN)Vision, Mission, and Values[11]

GBN Vision (What do we want to become, look like in the future?)

A global network sharing best practice knowledge to help public and private organizations achieve performance improvement.

GBN Mission (Who are we, what do we do, for whom and why?).

A network of benchmarking competency centres, which promotes and applies that knowledge, enhancing its communication, offers expert support, establishes ethical and protocol expectations, for Affiliates and their members, to demonstrate significant business results.

GBN Values (What do we believe in, want members to abide by?)

Professionalism—as evidenced by handling all relations between GB members in a professional way equally like relations to our members and customers.

Working Together—as evidenced by willingness to share and assist other members, participation in team or group activities and projects as appropriate and attendance at the annual meeting.

Excellence—as evidenced by developing expertise in benchmarking, leading or managing benchmarking activities and promoting the role of benchmarking in performance improvement.

Ethical Behavior—as evidenced by following the Benchmarking Code of Conduct and respect for confidentiality.

Source: GBN Web page; copyright©2004 by GBN.

The gurus who visited Japan after World War II focused on quality, reducing defects and in so doing eliminating waste. The Japanese did not solve their auto production problems overnight; however, in the 1960s, they began to make their presence felt, and by the 1980s, they had captured a significant share of not only the U.S. market but also the world market. They did a good job of reusing knowledge and recreating, capturing, and sharing it. The knowledge transfer concept is embedded in their culture and DNA, so that it has become second nature. This illustrates how the Japanese leveraged knowledge that they extracted from the United States, then leapfrogged to the forefront of new knowledge creation regarding the best auto manufacturing processes.

Reversing the Flow of Auto Industry Knowledge from Japan Back to the United States

In the 1990s and into the beginning of the twenty-first century, American automakers have staged a reinvention of their manufacturing, service, and sales. The flow of knowledge and learning for competitive advantage is now working in reverse. Many American companies realized that to move back into the forefront and become successful again, they had to adopt the most rapid learning approach. And that's what they did. American automakers have thus benchmarked the Japanese manufacturers extensively and have imported, transferred, shared, and reused the knowledge they've gained. As a result, American automakers have rejoined the knowledge transfer race and are competing for the lead.

As evidence of this the turnaround, American automakers scored first and second in the J. D. Power customer satisfaction rankings, and four of them were in the top seven. Table 7-2 gives the recently released (July 2004) J. D. Power and Associates 2004 Customer Satisfaction Index (CSI) Report summary[12]. The American autos Lincoln and Buick placed first and second, with 912 and 909 points, respectively. All in all, these results show that a huge turnaround has taken place since the 1990s, when Japanese, German, and other foreign autos dominated the top seven standings. According to Joe Ivers, executive director of quality/customer satisfaction at J. D. Power and Associates, "Ford's domestic brands—Ford and Mercury—also showed similar effects of improved quality performance, as did Land Rover."[13] It is also notable that all of the General Motors brand names scored above the industry average.

Phase 1 ("search for and import best practices") of the knowledge transfer race took place when the U.S. automakers aggressively benchmarked their Japanese counterparts on *Lean* manufacturing, on both a tactical and a strategic level. And then, during phase 2 ("learn, understand, and share"), American automakers adapted the Japanese best practices to the American automobile environment so that they could be used, accepted, and improved. Phase 3 ("create intellectual capital") is represented by the actual work improvements and changes made to manufacture autos that are much more competitive in quality and cost. Finally, to complete the cycle, the customer satisfaction metrics seen in phase 4 ("convert into value and profits") prove that customer value has been delivered, as evidenced by the J. D. Power survey rankings.

Table 7-2   Results of J. D. Power July 2004
Customer Satisfaction Rankings[14]

Name of Automaker	Points Scored
1. Lincoln	912
2. Buick	909
3. Infiniti	908
4. Cadillac	904
5. Lexus	902
6. Saturn	901
7. Acura	900

Source: J. D. Power and Associates

As this recent update shows, the top two models and three of the top four are now U.S. brands, and the Japanese manufacturers captured only three spots in the top seven. This is a testimony to the additional learning about quality that U.S. firms have acquired since the low point in the 1980s, when U.S. brands were often absent from the list. The Total Quality Management (TQM) movement, the Malcolm Baldrige National Quality Award, and the focus on *Lean* manufacturing sparked the North American quality revolution and forced learning in a crisis mode.

This revolution was fueled by reverse benchmarking visits to Japan and the passion of many proponents of improving U.S. operations, including the American Society of Quality, the Association of Manufacturing Excellence, and the American Productivity and Quality Center, among others. The big psychological step for the United States was to embrace humility and realize that the Japanese methods were producing superior results. Manufacturing and quality professionals began extensive studies of the Japanese methods, and although initially many of the individual best practices were lifted from the Toyota Production System, some of the leading proponents of change began identifying large chunks of the system that could be adapted to U.S. culture.

One of the first best practices transferred was the concept of lower inventory and "just in time" (JIT). Whole consulting companies and many books and workshops were produced to teach JIT to U.S. leaders and factory people. This learning was one of the first steps. U.S. firms had to concentrate on operational excellence in order to drive costs down and quality up. This, in turn, tends to lead to improvements in market share through customer intimacy and understanding that quality and customer perception are very important in a commodity industry.

The point being presented here is that international knowledge transfer in the form of "stealing shamelessly" has been around for a long time. Whether it is through ethical benchmarking, industrial espionage, illegal espionage, or just by reading books or surfing the Internet, knowledge transfer has existed for years. The world is a much smaller and a much quicker place, so it's important that people and organizations are prepared for the knowledge transfer race and are able to learn quickly.

Teleos and the KNOW Network[15]

Since 1998, excellence in international knowledge transfer has been the focus of Teleos and the Know Network's Most Admired Knowledge Enterprise (MAKE) Awards. These awards have grown in stature and now are recognized as the most prestigious for organizational knowledge and the use of intellectual capital.

The KNOW Network is an international Web-based professional knowledge-sharing network. Its principal aim is to help its members create the best possible level of performance across their organizations by building on the know-how and skills of world-class knowledge-based enterprises. Its mission statement reads, "The

KNOW Network is dedicated to achieving superior performance through networking, benchmarking and sharing knowledge best practices."[16] At the end of April 2005, it had 41 members in many industries, including consulting, computers, software, chemicals, steel, electronics, accounting, and others. The focus is on helping to identify, adopt, manage, and improve specific knowledge best practices, ranging from increasing the organization's intellectual capital through innovation to developing communities of interest to creating the learning organization. The KNOW Network provides Web-based services to expand and improve organizational performance by

- Developing new insights and strategies based on exclusive access to proprietary research, including the global and regional Most Admired Knowledge Enterprises (MAKE) studies and Most Admired Knowledge Leaders (MAKL) surveys.
- Using the KNOW Network databases of best knowledge practices to conduct regular organizational knowledge audits and enterprise MAKE assessments.
- Facilitating the transfer of best knowledge practices quickly and efficiently.
- Contacting the best minds in knowledge organizations around the world.
- Learning from network members with relevant expertise and experience.
- Keeping in touch with the latest thinking and approaches to knowledge creation.
- Facilitating knowledge creation, sharing, and use, such as the eight key performance aspects or criteria that are used to judge the MAKE Award winners.
- Integrating knowledge management practices into overall enterprise strategy.

Most Admired Knowledge Enterprise (MAKE) Awards

Teleos and the KNOW Network sponsor the Most Admired Knowledge Enterprise Awards, which have been established since 1998 to provide an international look at organizational knowledge transfer excellence. In fact, MAKE and the KNOW Network are service marks of Teleos. While not perfect, the awards serve as a good measurement tool for judging excellence.

The awards are based on eight key knowledge performance dimensions that are visible drivers of world-class knowledge-based organizations:

1. Creating an enterprise knowledge-driven culture
2. Developing knowledge workers through senior management leadership
3. Delivering knowledge-based products, services, and solutions
4. Maximizing enterprise intellectual capital
5. Creating an environment for collaborative knowledge sharing
6. Creating a learning organization

7. Delivering value based on customer knowledge
8. Transforming enterprise knowledge into shareholder value

To get an overall global perspective on the companies that are leading in the knowledge transfer race, one needs only to review the 2004 list of 20 global MAKE Award winners displayed in Figure 7-1. The winners are listed in alphabetical order. An analysis reveals that fifteen (75 percent) are North America–based, three (15 percent) are Europe–based, and two (10 percent) are Asian. So at this point, early in the twenty-first century, North American companies are still prominent and formidable leaders in the knowledge transfer race.

Asian Knowledge Transfer

During October 2004, the 2004 Asian MAKE Awards were also announced. A panel of Fortune Global 500 senior executives and leading knowledge-management experts selects the Asian MAKE winners, using research based on the Delphi methodology. This research methodology employs the panel's perceptual knowledge to identify organizations that are leaders in creating intellectual capital and wealth through the transformation of individual and enterprise knowledge into world-class products, services, and solutions. Displayed in Figure 7-2 are the 2004 Asian MAKE winners, listed alphabetically.

It is interesting to look at the types of industries that these 14 2004 Asian award recipients are engaged in. The winners are clustered in several industries. The

2004 Global *Most Admired Knowledge Enterprise (MAKE)* Award Winners

Enterprise	Industry
Accenture	Management Consulting
Amazon.com	Internet Products
British Petroleum	Oil and Gas
Buckman Laboratories	Specialty Chemicals
Dell Computer	Computer Systems
Ernst and Young	Management Consulting
General Electric	Diversified
Hewlett Packard	Information Technology Products
IBM	Information Technology
Infosys Technologies	Consulting and IT Services
Intel	Semiconductor Products
McKinsey and Company	Management Consulting
Microsoft	Software Solutions Provider
PricewaterhouseCoopers	Management Consulting
Royal Dutch/Shell	Oil and Gas
Samsung	Digital Technology Products
Siemens	Electronics and Electrical Equipment
Toyota Motor	Automobile Manufacturing
World Bank	Non-Profit
Xerox	Information Technology

SOURCE: A document entitled 2004Global MAKE Report, Executive Summary, prepared by Rory L. Chase, Managing Director, Telesos, p. 1, obtained from http://www.knowledgebusiness.com.

Figure 7-1 2004 Global Most Admired Knowledge Enterprise (MAKE) Award winners

2004 Asian *Most Admired Knowledge Enterprise (MAKE)* Winners

Enterprise (alphabetical)	Industry
Canon (Japan)	Computers and office equipment
Honda Motor (Japan)	Motor vehicles
Infosys Technologies (India)	Information technology products
Kao (Japan)	Household and personal products
Nissan Motor (Japan)	Motor vehicles
Samsung Electronics (Korea)	Electronics and electrical equipment
Samsung SDS (Korea)	Information technology services
Singapore Airlines (Singapore)	Airlines
Sony (Japan)	Electronics and electrical equipment
Taiwan Semiconductor Manufacturing Company (Taiwan)	Semiconductors/equipment manufacturer
Tata Consultancy Services (India)	Information technology services
Tata Steel (India)	Metal fabrication
Toyota Motor (Japan)	Motor vehicles
Wipro Technologies (India)	Information technology services

SOURCE: A document entitled 2003 Asian MAKE, Executive Summary, prepared by Teleos (United Kingdom) and the KNOW Network, a service of Teleos, p. 3, obtained from http://www.knowledgebusiness.com

Figure 7-2 2004 Asian Most Admired Knowledge Enterprise (MAKE) Award winners

electronics industry is the industry that is closest to high-velocity consumer prefer-ences and technology changes, and thus it is the fastest-moving industry that will drive the knowledge transfer race speed requirement to share and reuse knowledge in order to sustain competitive advantage.

- Electronics manufacturing: six companies
- Automobile manufacturing: three companies
- Service/IT: two companies
- Airlines: one company
- Steel: one company

"Besides solid organizational knowledge-driven leadership and product devel-opment," according to the MAKE Study Executive Summary, "the 2004 Asian, Japanese, and European MAKE finalists and winners also are exemplars in the areas of collaborative enterprise knowledge sharing and organizational learning. The rapid introduction of Web-based technologies and a focus on individual and team-based competencies have allowed these organizations to dramatically improve their capabilities in these two critical knowledge dimensions." To gain some in-depth understanding of the organizational journey required to achieve this level of knowledge transfer capability, the detailed Samsung example is provided.

Samsung Example

Samsung Group is South Korea's largest conglomerate. The group consists of over 60 affiliates and 14 listed companies and employs 175,000 people worldwide. Samsung has four main sectors: electronics, machinery and heavy industries, chemicals, and financial services. Electronics accounts for 43 percent of its sales and 67 percent of its profits.

On Samsung's fiftieth anniversary in 1988, it launched the second foundation of the company with the goal of becoming a world-class twenty-first-century corporation. And in 1993 it turned the corner with a "new management" company philosophy of "quality first." In 2000 it developed a vision of a "Samsung Digital World" with a goal of staying ahead of the great waves of digital changes engulfing the world. Samsung is focusing on winning the knowledge race in the context of a digital world of change. So it is changing its structure, management systems, and corporate culture in order to compete as a digital technology leader. The development of sharing and reusing knowledge (i.e., knowledge transfer) was a perfect fit with the company's future business vision.

Samsung has been rapidly expanding its enterprise intellectual capital since the late 1990s. In 1999, Samsung initiated a group knowledge management (KM) strategy as a precursor to the Samsung Digital World vision, but it fit perfectly. Hong-Ki Kim, CEO of Samsung SDS (Samsung Digital Systems) and CIO of the Samsung Group, was the initial driving force and visionary leader behind the adoption of knowledge management.[17] He proposed a strategic information plan for the twenty-first century that included five initiatives: customer relationship management, supply-chain management, e-commerce, knowledge management, and the information infrastructure to support the other top four initiatives. He identified the common IT needs of the Samsung Group using combined findings from a working group led by Anderson Consulting and a workshop held with the CIOs of each of the Samsung affiliates. Most affiliates reorganized based on the five initiatives after the workshop. They were rewarded with a sevenfold increase in productivity.[18]

Another concept that Hong-Ki Kim believed in was that Samsung SDS was not just the information technology support group but also the evangelist for the use of information to drive business decisions, much like some of the Six Sigma Black Belts. Samsung created its knowledge management systems using an intranet to encourage direct communication and sharing of knowledge at all levels. Hong-Ki Kim encouraged all employees to contact him directly whenever they had important ideas to share.

In 2002, Hong-Ki Kim implemented what he called phase 2 of the plan. It was titled "enhancement of competitiveness," and it showed Samsung's goal of adding value to the bottom line. With this strategic vision and support at the corporate level, each company and affiliate adapted its own approach to knowledge transfer depending on its business goals and objectives, and the KM managers formed a groupwide network to share best knowledge practices throughout the enterprise. There are several core KM activities that were common to all:

- Innovation and development of knowledge-based products and services
- Knowledge sharing and collaboration

- Individual and team-based learning
- Managing customer knowledge to gain market share

Samsung developed several internal systems (tools) to aid its efforts:[19]

- *SWIN.* A knowledge management system. SWIN is a knowledge-based storage and retrieval system established in 1998. This Web-based system contains information such as customer profiles, market information, financial data, and legal documents.
- *ARISAM.* An enterprisewide knowledge portal to support knowledge communities.
- *Process innovation-based knowledge management.* A KM database to facilitate knowledge sharing and best practices transfer:
- *KM path.* A tool for managing knowledge flows.
- *General KM tools.* Several tools have been developed to allow employees to work on virtual teams, recognize individual sharing, and encourage personal development.

Samsung has transformed itself into an innovative, knowledge-creating group of companies and is using a wide range of knowledge management/intellectual capital tools and techniques to generate new ideas and products, while at the same time reducing the costs of inefficiencies usually associated with the research and development process.[20]

According to a preliminary review of Samsung's progress in 2004 by the 2004 global expert panel, its investment in and focus on knowledge transfer is yielding significant results. According to the panel, Samsung has jumped over 20 places from its 2003 position on the Global Winners list and now ranks in the top 20 in the world.

European Knowledge Transfer

A panel of European business executives and leading knowledge management experts chose the 2005 European MAKE winners. Only organizations founded and headquartered in Europe were eligible for this award. The European MAKE Award finalists and recipients created value at an average rate of 13.5%, almost twice the top 600 European company average.[21] The 2005 European MAKE winners also are recognized for delivering superior returns on assets and revenues.

Displayed in Figure 7-3 are the 12 European MAKE Award winners for 2005.[22] The overall 2005 European MAKE winner was BP (British Petrolium (UK).

According to Rory Chase, managing director of Teleos, "The European MAKE winners are effectively transforming company knowledge into wealth-creating ideas, products, and solutions. They are building portfolios of intellectual capital which will enable them to outperform their competitors." Because it was the

2005 European *Most Admired Knowledge Enterprise (MAKE)* Winners

(In Alphabetical Order)

Enterprise	Industry
ABN AMRO (Netherlands).............	Financial services
BMW (Germany)........................	Motor vehicles
BP (UK)	Oil and gas
British Broadcasting Corporation (UK)	Media
Nokia (Finland).........................	Network and communications
Royal Philips Electronics (Netherlands)	Electronics and equipment
SAP (Germany).........................	Computer software
Schlumberger (France)..................	Oil and gas equipment/services
Schneider Electric (France).............	Electronics and electrical equipment
Siemens (Germany)....................	Electronics and electrical equipment
UBS (Switzerland)......................	Financial services
Unilever (Netherlands/UK).............	Household and personal products

Source: A document entitled "2005 European *MAKE* Report," Executive Summary, prepared by Teleos, UK, p. 3, obtained from Web site http://www.knowledgebusiness.com.

Figure 7-3 2005 European Most Admired Knowledge Enterprise (MAKE) Award winners

top-scoring European enterprise and has been considered the European benchmark for the years 2003 and 2004, there's good reason to take a closer look at Siemens (overall European winner for 2004) and its knowledge transfer race strategy.[23]

Siemens Overview

Siemens is a global leader in electrical engineering and electronics. The company has 417,000 employees in 190 countries with sales of $74.2 billion and net income of $2.445 billion. By any standard, it has a large international footprint. The 2004 European MAKE panel recognized Siemens for its enterprise knowledge-driven culture, developing knowledge-based products/services/solutions, and creating value from customer knowledge.

Groups and regions of the company with joint coordinating and proficiency-building efforts practice knowledge management (KM) at Siemens using a decentralized approach. Where necessary, knowledge management is driven by a companywide Community of Practice for the people involved. Siemens's approach is characterized by more than 1,600 registered Communities of Practice, over 85,000 users of IT-based knowledge marketplaces (tools), and dedicated processes for knowledge sharing and creation (process). Supporting this experience is the company's knowledge management consulting services.

Following are words summarizing the knowledge culture philosophy and strategy for Siemens Medical Solutions by one of Siemens's senior executives:

A knowledge driven corporate culture is one of the main success factors in global competition. In general, knowledge management means a two-dimensional approach: Foremost, the creation, distribution and discussion of new and innovative ideas through global collaboration. Secondly, the enhancement of quality and productivity within a company's core processes. Medical knowledge is growing dramatically; the need to manage and access this knowledge is mandatory for any efficiency improvement in health care. The infrastructural improvements by applying knowledge management internally thus create a new business opportunity for Siemens Medical Solutions.

—Dr. Hermann Requardt, member of the executive management board of Siemens Medical Solutions.

The combination of this depth of executive awareness with solid change management processes makes Siemens a model for the perfect knowledge management system. Keeping this in mind, Siemens Medical Solutions started to foster the development of knowledge along the business process lines. Accordingly, knowledge management is no longer an add-on, but an integral part of every employee's work tasks routine. In combination with a formalized knowledge-sharing process, global collaboration turns into pure global collaboration only when it includes customers and suppliers. Further improvements, such as well-defined processes, roles, and responsibilities, suggest that reliable information is available to users. Intelligent search mechanisms and target-oriented content ease the process of finding, recycling, and synthesizing company knowledge.

Focusing on the noted Siemens's innovations, the knowledge-sharing initiative at Siemens Medical Solutions implemented a market intelligence initiative that covers valuable market information available at Siemens Medical Solutions. The information is available through one single portal that is ready to be accessed for further dissemination, analysis, and decision making. The focus is not only on achieving a better understanding of the markets, but also on maintaining a competitive advantage over market rivals. It is a system that combines full availability of market information with clear information flow processes and very easy to use IT tools. This initiative makes it easy for employees to integrate knowledge sharing into their daily work routine, thereby securing the company's success. In short, our often referred to knowledge transfer race is typified by the Siemens knowledge management and knowledge transfer approach with the key result areas: the people, processes, and tools and the cultural change they are creating.

Japanese Knowledge Transfer

Finally, the 2004 MAKE winners for Japan are world-class competitors who've also received awards in North America, Asia, and Europe. They are listed in Figure 7-4.

The MAKE Award recipients for Japan are listed in alphabetical order. Still, Toyota has the distinction of being the overall Japan winner and is a five-time MAKE Japan winner. Toyota is a preeminent manufacturer of the highest order

Japan's
2004 *Most Admired Knowledge Enterprise* (*MAKE*) Award Winners

(Alphabetical Order)

Enterprise	Industry
Canon	Computers and office equipment
Fuji Xerox	Computers and office equipment
Honda Motor	Motor vehicles
IBM Japan	Computers and office equipment
Kao	Household and personal products
Nissan Motors	Motor Vehicles
Ricoh	Computers and office equipment
Sony	Electronics and electrical equipment
Toyota Motor	Motor vehicles

Source: A document entitled "2004 MAKE in Japan Report," Executive Summary, prepared by Rory L. Chase, Managing Director, Teleos, p. 2, obtained from http://www.knowledgebusiness.com

Figure 7-4 Japan's 2004 Most Admired Knowledge Enterprise (MAKE) Award winners

and is often referred to as the benchmark. That is why the Toyota Production System (TPS) and the "five whys" method have been illustrated as best practices in other chapters. Honda Motor, Kao, Nissan Motor, Canon, IBM Japan, and Fuji Xerox are also extraordinary organizations that are role models for transferring and reusing knowledge. Another MAKE recipient on the list is Sony, which will be discussed next in more depth. It's important to understand this company's journey and how it is addressing competition and its intellectual assets.

Sony Example

Millions of people know the Sony brand; it appears on products from TVs to the famous Walkman, music, videos, car radios, motion pictures, video cameras, and on and on. During 2004, Sony had 162,000 employees and worldwide annual sales of $72 billion.[24] Since the late 1990s, Sony has been driven by the Internet revolution, focusing on Internet delivery of games, movies, online shopping, and financial services. As illustrated in Figure 7-4, Sony was a 2004 MAKE Award Japan recipient, who also won for 2003.

Sony's challenges have been many, and it has moved into what's called a "silo of business," with both geographical and structural barriers restricting the sharing of knowledge. Sony seems to have hit the wall, staying in the innovation race with other competitors worldwide appears to be a challenge. Competitors from Korea and China have lower labor costs, and old-line American and European companies are attacking Sony in niche markets. By many accounts, Sony is no longer seen as an innovation leader.[25] Setbacks in Japan's Internet cell phone market and flat-panel displays have been highly visible failures. Because of quality problems, Sony even had to merge with Ericsson to survive in the Japanese cell phone market. In fact, since 1999, Sony has been trying to reinvent itself to meet the marketplace competition. Sony's future business model now focuses on selling movies, games, and Internet services rather than low-margin boxes (i.e., consumer products). The company has financed an internal good ideas initiative by acting as the venture capitalist to spur and relight the innovation flame inside its organization.

In contrast to Samsung, Sony does not have a visionary leader who sees knowledge sharing and reuse of intellectual capital as a primary path to excellence and has not made it part of the business strategy. Sony views itself as a knowledge-creating and innovation company, but it does not actively support a knowledge management framework that focuses on people, processes, tools, and culture. It does, nonetheless, actively concentrate on exceeding customer expectations with its products.

Sony has done well in the seven years of the MAKE Global Studies, being named a finalist in six of the seven years, but since 2001 its annual rank has slipped every year. In 2003 it was ranked twenty-fifth in the global ranking. While this is still good, the momentum is in the wrong direction. The preliminary 2004 Global Expert Panel review shows that Sony continues to decline across most knowledge management dimensions, especially organizational culture, innovation, and managing customer knowledge.[26] It is the opinion of the authors, therefore, that this means that Sony is not keeping pace in the knowledge transfer race and will have a difficult time until it integrates knowledge transfer into its business strategy so that it becomes a core competency and makes the necessary strategic cultural change.

Summary

Internationally, by joining a knowledge-sharing network, an organization can learn rapidly via best practices and lessons learned and develop its own path to growing and leveraging its intellectual capital. Prime examples given were the Best Practice Institute, the Global Benchmarking Network, and the KNOW Network, all of which operate internationally and can speed development and networking.

Examples have been provided to illustrate what it takes to win the knowledge transfer race. In the U.S. auto industry example, it was shown that even if a company drops behind in the race (e.g., Lincoln, Ford, and Buick), it can change its cultural emphasis toward learning and turn things around to accelerate back to top speed and become a leader. It just takes having a burning desire to change and a committed leadership and employee base. The other examples given (the IFIP Conference in Norway, Siemens, Samsung, and Sony) demonstrate that it's important to have a visionary leader, a commitment to change the culture, useful tools to aid the change, and recognition for knowledge workers who are good role models.

The Bottom Line for People in Small Global Organizations

The approaches that have been successfully used internationally by medium and large companies are available to the small international business owner, probably adjusted to a different scale. The same principles apply whether a company has 417,000 employees and operates in 190 countries, like Siemens or has fewer than 50 employees operating in two countries.

There are four points from this chapter on international trends that are listed as Tips 41, through 44 in the list of 55 tips for people in small businesses in Chapter 11. Briefly, they are

- Anticipate communicating in several languages and meeting the ISO 9000 quality management standard to be competitive.
- Encourage networks and a culture that brings people together to share and learn.
- Use the MAKE Award criteria because they're free and valuable.
- Study and learn from the MAKE Award winners.

First, management must concentrate on developing the company's culture for learning, comparing, and making improvements that add value. Do this every day; do not wait to be told or until a crisis occurs. Second, form networks of people that like to share and learn together. Use face-to-face meetings as much as possible (at least once a year) to build trust and familiarity. Feed off one another's enthusiasm and ideas. Form Communities of Practice (CoPs). These can be either inside the company or outside. The international consortiums are examples of this approach. If funds are available, go ahead and join the APQC's International Benchmarking Clearinghouse, Best Practices LLC's Global Benchmarking Council, or Teleos's the KNOW Network; the money will be well spent as an investment. Third, use tools that help reach inside and outside the business. Keep them simple, so that no one is intimidated. Fourth, make it easy to capture tacit know-how and to share; have a process that is well understood and used by all. Finally, look at and use the MAKE Award criteria to help your people focus on the long-term goal.

Endnotes

1. Based on a telephone interview of Rory Chase by Bill Baker during November 2004.
2. Ibid.
3. Ibid.
4. Melissie C. Rumizen, *The Complete Idiot's Guide to Knowledge Management*, [Indianapolis: Alpha (a member of Penguin Group), 2002], Foreword.

5. Peter M. Senge, *The Fifth Discipline: The Art and Practice of the Learning Organization* (New York: Currency Doubleday, 1990).
6. Asbjorn Rolstadas, *Benchmarking—Theory and Practice* (London: Chapman & Hall, 1995).
7. Robert C. Camp, *Benchmarking: The Search for Industry Best Practices That Lead to Superior Performance* (Milwaukee: Quality Press, 1989).
8. Best Practice Institute home page.
9. Robert C. Camp, *Global Cases in Benchmarking: Best Practices from Organizations Around the World* (Milwaukee: Quality Press, ASQ, 1998).
10. From the GBN Web page History, http://seth.ipk.fhg.de:8080/gbn1/history/.
11. Treacy, Michael and Wiersema, Fred, *The Discipline of Market Leaders*, Addison-Wesley, 1995.
12. July 20,2004, The J.D. Power and Associates 2004 Customer Service Index (CSI Study)
13. From Bill Baker's interview of Joe Ivers of J.D. Powers and Associates in November 2004
14. July 20, 2004, The J.D. Powers and Associates 2004 Customer Service Index (CSI Study)
15. From the Know Network Web site, http://www.knowledge business.com, 2005 European MAKE Winners Executive Summary, p.3
16. Information obtained from The Know Network Web site, http://www.knowledgebusiness.com
17. From the Teleos White Paper contrasting Sony and Samsung provided by Rory Chase in November 2004
18. Ibid.
19. Ibid.
20. Ibid.
21. From the Know Network Web site, http://www.knowledgebusiness.com, 2005 European MAKE Winners Executive Summary, p.3
22. Ibid.
23. From the Know Network Web site, http://www.knowledgebusiness.com/knowledgebusiness/projects/Knowledge_Library
24. From the Teleos 2004-2005 white paper contrasting Sony and Samsung, provided by Rory Chase, November 2004.
25. Ibid.
26. Ibid.

Chapter 8

Integrating and Leveraging Best Practices Knowledge into Six Sigma Strategies: Mastering Phase 4 of the Knowledge Transfer Race

Introduction

This chapter is about how to design, integrate, and leverage best practices benchmarking and knowledge transfer into Six Sigma strategies. In terms of the knowledge transfer race, the focus is on mastering phase 4 by creating knowledge that's convertible into customer value and profit. And while many references to Six Sigma have been made in earlier chapters, this chapter specifically addresses how to leverage intellectual capital to make a Six Sigma strategy deployment more successful. The authors believe that too often, Six Sigma deployments have neglected to consider best practices.

This discussion begins where the Chapter 6 overview ended, establishing that Six Sigma strategies, like the Baldrige criteria, the European Quality Award, the Shingo Prize, and ISO 9000, are reusable forms of intellectual asset transfers. What the authors contend is that while *Lean Six Sigma* is a codified road map that drives out defects and waste, when best practices benchmarking is not a key part of the approach, it is a suboptimal deployment. On the other hand, when best practices benchmarking is integrated into any Six Sigma or performance excellence system, it will create high-speed pathways that lead any organization to excellent performance. Thus, the integration of best practices benchmarking addressed in this chapter and the transfer and reuse of intellectual capital addressed in Chapter 9 will enable contestants to master phase 4 of the knowledge transfer race.

A Deeper Definition and Description of 6σ

In Chapter 6, the word *sigma* was described as the eighteenth letter (Σ or σ) of the Greek alphabet. When the English adjective *six* precedes σ and forms Six Sigma or 6σ, the phrase usually takes on a statistical and strategic meaning. Statistically, σ signifies the standard deviation of a population and measures the variation or dissimilarity among products or outputs. In truth, there's variation in almost everything, including, for example, the weather. But the concern in business and industry is the variation that exceeds the requirements of customers or the noncompliance of products and services with customer expectations.

Any instances of noncompliance or excess variation are considered defects. Therefore, using the example of an automobile, sigma or σ measures the variation against all the vehicle's specifications for the engine, transmission, drive train, braking, steering, power windows, and other apparatus, such as the air conditioning, defrost, ventilation, and heating systems. And so there is a statistical measurement of manufactured automobiles giving "output without defect" results for every million opportunities. Furthermore, σ is just as applicable to any output, whether it is electronic transactions, baked muffins, health-care services, tractor performance, water meter service, cable television availability, or any other manufactured goods or services. In ascending order, higher coefficient levels of σ indicate geometrically higher levels of defect-free output. As displayed in Table 8-1, the difference between 6σ and 2σ is tremendous, as was first illustrated in Chapter 6.

Consider instead a more realistic comparison between 3σ and 6σ performance. It's the difference between a 93.32 percent and a 99.99966 percent defect-free rate, meaning that there's a reduction of 66,803 defects per million. At the 4σ operating level, there's dramatic improvement, but there are still 6,210 defects per million outputs. Because most of the world's best organizations operate at between 3σ and 4σ, it's clear that 6σ is more of an end game or strategic goal. Even 5σ is extremely difficult to achieve, as it represents 99.98 percent defect-free output, or 233 defects per million opportunities (DPMO).

Table 8-1　The Differences between 6σ, 5σ, 4σ, 3σ, and 2σ

Sigma Level	Defects PMO*	Output Without Defect	Output with Defects
6	3.4	99.99966%	0.00036%
5	233	99.98%	0.02%
4	6,210	99.38%	0.62%
3	66,807	93.32%	6.68%
2	308,537.0	67.20%	32.80%

*PMO = per million opportunities

For most organizations, until they create more technological capability, it's nearly impossible to consistently achieve 6σ or 99.99966 percent defect-free output levels, except for a handful of processes for several months or several quarters. It's virtually the same as perfection. That is why managers need to think of 6σ as a strategic goal. It is synonymous with a business performance excellence strategy that requires a revolutionary culture change that's directed at eliminating variation and defects. In Chapter 6, 6σ was defined as a strategic approach to improvement. Motorola, AlliedSignal (now Honeywell), Bank of America, Citibank, DuPont, Dow Chemical, and Raytheon are prominent organizations pursuing such a strategy. These organizations are leveraging a relentless focus in their use of root-cause solutions to drive out wasteful rework. Table 6-4 was provided as a description of "The Characteristics of 6σ systems."

Four key characteristics were presented. First, 3.4 defects per million outputs should be thought of as an ultimate goal. This was discussed in terms of exceptional organizations operating between 3σ and 4σ while gradually elevating parts or "islands" of their operations to 5σ and sometimes to 6σ. For the foreseeable future, there will be oceans of opportunity where it will take all the efforts that a completely engaged, trained, and fully equipped organization can muster to achieve and maintain levels of performance between 4σ and 5σ. In an information age and amidst the knowledge transfer race, this will be as good as most will be able to achieve.

Second, the CEO and senior leaders need to have passion and be totally committed to doing this properly. Earlier glimpses of the actions of Larry Bossidy at AlliedSignal and Honeywell, Jack Welch at GE, Glen Barton at Caterpillar, and Dan Burnham at Raytheon illustrate the kind of passion and commitment required. It takes such a visionary CEO to launch Six Sigma and stay the course to succeed. Clearly, Six Sigma is not a strategy for the meek or nonchalant.

Third, the enterprise needs to have organizationwide deployment of process management and redesign. In Chapter 4, a case was made for using the APQC's Process Classification Framework (PCF) to classify best practices and intellectual capital as well as to support becoming a process-centered or managed organization. Value is created through processes, the mechanisms that transform inputs into outputs to fulfill the requirements and expectations of customers. Superior processes create superior value. The "managing by process" emphasis is essential to achieving *Lean Six Sigma* levels of excellence. IPO (Inputs-Processing-Outputs) analysis is the backbone for identifying root cause solutions for eliminating waste and for working with process suppliers on the input side and with customers' needs and expectations on the output side.

Last, having a common data-driven DMBAIC (define, measure, benchmark, analyze, improve, and control) improvement process is essential to creating a continual pipeline of root cause–based projects that individually and collectively move the organization closer to 6σ performance levels. The creation of the DMBAIC process is akin to Galileo's seventeenth-century development of the scientific method, which added structure to experimentation and required scientific findings to be based on facts. This requires a major culture change in organizations. An infrastructure is needed to train, equip, empower, facilitate, coordinate (Black Belts, Green Belts, process owners, champions, and so on), and sustain improvements installed in processes.

Raytheon's Approach and What Makes It Unique

We launched *Raytheon Six Sigma* in January 1999. The driver was that we were a company that had come together by acquisitions in '96 and '97. A number of deals were done very quickly of companies that while in the same market (defense) had been, in many cases, blood competitors previously. So, you can imagine the intensity of feelings that were taken on in this new company, as everybody came together under the same umbrella. It was clear that we needed to do something to bring this organization together. In essence, we needed to create a common language throughout the organization. I also had a view at the time that we were a technology company, an engineering company with over 25,000 engineers. What do you know about engineers? You know they're smart, that they love to solve problems, and that they're data-driven. It was clear to me that this confluence of things—the tension that existed in the organization, the need for a common language, and our competencies—all conspired to say there was one clear answer for us: Six Sigma.[1]

Dan Burnham, former chairman and CEO,
Raytheon Company

By the end of 2000, the new Raytheon, built by acquisitions and mergers and led by CEO Dan Burnham, had 100,000 employees and $20 billion in annual revenues. This "new" company consisted of the combination of Magnavox, CAE Link, E-Systems, General Dynamics Missiles, ST Systems (STX), Hughes Aircraft, Chrysler Technologies, Texas Instruments Defense Systems & Electronics Group, AlliedSignal Communication Systems, and the "old" Raytheon.[2] Consistent with Burnham's earlier quoted remarks, it was the confluence of several factors that led him to advocate and his board of directors to approve the implementation of Six Sigma, which they customized and have named *Raytheon Six Sigma* or *R6σ*.

To design R6σ, Burnham formed a blue ribbon team that used benchmarking to learn from the leaders of 6σ at that point in time. As detailed as a strategic benchmarking case study in Chapter 2, the blue ribbon team did benchmarking exchanges with Motorola, AlliedSignal, and GE and did significant secondary research at other companies, including Motorola and American Express. As a result, Raytheon combined *Lean Enterprise* principles and tools with Six Sigma tools and "change management" concepts into the design of R6σ. Classical *Six Sigma* concepts were borrowed from Motorola, influenced by Motorola's footing in hardware design and manufacturing. *R6σ* is based on five principles, which are listed in Table 8-2.

In the end, *R6σ* is much broader in scope than the approaches used by Motorola, AlliedSignal, and GE. Since Dan Burnham had been the former vice chairman of AlliedSignal and the head of its Six Sigma program, he helped to mold *R6σ*, taking advantage of his firsthand knowledge of the design factors that proved to be strengths, while ensuring that the historically weak areas were bolstered. Burnham also wanted to show improvement savings more quickly in order to establish Raytheon as having the "new and improved Six Sigma." With *R6σ*, all company processes and functions are targeted and included for improvement, as in TQM—it is a T6σ or Total Six Sigma model. But again, Raytheon's name for it is *R6σ*.

R6σ has been built on legacy company knowledge and talent, combined with customer focus, culture change, and tools. Employees are empowered to make improvements in their job and identify improvement opportunities elsewhere, which often leads to the creation of *R6σ* project teams, which are facilitated by Experts (Black Belts) and Specialists (Green Belts).

Empowering employees the way Raytheon does has led to culture change. First, it requires extensive internal communication to keep the focus on customers and customer value. Second, a huge commitment to education, training, and tools has been made to create the competencies that people need if they are to be successful. A support infrastructure was also created to provide employees and project teams with expert assistance from *R6σ* Champions, Master Experts, Experts, and Specialists. The Raytheon toolkit contains more than five forms of benchmarking and knowledge management.

In fact, Raytheon utilizes an Organizational Benchmarking Maturity Matrix, shown in Figure 8-1. The idea behind the maturity matrix is to be a model for corporate leaders and individual major business leaders that displays the competencies required for developing a mature benchmarking capability. Level 4 represents a mature capability, whereas Level 5 is considered world-class benchmarking for an organization. To be effective, an organization has to be active and competent in all four dimensions: the management culture has to appreciate the value of benchmarking and promote it; a focal point is necessary in order to develop a common

Table 8-2 The Five Principles of Raytheon's *R6σ*

I. Value in the eyes of the customer
2. Eliminate waste/variation in value stream
3. Make value flow at the pull of the customer
4. Involve, align, and empower employees
5. Continuously improve knowledge in pursuit of perfection

Source: Raytheon

process and be the recognized external and internal contact; a common process has to be well understood; and a set of tools has to be developed to reuse contacts and benchmarking projects. Raytheon uses this matrix in its in-house training and has shared it with many other companies.

As pictured in Figure 8-2, benchmarking has been integrated into the *R6σ* six-step closed process in steps: (1) visualize (2) commit, (3) prioritize, (4) characterize, (5) improve, and (6) achieve. Within step 1 of the *R6σ* improvement process, visualize, benchmarking is one of Raytheon's most powerful tools. *R6σ* project teams use benchmarks and best practices knowledge to create a quantified vision of the desired future state and target performance. Also in the visualize step, *R6σ* teams are trained to look for other similar *R6σ* projects, best practices, and lessons learned, to see if they are duplicating a previously completed project. Their goal is not only to understand their own process and metrics, but also to look for outside benchmarks and knowledge. To illustrate this, it's helpful to look at the work of one *R6σ* project team.

A *R6σ* project team leveraged best practices benchmarking and other tools to improve the invoice payment process for the B-2 bomber program of Raytheon's Air Combat and Strike Systems. Benchmarking enabled the team to envision a target of reducing outstanding invoices from $7 million to below $1 million.[3] The benchmark gap of $6 million created an immediate need for change. Best practices benchmarking, the discovery of ideal invoice processing best practices, process flow-

Organizational
Benchmarking Maturity Matrix

Level	Management Culture	Benchmarking Focal Point	Process	Tools
5	Benchmarking is • How we do our job • Learning & Sharing are valued	Network across • Functions • Sites	• Awards • Recognition • Communication	Integrated Knowledge Sharing • Intranet • Extranet • Internet
4	• Expects Long Term Improvement • Stretch goals based on benchmarking	Team	• Coaching • Key Priorities	• Broadcast Messages • Intranet • Push • Pull
3	• Takes Action • Assigns Resources	Full Time Person	• Formal Training • Success Stories	Electronic Database
2	Sees Need to • Compare • Learn	Part time Benchmarking Starpoint	• Defined Process • 1st Success	Document Files
1	Operates on • Short Term Fixes • Profit Driven	None	Industrial Tourism	• Word of Mouth • Memos

Figure 8-1   Organizational Benchmarking Maturity Matrix

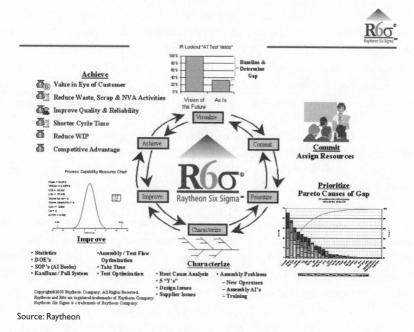

Source: Raytheon

Figure 8-2 Raytheon's Six Sigma Framework

chart comparisons with other best-in-class organizations, cause-and-effect diagrams, and root cause analysis were used. Before long, the *R6σ* project team became a joint Raytheon-Northrop Grumman team (Northrop Grumman was the customer in this case). In the end, the team used best practices to design new and better forms, standards, and communications while breaking down barriers to achieve the vision and close the performance gap. This is but one example of what hundreds of *R6σ* project teams are accomplishing with the help of best practices benchmarking.

Furthermore, to support the benchmarking needs of its *R6σ* project teams and organization, Raytheon created the senior management position of knowledge management and benchmarking champion. This position, formerly occupied by one of this book's coauthors, oversees the *R6σ* program and provides Raytheon leaders, process owners, Black and Green belts, and *R6σ* project teams with several forms of knowledge and best practices assistance that vary by project. This assistance includes, but is not limited to, benchmarking education and/or training, creation of aids such as Raytheon's Organizational Benchmarking Maturity Matrix (Figure 8-1), and opening access to intelligence by providing a conduit to a worldwide network of benchmarking contacts, partners, and suppliers of solutions. Representing all the needs of Raytheon, the knowledge management and benchmarking champion budgets for and acts as the Raytheon focal point on the Best Practices, LLC, Global Benchmarking Council (GBC) and the APQC International Benchmarking Clearinghouse (IBC) Consortium.

The Raytheon knowledge management and benchmarking champion also understands the value of and uses several important outside resources. Noteworthy among these are the GBC best practices database (www.BestPracticeDatabase.com), fast track benchmarking, and the IBC Best Practice Repository (www.apqc.org). These are sources or pathways to the knowledge that $R6\sigma$ project teams often need when they are in step 1, visualize, depending on their time and resource constraints. The sensibility involved in customizing the benchmarking assistance provided to any $R6\sigma$ team is captured by the belief, "An 80 percent solution is better than the 100 percent one that can't happen."[4]

Because many $R6\sigma$ project teams can't devote two to three months to a full-blown project, Raytheon developed what it calls the *Raytheon Blitz*. This is a short (often one-week) *kaizen* project, as pictured in Figure 8-3. In such cases, and when it's found beneficial, fast track quick-turnaround benchmarking (which will be discussed in Chapter 10) is used. Having a benchmarking champion focal point along with the tools, process, and management culture (as previously discussed with regard to Raytheon's Organizational Benchmarking Maturity Matrix), and resources (GBC and IBC memberships, and so on) has enabled Raytheon to fully integrate best practices benchmarking into $R6\sigma$. In addition, by including the knowledge transfer process in the mix, as is done in step 6, achieve, Raytheon also requires that $R6\sigma$ project teams share their best practices and lessons learned during execution of the project, so that other teams can take advantage of this new knowledge. Raytheon captures, shares, and reuses, better than most organizations, its process improvement knowledge throughout the organization.

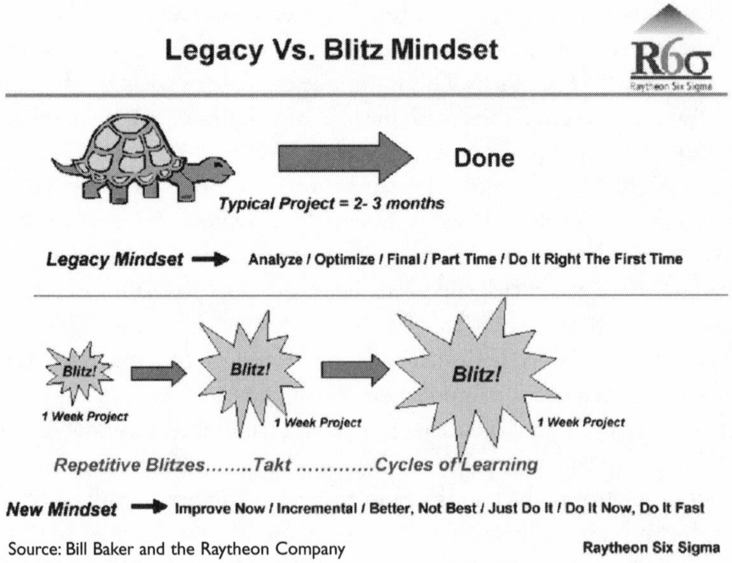

Legacy Vs. Blitz Mindset

$R6\sigma$
Raytheon Six Sigma

Done

Typical Project = 2- 3 months

Legacy Mindset ➡ Analyze / Optimize / Final / Part Time / Do It Right The First Time

Blitz! ➡ Blitz! ➡ Blitz!

1 Week Project   *1 Week Project*   *1 Week Project*

Repetitive Blitzes........Takt ....Cycles of Learning

New Mindset ➡ Improve Now / Incremental / Better, Not Best / Just Do It / Do It Now, Do It Fast

Source: Bill Baker and the Raytheon Company   **Raytheon Six Sigma**

Figure 8-3 Legacy vs. blitz mindset

As a result, Raytheon is a leader at importing innovations from the world's stockpile of knowledge. What difference does that make? In short, it means that the company has better, quicker, and cheaper performance. As a result, too, Raytheon's improvement pipeline has a continual fill, contains more innovation pulled in from outside, and is accelerating improvement from the 3σ to 4σ range to the high-performance 5σ to 6σ range. This concerted effort to drive out defects, and also remove waste and the costs associated with it, eliminates the causes of customer dis-satisfaction, improves profitability, and increases Raytheon's competitiveness. For 2001, the bottom line is that Raytheon's operating profit increased by $150 million, and cash flow improved by $300 million.[5] Raytheon's people achieved these remarkable results by using the *R6σ* process, strengthened by the inclusion and integration of best practices benchmarking.

Five Key Lessons About 6σ Results Learned So Far

This is a book about how to achieve 6σ excellence through the transfer and reuse of knowledge and best practices benchmarking. It is not another book about 6σ. Yet, unfortunately, most 6σ approaches and systems have neglected the systematic use of benchmarks and the identification and importing of best practices. The concept of best practices was explored and defined in Chapter 2. A best practice is a process, input, step, output, or enabling capability that fully satisfies customers, produces superior results in at least one operation, performs as reliably as any alternative, and is adaptable by others. The best practices of others are imported through one form or another of benchmarking.

It just makes good business sense to consider the experience of others. Those who rely totally on internally generated solutions are doomed to perennially rein-vent the wheel, since they do not learn and benefit from the progress in their industry and others across the globe. Many of the benefits of benchmarking were presented in Chapter 2. Perhaps one of the most important benefits of benchmarking is that it "teaches organizations new lessons in competitiveness."[6]

Speaking of lessons, there are five lessons to learn from the experiences of organizations that have been trying for years to achieve 6σ excellence. Clearly, one or more forms of benchmarking are useful in some of the lessons. When this is the case, a prescription will be made. Also, some, but not all, of the lessons presented involve how a 6σ system is implemented.

> **Lesson 1:** Integrate best practice benchmarking and internal knowledge management into Six Sigma. They provide the necessary learning and innovative adaptation to achieve the highest performance.

Too often, Six Sigma solutions have become internally focused because they haven't utilized benchmarking. Because Black and Green Belt facilitators have not been proficient facilitators of benchmarking, the teams they've assisted have instead been instructed to focus almost entirely on the DMAIC (define, measure, analyze, improve, and control) framework. This DMAIC focus has largely ignored leveraging breakthrough best practices that have already been developed elsewhere and had focused instead on the technical tools that a single Black Belt has available internally. This omission can be remedied. For one thing, experts (Black Belts) and specialists (Green Belts) need to be trained and certified in benchmarking techniques. Up until now, almost all the training they receive has to do with controlling variation. Benchmarking training has rarely been emphasized because of the misperception that benchmarking studies are lengthy and require outside contacts that are not conveniently available. Yet, Black Belts and Green Belts may also be supported by, say, a program office for benchmarking, where memberships, networks, Internet fast turnaround benchmarking, informal benchmarking, and other tools and techniques may be rapidly accessed and used to gain intelligence.

In addition, a proven remedy may be formulated through the study of organizations that have already successfully integrated benchmarking into their 6σ methodology. One such organization is the Bank of America. When it first began 6σ, benchmarking was already apart of it. Figure 8-4, "Bank of America's Integrated Benchmarking Process," displays how the bank has integrated best practices benchmarking and *Hoshin* into how it strives to achieve Six Sigma.

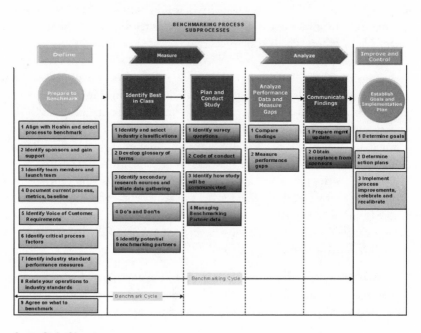

Source: Bank of America

Figure 8-4 Bank of America's Integrated Benchmarking Process

Importance of Benchmarking for Bank of America

During 2001, Bank of America created a position with the title senior vice president, integration and benchmarking. Since filling this position, as the title suggests, the bank has made a concerted effort to integrate benchmarking into all of its improvement work on quality, productivity, and cost projects. Bank of America is one of the three largest banks in the United States and one of the world's leading financial services companies. In the United States, this bank has a coast-to-coast presence in 21 states, with 4,400 offices and 13,000 ATMs in 2002.

The bank launched a customer-focused strategy during 2001 along with its customized version of a Six Sigma strategy.[7] Almost simultaneously, the bank integrated benchmarking into its Six Sigma platform, as shown in Figure 8-4. Benchmarking was integrated into the bank's adoption of the traditional 6σ DMAIC process, which all of its 6σ project teams follow. To that end, here are the DMAIC process step definitions that Bank of America uses:[8]

Define: Identify activities/processes to benchmark; align your project with strategic goals; study/measure your own processes; relate your operation to industry standards.

Measure: Identify best-in-class organizations by leveraging secondary research; if necessary, directly contact best-in-class organizations for exchange and or new learning.

Analyze: Compare findings to our current processes; determine gaps; and communicate findings.

Improve and Control: Determine process improvement goals; develop action plans; implement and validate success.

As can be seen from Figure 8-4, there are nine steps in the process of "Prepare to Benchmark." First, there needs to be alignment with *Hoshin* when selecting processes to benchmark. The processes selected must be tied to strategic goals. Then, there's a series of steps to identify sponsors and team members, document the current process, and identify the voice of customer requirements, critical process factors, and industry standards (i.e., benchmarks), resulting in agreement about what process to benchmark.

Next, there are five steps for the process "Identify Best in Class," resulting in a list of benchmarking partners. Third, there are four steps for "Plan and Conduct Study," resulting in "managing benchmarking partner data." Fourth, under "Analyze Performance Data and Measure Gaps," there are two steps producing the output of measured gaps. Fifth, under "Communicate Findings," there are two steps for preparing a management update and obtaining acceptance from sponsors. Last, for the process "Establish Goals and Implementation Plan," there are three steps for determining goals and action plans, ending with "implement process improvements, celebrate, and recalibrate." Together, these processes and subprocess steps effectively integrate benchmarking into the way 6σ project teams operate at Bank of America.

> **Lesson 2:** Speed up the cycle time for improvement projects. Use of *Kaizen* (like) *Blitzes, Lean* methodology, and fast turnaround benchmarking will all help. Avoid tendencies toward bureaucracy and "know it all" attitudes.

When new Six Sigma project teams are formed and seek help, the answer to the question, "How much time do you have to get the information you need?" will usually dictate what's done. With few exceptions, speed is of the essence. The current business climate dictates *faster, faster, faster* as the mode of operation. Thus, more techniques that speed up the processes are needed. In addition, the need for speedy results will continue to increase, so everything will have to be compressed. Don't try to fight it; accept it and work on speed every day. This is the knowledge transfer race, and the internal need is for speed.

Time constraints may limit the search for knowledge to do a data search or a best practices database search instead of a full benchmarking study or surveying a network of experts. Well, then, maybe organizations should be obtaining access to continually updated best practices databases and networks, so that when those quick-turnaround requests come, the knowledge will already be on hand. The authors call this "off the shelf" or "just in time knowledge."

Knowledge has been found to be "sticky," meaning that it tends to stay right where it is unless it's transported using the transfer process. Facilitated knowledge transfer (FKT) occurs when a benchmarking expert helps 6σ project teams locate best practices. Until that happens, 6σ project teams often flounder, trying to find out how other organizations are performing the very process the team is trying to improve. Individuals usually access their own private network of experts, to the exclusion of everyone they don't know. FKT broadens the network of experts exponentially and provides teams with quicker access to much more knowledge. Systematic use of FKT, however, usually requires an organization to have a clear knowledge management strategy, which is recommended. This strategy should include targeted and systematic transfers of specific tacit (unwritten) knowledge into explicit (codified) knowledge. The strategy needs to be specific enough to locate the correct tacit knowledge, so that it is captured, documented, made accessible, used, and reused as needed. It's important that organizations also develop networks of subject-matter experts who are accessible to process owners and 6σ project teams. Fast-turnaround benchmarking will be reviewed in Chapter 10. The issue is speed, continually achieving it for improvement projects.

Lesson 3: Create more focus on improvement projects that improve financial performance and competitiveness. Strategic importance tests and better prioritization techniques are needed to ensure that enough of the right improvement projects are done right.

First, better linkage with the attributes that are of greatest importance to customers is needed. When documented and weighted, such techniques as quality function deployment (QFD) introduce discipline into prioritizing improvement projects and aligning them with those attributes that are of greatest importance. More focus should be placed on being better than the competition on the attributes that are of greatest importance to customers. Benchmarks, gap analysis, and performance targets will aid the effort. The preoccupation with defect reduction can't ignore competitive advantages and disadvantages, including core competencies.

Second, the need to improve financial performance is of high priority and never-ending. In fact, from the results of several studies, including the Bain & Company annual management tool usage mentioned in Chapter 1, not only is financial performance the top priority for senior managers, it's four times more important than any second priority, such as creating long-term performance capability. Obviously, Six Sigma—or any other management tool—must support executive priorities. Therefore, financial performance should receive more attention when prioritizing, ranking, and deciding where to deploy Black Belts and Green Belts to work on 6σ projects. The financial folks need to participate in the selection of projects and also in reporting the financial results to management. On the other end of the spectrum, too often, 6σ project teams are created to address performance areas where the potential cost savings or return on investment is not significant to management.

Lesson 4: Instead of being difficult, Six Sigma needs to be simplified and made easy for small organizations, so that they can make a minimal investment and achieve a 100 percent payback in six months. Because large organizations have thousands of people at many locations using different vocabularies, have hundreds of suppliers, and so on, it is difficult to make it simple. All this complexity has made Six Sigma complicated and difficult for small organizations to deploy.

Every aspect of change management—CEO involvement, education, 6σ project team materials, Black and Green Belt facilitation—needs to be made clear, simple, and easy to understand. At the minimum, a CEO must do four things to simplify Six Sigma: (1) become passionately committed to Six Sigma and to making it as uncomplicated as possible; (2) designate one person as the focal point for facilitating, orchestrating, and overseeing communication that meets people's needs for under-standing; (3) ensure that everyone is trained to at least the level of awareness, so that everyone will be "in on" the jargon; and (4) empower the workforce through a vision, strategy, and policies. Creating simplicity begins with having simple goals that are easily communicated. For example, there is straightforwardness in giving Black and Green Belt facilitators the goal of encouraging 6σ teams to target a full payback on the investment they make within six months and having a combined goal for an annual return of at least 6 percent of gross revenues.

In addition, just as the simple concept of span measurements removed some of the statistical complexity of 6σ for GE employees, a lot more needs to be done to make 6σ simple. Often, such straightforward tools as checklists are suggested. To "walk the talk," in Chapter 1 and at the end of later chapters, the authors have added a subsection entitled, "The Bottom Line for People in Small Organizations." In that section, the authors have tried to simplify everything in the chapter for people in small organizations. What's said answers the question, "What would an organiza-tion with only 20 employees need to do?" What's the bottom line for that organi-zation? Every effort is being made to make the knowledge as simple to understand as possible. In the same way as for the imaginary small company, it is suggested that Six Sigma be made less complicated and easier to understand and apply.

> **Lesson 5:** Instead of worrying about whether you are at 3σ, 4σ, or 6σ, the idea is to know how your performance compares and to keep filling up your "improvement pipeline" so that improvements can be made as fast as possible. Let's face reality; all organizations are driven by financial success. To succeed, each year, every individual needs to prove that she or he has made enough of a contribution. Thus, everyone needs to be on the lookout for new opportunities to fill the pipeline.

Too often, people get so preoccupied and distracted in a forest that they forget to search for light and find the way out. The reality is that few organizations will actu-ally achieve 6σ for all their products and services. But some preoccupy themselves with the goal when, in reality, it's the journey that's important to focus on. This is why the authors describe the knowledge transfer race as never-ending. Incredibly, improving a process from 3σ to 4σ reduces defects by a factor of ten times. And, equally astonishing, bettering a process from 4σ to 5σ produces a 26 times improvement! So the journey to 6σ is a tough and exhausting marathon that, like climbing Mount Everest, is not for the fainthearted or for people who aren't fully committed. Nonetheless, just as equipment for mountain climbing speeds the ascent and makes it more secure, best practices benchmarking speeds the journey to 6σ and makes it less painful. It's a heavy-duty tool for the tough journey. It's all about the process of achieving excellence, and it's unlikely that everyone will arrive at the 6σ destination. Since this is about a journey, therefore, what's suggested is to focus on keeping the improvement pipeline filled with ample new projects so that enough improvement is actually achieved each year to consider the total company performance as remarkable. For this reason, the answers we consider most helpful are replies to three questions: "How do I compare?" "Who's the best at this?" and "What am I doing to improve and become the best?"

Table 8-3 displays a list of pitfalls to avoid during the journey.

Best practices benchmarking is a huge help because, like a faucet of water turned wide open in a desert, it's a perpetual source of new ideas that can help quench an organization's endless thirst for innovation. Like a river that never dries up, benchmarking never stops identifying practices and knowledge that have produced outstanding results in one circumstance and can be reused in new situations to produce similar results. It's been said time and time again that necessity is the mother of invention. Likewise, it can be said that an extremely unfavorable benchmark comparison creates such a necessity for improvement that it is the father of "borrowing shamelessly." *Borrowing shamelessly* is the homegrown phrase of 1989 Baldrige Award recipient Milliken & Company, which coined the phrase to describe the company's approach to benchmarking.

Key Success Factors for the Long Haul

1. A multi-year plan will be needed in order to achieve 6σ excellence. Culture change is intense, confusing, conflicted, hard, painful, and difficult. Just going from 3σ to 4σ will be an enormous challenge. Then, the difficulties in going from 4σ to 5σ will only be greater. So the plan should anticipate obstacles and provide for the capability and resourcefulness to overcome them.

Table 8-3　Authors' List of Pitfalls to Avoid

- Don't focus on winning a defects elimination game.
- Don't create projects of lower priority.
- Avoid arrogance and know-it-all attitudes.
- Don't focus only on internally created solutions.
- Don't ignore the "soft" administrative side of the business.
- Don't ignore benchmarking because of time urgency.
- An 80 percent solution is better than the 100 percent one that can't happen.
- Don't create projects that take too long.
- Avoid anything that makes Six Sigma bureaucratic.
- Make sure Six Sigma projects are linked to the business strategy.

2. Establish a position for a leader who champions best practices benchmarking and heads the corporate program office that is responsible for the process, as Raytheon and Bank of America have done. Establishing such a position indicates a commitment to incorporating enough methods (e.g., the Benchmarking Maturity Matrix); resources (e.g., Global Benchmarking Council and APQC membership); education and training; integration into the strategic plan, the improvement plans (e.g., Six Sigma), and a network of subject-matter experts and benchmarking contacts. Proactive organizations may be able to cost-justify such a position by including knowledge management as another part of the position's responsibility, as Raytheon did. After all, in the long run, organizations will need to create, identify, collect, and organize best practices and internal knowledge. Once best practices are collected, it's knowledge management that enables them to be spread around the organization for transfer and reuse. For small organizations, instead of establishing a new position, it's recommended that this responsibility become one-third of the responsibilities of an existing manager, preferably a respected rising star who has the visionary capability to lead change.

3. Strive to make benchmarks, benchmarking, and the use of best practices an everyday core competency of management people in the organization. Just as the exercise in Chapter 1 identified four stages leading up to unconscious competence, connect benchmarking to information cycles feeding the strategic plan, to daily and weekly decision making, and so on. "How does your plan compare to the benchmark?" can be a question that drives constructive change.

4. Embed best practices benchmarking and knowledge transfer into the training, performance reviews, and career growth experiences of Six Sigma Black Belts and Green Belts. Successful 6σ organizations have found it effective to require their high-potential managers to become trained and serve for specified periods as Black Belts supporting 6σ project teams. They need to become competent in benchmarking. This kind of rotation satisfies the requirement for support of the teams, while sending a message to the organization about the importance of 6σ, benchmarking, and knowledge management expertise to aspiring managers in the organization.

5. Leaders need to inspect in order to see the extent to which people in the organization are going external to capture ideas and to see that the knowledge gained is being shared throughout the organization. Such inspection will continually reinforce the importance of benchmarking and sharing of knowledge.

6. Modify the rewards and recognition processes so that the right benchmarking behaviors are rewarded and reinforced. Indeed, benchmarking could become a core competency, and this, over time, will cause employees to develop considerable proficiency in best practices benchmarking along with employee problem-solving techniques, process management, change management, and other 6σ tools and techniques.

The Meaning of "*Lean Six Sigma*" and Why to Care About It

Lean is a relatively new term that has been added to the vocabulary of improvement practitioners within manufacturing and beyond in recent years. Depending on who's asked, *Lean* is a manufacturing philosophy that shortens the lead time between customer order and shipment, or it's a systematic approach to eliminating waste.[9] But wait, others contend that *Lean* is merely focusing on the value-added expenditure of resources from customers' viewpoints. These two interpretations, however, seem too limited and vague to explain what it means to be *Lean* in a context other than thin. A definition that's more helpful is:

> *Lean* is a systematic approach to identifying and eliminating waste (nonvalue added activities) through continuous improvement by flowing the product only when the customer needs it (called 'pull') in pursuit of perfection.[10]

With roots back to the 1950s, the Japanese auto maker Toyota is credited with first introducing the new manufacturing system, called the Toyota Production System, that concentrates on reducing and eliminating non-value-added tasks. This system eventually was popularized in the United States under the umbrella name of "*Lean* manufacturing." The central concept was that customers should not be required to pay for the costs of any wasteful activities, those that do not add value to the manufacturing process. Therefore, such waste should be identified and eliminated. Over time, these *Lean* concepts have been broadened beyond the manufacturing shop floor and are known today as "*Lean* Enterprise" and "*Lean* Thinking."[11] Now, *Lean* concepts apply to all business processes, beginning as early as the order placements process and continuing all the way downstream until the final payment is received. From start to finish, processes are streamlined, bottlenecks removed, and non-value-adding steps purged.

A key to achieving business excellence is integrating *Lean Enterprise concepts* and 6σ and deploying them together to complement each other as a "one-two punch."[12] In fact, Bonnie Smith observes, "By looking at projects through both the *Lean* and Six Sigma lenses, you have the precision, actionable tools needed to find hidden problems while making sure you don't overlook the obvious."[13] The argument is that while Six Sigma is effective in controlling variation, Six Sigma projects often take too long (from six to nine months) to complete. Another drawback is that the expert Black Belts and Green Belts are often cut off from what's happening on the shop floor. To compensate for these two shortcomings, it is argued, *Lean* initiatives are well suited for quick action by attacking low-hanging fruit with quick-hitting *kaizen* events to reduce non-value-added process steps. The idea is to get both initiatives working together to achieve results that are consistently superior to what either system could achieve alone.[14]

To illustrate this concept, consider Raytheon, which has designed *R6σ* in order to combine quick hits with longer-term improvements as part of the same improvement project. The Raytheon argument became, "If you eliminate defects à la Six Sigma, it helps the organization also reduce nonvalue efforts and also reduce cycle time and defects." Accordingly, the organization has a double-barreled approach to achieving excellence. In many cases, organizations will be able to make initial *Lean* cycle-time improvements and then follow-up with Six Sigma variability reduction efforts to drive the overall project results to new levels. Thus, by combining *Lean* tools and 6σ tools, the Black Belt has an large array of options to draw from when developing a plan for a project.[15] One group of tools that needs to be in the Black Belt toolkit is benchmarking.

Authors' Process to Achieve 6σ Excellence

Though it's not the only approach, the commonly accepted and growing approach to achieving 6σ is to implement a proven or customized version of strategic Six Sigma. Total Quality Management (TQM) updated business process reengineering; the European Quality Award criteria and the Baldrige criteria are other systematic approaches that (in varying degrees) also lead to 6σ levels of performance. In any case, what's important is that best practices benchmarking be an integral part of the approach. Like the four-year process to achieve an Olympic gold medal, whatever approach is adopted should pave a road to the same 6σ excellence. While strategic Six Sigma is promising and shows results, so was business process reengineering (BPR) in the 1990s. An approach can even be a combination of several systematic endeavors, including *Lean Enterprise* concepts. Accordingly, the authors suggest the improvement process in Table 8-4 as the steps to be taken to achieve excellence.

In the first column is the traditional or standard Six Sigma DMAIC process used by many organizations that, with one exception, have already deployed Six Sigma in one form or another. For example, DMAIC is used by Bank of America and many others. The one exception to DMAIC in column 1 is that, for obvious reasons, "Benchmark" has been added as step 3 to form DMBAIC. In the second column, Raytheon's process is portrayed because it exists, is proven, and isn't solely Six Sigma dependent. The third column represents the authors' suggested process steps to achieve 6σ excellence. The authors' process starts with the DMAIC process and incorporates "Benchmark" (generic for best practices benchmarking) along with steps for "Plan," "Commit," "Achieve," and substitutes "Sustain" for "Control."

The key addition is step 5, "Benchmark," which is a generic term that incorporates any and all aspects of benchmarking to gain world-class knowledge before embarking on improvements. In Chapter 2, benchmarking was defined as "the

Table 8-4 Authors' Process for Achieving 6σ Excellence

DMBAIC Modified	Raytheon Process	Authors' Process
	1. Visualize	1. Plan
	2. Commit	2. Commit
1. Define		3. Define
2. Measure		4. Measure
3. Benchmark (added)	3. Prioritize	5. Benchmark
4. Analyze	4. Characterize	6. Analyze
5. Improve	5. Improve	7. Improve
	6. Achieve	8. Achieve
6. Control		9. Sustain

systematic process of seeking out and adapting best practices and using benchmarks." Following step 5 will thus result in importing best practices during Six Sigma projects. Best practices management was also defined in Chapter 2 as the "transfer of the right knowledge (best practices) to the right people at the right time to improve performance and achieve excellence." Consequently, the addition of step 5 will infuse intellectual capital into Six Sigma projects and thereby supercharge more and more projects to achieve excellence through knowledge transfer. The types of intellectual capital discussed in Chapter 5 (human capital, intellectual assets, and intellectual property) may be pursued, and the types of knowledge transfer (serial, near, far, strategic, and expert) reviewed in Chapter 3 may be incorporated. Depending on the receiving team, the impact on the entire organization, and the type of knowledge, the Dixon Decision Tree (Figure 3-5) is a tool that can help the change agent use the right type of transfer. All of this work can be done as part of step 5.

Otherwise, the steps "Plan," "Commit," and "Achieve" are easy to explain. Step 1 is "Plan," and it is a generic equivalent of the corresponding Raytheon step, "Visualize." This step is needed to baseline the present levels of performance and anticipates through targeting what the needed level of performance is for the future. This step thus defines the extent to which a gap exists. It is essential to frame the breadth and depth of improvement that must occur. Step 2, "Commit," is borrowed from Raytheon and advocated for the same reasons that company includes it. Simply put, an approval is needed in the form of committed resources to undertake and implement the project. Leaders have to be committed in order to make real changes. The same is true for step 8, "Achieve." In Raytheon's case, it targets value in the eyes of customers, reducing waste, scrap, non-value-adding activities, and so on. The targets may vary by organization, but they need to be defined.

Except for "Sustain" instead of "Control," the authors advocate all the other steps in the process for achieving Six Sigma excellence come from the traditional DMAIC framework, except for the addition of benchmarking, which has already been explained. The authors believe that "Sustain," in the sense of "sustain the gains," is a much more proactive description of the step than the old terminology of "Control." All in all, it is the authors' opinion that the nine-step process outlined in Table 8-4 will create for organizations—large or small, service or manufacturing—better and faster acceleration to achieve excellent performance using the context of the knowledge transfer race.

The Bottom Line for People in Small Organizations

Best practices benchmarking has been overlooked by most Six Sigma training and implementations. Likewise, Six Sigma solutions have been too internally focused. Yet best practices benchmarking—the systematic search for best practices, innovative ideas, and highly effective operating procedures that lead to superior performance—is a powerful tool.[16] In fact, benchmarking is the second most used management tool in the world. Satisfaction with the tool is also high. With it, efforts to achieve 6σ excellence are greatly enhanced. Definitions, examples, and much more about best practices are provided in Chapter 2. Converting knowledge to profit and managing the change in order to get there are the subject of Chapter 9.

Every one of the five types of knowledge transfer discussed in Chapter 3 is of benefit to small organizations, especially serial, far, and strategic transfers whenever tacit knowledge is involved. It behooves small organizations—informally or formally—to be highly effective in making knowledge transfers. Indeed, it is suggested that small businesses focus on being especially competent at two or three of these types of transfer.

While the PCF (APQC Process Classification Framework) presented in Chapter 4 may seem to be more complicated than necessary, actually, it's relatively easy to understand and will surely benefit small organizations. This is because of how precise and clear the language and definitions are, along with how they apply to companies in every industry and of any size. Small organizations benefit from process management. However, small organizations may wish to start by identifying two to five core processes and focusing on improving the end-to-end performance of each. This will require working with the PCF and customizing it for a given organization's business circumstances. The crucial knowledge of the organization will need to be identified, too. And then, answers need to be considered to questions like: Is the crucial knowledge being grown enough? Is that knowledge being shared and transferred in ways that add the most value? Will use and reuse of this crucial knowledge enable the future success of the enterprise?

In fact, tips 45 and 46 of the 55 tips in Chapter 11 for people in small business come from this chapter and are pertinent. They are

- Rather than undertaking a comprehensive Six Sigma approach (as it tends to be too complicated for small business), the authors suggest adopting their process for achieving 6σ excellence, which is displayed in different forms as Tables 8-4 and 11-1. The authors recommend making investments that can be 100 percent recovered within six months.
- People in small organizations are urged to add the use of a benchmarking step as one of the steps detailed in Tables 8-4 and 11-1 (DMBAIC). Without benchmarking, an organization is flying blind in a storm.

The time invested in these actions will pay big dividends. For the processes selected, it will be important to formulate key performance indicators (KPIs) or metrics, benchmarks, and best practices, internal and external. Financial return is an important consideration.

People in small organizations need a simple and easy 6σ excellence and benchmarking process with low investment that generates returns in three to six months and a total return on investment within twelve months. Accordingly, people in small organizations are encouraged to test and pilot the authors' nine-step process displayed in Table 8-4. It is a very good starting place. If after three or four trials or tests, it is determined that the nine steps need to be simplified, consider adopting the DMBAIC 6-step process in the left column of Table 8-4. It is somewhat simplified. Nonetheless, the authors do <u>not</u> recommend leaving out the "Benchmark" step. If it does so, the organization involved is driving blind in the knowledge transfer race.

In Chapter 10, new forms of benchmarking will be reviewed. Some of these—such as quick-turnaround benchmarking, database searches, and other tools—are well suited for people in resource-strapped small organizations. Please review and pilot several, if not all, of the new techniques presented in this upcoming chapter. The call for action and tips presented in Chapter 11 should also be reviewed for those suggestions that have the greatest value for a given small organization.

Summary

After everything is said and done, to be a winner in the knowledge transfer race, whether in a large or a small organization, people need to acquire more than the usual amount of humility. When they acknowledge to themselves and their colleagues that the problem they are trying to solve has already been solved (partially or completely) in the same, a similar, or a different context, they are open to rapid learning. Such humility and aggressive learning will lead to breakthroughs, knowledge transfer, speed, and success. In the end, it will also create leaders in the knowledge transfer race.

Endnotes

1. Dick Smith and Jerry Blakeslee, with Richard Koonce, *Strategic Six Sigma: Best Practices from the Executive Suite* (Hoboken, N.J.: John Wiley & Sons, 2002 p. 44.
2. Raytheon's 2001 Annual Report.
3. From Bill Baker's presentation to the QuEST Forum's Third Annual Best Practices Conference, Richardson, Texas, September 2002.
4. A motto of Bill Baker, coauthor of this book.
5. Information cleared through Raytheon's *Raytheon Six Sigma*™ Office and used in Bill Baker's presentation to the QuEST Forum's Third Annual Best Practices Conference, Richardson, Texas, September 2002.
6. Christopher E. Bogan and Michael J. English, *Benchmarking for Best Practices: Winning through Innovative Adaptation* (New York: McGraw-Hill, 1994), p. 14.
7. From Bank of America presentation shared by Leslie Pemberton during a Global Benchmarking Council meeting, July 2003.
8. Ibid.
9. George Alukal, "Create a Lean, Mean Machine," *Quality Progress*, vol. 36, no. 4, April 2003, p. 29.
10. Ibid., p. 29. Alukal credits this definition as having come from the National Institute of Standards and Technology Manufacturing Extension Partnership (NIST/MEP).
11. Ibid., p. 34.
12. Bonnie Smith, "Lean and Six Sigma-A One-Two Punch," *Quality Progress*, vol. 36, no. 4, April 2003, pp. 37-41.
13. Ibid., p. 37.
14. Ibid.
15. Bill Baker's viewpoint regarding Raytheon's use of Lean as part of R6σ® as a process improvement strategy.
16. Bogan and English, *Benchmarking for Best Practices*, p. 1.

Chapter 9

Converting Knowledge into Value and Profit: Part Two of Mastering the Innovation and Change Involved in the Payoff Phase 4 of the Knowledge Transfer Race

Introduction

Readers understand by now what it takes to master phases 1, 2, and 3 of the knowledge transfer race. While various paybacks begin to accrue during those first three phases, the big payoffs happen through mastering phase 4, where knowledge begins to be systematically transformed into greater value and profits. The knowledge that is being converted is intellectual capital, the subject of Chapter 5. The first part of the discussion of mastering phase 4 was given in Chapter 8. There, it was shown how, by integrating best practices benchmarking into Six Sigma strategies, literally hundreds of intellectual capital gold nuggets could be mined and "cashed in" to fully optimize the impact of Six Sigma strategies and achieve stunning results. Here in Chapter 9 is the second part of the discussion about mastering phase 4 of the race, a discussion that focuses on the reuse of existing intellectual capital through new applications in different contexts.

Returns have been realized during each of the preceding three phases. Best practices were imported during phase 1, and this enabled organizations to deliver to customers, products and services that are better, faster, and cheaper. A greater capacity for learning and sharing was instituted during phase 2, which enabled the organization to systematically translate the experiences of its teams and individuals into knowledge. Teams now reflect back on their actions and outcomes before moving forward. They extract knowledge from their experiences. The organization also transfers knowledge across time and space through at least five transfer methods. And during phase 3, the organization is benefiting from the way it creates and manages intellectual capital. Together, these benefits have reduced cycle time, improved productivity, reduced costs, and begun to produce features, functions, or services that customers are willing to pay for. But it's in phase 4 that the big paybacks occur. Intellectual capital is transformed into never before imagined new products, services, markets, revenues, and cost savings. In simple terms, this is the new twenty-first-century mastery of the innovative use and reuse of intellectual capital knowledge.

To begin with, how have organizations reached phase 4? They became proficient at searching out and importing best practices, often referred to as hundreds of knowledge nuggets. They became learning organizations, regularly using at least five methods (serial, near, far, strategic, and expert) to transfer the knowledge gained by source teams to receiving teams, who put that knowledge to work making the enterprise more competitive. Such organizations create more human capital. Tacit knowledge (human capital, or people's experience, know-how, skills, and creativity) is growing and spreading as the source of all new intellectual knowledge creation for the organization. Also, policies and processes have been developed for inventorying and managing intellectual assets (programs, inventions, processes, databases, methodologies, documents, drawings, and designs), including intellectual property (patents, trademarks, copyrights, and trade secrets). Pit stops were made as necessary to create the capability or mastery to move on. All the while, it became necessary to build a knowledge-enabled culture.

What It Means to Convert or Transform Knowledge into Value or Profit and to Master Phase 4 of the Race

This is where people (human capital), as individuals and as members of knowledge-creating (source) and knowledge-receiving (reusing) teams, have grown new combinations of synergistic capability (experiences, know-how, skills, and creativity) and routinely demonstrate newly formed proficiencies for generating imaginative and relevant ideas. This occurs when all five of Senge's disciplines of learning (systems thinking, personal mastery, shared vision, mental models, and team learning) take hold synergistically in environments (cultures) where opportunities to effect significant change are provided and people are empowered and encouraged to do better. People grow, feel stretched, begin experimenting, and take risks. Ideas about how to be better at what they're doing fill people's minds—especially as they collaborate on teams.

This approach to vitalizing human capital so that teams and individuals eagerly want to and do generate new ideas resembles employee involvement (EI) deployments, but is clearly different. To illustrate the effect of employee involvement on teams, consider *Industry Week* magazine's annual competition for the best plants in the United States. One of the by-products of *Industry Week's* sponsorship of the competition among applicants is the identification and continual refinement of a standard set of criteria that defines or embodies what it is that constitutes a best plant. One of the five major categories of criteria examines employee involvement, as evidenced by the deployment of self-directed work teams.

Considering the 2004 best plant finalists, *Industry Week's* editor, Patricia Pancheck, discovered that 85 percent of the finalists had more than 50 percent of their production done by self-directed work teams, compared to 26 percent in the general population.[1] With production workers involved in self-directed teams, the workers at the best plants are outdistancing the workers of competitors. Like those who work in a learning organization, workers on self-directed teams feel that their ideas count, that they're learning, that they're stretched, and that they're doing something that matters. Workers who are so actively involved engage their minds and use knowledge to achieve the highest performance. Pancheck of *Industry Week* sizes up the importance of employee involvement in plants as follows: "U.S. Manufacturing leaders who haven't implemented proven employee best practices on the plant floor haven't begun to tap the potential of their companies' production employees."[2] Self-directed work teams manage their own work group assignments, schedules, communications, training, quality assurance, safety, and performance evaluations. By sharing, using, and reusing knowledge within the team, workers are more intelligent together than they are apart, and, together, they generate high performance. This is an illustration of how knowledge is turned into value during phase 4 of the knowledge transfer race.

What the authors advocate is engaging everyone in the organization to generate ideas about reusing the intellectual capital that already exists. The reuse or repurposing of knowledge that already exists has phenomenal payback possibilities. It makes much more sense to start where others have left off than to start from scratch on every new creation. Existing knowledge may be reused in a different context, setting, industry, country, or environment. It's the mindset of reusing 75 percent of the knowledge that already exists. Consider, for example, the Hummer—a High Mobility Multi-Purpose Wheeled Vehicle (HMMWV) that American Motors General began building for the U.S. Army in 1982.[3] The knowledge embodied in the Hummer's systems was reused in 1992 to create the first civilian model—the H1.[4] In 2003 the same reuse mindset applied 75 percent of the H1 model knowledge to the design of the very popular H2 model Hummer, which was introduced into the world SUV (sport utility vehicle) market. The Hummer H2 is a consummate example of knowledge reuse. It's easy to imagine organizations launching campaigns like "reuse 75 percent of the knowledge that exists." The savings potential is huge. The time and cost of certain types of product development and manufacturing could be cut by 25 to 50 percent, and maybe more. In manufacturing, it has become a regular practice to reuse common parts to reduce cost and development time.

On the other hand, employee involvement, which began in the 1980s, concentrates on engaging employees to solve problems that they experience in their daily work. Introduced as an early part of the Baldrige criteria and Total Quality Management thinking, the idea has been to tap into the full potential of the workforce to make improvements. This is usually advocated through the combination of four concepts.

1. Implement a deliberate strategy with tactics for keeping employees informed (about the vision, mission, strategies, key performance indicators, objectives, results, deficiencies, gaps, and problems), so that they will focus their attention and energies on the things that matter. Some describe this as creating alignment with the corporate goals.
2. Provide employees with knowledge (skills, experience, and problem-solving tools and techniques), so that they have a framework and the know-how to figure out how to solve the problems they encounter in their daily work.
3. Empower employees to act and make improvements in how they perform tasks and follow a process to solve problems that are broader or that require resource funding or reallocation.
4. Recognize, reward, and encourage people for the work they do and the risks they take to achieve improvements.

While these EI deployments are as valid as ever, they have not been designed to grow human capital and reuse knowledge that already exists.

The present-day EI tends to focus on improving end-to-end process performance, but not necessarily on reusing intellectual assets that are already in existence, such as software, products, methodologies, programs, or databases. Even Six Sigma project teams tend to narrow their focus to addressing the root causes of variation and waste. These teams are usually ill equipped to do the research needed to identify the body of knowledge that already exists in other domains, which is a prerequisite to the systematic reuse, repurpose, or building on top of knowledge that already exists.

Organizations have their own unique EI approach. For example, GTE Directories—a 1994 recipient of a Baldrige Award—formulated a successful EI approach based on teamwork that it named QIT (Quality Improvement Teams). Whatever the name, early EI efforts started with quality circles, evolved into EI teams that solved problems, and today, tend to be process improvement teams. In organizations that have become process-centered and process-managed, these teams work within an infrastructure of process owners (introduced in Chapter 4) to prevent upstream and downstream disconnects using IPO (input-process-output) analysis. All of the problem-solving techniques (within the stages of define, analyze, solve, implement, and report), like brainstorming, triple-ranking, Pareto (80/20 rule) analysis, cause-and-effect or fishbone analysis, sampling, and cost-benefit analysis, are still relevant and effective. But EI teams are not enough to master phase 4 and win the knowledge transfer race.

What's necessary is to become a learning organization (as advocated in Chapter 3), to become a process-centered organization (as advocated in Chapter 4), and to have a modest knowledge specialist infrastructure (librarians, benchmarking, and best practices experts) that, together, engages and encourages everyone to reuse existing intellectual capital (knowledge). The emphasis must be on applying existing knowledge in new ways, contexts, and circumstances to support the organization's present-day vision and strategies. This convergence differs with but should complement the work of EI teams aimed at optimizing end-to-end process performance. In this regard, the authors are not at all certain that both EI and knowledge reuse/sharing are best achieved through one combined and integrated deployment. It is the opinion of the authors that any and all work done by teams—whether it is teams of executives, managers, workers, or any combination—needs to consider and incorporate existing and relevant knowledge before the team proceeds. The key is for everyone to recognize that pertinent knowledge exists and to share it with those who can use or reuse it in a different context with experiments and refinement. The intended outcome is to create a stream of tacit knowledge ideas that create intellectual assets, which produce greater customer value and profits.

Soon ideas fill an *enterprise innovation pipeline* as they travel through different life-cycle stages of evaluation and adoption of knowledge reuse ideas. Many ideas are brainstorming solutions that are refined by piggybacked suggestions. Yet other ideas aim at correcting problems that customers unhappily experience. As pictured in Figure 9-1, *pipeline* is the term used to describe the flow of ideas through consideration, starting with when the idea is expressed and ending after findings about concept development, demonstration, evaluation, test, refinement, trial, and adoption or rejection are shared. At first, ideas trickle into the pipeline. Then, as managers become aware of and appreciate the full potential of the human capital knowledge base, more and better ideas are nurtured in an expanding pipeline. With encouragement, the pipeline becomes a key source of leading-edge innovations. Ideas center on applications that customers are willing to pay to have, which means things that have value. Some ideas may seem ahead of their time or need refinement or trial, or managers may need to enlarge their mental models so that they can see new possibilities outside the paradigms or patterns of thinking that prevent the mind from being receptive to certain new possibilities.

The enterprise innovation pipeline is also separate and distinct from the research and development (R&D) technology innovation process that knowledge-enabled organizations also must undertake. To clarify the difference, consider the example of the Xerox Corporation. The difference is that Xerox's enterprise innovation pipeline engages all of the company's 61,100 worldwide employees to generate ideas for reusing knowledge that Xerox already possesses. Xerox's R&D technology innovation effort, on the other hand, engages a total of 1,100 researchers, scientists, engineers, and intellectual property experts to explore the unknown and invent the next generation of technology.[5] The enterprise innovation pipeline captures the ideas of Xerox's 61,100 employees on any and all business processes, whereas the R&D technology innovation pipeline captures the work of 1,100 scientists working on marking systems, materials, digital imaging, technology, and new solutions. Knowledge reuse needs to be undertaken by the entire employee population, not just the R&D staff. Nonetheless, the scientists need to apply the concepts of knowledge reuse or piggybacking to their R&D work as well.

Three driving forces fill the enterprise innovation pipeline. The first is necessity. This is explained by the adage "necessity is the mother of invention." If people are stranded on an island, *necessity* will lead them to reuse any knowledge they possess in order to survive and escape. Consider Ford Motor Company, which claims to have achieved $34 million in savings during one year by transferring ideas between plants.[6] Ford gives each Vehicle Operations plant an annual 5 percent productivity improvement target. The local plant must figure out how to achieve this improvement. The 5 percent target translates into a necessity for plant managers to find savings; thus, it's an incentive for them to look at Ford's intranet weekly for

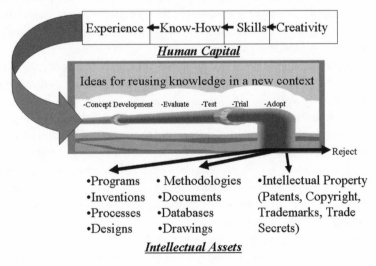

Figure 9-1   The enterprise innovation pipeline

new ideas posted that have actually been adopted elsewhere and proved to create savings in other plants.[7] Necessities—be they the Ford-imposed type, a problem that's become critical, or something that can bring the enterprise to its knees—will generate ideas and inventions. Often, the invention can be the reuse of existing knowledge, but applied in a new way.

Consider another *necessity* example involving the 3M Corporation and a knowledge-reuse solution. 3M's in-house tests of one of its R&D cement formulas revealed that the bonding strength of the adhesive compound was inferior to that of competitors' products and even other 3M products. 3M faced the prospect of having a defective cement that had no market in the traditional sense. However, the cement had a sticky, flypaper-like characteristic, and this became a knowledge tidbit that opened the imagination of 3M project employees. The formula was found to be an excellent bonding agent that would holds papers together temporarily. The knowledge involved was reused in an entirely different context to create a different product to meet an as yet undefined market need of customers. The new product became *Post-it Notes*, which not only became amazingly successful but also created a new niche market and a major source of income for 3M. This is an example of converting intellectual capital into profit and doing it by taking knowledge that already exists and applying it in a new context.

A second important driving force filling an enterprise innovation pipeline is a *shared vision*. When employees share the same vision that their organization has for itself, they tend to behave in ways that bring that vision to life. For example, when a vision calls for helping customers find better ways to do their work, employees will try to discover any recent success stories about performing work and try to adapt them to their present clients for reuse in a context at hand. This is reusing existing knowledge.

Consider again Figure 5-3 along with the continuing example of the Xerox Corporation. Figure 5-3 shows how human capital forms the capacity to provide reuse solutions to customers (which creates value for them) and is the source of the enterprise's new knowledge creation. Relate this to Xerox and its shared vision. Xerox, a $15.7 billion worldwide enterprise at the end of 2003, shares with its employees the vision that the company exists "to help businesses deploy smarter Document Management strategies and find better ways to work."[8] As a result of Xerox's vision and the advertising it does for its brand, the consuming public and Xerox's employees form a mental image of Xerox as the "Document People." In addition to a substantial R&D investment, Xerox encourages its employees to contribute ideas that bring its vision to life, making it real and, in effect, aligning everyone with the company's vision. Thus, employees see themselves as the Document People. In this and a number of other ways, Xerox grows its human capital and proactively nurtures it to fill a growing enterprise innovation pipeline that keeps generating value for its customers and commercializes new products that renew profits. Xerox employees are encouraged to reuse existing knowledge about better ways to work and apply it in new contexts for other sets of Xerox customers.

A third driving factor is the encouragement and learning organizational capabilities built in phases 1, 2, and 3, along with the vast new possibilities opened up by having a knowledge-enabled culture. The human capital capability to innovate—supported by the environment of a learning organization—is a Herculean force for bringing to the surface ideas for reusing knowledge or converting it into profitable products.

Consider the IBM Corporation, the world's largest information technology company, which operates in 160 countries and had 2003 revenues of $89.1 billion.[9] What IBM says about itself is, "At IBM, we strive to lead in the invention, development and manufacture of the industry's most advanced information technologies including computer systems, software, storage systems and microelectronics. We translate these advanced technologies into value for our customers through our professional solutions, services and consulting businesses worldwide."[10] As a testament to its knowledge leadership, IBM received its fourth Most Admired Knowledge Enterprise (MAKE) award for North America during 2005. It was also a global MAKE Award winner for 2004 because of how it delivers knowledge-based products, develops value based on customer knowledge, and transforms enterprise knowledge into shareholder value. IBM also received the most U.S. patents— 3,415 U.S. patents in 2003—for the eleventh consecutive year. During the past four years, IBM inventors received over 13,000 patents.[11]

Clearly a knowledge-enabled company, IBM claims to be the world's largest information technology research organization, with more than 3,000 scientists and engineers working at eight labs in six countries.[12] Nonetheless, what is most relevant about what IBM is doing is the way it empowers its 319,000 employees (not just its 3,000 scientists) to reuse knowledge that already exists and apply it in the new context of the present. Software reuse is one category of applications in which IBM is making considerable headway. Regarding the IBM strategy, it is noteworthy that IBM sold its famous personal computer business at the end of 2004. This suggests that IBM is concentrating on more knowledge-intensive products and services (e.g. Intel-based server systems, supercomputing power, and so on) and moving away from the low-margin, commodity-like hardware business.

Reusing Innovation is the "Name of the Game": It's a Powerful Lever for Transforming Intellectual Capital into Profits

To innovate is to create a new—and presumably better—way of doing something. The new way of doing things, however, doesn't have to be invented; it just as easily can be the result of creative imagination. A solution that has already been invented may be connected or extended and applied in another context.

Consider, for example, the reuse of architectural plans for a restaurant. The specifications provided by an entrepreneur who wants to design and open a restaurant are: one floor, seating capacity of 200 inside and at least 30 outside, at least 1,000 square feet of kitchen space, parking for 75 cars, a cocktail lounge that seats 50, and a design that fits with an art deco theme. For illustrative purposes, say that a database search comes up with 250 possible architectural plans from a population of 7,000 restaurant plans that already exist. Using knowledge reuse principles, it makes sense to examine the 250 potentially qualifying plans, narrow them down to perhaps the three or four best ones, and reuse those as 75 percent or more of what's needed to meet the present-day requirement. Why start from scratch when 75 percent of what's needed is knowledge that already exists?

As a result, the architectural plans are produced in half the time and at half the cost, and probably produced a superior design (taking the best of 250) than could have been reinvented. This is just one example of potentially hundreds. Why reinvent knowledge when it already exists and the best of what already exists is probably superior to what can be reinvented? Selecting the best and adapting it to the current situation is a form of innovation and creativity to generate a positive result.

In the twenty-first century, knowledge reuse already plays a big role in defining an organization. Web sites, voice response systems, e-mail, supply-chain systems, customer service systems, and billing systems influence how organizations are defined. It used to be that what defined an organization were its products, services, advertising, storefronts, and sales and customer service people. These are still factors. In any case, some or all of what defines an organization should not be built from scratch. Many best practice approaches for doing these things already exist and should be leveraged or reused. Even the software supporting all the aforementioned systems already exists and should be reused, adapted, tweaked, or repurposed instead of being built from scratch. In the end, it comes down to knowledge that defines an organization's relationships with its customers, competitors, and partners. If properly managed, knowledge is an asset. If not, it's a liability and costly. Many knowledge reuse tools will be needed in the twenty-first century, and those for software reuse will be near the top of the list.

It is not productive or cost-effective to reinvent knowledge that has already been invented two, three, or four times inside the same organization. And if the reinvention is something that's already been invented elsewhere in business and industry fifty times, it's inefficient and disadvantageous to start from scratch again. Accordingly, to win the knowledge transfer race, organizations need to look at reusing intellectual assets every way they can. The following is a starting list of assets to explore for reuse possibilities.

Programs and Databases

■ *Software reuse.* Software reuse management is an emerging discipline. It is not well understood or developed, and it clearly is not yet well managed. Nonetheless, because of the ever-increasing importance and growth of software, reuse of it has colossal payback potential. The case for reuse is solid because it reduces schedule time frames and costs by reusing software assets instead of building them from scratch. It has been a standing principle that using an industry standard software tool also ensures that technical support and maintenance for this tool are relatively lower because the fixed costs are spread over a large body of users. In contrast, the costs of unique and stand-alone software solutions tend to be a drag on profitability. Now, newer technologies like component-based development and Web services exist. New tools are needed to enable reuse initiatives. Developing software assets once and encouraging others to reuse them rather than developing new software from scratch yields benefits in terms of quality, time, and cost. There is a relatively new but growing market for commercial off-the-shelf (COTS) software where horizontal reuse has proven successful (math routines, screen formatting, graphics, data visualization, and database building). Reuse benefits are potentially stunning—a threefold or greater reduction in time to market. Reuse manufacturing reference models are under development, which will pave the way for organizations to align reuse with their vision and strategic goals. Because software consists of entire sets of programs, procedures, and related documentation for systems, it makes perfect sense to avoid starting from scratch for each new future need. Consider the all-encompassing categories of software that exist and are growing:

  ◆ Business and office (which includes database, e-mail and contact management, fax and scanning, office suites, office applications, project management, publishing, and PDF documents)
  ◆ Antivirus and security
  ◆ Finance and accounting (which includes payroll and taxes)
  ◆ Graphics and design (including photo editing and Web design)
  ◆ Kids and education (including games)
  ◆ Operating systems
  ◆ Personal productivity (including music, foreign language, and travel)
  ◆ Server applications
  ◆ Storage and backup

■ *Servlet reuse.* Java Server Pages (JSP) technology supports application object reuse using JSP tag templates. The point is that there are several ways to reuse the knowledge embodied in software code in servlet environments. The Java Servlet API is a standard extension to the Java platform that provides Web application developers with a simple and consistent mechanism for extending the modules of Java code that run in a server application (hence the name servlets, similar to applets on the client side) to answer client requests. Servlets are not tied to a specific client-server protocol, but they are most commonly used with HTTP. (The word *servlet* is often used with HTTP and used with a meaning of HTTP servlet). Since servlets are written in highly portable Java language and follow a standard framework, they provide a means to create sophisticated server extensions in a server and operating system. One way to reuse code is described as using "inheritance." Another way is in the Java servlet specification, which defines natural mechanisms to chain execute from one servlet to another. There are disadvantages because reuse requires programmers to explicitly wire servlets together in the code, which means that reuse must be planned for during development.

- *Database management systems.* Overlapping with software reuse, these are collections of programs that enable users to store, modify, and extract information and knowledge in and from databases. Rather than reinventing such a system from scratch when a growing body of knowledge already exists, reusing knowledge applies, for example, to computerized library systems, automated teller machines, flight reservation systems, and computerized parts inventory systems. Furthermore, a growing domain of related knowledge might also be reused for data mining, data warehousing, decision support, information retrieval, and security.

- *Franchises.* Franchises are excellent examples of knowledge reuse and may be expanded further. The franchise concept is built on taking knowledge that has proven successful in several locations and then replicating it in many other locations. Knowledge replication applies to store architectural plans, space and storage space utilization, menu design, supplier sourcing agreements, advertising programs, human resource practices and procedures, and so on. While there are many successes in the fast food industry (e.g., McDonald's, Burger King, Jack in the Box, Taco Bell, Kentucky Fried Chicken, Dominos Pizza, Arby's, Denny's, Pizza Hut, and Wendy's) the concept (which embodies knowledge reuse) may be efficiently extended into other industries. Wal-Mart, Target, Home Depot, and Lowe's are other very successful examples of knowledge reuse between stores and outlets.

Inventions

- *Organizations can reuse concepts and technology to create new products and services.* As displayed in Table 9-1, the knowledge that exists regarding one technology (e.g., headphones) may be combined and reused with another (e.g., sunglasses) and extended to create, for example, the Oakley Thump

Sunglasses, one of *BusinessWeek's* Best Products for 2004. In fact, ten of the other Best Products for 2004 are also identified in Table 9-1, and highlighted in italics is a brief description about how knowledge reuse may have led to the creation of each listed product. The product name and description are also provided. The point is that rarely should new product development start from scratch.

■ *In certain circumstances, organizations may give priority to reusing utility patents that already exist and making novel improvements to them.* A utility patent may be sought for mechanical, electrical, chemical, and process (including business method) inventions that are not completely new (few are). During 2000, the U.S. Patent and Trademark Office (USPTO) received 315,015 patent applications and granted 175,983 patents, which was an 80 percent increase over the numbers for 1990.[13] Of the 315,015 patent applications for 2000, 295,926, or 93.9 percent, were utility patents; 18,292, or 5.8 percent, were design patents; and 797, or less than 1 percent, were plant patents.[14] The USPTO approves about 72 percent of the applications received.[15] The courts have been allowing business method patents since 1998. Utility patents provide their owner a 20-year monopoly (enforced against anybody who infringes on the patent by making or selling a patented invention without permission) and are the most important of the three types, accounting for 90 to 95 percent of the patents applied for in any given year. There are still three USPTO hurdles to clear before a patent will be issued: (1) Is the invention new? (2) Is the invention useful? (3) Does the invention work? The bottom line is: why invent something from scratch when 50 to 75 percent of the knowledge required can be reused from knowledge that already exists, so that the invention need include only 25 to 50 percent new ideas?

■ *Organizations need a patent policy and need to be able to conduct patent searches.* While this is more relevant to Chapter 5 (creating intellectual capital), a policy, process, and patent search methodology is needed to inventory and manage intellectual capital assets. Internet searches may be conducted by going to www.USPTO.gov.

■ *A policy and process may also be needed for copyrights and trademarks.* To the extent that these are deemed necessary, it makes much more sense to reuse or piggyback on knowledge that already exists for these policies and processes.

Processes

■ *Free reuse of the APQC copyrighted Process Classification Framework (PCF) provided in Chapter 4 is highly recommended.* This intellectual capital taxonomy

Table 9-1 Eleven of *BusinessWeek*'s Twenty-Three Best Products for 2004

Concept	Product Name	Description
Hear-Sighted		
Reuse of two concepts (headset and sunglasses)	Oakley Thump Sunglasses	Sunglasses with a digital audio player built in. The 256-megabyte version ($495) holds 120 tunes, and its battery plays for six hours.
Moving Music		
Reuse of remote control concept in PC context	Roku SoundBridge	Elegant way to get digital music stored on a PC or Mac to play on a stereo. Two models with easy hookup, wired or wireless network ($250).
Cell Sensation		
Reuse of headset and microphones with special filters	Aliph Jawbone Headset	Headset for noisiest places because it drowns out noise. The headset ($150) uses two microphones; one picks up sound and the other rests on the jaw; subtracts out noise.
A Steady Beam		
Reuse of laser technology in new application	Ryobi AIRgrip Laser Level	This level uses a tiny vacuum to stick to painted, papered, and paneled walls. The laser is visible for 30 feet and turns 90 degrees. It's $40 only at Home Depot.
Big Red Goes Green		
Reuse of motorcycle knowledge	2004 Honda CRF250X Motorcycle	A race-ready off-road bike ($5,999) that meets emissions rules in 50 states. It is a year-round ride built for fun.
Pretty Picture Perfect		
Reuse and extension of digital camera knowledge	Hewlett-Packard Photosmart R707 Digital Camera	This 5.1-megapixel, pocket-size shooter ($300) fine-tunes high-contrast photos and takes up to five shots to see a panorama on the camera's 1.5-inch screen.

(continued)

247

Table 9-1 Eleven of *BusinessWeek*'s Twenty-Three Best Products for 2004 (*continued*)

Concept	Product Name	Description
Closet Case *Reuse and extension of dryer designs*	Maytag Neptune Drying Center	Speed-dry sneakers and sweaters in this unique drying cabinet ($1,200) built on top of a traditional tumble dryer. A top clothes rod swings in heated air to remove wrinkles.
One Smart Phone *Reuse and extension of cell phone and camera technology*	Motorola Razr V3	This $500 pocket-pleaser hides a camera buried in 3D graphics beneath keypad; great acoustics and images from a thin sharp-looking phone.
Open-and-Shut *Reuse of borrowed convertible design*	MINI Cooper S Convertible	Weekend runabout ($24,950) with ragtop that produces a sunroof with one press. Press again, and the top retracts completely.
Brush and Run *Reuse of toothbrush concept using finger instead of brush*	Oral-B Brush-Ups Finger Toothbrush	A disposable fingertip toothbrush that freshens your breath and gives you that just-brushed feeling ($2.49 for a package of 12). The toothpaste is built in. No rinsing needed.
Going Mobile *Reusing AM/FM radio knowledge in satellite context*	Delphi MyFi Portable Satellite Radio	A battery-powered satellite radio you can take with you ($350; $10/mo. for XM radio service). Clip it to your belt; records five hours for subways and places no signal exists.

Source: Information for the first 11 of the 23 Best Products for 2004 at the Web site http://images.businessweek.com/mz/04/50/0450best_products/0450best_products12.htm

reused a earlier 1994 version and has been updated during 2004 and 2005 through a collaboration of 20 worldwide organizations. Any effort to reinvent it would unnecessarily cost tens of thousands of dollars and take as long as a year, and afterwards it would lack (in benchmarking exchanges) the international and cross-industry support that the PCF has already achieved. The APQC encourages wide distribution, discussion, and use of the AQPC PCF as an open standard for classifying and defining processes. Accordingly, it has granted permission to use and copy the PCF free of charge as long as an acknowledgement is made to the APQC.

- *To the extent the new, modified, or customized variations of the PCF are needed, reuse of existing process development work is suggested rather than starting from scratch.*
- *Reuse of best practices processes.* Best practices already exist for developing and managing human capital (recruitment, policies, compensation, diversity, training, competency development, recognition and rewards, and so on), customer service, information technology, financial resources (accounting, accounts receivable, accounts payable, and so on), property, environmental health and safety, legal and ethical issues, and improvement. In fact, Chapter 6 addressed reusing the knowledge that has already been developed and is embodied in the Baldrige criteria, European Quality Awards, Shingo Prize, and ISO 9000.

Designs and Drawings

- *Architectural plans.* As previously mentioned, reuse of architectural designs makes perfect sense. Reuse depends on a research capability, which probably would require a database from which to conduct searches.
- *Engineering configurations.* In energy, cable television, including high-speed Internet, and the telecommunications industries, for example, there are standard and proven configurations for outside plant (cable, junction boxes, switching systems, distribution and feeder methodologies, and so on) that may be reused as templates.
- *Surveys.* Geological and land use survey knowledge has grown sufficiently to form a base for knowledge reuse, so recurring needs do not have to be met by starting from scratch.
- *Vehicle and machinery designs.* Successful motorized vehicle designs may be reused for consumers at large and for applications in the military, agriculture, 18-wheel transportation, taxi and limousine, or construction (tractors, backhoes, and so on). And like the Hummer example provided earlier, existing knowledge may be reused in a different context, setting, industry, and application. Even engines, whether they are fueled by gasoline, alternative

fossil fuels, steam, or electricity, may be reused in another context, like the now popular electric-powered golf cart. Once again, it makes perfect sense to capture knowledge that already exists and reuse it in another context, making modifications as needed.

Documents and Methodologies

- *A document management system* has become essential for organizations that become ISO 9001 certified. The initial focus is on controlling, by dated releases, the updates and revisions to quality management system manuals, procedures, and practices.

- *When document management and records management are integrated,* opportunities for reusing knowledge pertaining to policies and procedures, corrective actions, customer complaints, internal audits, meeting minutes, tracking proposals and projects, forms automation, training records, vendor management, strategies and objectives integration, and so on can be identified.

- *Reuse of medical treatments, cures, vaccinations, experiments, and medicines has tremendous potential.* It's not enough to await new research when it's published in medical journals. Why not explore many more ways in which the knowledge that already exists may be shared and reused instead of having so many unnecessary attempts to reinvent solutions to problems already solved? There is no need to have each new research project start from ground zero. The types of devastation that have struck various regions of the world, such as the killer waves of the December 26, 2004, tsunami that initially killed 150,000 people in 12 countries, may be mitigated through applications of knowledge reuse that prevent or treat outbreaks of infectious diseases such as malaria, cholera, and tuberculosis. The same applies to AIDS prevention and treatment.

- *Agricultural knowledge reuse can help supply food to the starving.* Methodologies for crop rotation, genetic engineering, planting, replanting, pesticide treating, and harvesting crops such as corn, wheat, rice, and many others are well developed. Knowledge that has been developed and had successful results in one region of the world may be reused in other countries, geographies, or plant sites to great success. With up to a third of the world's population of 6.1 billion (at year-end 2003) in danger of starving, especially in heavily populated parts of Africa, China, and India, among others, knowledge reuse will supply more food to those who need it.[16] Also, while the Earth is 70 percent water, only 2.5 percent of that water is fresh and drinkable.[17] Considerable knowledge has been accumulated regarding conservation and water reuse. In fact, efficient irrigation techniques are prime examples of how existing knowledge may be reused in different but related circumstances throughout the world. Fortunately, rather than only being involved with financing international projects, the World Bank has accepted a role, through its agents and programs, of being the champion of sharing and reusing this type of water and agricultural conservation knowledge.

Life Cycle Is a Consideration in Reusing Intellectual Capital

Intellectual capital has varying life cycles that must be managed and harvested to optimize payoff. Short life and vulnerability to piracy are reasons to "cash in" intellectual capital during recurring life cycles. Because of new technologies (new microchips, inventions, and so on), some forms of intellectual capital may age quickly. First or second-generation technologies are made obsolete when third or fourth generations are introduced into markets. In the example of software, updates have become a necessity. Also, in the twenty-first century, intellectual property is easily stolen, pirated, or infringed upon. Patents expire, too.

Except for very secure and safeguarded trade secrets (e.g., the Coca Cola and Kentucky Fried Chicken recipes mentioned earlier), few forms of intellectual property are safe from infringements that are hard to locate and prosecute or to loss caused by industrial espionage. Therefore, profits need to be harvested, and knowledge reuse helps. Earlier, the Napster copyright infringement case was mentioned, which exposed thousands of individuals to prosecution for file-swapping copyrighted music. Pirated software is available and regularly used for every conceivable purpose, including tax preparation, antivirus protection, language, education, and every kind of game imaginable. And in countries like China and Russia, the capture, production, and sale of pirated (illegal) content has become a major business enterprise.

Knowledge also leaves organizations in several other ways. It leaves when people leave by way of transfers, retirements, or being hired away by competitors. In the twenty-first-century world economy, people don't stay employed with the same organization as long as was once the case. The demographics of the baby boomer retirement bubble indicate that the risk of loss in the near future is higher because of the increase in the retirement-ready age groups.

Payback Examples of Reusing Knowledge That Already Exists

The focus on payback involves using or reusing knowledge in ways that create customer value and increase profitability. But there are many ways to create value for customers. Increased profitability is also the result of a variety of actions. Examples help to illustrate how payback can occur. Accordingly, a partial list of the types of payback that can result from reusing knowledge that already exists rather than reinventing new solutions from scratch follows.

Reuse of Best Practices Knowledge Creates Profits

Consider an example from the Public Service Electric and Gas Corporation (PSEG). PSEG is a publicly traded (NYSE, ticker symbol PEG) Fortune 500 company providing diversified energy and energy services in New Jersey. With assets of $26 billion and revenues of $10 billion in 2002, PSEG utilizes a Balanced Scorecard to identify opportunities for improvement. During 2002, an identified gap in the financial quadrant of the scorecard led PSEG to create two Six Sigma projects to increase recovery of third-party damages and reimbursements for having to relocate or move electric or gas facilities because of new construction.

The first of PSEG's two Six Sigma projects involved accidental damage to PSEG's facilities by others who dig (TV cable, telephone companies, builders, or individuals) or damage power lines (heavy road equipment and construction equipment). These accidents cause in excess of $5 million in damage to PSEG's electric and gas facilities each year.[18] Despite attempts to hold the culprits responsible, annual recoveries were running less than 60 percent, and the average cycle time to receive payment exceeded 300 days. PSEG's first Six Sigma project focused on redesigning its process to recover closer to 100 percent in less than one-third the time. Using a cross-functional team made up of people from operations, accounting, and business planning, the team redesigned the process, reviewed internal and external practices, and reused best practices across locations. As a result, PSEG made substantial improvements.[19]

Second, PSEG did a similar project for recovering the costs it incurred in relocating facilities for highway and other construction purposes in a shorter time. These were instances where electrical transponders or physical plant had to be physically moved because a new road was being constructed. Annual third-party billable amounts exceeded $50 million, and only 60 percent was being recovered, with the average time to recovery being 365 days, or a full year afterwards. As a result of reusing best practices from elsewhere in PSEG's operations, the company increased billing by $46.7 million and increased annual recovery for 2002 by $22.7 million, from $8.5 million to $31.2 million. Indeed, both projects together increased billings by 760 percent, increased amounts recovered by 270 percent, and reduced cycle time by 40 percent.[20] The benchmarks in the financial portion of PSEG's Balanced Scorecard created a compelling case for PSEG to improve.

Knowledge Reuse Dramatically Reduces the Time Required for Product Development

Verizon Communications, a Fortune 10 U.S. publicly held corporation (NYSE, ticker symbol VZ) with $67 billion in operating revenues for 2002, reuses existing best practices knowledge that enables it to make fast product development updates to its Investor Relations Web site, www.verizon.com/investor, nearly every week. During 2002, just a year and nine months after the merger of Bell Atlantic and GTE that created Verizon, its Web site was named the Best U.S. Investor Relations Web Site in the mega-cap company category by Investor Relations magazine. During 2003, the Web site also placed a prestigious fourteenth in the U.S. Grand Prix Ranking of the top 200 investor relations programs. Because 50 percent of its investors are institutions, Verizon puts a priority on solutions designed into the Web site that professional portfolio managers can use to satisfy their individual needs. Drop-down menus have been built into Verizon's Web site to give visitors easy navigational choices, allowing them to select or ignore deep layers of information.

According to Kevin Tarrant, Verizon's executive director for investor relations, "Given that we're dealing with a limited space panel, drop-down menus enable the deep layering of detailed information."[21] And while it's not a formal process, Tarrant and his staff devote time and attention to visiting, examining, and picking up ideas from the Web sites of IBM, Intel, Microsoft, and Cisco Systems. Those Web sites have also been finalists year in and year out for the same awards as Verizon. Verizon's investor relations manager, John D. Adams, says, "We look at what these other corporations are doing because, like us, they tend to make available tons of product and financial information. And make no mistake about it, this is about information—financial information—having it, posting it, and being quick about it."[22] Listening to the needs of investors and benchmarking improvements made by others has led Verizon to adapt innovations quickly. For example, Web site visitors can now enroll in VZ Mail, an innovation that dates back to the Bell Atlantic days. In May 2003, about 8,000 portfolio managers and individuals had enrolled in VZ Mail, which puts enrollees on automatic distribution to receive e-mail announcements and news about Verizon as it happens.[23] This is but one example of how reusing existing knowledge speeds up product development and addresses customer satisfaction at the same time.

In another example involving Raytheon, knowledge reuse enabled the elimination of product development delays. By using collaboration in what are called integrated product teams (IPTs), Raytheon is able to have all disciplines, including engineering, manufacturing, and quality, along with customers and suppliers, involved up front in the critical design phase. While there are risks in having this kind of face-to-face communication, it's proven time after time to be a winning approach for addressing problems and shortening the required communication loops to obtain approvals, which was troublesome in the previous arms-length approach. A surprise benefit to Raytheon is how effective and immediate it is to use suppliers' knowledge in the design phase to cut cost and increase "producibility." Cycles of learning are reduced. Saving time and cutting cost are the big paybacks.

Customer Relationship Management (CRM) Reuses Knowledge to Broaden and Deepen Business with Customers

The development of knowledge-enabled systems now supplies rich and revealing intelligence, and organizations have become markedly better at reusing it to develop responsive solutions. The knowledge-enabled CRM axiom has become "know thy customer." In the process of doing so, organizations are discovering how much more there is to understanding their customers and what's involved in achieving the kind of dialogue that leads to mutually beneficial collaboration. Reused software captures data (pertaining to customer interactions, buying patterns, product preferences, and so on), so it's easier to convert that knowledge into solutions that optimize an organization's relationships with customers and prospects.

In Chapter 5, knowledge-enabled customer relationship management was reviewed. The Ritz Carlton Hotel's customer intimacy approach was provided as an example. Also provided was a list of results achieved using software solutions, including call avoidance, shortened call times, problem avoidance, and lower information technology costs. Clearly, knowledge reuse is paying dividends for customer relationship management.

Knowledge Reuse Also Enables the Success of Strategic Improvement and Change Management Initiatives

Knowledge is the crucial element in achieving strategic change across an organization. Sharing the vision, goals, and detailed knowledge about such initiatives as *Lean* Enterprise, Six Sigma, *Lean* Six Sigma, TQM, the Baldrige criteria, ISO 9000/14000, and process excellence involves, energizes, and empowers the workforce to be active participants in making these changes come to life, take form, become real, and succeed. This has certainly proven to be the case at Raytheon.

For example, as a result of benchmarking, Raytheon was able to learn and reuse *Lean* best practices knowledge that already existed. Following is a partial list of the targets for reusing *Lean* knowledge to improve end-to-end speed: (1) reduce bottlenecks; (2) reduce the number of inspection sites; (3) reduce and eliminate decision and approval points; (4) simplify the decision-making process; (5) standardize information, reporting forms, and procedures to reduce variation; (6) avoid frequent process handoffs; (7) improve plant or office layouts that separate work groups or disrupt processes; (8) "pre-stage" tools and packages of paperwork for rapid processes; (9) eliminate unnecessary variation in design; (10) automate operations that are repetitive in nature; (11) perform simultaneous rather than serial processing or distribution of outputs that are inputs downstream; (12) eliminate non-value-added steps; and (13) use one-piece flow rather than batch building.

Knowledge Reuse Reduces Risk and Enables Quicker Decisions

The most rapid way to make process improvements is to generate fast cycles of learning. However, such fast progress involves more risk, as less is known going into new projects. Going after opportunities aggressively means running toward rather than away from risk. This means that organizations must remove the personal fear of failure, because nonsuccesses will occur and more often; however, they, too, produce enlightened learning or knowledge, which paves the way for faster and more successful new undertakings. Without encouraging enough risk taking, organizations, ironically, take the higher risk of inviting a *know-do gap* and becoming complacent, stale, and irrelevant.

Indeed, fast-learning organizations have learned to practice risk management, which substitutes risk tolerance for finger-pointing and makes distinctions between technical, management, contractual and legal, financial, and personnel risks. With fast learning cycles, greater tolerance may be permitted with management risks, where problems usually result from a lack of experience, inadequate training, insufficient project planning, inaccurate estimates, communications and project tracking breakdowns, and the like. On the other hand, lower tolerance is permitted with technical risks, where real disasters must be avoided. Also, some companies have created formal programs of "hatching" new businesses in a protected environment, so that they can devise new ideas and concepts that provide innovation and the promise of eventual P/L success. Whether the result is failure or success, the key is the learning messages transmitted when the experiences are communicated and the knowledge gained from what happened is shared with everyone across the organization. This is the mantra of sharing best practices and lessons learned from experiences.

Despite the Need to Pay Licensing Fees, Reuse of Intellectual Capital Developed Outside Can Speed Innovation and Leapfrogs What One Organization Can Do Alone

Rather than trying to reinvent capabilities inside an organization that are not within the organization's core competencies, it makes sense to purchase (via licensing) a brilliant invention that has already been built and proven to work. This is a reuse of knowledge that already exists, except that this time someone else owns the knowledge. There are two key points involved with this. First, the intellectual property knowledge involved should lie outside the commercial interests of the organization. For example, an energy company like Royal Dutch/Shell is comfortable creating intellectual capital knowledge involving oil and gas extraction, but would rather outsource the need for advertising intellectual capital to those who specialize in it. Second, it is inefficient, costly, and risky for one organization— even reusing knowledge that exists—to try to create a solution when a brilliant one can be purchased at one-fourth the cost it would take to build it in-house.

Consider how Verizon Communications has introduced innovative reuse of intellectual capital knowledge into its accounts payable operations. For years, Verizon and its predecessors, NYNEX, Bell Atlantic, and GTE, have conducted benchmarking exchanges to reuse the knowledge learned from others by importing best practices approaches, technology, and methods that improve performance. Exchanges of nonproprietary information took place with benchmarking partners Bank of America, Colgate, Disney, General Motors, Shell Oil, IBM, the International Accounts Payable Professionals (IAPP), and many other telecommunications companies. "Since about 1996 we have participated in and partnered with a number of professional accounts payable and benchmarking organizations that included a number of other Fortune 500 Companies," says Marsha Krashoc, Verizon's former staff manager for accounts payable. Such learning was essential when Bell Atlantic merged with NYNEX in 1998 and then Bell Atlantic and GTE merged during 2000 to form Verizon.[24]

As a result of these mergers, Verizon's list of vendors more than doubled. Innovations in the accounts payable processes were required to ensure that vendors were properly paid according to the required terms for equipment, supplies, software, utilities, vehicles, land, services, and whatever else Verizon needed to procure. Also, the proper treatment of employees was involved because accounts payable processes are involved in reimbursing employees for out-of-pocket expenses. If these processes are not performed well, the reputation of the organization is at stake, not only with its suppliers, but also with its employees. Done well, accounts payable can be a strategic advantage. Done poorly, it can be a strategic disadvantage. Verizon has made it an advantage with the help of benchmarking, which enabled Verizon to identify and adapt a number of noteworthy innovations.

Displayed in Table 9-2 is a list of innovations that Verizon introduced into Accounts Payable that reused knowledge already created from applications in another context. Listed are the knowledge reuse of electronic funds transfers (EFT) to pay vendors, the reuse of imaging software to process vendor invoices electronically, and the reuse of corporate debit/credit charge cards and downloads. Benchmarking site visits were quite effective in bringing to the surface data, evidence, best practices, and success stories that inspired and motivated key people at Verizon to initiate constructive change.

Table 9-2 Verizon's Innovations in Accounts Payable

Verizon's Accounts Payable	Innovations via Knowledge Reuse
Electronic Funds Transfer (EFT), which enables paying vendors using electronic payments rather than checks. *The payback:* A 20 percent reduction in checks written, a corresponding reduction in lost checks and the unproductive time to investigate them, improving productivity in accounts payable, reducing time required by Treasury in funds management, and improving performance in making payments within 30 and 45 days of invoice. And nearly all the vendors that have switched to EFT prefer it to being paid by check.	*Knowledge reuse involved:* Verizon explored via benchmarks what superior results others had achieved in such measures as "cost to issue payment," "cost to process bills," and "total time researching lost checks." Then, Verizon used benchmarking probes to identify and reuse successful methods, software, and suppliers. One adapted method put a message on vendor check payment stubs to trigger those interested in EFT to telephone Verizon. As such calls were received, Verizon faxed back to the vendor a form letter to set up an EFT account. Over time, this practice enabled vendors to transfer to being paid by EFT rather than by check.
Imaging software: This enables the scanning and faxing of vendor bills and employee expense receipts, which are linked to an electronic payment transaction and are processed and approved online with a click. *The payback:* Time saved by eliminating processing, mailing bills or receipts, and seven-year storage of receipts.	*Knowledge reuse involved:* The outreach learning about which software others had used, what upside and downside exists for each, what mistakes need to be avoided, and do's and don'ts from the experience of those already using imaging software. Benchmarking enabled Verizon to identify, select, and reuse the best software available to achieve this innovation.
Downloaded corporate card statements: This is an improved method of processing employee expense payments. *The payback:* This "paperless" method is quick and easy to review, certify, route, approve, and make payment.	*Knowledge reuse involved:* Learning began at an accounts payable conference. Best practices study identified as ideal a collaboration with a corporate credit card supplier that reuses debit/credit charge download knowledge at agreed-to intervals and simplifies transactions for employees.

Source: Verizon Communications. (In-person interview of Marsha Krashoc by Mike English in Dallas on Oct. 1, 2003.)

The excitement and passion of people at organizations like Verizon, Raytheon, DuPont, IBM, Xerox, Buckman Labs, and dozens of others as they enter into face-to-face knowledge exchanges to share and learn is contagious. Following a code of conduct, each shares its performance successes and failures for the sake of learning from the experiences of those who have already walked down the path involved.

Actually, it's "infectious," inspiring, and trust-building when people share their potentially embarrassing problems and how those problems were overcome. To become a best practices organization, companies had to close performance gaps and often adopt a new way of thinking that originated in another industry. This is where "out of industry" benchmarking can be a real eye-opener. Best practices benchmarking takes advantage of the other organization's learning and leapfrogs from the existing organization's current state over its benchmarking partners' organizations to an even better future state. Such efforts inspire beneficial change.

Avoiding the Know-Do Gap as a Prerequisite to Managing Change

A trap that organizations must avoid is the *know-do gap*, which is the difference between what the organization knows should be done and what is actually done. This pertains to managing the changes associated with reusing knowledge or simply making improvements. Unfortunately, in some organization, very skillful Microsoft PowerPoint presentations are mistaken for actually doing something about the knowledge presented. Many meetings occur simply to "get people on board" (i.e., to create awareness and identify concerns to address before proceeding). Nevertheless, too many meetings end with a vague understanding about what action has been decided upon or what agreement was reached about the next steps that will be taken. To avoid this, it makes a great deal of sense and it's a best practice to put up a sign in the meeting room that reads:

> At the end of this meeting, let's agree to spell out in writing exactly what action has been decided. For each action item, we will identify who will be responsible for completing the action, with a date for completion. If the knowledge did not get converted to action, a know-do gap exists.

The point is, knowledge isn't always implemented. Knowing what to do falls woefully short of being enough; nothing is accomplished unless the knowledge gained is translated into action. While all four phases of the knowledge transfer race are important, action needs to be taken in phase 4 in order to convert knowledge into profit. This is where intellectual capital is reused and the payoff occurs. However, there's compelling evidence that in many organizations, there is a significant gap between what's known and what's been deployed or implemented.

In their 2000 work, Pfeffer and Sutton investigated why knowledge of what needs to be done often fails to result in action or behavior consistent with that knowledge.[25] They discovered evidence that substantiates the existence of what they labeled a *knowing-doing gap*, which is the difference between the known superior ways of managing people and organizing work and what's been actually implemented. They found gaps in modular production in apparel manufacturing, flexible or *Lean* production in automobile assembly and semiconductor fabrication, and inconsistencies between what CEOs say their organizations should have and what they actually have.[26] They also produced evidence that knowledge not only isn't transferred *across* firms, but also isn't readily transferred *within* firms, as differences of 300 percent were found between the best and worst-performing plants in the same company.[27]

With a focus on urging organizations to engage in more frequent thoughtful action, Pfeffer and Sutton identified eight themes for every organization to act upon to prevent a know-do gap. One important insight is that knowledge that has actually been implemented is much more likely to have been acquired from experiences than from reading, listening, or even thinking.[28] Following are recurring themes that Pfeffer and Sutton identified to help organizations understand the source of problems and, by extension, identify ways to prevent and solve them:[29]

1. *Why before how: philosophy is important.* The authors contend that to learn from Saturn automobiles, the Toyota Production System (TPS), Men's Wearhouse, the SAS Institute, or other such operations, people have to understand the philosophy underlying each of these organizations' processes or approaches to realize why they are successful. The processes for each have been founded on an overarching philosophy that may be different and unique. Founder George Zimmer of the Men's Wearhouse, for example, believes that people have tremendous human potential and that it is his job to help them realize that potential.[30] And Zimmer's philosophy may account for how the Men's Wearhouse can use the same "how-to" methods as others, but achieve superior results.

2. *Knowing comes from doing and teaching others how.* Simply put, doing something is much more powerful than hearing or reading lots of words. Pfeffer and Sutton furnish examples from McKinsey's apprenticeship approach to learning and General Motors' "being thrown into situations" approach to support this finding, which is common sense. To illustrate this further, when a person is thrown into a swimming pool to learn how to swim, he or she is directly involved and will learn by doing.

3. *Action counts more than elegant plans and concepts.* The contention is that there are virtues to "ready, fire, aim" insofar as it creates opportunities for learning and establishes a cultural tone that action is valued by the organization. Greg Brenneman, COO of Continental Airlines, for example, is quoted as saying, "If you sit around devising elegant and complex strategies and then try to execute them through a series of flawless decisions, you're doomed. We saved Continental because we acted and we never looked back."

4. *There is no doing without mistakes.* Things can go wrong, and when they do, people must not be treated so harshly that they fear taking action in the future. Mistakes must be viewed as learning, an extension of the word *try*. Mistakes do need to be owned and acknowledged for what they are. But they

also must be considered a valuable source of learning. Fortunately, some organizations are experimenting with the recognition for employees who practice "taking a shot" risk taking.

5. *Fear fosters knowing-doing gaps, so drive out fear.* As stated by COO Greg Brenneman of Continental Airlines, "Pressure and fear often make managers do erratic, inconsistent, even irrational things." The point is that organizations need some sort of a forgiveness framework instead of a failure framework. Driving fear out is easier said than done. Nonetheless, more and more best practices are emerging on how to be successful at it.

6. *Beware of false analogies: fight the competition, not each other.* Just because the competition is winning in some markets doesn't mean that the same kind of competition ought to take place inside the organization. Unnecessary rivalry and contention undermine teamwork. Find ways to promote unity and common "win-win" teamwork.

7. *Measure what matters and what can help turn knowledge into action.* What's measured is what gets done, so narrow the focus to what matters. Too many organizations measure the past and measure too many activities. Measure knowledge implementation and reuse.

8. *What leaders do, how they spend their time, and how they allocate resources matter.* The difference between turning knowledge into action in one organization and not in another has as much to do with the daily management practices as anything. Highly successful CEOs understand that, instead of trying to know everything, they need to create environments that contain many people who know what to do and are empowered to act on it. When it comes to a knowing-doing gap, it matters what senior leaders do.

Managing Change Is Required to Derive Value from Intellectual Capital Knowledge

To improve is to change. It's making something better than it was before. If intellectual capital is involved, change usually makes it more valuable than it was before. Simply put, organizations cannot improve to a "future" state from an "as is" state without making the major changes (initiatives) needed to move from one to the other. Many organizations tend to be static, and most of their people must be sold on the reasons for change before they will lift a hand to enable it. The old adage, "If it ain't broke, don't fix it," comes into play. So right from the beginning, change management begins with meeting peoples' needs for understanding why the change is necessary. Then, there's managing how the work tasks may be restructured and how the culture will be affected. Therefore, change management must be part of transforming knowledge into customer value and profit. Managing change can also be enhanced through knowledge reuse by building on the accumulated knowledge that already exists from managing past changes.

Consider all the change that must be managed for an organization to go from being a Three Sigma (or 3σ) company to a Six Sigma company. Going from one to the other requires gigantic change. It means going from a 93.32 percent defect-free output to a 99.9966 percent defect-free output. In actual numbers of defects, it's going from 66,807 to 3.4 defects per million opportunities. This is revolutionary change! The culture of the organization must be turned upside down and all the processes and tools recalibrated. Obviously, the knowledge regarding all relevant aids, tools, techniques, methods, and technologies should be reused rather than starting from scratch to invent what will be needed to manage the colossal change involved.

To illustrate the magnitude of the change involved, imagine a 3σ organization that completes three billion transactions annually. These transactions include everything done inside that organization, be it a hospital, a school, an auto repair service, or any other type of organization that comes to mind. At 3σ, defects would run at a rate of about 200 million per year. To move from 3σ to 6σ, defects would have to be reduced to the 10,500 per year level. This is massive change! And to get there, many projects will have to be accomplished.

Indeed, for a 3σ organization to become a 6σ organization, three key things must occur. First, the organization must have the capabilities to competently design, test, validate, and implement improvements in manageable increments, usually referred to as projects. This requires tools, processes, methods, education, and, as it turns out, an infrastructure that supports innovation and change. Without exception, employees and teams must be educated, empowered, and rewarded if they are to build and bring to life the enormous improvement capability that's necessary to achieve 6σ excellence. The culture of the organization must be capable.

Second, to close the gap between 3σ and 6σ performances, the organization must tap this newfound improvement capability by continually creating and implementing a pipeline of improvement projects aimed at eliminating variation and defects. This is a monumental undertaking that, even with all-out commitment, requires years of sustained progress. Management must engage everyone in the organization so that their minds are in the game; and they need to be empowered as individuals and on teams to contribute to 6σ projects that bring about the needed changes. However, despite every intention to improve, not every improvement project is totally successful. In fact, of every 20 projects an organization may undertake, only 12 to 15 actually produce better performance. One or two may actually be found to have a negligible impact. On occasion, too, projects may be found to have had unintended consequences that, on the whole, net out to negative improvement. For instance, in the case of productivity, the revised process may actually require more time to perform than the pre-change process did. Furthermore, there are isolated instances in which the originally planned change was incorrectly deployed and produced no improvement.

Even after five years, an organization may only have become a 4σ to 5σ company. But this in itself is a major and successful change. As mentioned in Chapters 6 and 8, going from being a 3σ company to a 4σ company reduces defects by a factor of 10 times. Incredibly, going from 4σ to 5σ is a 26 times improvement. The point is, this is a tough, exhausting marathon that was compared in Chapter 1 to climbing Mount Everest. It's the biggest challenge most people will face during their entire careers. For this reason, throughout this book, the authors make repeated reference to the idea that 6σ is more of a journey than a destination. Indeed, most professionals are unlikely to achieve 6σ performance levels consistently during their career. The goal of achieving 6σ is not for the meek; a 10 to 15 percent improvement each year will not be aggressive enough. So this journey has to be based on a realization that major fundamental changes must take place. Many times, this realization must be based on either survival or charismatic leaders who show the way, or both.

Knowledge about achieving speed in the domain of process management that already exists may be reused to achieve speed in managing change. It is knowledge about speed that is repurposed in another context. Speed can be accelerated in at least four ways. First, cycle-time benchmarks or comparative performance measurements provide an early warning system that raises red flags as signals to the organization when its processes are running sluggishly or poorly compared to those of other competitors and process leaders. A gap in the process-cycle-time benchmark indicates the presence of non-value-added steps, too much rework, or both. Second, benchmarking then helps identify exactly where nonvalue and/or waste is excessive by providing examples of faster, leaner, and more effective operating systems. Third, knowledge management transfers breakthroughs in speed from one area to all other parts and locations of an organization, creating a learning organization. Lastly, benchmarking helps generate time-compression solutions by identifying the best practices and approaches of faster companies with less risk because they have already been proven through deployment at those other companies.

Knowledge Reuse Identifies Best Practices for Managing Change.

Bogan and English pointed out how best practices benchmarking helps organizations find their way through two frontiers of change.[31] First, it provides navigational maps or blueprints describing the most effective practices and approaches for structuring and accomplishing work. Second, it provides insight and information about how to accomplish cultural change. These two frontiers enable successful change efforts.

The metaphor of a ship navigating 15-foot-high waves as it crosses the Pacific Ocean is helpful for envisioning the two types of change. The work process is the surface ride over the waves. Controlled by the view from the ship's deck, the work process activities keep the ship on course and are above the water line and visible. Likewise, environmental factors related to the work process, such as the weather, landmasses, birds, whales, and other sea life, can be considered to be above the waterline. However, below the waterline are water currents, eddies, plant life, fish life, and geologic activity that are abundant, but are not visible from the ship. The work processes are essentially "above the waterline" activities that enable change within the process. "Above the water level" is *how work is done.* Benchmarking provides valuable design and operating information that can help employees see ways to improve important above the waterline work processes. This occurs in varying ways for such PCF process categories as "2.0 Design and Develop Products and Services," "3.0 Market and Sell Products and Services," "4.0 Deliver Products and Services," and "5.0 Manage Customer Service."

Cultural transformation occurs below the waterline. This embodies the people side of change. It's about people's feelings, buy-in, and ownership of the changed work processes. If this type of change is properly managed, work-related fears, phobias, and resistance will be minimal, whereas acceptance will be high. This *soft* stuff is really the hard stuff. Not surprisingly, people often try to avoid change; when confronted with strange or new experiences, they resist. All change happens through people.

Another metaphor is the story of the biplane wing walkers and their prime rule: don't let go of one strut until you have a hold on the next strut. This is also true of change and how people react to it. Everyone wants to know about the next step being taken and feel safe taking it. People must trust that they are safe. Frontline worker resistance is frequently reinforced by traditional "keep-them-in-the-dark," "what-they-don't-know-won't-hurt-them" management behaviors. Sadly, too many organizations have neglected to focus enough on the cultural level of change management.[32]

Change management, at the metaphoric underwater level, identifies the roadblocks, restraints, or causes of employee resistance to changes in the work processes and allows organizations to chip away at them one by one to remove, eliminate, or neutralize them. On the positive side, good change management also puts a focus on strengthening and leveraging the forces that are already helping employees embrace the changed work processes. Consider the example of Verizon Communications benchmarking of 2001 Baldrige recipient Clarke American Checks' call center processes during 2002.

At the time, Clarke American filled over 50 million personalized orders with 24-hour service, handling more than 11 million calls annually. Verizon focused its learning from benchmarking Clarke American on how to build the correct call center environment for a 24-hours-a-day, 7-days-a-week operation. In an above the waterline change, Verizon's Customer Response or Repair Center for West Operations adapted Clarke American's leadership scorecard, turning it into a daily tracking format, which they later rolled up into weekly and monthly reports.[33] This management tool change enabled Verizon to eliminate $1.4 million in avoidable cost during the last four months of 2002.[34] Below the waterline, Verizon's leaders had enough change management savvy to conduct trial use of the tool and then utilize supervisor and employee feedback to further refine the tool.

As a result, within a year, Verizon's feedback and management tool had been improved through daily tracking and rolled up into weekly and monthly reports. The various uses of the tool have exceeded expectations and have enabled Verizon team leaders to successfully manage headcount to call volumes, target ideal performance, and devise and use options that control and reduce costs while maintaining high service quality standards. By addressing both frontiers of change, Verizon's changes also led to a transformed and better call center culture. Not only does the new culture excel in the extraordinary daily challenges of operating in a 24/7 telephone response environment that is both regulated and unionized, but the environment is well suited and committed to providing the very best customer service.[35] Figure 9-2 displays the two levels of conceptually managing change—above and below the waterline.

Learning from benchmarking has made it clear that successful cultural change efforts by organizations must take both a people-oriented and a process-oriented approach to making major organizational change. Managers must manage change by helping employees to understand the intended vision or endpoint of the change so that their minds will be in the game. Only then will employees own the behaviors and actions needed to successfully make the journey. One sure way to develop and sustain the employee ownership needed is to meet the employees' individual needs to understand the organization's vision and the rationale for it. It is also essential to realign the organization's recognition and rewards systems, so that the right behaviors take place, get noticed, are rewarded, and thus are reinforced. Managers and employees tend to view change as being at one of two extremes: it represents either an appealing opportunity or a serious threat. For those who see change as threatening, the response will be either flight or fight. If they flee, both the employees and the organization usually lose. If they fight, good ideas are killed off during the conflict, and breakdowns in trust often occur because managers and employees differ about the purpose and benefits of making the changes. Such flight or fight reactions injure or weaken corporate cultures and business operations.

Unlike an engine that's turned on and off with a key, cultural change is a process that takes form over time. As pointed out by Bogan and English, it is

Managing Change Above the Waterline
Visibly changing how a process is performed

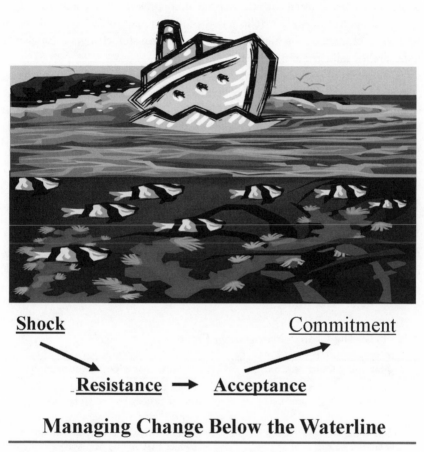

Shock   **Commitment**

Resistance → **Acceptance**

Managing Change Below the Waterline

Figure 9-2 Managing change above and below the waterline

similar to the process a journeyman photographer uses to develop a picture in the darkroom.[36] When all the proper elements are in place, the picture slowly appears on the photographic paper, beginning as a ghostlike image. Moment by moment, the picture grows in sharpness and clarity. The photographer—just like a change manager—takes great care not to underexpose or overexpose the image in the development process. Transforming corporate culture requires a well-developed and highly effective approach to managing change, including the use of every sophisticated tool available.

As an instrument for undertaking and managing such change, benchmarking helps managers to enlighten employees about the need, urgency, benefits, and path to achieve change better than any other tool can. Table 9-3 illustrates how knowledge reuse enables cultural change. Each and every project, when combined, forms an organization's change portfolio. Such projects refine initiatives, projects, or advances and must be carefully designed. To be successful, changes must also be tested and/or validated and adapted.

Changes must also be managed, deployed, and sustained properly. Deployment determines whether the change will be successful or not and must be crafted in such a manner as to address the old adage, "What's in it for me (WIIFM)?" Change must be addressed on philosophical and intellectual levels. Yet to make it really stick, change must also be addressed on a personal and emotional level. The individual must see personal gain from the change.

Knowledge Reuse Helps to Evaluate the Impact of Earlier Changes

Any time major change is undertaken, there needs to be a pre-change baseline established for the process, including benchmark performance measures that will enable post-change comparisons. Management will always want to know the benefits of

Table 9-3   The Change-Management Process

Managing Culture Change	How Knowledge Reuse Helps
1. Identify what is working and not working in the old culture.	Avoids starting from scratch by identifying what is already known to be working and not working.
2. Describe the changes needed for the new culture to succeed.	Identifies what is already known and the changes that will be necessary
3. Model new culture from the top.	Identifies role model behaviors for those who will lead the cultural change.
4. Train people for the new culture.	Identifies which behaviors and skills are necessary to support the change and to deliver the training.
5. Reward people for taking on the new culture.	Identifies which recognition/reward systems have proven to be most effective in supporting change to the new culture.
6. Structure for the new culture.	Identifies organizational structures that have best supported the new culture.
7. Assess and maintain the new culture.	Provides an ongoing monitoring system based on history of past successes.

Source: Adapted from John Scherer, "Changing the Game." An unpublished white paper prepared during 1992

the change, so the current starting baseline is a necessity. One of the other aspects of change that is fairly unusual is that when the members of a team of stakeholders in a process, for example, talk about the process, they most often do not understand the total process. It's like the cartoon in Figure 9-3, where if everyone was blind-folded and was trying to describe what his part of the elephant looked like. They cannot agree, but they are all correct; however, as pictured in Figure 9-3, no one can see or feel the whole elephant or understand the complete end-to-end picture.

The same thing is true of business processes and baselines. The process needs to be mapped and understood by all stakeholders before changes are initiated. Often, this develops into a new realization and a great learning experience for the whole team. Once everyone understands the process in the same way, sound and rational decisions about changes can be made. Value-stream maps, process maps, and associated benchmarks are also key elements to share with benchmarking part-ners so that a "win-win" attitude of beneficial exchange is achieved. Often, a new realization takes place among the members of the stakeholder group as they gain knowledge that they didn't have before. Also, this is when stakeholders realize that duplications and omissions exist, which are conditions that they not previously thought existed. This is a key aspect of *Lean* process improvement.

Linkage to Balanced Scorecards

Ever since Kaplan and Norton's trailblazing work in the early 1990s on managing performance measurements through a *balanced* and integrated system, their con-cept of a Balanced Scorecard has prevailed as the *best practice* approach to organi-zational measurement.[37] As shown in Table 9-4, a balanced scorecard typically contains four quadrants. In the financial portion of the scorecard, answers are pro-vided to questions about what success will look like to shareholders or investors.

Figure 9-3 The elephant has many facets

Certainly, there must be profitability. In addition, in the example in Table 9-4, top-line growth and return on investment are included and would have performance targets. Similarly, the customer portion of the scorecard answers the question, "To be successful, what would performance need to look like to customers?" In the internal business process perspective, the questions might be, "To achieve customer and financial success, what organizational processes must the organization excel at?" In the example, defects PMO (per million opportunities), productivity, and cycle time are specified.

Finally, in the organizational learning portion of the scorecard, the question is, "To achieve the organization's vision, how must the organization learn and improve?" The Balanced Scorecard approach puts a premium on the leading indicators rather than the traditional lagging financial results, thus enabling organizations to focus on business process improvement as the means to drive future results.

The point is that an organization's Balanced Scorecard must contain key performance indicators (KPIs) for which benchmarks can be obtained to compare past performance and target future accomplishment. Thus, every KPI in an organization's Balanced Scorecard must be traceable back to the measurement and benchmark architecture.

The Bottom Line for People in Small Organizations

It is just as pivotal for small organizations to become learning and process-centered organizations and to have a modest knowledge infrastructure (e.g., people who act as librarian types or best practices specialists part of the time), only scaled down and simplified. Everyone still needs to be engaged and encouraged to reuse existing intellectual capital. What seems to be a practical approach is to designate, probably on a rotational basis, a person to be the organization's *lead person* or knowledge reuse

Table 9-4   Illustration of a Balanced Scorecard

Financial Perspective	Customer Perspective
Profitability	Defect-free product
Top-line growth	On-time delivery
Return on investment	Value for price
Internal Business Process Perspective	**Organizational Learning Perspective**
Defects PMO	Innovation in new products
Productivity	Use of intellectual assets
Cycle time	Continual improvement

SME (subject-matter expert). This means that one person works with the owner or CEO to create a strategy for intellectual capital reuse. Then, the two of them simplify it and roll it out to everyone else, along with any related policies and procedures and communications with Q&A. One way to start, among many alternatives, is for the SME to facilitate a two-hour meeting-discussion with all employees on Friday mornings, initially weekly and then tapering off to monthly or quarterly as the concept becomes a part of business as usual. The emphasis should be on having people apply existing knowledge to solve present-day and future problems. It is applying existing solutions or reusing knowledge in new contexts.

Indeed, the reuse of existing intellectual capital is tip 47 of the 55 tips for people in small business in Chapter 11. All told, there are five tips from this chapter that have made it into the summary, numbered 47, through 51. In capsule form, they are

- Designate a lead person to help formulate and deploy a strategy for the single most important concept to emphasize: reuse of intellectual capital that already exists.
- Owners must personally make knowledge reuse systematic.
- To fill up an *enterprise innovation pipeline* requires a well thought-out, best practices-like methodology for managing all the life-cycle stages for ideas that reuse knowledge. The process for submitting, evaluating, and adopting ideas should encourage an increasing flow of ideas.
- There needs to be a bias for action in deciding and leveraging ideas in the enterprise innovation pipeline. A know-do gap must be avoided.
- Software reuse needs to be explored, especially reuse of commercial off-the-shelf applications.

The best practices approach is still to create and fill an *enterprise innovation pipeline* that travels through different life-cycle stages of evaluation and making use of knowledge reuse ideas. For the small organization, everything is scaled down and simplified to a two-page list. Brainstorming is a valid approach, and ideas for reusing knowledge may be refined through the piggybacking of refinements. The list for a start-up company will differ from that for a company that has existed for several years. There does need to be a bias for action to avoid a know-do gap. The size of the pipeline may depend on the extent to which a given organization is knowledge-enabled and on what opportunities for reuse exist. There should be a speedy process to decide whether to adapt or reject ideas while encouraging people to participate and grow the number of ideas flowing through the pipeline. Recognition and rewards should be considered to encourage the behaviors needed.

The knowledge reuse SME or focal point should arrange education and training to elevate awareness and understanding and get ideas first trickling and then flowing rapidly into the pipeline. Just as in large organizations, managers need to become aware of and appreciate the full potential of the human capital knowledge base, so that more and better ideas are nurtured into an expanding pipeline. The pipeline still needs to become a key source of leading-edge innovations. Customer applications are always good places to begin brainstorming. Software reuse should be explored, including brainstorming about applications of commercial off-the-shelf software, which, as mentioned earlier, has proven successful when math routines, screen formatting, graphics, data visualization, and database building are involved. Reviewing the list of knowledge reuse examples provided earlier in this chapter is worth doing with employees as part of an education process and to generate ideas for the idea pipeline. Some of these examples can prime the pump of the pipeline.

Even in small organizations, improvement = change + need to manage the change. There is just as much benefit from having a know-do sign in conference rooms to prevent or address the eight research findings or themes of Pfeffer and Sutton. Because of the importance of culture and leadership, the knowledge reuse SME may need to spend time with the owner, CEO, or manager to be sure that the correct culture exists. There must be a bias for action, and there is a need for a forgiving framework when mistakes are made and a commitment to drive fear out. Encourage risk taking within limits.

People, even though they are in small organizations, can still leverage best practices benchmarking to help them manage change. This involves (1) creating the data and comparative gap information that provokes change, (2) helping managers decide what to change, (3) building a picture of what the organization will look like after the change is made, (4) creating a desire for change by the people who must make the change work, (5) identifying the best practices for managing the change, (6) reducing the cycle time to accomplish change, and (7) establishing a baseline to evaluate the impact of earlier changes.

To help small organizations manage the change associated with reusing knowledge and making improvement, the following is a short list of possibilities.

- Begin with benchmarking, change management, and knowledge reuse opportunities when searching for and using off-the-shelf training software packages.
- Arrange customized "just-in-time" training to enable specific people to apply knowledge reuse to specific projects they are working on.
- Use a day each month to educate, train, equip, and empower employees to be proficient at knowledge reuse, sharing, learning, and/or benchmarking.
- Meet employees' needs for understanding the small organization's vision, strategy, key business factors, competitors, suppliers, and keys for success. This alignment gets people's minds in the game and prevents what would otherwise be obstacles when drastic change becomes necessary. When all the employees are aware of the goals, they will take ownership and make individual decisions to support the path of improvement.

- Redesign and/or restructure jobs to make them accountable for customer-focused outcomes, with sufficient empowerment and sufficient rewards and recognition to encourage and reinforce knowledge reuse.

Endnotes

1. Patricia Pancheck, "Production Workers Can Be Your Competitive Edge," *Industry Week*, October 2004, p. 11.
2. Ibid.
3. Information obtained from "History of the Hummer" at Lynch Hummer's Web site, http://www.lynchhummer.com/History.html
4. Ibid.
5. Information obtained from Xerox's Online Fact Book at the Web site http://www.xerox.com/ and Xerox's innovation Web site http://www.xerox.com/innovation/index.shtml?Xcntry=USA&Xlang=en_US.
6. Nancy M. Dixon, *Common Knowledge: How Companies Thrive by Sharing What They Know* (Boston: Harvard Business School Press, 2000), p. 20.
7. Ibid., p. 54.
8. Information obtained from Xerox's Web site, http://www.xerox.com/.
9. Information obtained from IBM's "About IBM" Web site, http://www.ibm.com/ibm/us/.
10. Ibid., "About IBM" and "Fast Facts."
11. Ibid., "IBM Press Room—Background—Fast Facts."
12. Ibid.
13. Craig Hovey, *The Patent Process: A Guide to Intellectual Property for the Information Age* (New York: John Wiley & Sons, 2002), pp. 1–3.
14. Ibid., pp. 1–3, 119–120.
15. Ibid., p. 1.
16. Borgna Brunner (ed.), *Time Almanac 2004* (Needham, MA: Time, Inc., 2004), pp. 580–581.
17. Ibid., p. 581.
18. Joseph Martucci, Performance Leader of PSEG, "Integrating Six Sigma with Process Improvement and Best Practice Replication," presentation at Global Benchmarking meeting, Denver, Colorado, Aug. 8, 2003.
19. Ibid.
20. Ibid.
21. Telephone interview of Kevin Tarrant, executive director, investor relations, and John D. Adams, manager, investor relations (both of Verizon) and Mike English on May 14, 2003.
22. Ibid.

23. Ibid.
24. In person interview of Marsha Krashoc by Mike English in Dallas on October 1, 2003.
25. Pfeffer, Jeffrey, and Sutton, Robert I., *The Knowing-Doing Gap: How Smart Companies Turn Knowledge into Action*, (Boston: Harvard Business School Press, Boston, MA, 2000), p. 5.
26. Ibid., pp. 7–9.
27. Ibid., pp. 7–9.
28. Ibid., pp. 5–6.
29. Ibid., pp. 246–262.
30. Ibid.
31. Bogan, Christopher E., and English, Michael J., *Benchmarking for Best Practices: Winning through Innovative Adaptation*, (New York: McGraw-Hill, New York, NY, 1994), pp. 211–232.
32. Ibid., pp. 211–232.
33. Telephone interview of Claudia Loffler, director of Verizon's Customer Response (Repair) West, by Michael English on Mar. 12, 2003.
34. Ibid.
35. Ibid.
36. Bogan, Christopher E., and English, Michael J., *Benchmarking for Best Practices: Winning through Innovative Adaptation*, McGraw-Hill, New York, NY, 1994, pp. 211–232.
37. Kaplan, Robert S., and Norton, David P., "The Balanced Scorecard—Measures That Drive Performance," *Harvard Business Review*, January–February 1992, pp. 71–79.

Chapter 10

Twenty-First-Century Tools, Techniques, and Methods for Importing and Leveraging Intellectual Capital, Including Benchmarking

Introduction

In any job, it is extremely important and useful for the person performing the job to have his or her own toolkit containing a complete assortment of familiar tools (whether machines, devices, instruments, gear, or software), that will allow him or her to successfully solve most problems faced every day. It's all the better if the toolkit also enhances each person's productivity and makes his or her job easier. Like a forklift, a sewing machine, and a personal computer, a tool can help each worker lift heavy weights like Superman, make a sow's ear look like a silk purse, and solve mathematical problems like Albert Einstein. These similes paint clear pictures of what is possible and expected of tools in the twenty-first century.

Like the tools for growing wheat, the tools for growing intellectual capital must treat these valuables like the precious seeds they are. An organization's intellectual capital is a nebulous concept; it can't be laid out on the table and measured physically, and we can't weigh it, but by all accounts it's the only thing an organization has that is of lasting value. The enterprise innovation pipeline that was discussed in Chapters 8 and 9 is real and can be measured in terms of the number of ideas, patents, new products, and new markets that an organization enjoys. Ideas, programs, inventions, methods, designs, and databases act as seeds. Tools are needed to find ideas, plant ideas, cultivate ideas, care for and grow ideas, harvest ideas, and sell ideas for a profit. The life cycle of intellectual capital is a very close match to that of farm products because in both cases, the crops are fragile and are dependent upon environmental and market factors, including prices. In this chapter, these newer tools will be introduced to readers for use in a twenty-first-century toolkit to help deliver intellectual capital value

- Job-specific knowledge
- Knowledge workers
- Business strategy alignment—the Balanced Scorecard and policy deployment
- New forms of best practices benchmarking
- Benchmarking memberships, networks, and forums
- Quick-turnaround benchmarking
- Fast-track data searches
- Best Practice Database memberships and searches
- Industry best practices conferences
- Communities of Practice (CoPs)

Job-Specific Knowledge: The Knowledge Needs of People by Job Type

People with different types of jobs have basic common needs, but they also have different requirements for specific information in order to execute their job well. To dive deep into a specific process in the PCF, we need to understand the inputs, process steps, and outputs of that process. A manufacturing manager, for instance, will need access to factory data on an hour-by-hour, day-by-day, and weekly basis. He or she will be concerned with production flow, test yields, quality levels, "cost-actuals," and any bottlenecks that occur.

A manager implementing *Lean* Enterprise concepts will also be interested in value-stream mapping and benchmarks of performance versus the annual plan in the areas of setup times by machine, inventory, and cost per unit. In addition to these tactical data requirements, he or she will be interested in learning how similar operations are being performed within the company (internal benchmarking and forming Communities of Practice) and how other organizations in the industry are approaching the same problems (external benchmarking). For these needs, the manager will want to link to external Web sites and databases specializing in current manufacturing benchmarks, best practices, and articles on new innovations. *Industry Week* magazine, the Association of Manufacturing Excellence, the Society of Manufacturing Engineers, the Shingo Prize, the *Superfactory* Web site (www.superfactory.com), and the Best Manufacturing Practices program (www.bmpcoe.gov) are some excellent sources of manufacturing excellence that come to mind. For a broader view of enterprise excellence, practitioners might use the *Harvard Business Review, Fortune, Sloan Management Review*, Malcolm Baldrige National Quality Awards, National Institute of Standards, QuEST Forum, the Best Practices, LLC, Global Benchmarking Council membership and database, and American Productivity and Quality Center (APQC) membership and databases.

For a different type of job, such as one in finance, the manager will also want to look inside the company at similar operations by using the company's internal network of contacts and setting up a Community of Practice to share ideas on a regularly scheduled basis. The focus might be on accounts payable, accounts receivable, corporate loans, treasury processes, cost accounting practices, government reporting, or some other such area. To stay in touch with the outside world, the manager will want to tie into professional organizations, financial Web sites, Certified Public Accountant (CPA) groups, and chief financial officer (CFO) groups and conferences. In addition, the databases of *Industry Week*, Best Practices, LLC, and the APQC provide relevant benchmarks and information on best practices of leading companies. Using the PCF will help employees isolate those processes that may have gaps in performance and need improvement.

The common need here is that managers and individuals must access several types of information if they are to be effective and productive. Specific information on process performance is needed to help make the day-to-day, hour-to-hour operating decisions. Information on yields, outputs, inputs, flow, defects, and customer feedback are good examples. Internal network knowledge of how others in the company are doing in comparable situations is a great source of internal best practices that have already been proven in the company environment. By forming Communities of Practice (CoP), individuals and managers can share and learn together in order to improve faster. If the company sponsors and facilitates these CoPs, it makes it easy to participate. The sharing will involve ideas, best practices, lessons learned, and benchmarks to guide goal setting. External knowledge networks and ties to external databases can help solve immediate problems as well as help set longer-term process improvement goals and direct projects which assures a lead in the knowledge transfer race.

Knowledge Workers: Those Who Create the Intellectual Capital of the Organization

Everyone is a knowledge worker to some extent. The value that people bring to their job comes from the skills, know-how, experience, and creativity that they apply to an ever-increasing array of unique problems and challenges. After all, it's the "smarts" of the organization that the customer wants and is willing to pay for. For instance, a person who had enough time, money, and patience could build her or his own house. He or she could develop the floor plans, the plumbing layout, and the electric wiring plan, and also do most of the work, albeit with a few errors and a certain amount of waste. Indeed, some rugged individualists have done just that, and they have learned quite a bit along the way. Some of them would never do it again, but some would, based on their positive and negative experiences. However, most people would either buy a used house, where they could see what they were getting, or contract with an established builder to take advantage of the builder's learning, experience, know-how, and creativity.

Of course, when people do this, they have decided to pay for the builder's intellectual capital, and they expect a "professional" job, including adherence to the planned schedule and cost budget, and to receive a completed house with few defects. The builder in this case is a knowledge worker, and he is cashing in on the dues paid in all those previous construction events. Just as a builder grows this expertise, professionalism, and good reputation, organizations do the same, and this contributes to the value that customers receive.

Individual knowledge workers need to be involved in keeping their skills sharp. The knowledge in the world is changing rapidly, even exponentially, so what are the twenty-first-century tools that will allow knowledge workers to stay at the top of their game? This is the question that is addressed in this chapter. The knowledge workers themselves are the most potent new tool (i.e., human capital), once the organization realizes it and drives the growth of intellectual capital. The real-world discussion with new college graduates concerning "Now that you've graduated, the real learning begins" has never been more true. In this age of rapidly changing science, technology, information, and inventions, and the knowledge transfer race, the life cycle of current knowledge is very short, and knowledge must be continually renewed. Fortunately, Generation X and Generation Y individuals are ideally suited for this continual learning approach; in general, baby boomers are not as adaptable and learning-driven.

The main challenge in getting Generations X and Y on board, however, is aligning their personal goals with the goals of the organization. Personal learning is crucial for two reasons: First, it keeps the organization vigilant and knowledgeable, which is a key to being a learning organization. And second, it provides individuals with more know-how, skill, and creativity, which makes them more valuable in the jobs and careers marketplace. Ideally, these two by-products must be balanced for both the organization and the knowledge worker to prosper.

Individual recognition and rewards for sharing and reusing ideas, concepts, knowledge, and processes are excellent tools to promote the correct cultural behavior. Hearth & Home Technologies (HHT), a mid-sized manufacturer of fireplaces in Minnesota and the market leader in fireplaces, provides an excellent illustration of one way of going about this. The Lake City plant, with about 500 employees, has adopted *Lean* manufacturing techniques and strives to involve the workforce in generating ideas for improvement in their daily jobs. The company's annual goal is for each member (employee) to generate ten improvement ideas. HHT has a simple form that the work group supervisor reviews and approves for implementation.

The company tracks ideas by work teams, and social and competitive pressure helps each team reach the goal, so that the members can be both recognized and rewarded. The progress of each team is kept on a visual horse race display board that is available at a central place in the factory for all to see. So for 2004, the company wanted to involve all employees and had a goal of 5,000 ideas for the total plant. In addition to Manufacturing, every department is involved, including Finance, Engineering, Human Resources, Warehousing, and so on. This is a simple example of how one company encourages creativity and captures the know-how and intellectual capital of its most experienced knowledge workers within each work process. In 2004 HHT was a recipient of the Shingo Prize.

Business Strategy Alignment: Combining the Balanced Scorecard and Policy Deployment

One of the more prevalent management tools in use today is some version of the Balanced Scorecard.[1] Many companies use a scorecard or management dashboard, but do not refer to it as a Balanced Scorecard. Yet there are big differences between a balanced and an unbalanced approach in terms of philosophy, priority, emphasis, and value received. Think about Kaplan and Norton's original concept, and consider the main attributes and advantages of being balanced. The four quadrants that they identified on the Balanced Scorecard are "Customer Perspective," "Financial Perspective," "Internal Business Process Perspective," and "Organizational Learning."[2] If an organization picks a few key performance indicators (KPIs) that drive improvement in each of these equally weighted four quadrants, the resulting balance will drive organizations to achieve high performance that is sustainable for the long term. These KPI measures in every quadrant need to be tied directly to the overall business strategy. Table 9-4 displays an example of a Kaplan and Norton Balanced Scorecard.

The advantages of using a Balanced Scorecard are:

1. Its use aligns all four quadrants and their focus with the vision of an organization.
2. It balances goal attainment by asking the questions, "To achieve our vision, how must we look to our shareholders?" and "How must we look to our customers?" Then, gives the answers to the two preceding questions, "What management processes must we excel at?" And, last, "How must the organization learn and improve?"
3. Scorecards are graphic and picturesque and well suited for communicating goals and current status to employees.
4. The concept of balancing performance in four different areas is intuitively easy to grasp, and performance goals and accountability can be cascaded throughout the organization.

The answers to the four questions in the second advantage above will lead organizations to achieve continuous improvement while broadcasting their goals to everyone in the company. This approach can be a very powerful force for getting everyone to pull in the same direction. Alignment and cascading goals throughout the organization multiply the force many times. This is alignment because performance is concentrated in the four key areas (customer, shareholders, internal, and learning) and the results for each are identified as being of equal importance. This alignment and balancing act, coupled with a common understanding of the KPIs and a common language, becomes ultra-powerful.

The KPI measures used to review performance in these four quadrants need to have several attributes if they are to be effective:

- They must be simple to calculate and report.
- They should be leading and not lagging indicators.
- The definitions for each KPI metric need to be precise.
- There need to be few rather than many. Fewer than ten is preferred.
- The metrics should roll up from work group to business unit to business group to business division to the corporate level to be most effective.
- A metrics oversight team should manage the Balanced Scorecard processes.
- It is preferred that the metrics be rolled up monthly and quarterly to measure progress against the annual plan.

There are three different terms used to describe this type of measurement process. One is policy deployment, another is "catchball," and the last is *Hoshin* planning. They are all very similar. The effective use of this process has a unifying effect on setting goals that contribute to the overall business strategy. To be effective and competitive, this measurement system, like all measurements, needs to have a methodology for setting goals and plans. This is where the use of benchmarks and best practices becomes a part of planning strategy. "Where are we now?" and "Where do we need to go?" are the key questions for driving a strategy toward a continuous improvement solution in the knowledge transfer race. Benchmarking is the process that can uncover answers to both questions. Once the appropriate annual goals that will allow the business to stay competitive have been established for the KPI measurements, then the measurements are cascaded down the hierarchy and aligned goals are set at each successive level.

In catchball, a negotiation takes place at this point. The question is whether the lower-level managers are willing to accept the passed-down goal or whether they see barriers that will prevent the attainment of that goal that need to be removed. If the barriers are significant, upper management must accept the task of clearing the barriers for the good of the organization, and a real team effort takes place. This negotiation continues all the way down the organizational chain until all goals have been either accepted or modified based on identified barriers, and realities have been faced.

Once the measurement system and goals for the year are in place, there is also a need to monitor performance against each goal and to initiate action when any business unit needs help or is at risk of not making a KPI goal. Every level of the organization has its own set of measurements, and they should be tied directly to the business strategy. This hierarchy of measurements is a very powerful tool to facilitate knowledge sharing, communication, and a coordinated approach to achieving business excellence. In large organizations, a full-time manager of the measurement deployment process may be justified. Certainly, there are many consultants that are capable of assisting in developing and deploying this cascading approach to the Balanced Scorecard.

These aligned KPI measures should include both forward-looking leading indicators to improve the business processes and also some all-important financial measures that are lagging indicators. The age-old rule is, if you do not survive this month or this quarter financially, you will not be around to implement long-term improvement.

New Forms of Best Practices Benchmarking

Benchmarking has gone through numerous cycles of refinement since Robert Camp wrote his first book in 1989.[3] The authors have been directly involved and have contributed to many of these refinements. Over 15 years later, the benchmarking process is tied for second in worldwide usage and is considered one of the most valuable management tools. However, when the "B word" (benchmarking) is used, it conjures up different visions and understandings in people's minds depending on which organizations and individuals are involved in the conversation. Even after Robert Camp published his second benchmarking book,[4] which added a step zero to his 10-step benchmarking process, many different organizations and individuals continued to tinker with, improve, and customize the process they used to fit their needs. Originally, step zero was, in general terms, the baselining of the business process so that it is well understood, including inputs, process, outputs, suppliers' capabilities, and customers' needs. It is important to have this understanding before launching a benchmarking study. During the ensuing more than 15 years, practitioners have seen organizations use everything from a general four-step process to a more complex sixteen-step process. Some may describe the phases as "planning," "data collection," "analysis," and "implementation." Yet in truth, there is no violent disagreement over which benchmarking process is used as long as each accounts for, in one form or another, the five phases (initiate, plan, import, formulate, and act) presented in Table 2-8.

Figure 10-1 shows the input-process-output (IPO) diagram that Raytheon presented to the APQC Advanced "Benchmarkers" working group in 1998. At the time, this team was considering the future of benchmarking.

Source: Bill Baker, from the Raytheon Benchmarking Overview presentation presented in 1998.

Figure 10-1   The Raytheon Benchmarking Study Input-Output Chart

Under "Input," Figure 10-1 lists the four primary questions or issues typically posed during that time period that triggered a benchmarking process. "I need to benchmark" was a typical outcry by someone in the organization who wanted help. Sometimes people would say, "I need to compare my operations to see how well my organization compares to others outside." In response, research processes were initiated to identify "benchmarks," "best practices," and so on. The output could be a fast track benchmarking study, core team coaching, chartering a study, identification of best practice companies, or several other services. Looking at the input side, it's apparent that many people did not realize that their need for data actually generated the need to conduct a benchmarking study, but they usually ended up authorizing a benchmarking study to collect the data needed.

Benchmarking Memberships, Networks, and Forums

The creation of and reliance on sharing networks has become the biggest and most successful tool that's been developed going into the twenty-first century. Creating a network that survives and thrives often requires an organization or individual to become dedicated—almost passionately—to launching, promoting, and sustaining a mutually beneficial sharing network. Facilitating a network is a real job because with all the varied interests, the common thread needs to be constantly reevaluated to be sure that sufficient value is being added by keeping members active, interested, and contributing. And an intercompany network requires attention to the same four key result areas that have been espoused for organizations in earlier parts of this book: people, process, tools, and culture.

- *People.* Interested people who have a desire to share and learn.
- *Process.* A process to create, capture, and share learning as a group.
- *Tools.* Aids that everyone is comfortable using, including conference calls, Webex conferences, e-mails, and so on.
- *Culture.* The participants have to trust one another and have a positive feeling about the direction of the group. "What's in it for me?" has to be answered.

In this book, the experiences and best practices of the leading knowledge-sharing and benchmarking organizations in North America and the world have been shared. A membership in any of these organizations requires an annual membership fee so that the organization can provide dedicated service, assistance, and databases. Just purchasing a membership does not guarantee value, however; once a membership has been secured, a company focal point or team must familiarize itself with its counterparts in other member organizations and become proactive and aggressively involved in forging a network of contacts eager to share mutually beneficial knowledge for the sake of improvement. Proactive participation in networks can yield tremendous benefits, whereas casual participation may not yield benefits at all.

A significant new tool and service offered by memberships is what is called "facilitated networking/benchmarking." In this situation, a member might express a need for knowledge about a particular process. The contact or account representative at the supplying organization would act as facilitator and initiate an introduction and meeting between the manager needing the knowledge and a member who has identified that process as an area of excellence. This introduction and facilitated help can be very valuable to two organizations that may not already be part of each other's trusted network.

The authors' composite listing of leading membership (supplier) networks is provided here in alphabetical order:

American Society for Quality (ASQ)

American Productivity and Quality Center (APQC) International Benchmarking Clearinghouse

Association of Manufacturing Excellence (AME)

Best Practices, LLC, sponsored Global Benchmarking Council (GBC), Financial Services Forum, Quality and Performance Forum

The Global Benchmarking Exchange (GBE)

The Global Benchmarking Network (GBN)

The KNOW Network

The *Lean* Aerospace Initiative (LAI)

Quality Excellence for Suppliers of Telecommunications (QuEST Forum)

The Shingo Prize

The Best Practices, LLC–sponsored memberships and the APQC International Benchmarking Clearinghouse offer several unique menus of research and optional benchmarking services. To illustrate, Best Practices, LLC, sponsors the Global Benchmarking Council and other knowledge exchange forums that offer an array of services. The GBC enables expert practitioners to present business strategies and action plans with real best practices, comparative benchmarks, and lessons learned.

When an organization becomes a GBC member, it receives six key services.

Custom Benchmarking Survey Research

The GBC offers its members "Internet benchmarking exchange" surveys to gather comparative benchmarks on a topic of their choosing. According to Kristen Smithwick, manager, Best Practices, LLC, "Each member receives custom research through these fast exchange surveys. Internet benchmarking exchanges gather a broad base of information and deliver directional insights for any initiative (Six Sigma, *Lean* Six Sigma, etc.) the member is considering."[5] In January 2005, Best Practices, LLC, for example, facilitated six Internet benchmarking exchange surveys on topics ranging from "Benchmarking the Outsourcing of Technical Support" and "Ensuring Brand and Health Safety from Parallel Importation and Counterfeits" to "Rewarding Contract Center Employees." At any given point in time, the Best Practices, LLC staff facilitates anywhere from three to ten surveys that have been originated by client members seeking rapid knowledge transfer from others.

Peer-to-Peer Benchmarking

GBC members have 24/7 access to cross-industry and cross-functional executives through an online member directory. This directory enables them to call or e-mail over one hundred contacts in the network to discuss or exchange information on topics of mutual benefit.

Face-to-Face and Virtual Conferences

GBC member organizations gain a wealth of knowledge and share best practices across industries and functions at GBC conferences. According to Theresa Esposto, the senior associate who manages GBC conferences, "While Best Practices, LLC, is not a conference organization, when enough members experience 'pain' on a given topic, the GBC staff produces world-class quarterly meetings and arranges for the very best speakers from organizations who are at the forefront of developing the new wave of best practices involved."[6] This provides members with key insights that can enable them to avoid the pitfalls and false starts and to enable knowledge reuse. The more than 20 conferences that have been held have addressed the topics that are most important to businesses, including leadership development, trends in process excellence, branding, *Lean* Six Sigma, portfolio optimization, and change management. Meeting proceedings are archived for reuse at www.globalbenchmarking.com.

Online Archive of Benchmarking Research

Members have instant access to an online repository of all research conducted by Best Practices, LLC, through the Best Practice Database (www.BestPracticeDatabase. com). According to Chris Bogan, founder, chairman, and CEO of Best Practices, LLC, "This database represents over $30 million in best practices benchmarking research from hundreds of top companies in every industry throughout the world."[7] Adds Bogan,

> Instead of starting with no knowledge on a given subject and having to "reinvent the wheel" time and time again, GBC members, by accessing the database, learn all the insights, lessons, and knowledge nuggets of those who have already undertaken the journey that the member is contemplating. And in terms of knowledge reuse, it's a fantastic starting point for learning the body of knowledge that exists on a given subject.[8]

Benchmarking Study Participation and Published Reports

The last two services that GBC members receive involve participating in and receiving original research. The fifth service is automatically qualifying for benchmarking study participation. Free of charge, GBC members may participate in benchmarking studies that Best Practices, LLC, undertakes on behalf of other clients. Finally, GBC members receive a discount on all published reports. Considering that Best Practices, LLC, has over eight years of published reports, this is a significant benefit. All in all, there are considerable benefits and value received from a membership in the Best Practices, LLC–sponsored GBC or the APQC IBC.

Quick-Turnaround Benchmarking

In the early 1990s, benchmarking guru John Hendricks of AT&T designed a speedy benchmarking process that was the first known formal attempt to shorten the benchmarking process and generate value in a rapid manner. Among a network of leading practitioners at an APQC advanced benchmarking practitioners' meeting, he shared the process used at AT&T and mentored others to help them understand the rationale and process steps. At the same time, Andy Gerigk, then the benchmarking group director at AT&T Bell Labs, presented the concept to the former Strategic Planning Institute's Council on Benchmarking. Before long, most of the prominent practitioners (Orval Brown at Ameritech, Bob George at DuPont, Nancy Wells at Sprint, Fred Bowers at Digital, Jim Madigan at Eastman Kodak, Al Pozos at Pacific Bell, the coauthors at TI and GTE, and unknown others) began experimenting with shortened forms of benchmarking. This gave birth to the Texas Instruments Fast Track Benchmarking process, which, upon the sale of Texas Instruments Defense Systems & Electronics Group to Raytheon, was further improved to become the Raytheon Fast Track Benchmarking process. Up until then, benchmarking had been viewed by critics, cynics, and many practitioners as a long, tedious process, and the fast-track process aimed to streamline to 90 days or less what had been taking four to six months. The new and faster solution was well received by the sponsors of benchmarking studies and the speed achieved re-calibrated the expectations for both managers and benchmarkers.

In the early 1990s, the business process reengineering (BPR) movement became a prevailing driving force that also required speedy forms of benchmarking to be integrated into modules for fast-paced reengineering teams. Enormous reengineering undertakings were undertaken at both GTE and TI that required quick-turnaround forms of benchmarking. Firm action plans had to be completed within 90 days or fewer and usually included three to four site visits and the participation of a cross-functional team. In fact, the 90-day process was a detailed day-by-day process that could be put on a project management timeline that management understood. For higher-priority projects, the 90-day timeline could be shortened considerably by nearly doubling the dedicated resources. It has been done successfully in 30 days.

The Raytheon Fast Track Benchmarking process is displayed in Table 10-1. The Fast Track Benchmarking process can be modified to add additional resources and to shorten the life cycle, but the key learning is that these key milestones should not be skipped, although they can be worked in parallel to speed up the race.

One of the eye-opening features of benchmarking is that the process produces comparisons between an organization's current process and the processes of outside leaders that include corresponding benchmarks and best practices. The authors suggest collecting data on a standard set of questions and comparing them side by side in a matrix of answers in order to view the collected data and results objectively. A simple, but effective analysis is to identify the best results on each question and use a marker to circle that answer to show that no one company is best in all areas and that by combining the best of the best, a new and innovative process can be created for all to see and appreciate. See Table 10-2, where the best results

Table 10-1   Raytheon Fast Track Benchmarking Study Milestones

Event Milestone	Activity Duration (days)	When	Maximum Elapsed Time (days)
Determine scope of study	1	—	1
Identify team and leader	1	—	2
Agree on current map baseline and process	1–3	First team meeting	5
Conduct literature search of topic			
Brainstorm 15–25 partners and draft 7–10 screening questions	1–3	Second team meeting	8
Draft 1–2 page survey and cover letter, and identify phone contacts for partners	1–3	Third team meeting	11
Complete cover letter and survey and finalize phone contacts. Team members volunteer to split up contacts. Ask for initial responses in 2–5 days; 2–3 weeks maximum	1–5	Fourth team meeting	16
Make contact, find the right contact, get agreement to partner, and fax or e-mail letter and survey to those agreeing	1–5	—	21
First review of contacts, successes, and new approaches	1	Fifth team meeting	22
Second review of contacts, successes, and new approaches	1–7	Sixth team meeting	29
Third review of contacts, successes, and new approaches	1–7	Seventh team meeting	36
Fourth review of contacts, successes, and new approaches	1–7	Eighth team meeting	43
Summarize responses; identify 3–4 best practices and 3–4 best practice follow-up partners	1–7	Ninth team meeting	50
Complete detailed half-day meeting with best practices partners. Site visits or teleconference	30	—	80
Generate best practice matrix and process improvement plan by adapting best practices. Gain acceptance from process owners and stakeholders. Start implementation. Submit final report and best practices to KT&B Office and send blinded copies to partners	1–10	—	90

Source: Raytheon. Used with permission. Copyright 2003 Raytheon Company. All rights reserved. Raytheon is a registered trademark of the Raytheon Company.

have been shaded and can be considered as benchmarks for this limited but typical third-party study. By looking at the three best answers provided by Company A, the two shaded areas for Company B, and the one area for Company C, researchers have a good start on designing the "best of the best" process for their organization.

Fast-Track Data Searches

Fast-track data searches are the simplest and fastest approach to gain some knowledge in a short period of time. Increasingly, on very short notice, managers need to gather and report various kinds of intelligence about what competitors or others in the same industry are doing better in a problem area of their organization's performance. It's not unusual for such a meeting to be set up with only a day's notice. The request may range from, for example, a vice president's interest in how to do "mystery shopping" to a line manager's concern about why customers are increasingly unhappy about a product for which the line manager is responsible. On another day, the request might be about which companies introduce products into the market the fastest.

The natural instinct of anyone being asked is to want to look good to her or his manager or peers. Let's say, for example, that today a request comes in for some factual data about who the leaders are in PCF process 5.4.1, "measure customer satisfaction level for customer requests/inquiries." Two usual follow-up questions are: "How do we compare?" and "What level is considered world-class performance?" At Raytheon, because managers are encouraged to ask questions of this type, Raytheon created a visual graphic, shown in Figure 10-2, that provides a framework for managers facing these kinds of quandaries. The intent is to translate the manager's request into the type of information that he or she requires, so that a service approach that will yield a solution that fulfills the requirement can be

Table 10-2 Typical Benchmarking Matrix

Questions	Company A	Company B	Company C
Staffing headcount?	5	10	7
Communication techniques?	Internet, e-mails, face to face	Water cooler face to face	E-mail
Monthly output?	25	75	50
Quality?	5σ	4σ	3σ
Ideas program Ideas/month	10	20	30
Attitude survey rating	90	95	88

selected. It might be internal, external, or a combination of both. Once the services are agreed to, they are scheduled and provided.

Usually, the information that managers need rapidly is limited in breadth and depth, but it's still very important. Many managers want comparable performance results for primary competitors. This may be harder to obtain, but, assuming that funding exists to finance these needs and that the data are not proprietary, there are always at least two legal ways to collect most required data and/or knowledge. Financial data on specific products and future marketing plans are the most sensitive proprietary data.

There are various quick-access sources of information, but, typically, most data collection will come from close personal networks (including memberships) of people, subject-matter experts (SMEs), and key trusted databases. Figure 10-2 also shows both internal and external sources that can be queried and tapped for relevant knowledge within the timeline. A limited two- to three-hour search by the Raytheon Knowledge Transfer Office or a knowledge champion is not uncommon. Corporate information specialists (librarians) also can be very valuable, since they have access to many external databases. If the data search is a top priority, several researchers may be asked to search in parallel to allow enough time to edit, screen, validate, and interpret the results for the requesting manager.

One of the most important steps in the data search is to clearly define the scope of the business process being examined, key words, and the time frame of the data needed. A question like, "Are we looking for current data, last year's results, or the last five years?" always needs to be asked up front to prevent missteps and

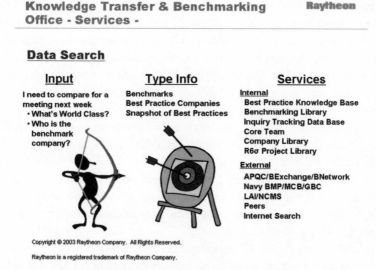

Knowledge Transfer & Benchmarking   Raytheon
Office - Services -

Data Search

Input	Type Info	Services
I need to compare for a meeting next week • What's World Class? • Who is the benchmark company?	Benchmarks Best Practice Companies Snapshot of Best Practices	**Internal** Best Practice Knowledge Base Benchmarking Library Inquiry Tracking Data Base Core Team Company Library R6σ Project Library **External** APQC/BExchange/BNetwork Navy BMP/MCB/GBC LAI/NCMS Peers Internet Search

Figure 10-2   Raytheon's Data Search Input Output Chart

rework later. This ends up being, in effect, a contract between the requestor and the data searcher.

Another aspect of the search to be defined in this contract is when the data are needed. It may be in two to three hours, two to three days, or two to three weeks. The time schedule will have a major impact on how many databases, contacts, and resources can be searched. The last aspect is to define the expected deliverable. Does the manager want a summary, a list of articles to read, or copies of the ten best articles? Rarely does he or she want ten pounds of paper or electronic attachments to dig through.

Best Practice Database Memberships and Searches

As shown under the "Services" subheading in Figure 10-2, external memberships are recommended in progressive organizations that provide access to databases that can be searched for real-time solutions to hundreds of questions. For any organization that embraces benchmarking along with the filling up of an enterprise innovation pipeline with knowledge reuse ideas, these memberships are vital. When a rapid snapshot of the industry benchmarks or a process scenario and activity are needed, these database memberships are usually the perfect source to locate the knowledge needed. Rarely, however, does a quick data search—sometimes called secondary research, since one is reviewing data secondhand rather than dealing with the primary data source—provide an in-depth understanding of the knowledge, best practices, and lessons learned by others who've performed the process.

Several of the benchmarking organizations mentioned earlier under the subheading "Benchmarking Memberships, Networks, and Forums" are primary research–driven and use ongoing findings to refresh and invigorate the value of their content for members. And if the content is not current enough or doesn't exist, the research-driven providers offer the option of five to fifteen or so members banding together and sponsoring new research on a hot topic to meet the new need. Information and knowledge gained from these various types of benchmarking studies provide research services to the organizations' members that cannot be found elsewhere. In alphabetical order, the APQC, Best Practices, LLC, the Global Benchmarking Council (GBC), the KNOW Network, and the QuEST Forum all require a membership fee before providing access. Best Practices, LLC, and the APQC Benchmarking Clearinghouse have account relationship managers to oversee the needs of members, coordinating whatever research or other solutions may be required to satisfy all the members' needs.

In addition, these providers usually publish special reports and studies that can be purchased by members with special needs. This content is often referred to as "off-the-shelf" benchmarking. It is often difficult to find an off-the-shelf study that exactly matches the needs of a specific organization. But often these existing reports contain relevant data, benchmarks, or results that can be updated and used as part of a current or new study.

Not-for-profit organizations that promote business excellence initiatives such as the Malcolm Baldrige National Quality Award, Shingo Prize, Best Manufacturing Practices, and ISO 9000 have also found it valuable to consolidate their collected knowledge. As explored in Chapter 6, this type of captured knowledge provides relevant and inspiring accelerated improvement models showing how the best companies use best practices and lessons learned to fuel their success. Most of these organizations take telephone calls from the public and provide free access to their valuable intellectual assets, since it is in their charter to make this knowledge available for reuse. This may be accomplished through their Web sites, which are cited in the endnotes for Chapter 6.

Best Manufacturing Practices Program

The Best Manufacturing Practices Program (BMP) contains a free database of role models and best practices success stories; these were originally focused on U.S. Navy suppliers, with the expectation that sharing best practices would increase Navy effectiveness. The BMP Program was created in 1985 to help businesses identify, research, and promote exceptional manufacturing practices, methods, and procedures. Its objective is to empower defense and commercial customers to operate at a higher level of efficiency and effectiveness. BMP operates out of the BMP Center of Excellence, a partnership among the Office of Naval Research's BMP Program, the Department of Commerce, and the University of Maryland.

To this end, BMP has three core competencies represented by tools and resources that enable organizations to identify and apply best practices and become part of a vast, mutually supportive information exchange network. These are

- *Best practices surveys.* These are conducted to identify, validate, and document best practices and to encourage government, industry, and academia to share information and implement the practices.
- *Systems engineering.* This is facilitated by the Program Manager's WorkStation (PMWS), a suite of electronic tools that provides risk management, engineering support, and failure analysis through integrated problem solving.
- *Web technologies.* These are offered through the Collaborative Work Environment (CWE) to provide users with an integrated digital environment to access and process a common set of documents in a geographically dispersed environment.[9]

The BMP's mission is to continually search for new best practices and organizations that would like to showcase what they do well. In-depth, on-site, voluntary surveys are the heart of the BMP Program, which identifies and documents best practices in industry, government, and academia. It also facilitates the sharing of information through technology transfer efforts; and it helps strengthen the global competitiveness of the U.S. industrial base. BMP publishes the documented practices after review by the hosting organization. The survey reports are distributed electronically on the BMP Web site and are available in hard copy throughout the United States and Canada. The actual exchange of detailed data is, like benchmarking itself, between organizations at their discretion.

BMP surveys are not audits, but rather an opportunity for an organization to showcase its best practices and have them evaluated by an independent team of experts. BMP surveys provide the participating organization with valuable benchmarking information at no cost, as well as giving their organization greater visibility throughout the country. The overall survey process consists of the request, the presurvey visit, the survey, the report publication, and the sharing.

The structure of the survey process, as well as the published report, involves six technical areas (design, test, production, facilities, logistics, and management) that are highlighted in the Department of Defense's manual 4245.7-M, "Transition from Development to Production." This publication defines the proper tools that constitute the critical path for a successful material acquisition program, describes techniques for improving the industrial process, and focuses on a product's design, test, and production phases, which are interrelated and interdependent disciplines.[10] By going to the BMP Web site, a search can be conducted for best practices by process, or data from individual organizations as varied as Lockheed Martin, Bell Helicopter, Raytheon, the City of Chattanooga, and Polaroid that have shared their best practices. See http://www.bmpcoe.gov.

Industry Best Practices Conferences

There are several annual conferences that specifically focus on knowledge sharing and reuse processes as well as promote the improvement of all knowledge transfer activities. Listed here are those that have major impact and could benefit the readers.

American Productivity and Quality Center Knowledge Management Conference

In 2005, the APQC held its Tenth Annual Knowledge Management Conference. Since the APQC was one of the early leaders in the knowledge management realm, it has continued to feature leading speakers and best practices organizational practitioners. Some of the leading speakers have included Tom Davenport, Thomas A.

Table 10-3   APQC KM Principles and Beliefs

You can measure the impact of Knowledge Management (KM), and the return on investment is high. Best-practice organizations double the return on their KM investments. Best-practice organizations have a deliberate and robust KM strategy to solve business problems. APQC's Road Map to Knowledge Management: Stages of Implementation can guide the maturing organizations' progress.

Best-practice organizations use communities of practice (CoPs) to identify and close knowledge gaps, transfer successful practices, and develop and perfect state-of-the-art processes. Communities of practice increase participants' awareness of and involvement in the core business. Using best practices, APQC's CoP Implementation Guide is a step-by-step guide to CoP Startup and maintenance.

Knowledge maps help organizations uncover areas of vulnerability, ascertain the whereabouts of key knowledge, and understand the impact of knowledge within key business processes. The knowledge mapping process, coupled with knowledge harvesting, can help identify key areas of expertise, prioritize relevant knowledge, understand where gaps exist, and develop plans to improve.

PowerMARQ, APQC's comprehensive database of standardized process measures and benchmarks, provides more than 1,200 commonly used measures and individual benchmarks to track performance of core operational functions. Looking to constantly improve processes, professionals can share their data through the PowerMARQ online database and, in return, receive a comparative report with quantitative and qualitative information.

Source: APQC Web site, www.apqc.org

Stewart, Roseabeth Moss Kanter, and, of course, APQC's president Carla O'Dell, and director of custom solutions, Cindy Hubert.

As an illustration of the depth and passion of this conference's speakers, Thomas A. Stewart, a member of the board of directors of *Fortune* magazine, made a very dynamic statement in the foreword of his book *Intellectual Capital,* which reads: "Information and knowledge are the thermonuclear competitive weapons of our time. Knowledge is more valuable and more powerful than natural resources, big factories, or fat bankrolls."[11]

Leading companies that have made best practice presentations at the APQC conferences have included Ford Motor Company, Buckman Labs, Raytheon, Best Buy, and many, many others.

APQC and its conferences have adopted an understanding of knowledge transfer similar to that of this book's authors. Table 10-3 gives a snapshot of the APQC's guiding principles, which have been summarized from information at the APQC Web site.[12] In the opinion of the authors, these principles are forward-thinking.

Braintrust International Conference

The annual Braintrust International Conference is usually held in February and is considered by many as a fitting kickoff conference to begin each new year. It is considered a highlight of the year, with top-level speakers and practitioners drawn from around the world. It is sponsored and produced by the International Institute for Research (IIR), which also sponsors many other events. The Braintrust Conference appears to be the IIR's premier event, and, in 2005, it hosted its seventh annual conference.

Table 10-4 displays the mission statement for the conference, which provides insight into how the conference agendas center around the role of knowledge management in responding to changes in the economy, workforce changes, globalization, and making organizations more innovative. The statement also reveals a flavor of the conference.

This annual conference attracts leading thought leaders and speakers, such as Dave Snowden, director of the Cynefin Center; Dr. David DeLong, researcher, consultant, and author of *Lost Knowledge*; and Dr. Melissie Rumizen of SAIC, author of *The Idiot's Guide to Knowledge Management*. The Web address for the conference is http://www.iirusa.com/braintrust.

Industry Week's Best Plants Conference

The *Industry Week* Best Plants Conference features the Best Plant winners from the yearly competition and has a "hands-on" feeling and approach. Table 10-5 gives the criteria for the Best Plants Awards. The networking and firsthand plant tours offer an unparalleled opportunity to talk to practitioners and see firsthand plants that are considered benchmarks. The focus is on the individual plant site, so all the plant business processes must meet the criteria prescribed by the Best Plants Awards.

David Drickhamer, editorial research director and *Industry Week's* Best Plants Award Program coordinator as of December 2004, provides some valuable insight about the awards and the conference in the November 2004 issue of *Industry Week*, which reads:

> How well organizations themselves actually learn from their flops and fiascos depends upon a company's tolerance levels for both risk taking and failure. Those with a higher level of control, that have well defined steps for bringing a

Table 10-4   Braintrust International Conference Mission Statement

Now more than ever before, organizations need to be increasingly agile, resilient, adaptive, responsive, and innovative. Changes in the economy, evolutions in workforce composition, continuing globalization, increased merger and acquisition activity, and ongoing process excellence programs represent both key issues and critical opportunities for today's organizational leaders. In response, knowledge management is playing an increasingly important role in enabling organizations to become more action and results-oriented through improving productivity, growth, and profits.

Source: International Institute for Research Web site, http://www.iirusa.com/braintrust.

Table 10-5 *Industry Week's* Best Plants Criteria

A panel of *Industry Week* magazine editors, who may solicit independent evaluations from manufacturing experts and other knowledgeable persons, judges candidate facilities. The panel looks for evidence of:

- A comprehensive effort to achieve world-class manufacturing capability.

- Management practices geared to motivating achievement of breakthroughs in operating performance and customer satisfaction, as well as cultivating continuous improvement.

- Strong quality systems and results, including evidence of low defect rates and good process-control capability.

- Extensive employee involvement and empowerment programs, especially efforts to create and provide training for high-performance work teams.

- A strong customer focus, including formal customer-satisfaction programs, customer involvement in product design, employee contact with customers, and efforts to reduce customer lead-times.

- Effective supplier-partnership programs, including efforts to solicit supplier evaluations of plant practices.

- Appropriate use of technology, as required by changing business needs.

- Flexible and/or agile production systems capable of responding quickly to customer needs and shifts in the marketplace. The flexibility may be the result of intelligent automation and information technology, just-in-time/continuous-flow production systems, use of quick-changeover methods, a multi-skilled workforce, small-lot production, focused-factory plant design, or other lean initiatives.

- Improvements in manufacturing operations, including shortening of manufacturing cycle times, improvements in productivity, and reduction of inventories.

- Proactive environmental and safety practices.

- Meaningful community involvement and support programs.

Source: *Industry Week* Web site, http://www.industryweek.com/iwinprint/BestPlants/naguide.asp.

product to market or making a capital investment often have a greater understanding of and tolerance for risk taking and a greater ability to learn when things don't work out.[13]

In addition, *Industry Week*, a publication of Penton Publishing, offers several benchmarking tools, including an annual subscription to its Census of Manufacturers Database and Best Plants Database, free white papers, a financial benchmarking tool, and its management resource directory. For access to *Industry Week* services and tools, go to its Web site, http://www.industryweek.com/Tools.

The QuEST Forum's Annual Best Practices Conference

The Quality Excellence for Suppliers of Telecommunications (QuEST) Forum is a unique partnership of telecommunications suppliers and service providers. The

QuEST Forum helps its member organizations pursue global telecommunications quality and performance excellence through the implementation of a common quality standard, the collaborative activities of its global work groups, an emphasis on industry best practices, and the delivery of a leading-edge measurement system. Its history, mission, and annual Best Practices Conference have already been described in Chapters 2 and 6. The conference is held in the fall and highlights the diligent efforts of the forum's work groups to transfer, share, and reuse best practices to improve the quality of telecommunications worldwide. Leading-edge topics and practices are presented by knowledgeable practitioners and experts from inside and outside telecommunications. Submitted abstracts are judged and selected for presentation, and several involve interactive discussions. This is truly a successful example of industry-specific sharing of knowledge and best practices knowledge. Access to the QuEST Forum's Web page and Best Practices Conference can be found at http://www.questforum.org.

Global Benchmarking Council Meetings

As previously discussed, Best Practices, LLC, produces quarterly GBC conferences on subjects of members' choice, often to share knowledge best practices in areas where the members are feeling competitive pressure. Usually, this translates into several members coming under increasing pressure inside their organizations to identify the superior best practices in an area of weak performance. In 2002, this may have been ethical governance and accounting standards after the 2001 Enron (the second-largest bankruptcy in U.S. history) and 2002 WorldCom bankruptcies. In 1999, it was mergers and acquisitions after a string of mergers were found to be unsuccessful in achieving premerger expectations. And in 2003, because of the pressure to focus on customers and reduce cost, one of the topics was "*Lean, Six Sigma TQM: Beyond Manufacturing.*" During 2005, one of the topics was "Managing Virtual Global Teams and Remote Project Management."

The meetings are coordinated, staffed, and facilitated by Best Practices, LLC, and there is good attendance, determined by members' interest levels. Topics not already mentioned have included customer relationship management, driving sales through customer service, performance measurement tools to drive growth, portfolio optimization, quality, and cost-cutting breakthroughs. The membership is actively engaged, and excellent practitioners relate their success stories and lessons learned openly. Chris Bogan, president and CEO of Best Practices, leads the discussion and provides feedback and an overview of what was presented for members to use. The maturity of the attendees is high, and good networking opportunities exist. Some of the leading practitioners have included 3M, Bank of America, Northrop Grumman, Raytheon, Dow Corning, Sprint, and Land's End, among many others. Information about upcoming conferences can be found on the Web at http://www.best-in-class.com.

Communities of Practice

Communities of Practice (CoPs) have existed for a long time, but until recently they were not called by that name. People have had social networks throughout grade school, junior high, high school, and college. A CoP consists of a group of volunteers who share something in common and like to meet and trade stories. They don't have to meet; they meet because they want to.

A typical example of a CoP might be a special-interest group or a college fraternity or sorority that people join in order to form a social group that focuses on academics, leadership principles, and social activities. In the fraternity and sorority example, it can also produce "brothers" and "sisters" who support and help one another. Most fraternities and sororities act as extended families. They provide a support group that is an intermediate step between the real family, the high school social group, friends, and future coworkers once the graduate moves on into industry and the workforce. The fraternities' older "big brothers" act as mentors and subject-matter experts for new members to help them get up to speed concerning both college academic and fraternity expectations. New members are called "pledges" and must endure a semester of learning, making a minimum grade point average in their classes, and attending fraternity functions. Only then may they be initiated and become fully functional members.

In business, a CoP can create colleagues and the same kind of fellowship that leads to collaboration at work. There are many similarities between fraternities and CoPs. In business and industry, however, there is usually a common professional interest (e.g., knowledge management, performance improvement, mechanical engineering, Six Sigma, intellectual capital, TL9000, librarians, or marketing) that leads members to share, transfer, and reuse knowledge while supporting and helping one another.

Once an individual is hired or transferred into an industry organization, his or her immediate goal and challenge is to quickly grasp and master all the knowledge and intellectual capital that he or she is able to in order to become productive and successful. There are knowledgeable people (e.g., subject-matter experts) in the organization who can mentor these individuals or so-called rookies. The mentors can also teach the rookies the ropes and guide their activities so that they can get up to speed fast. In the majority of companies, this happens because of the company's culture, but as companies grow, it becomes more and more difficult for the organization to keep track of all the people who need to be included in certain groups and to mentor them in social networks. People get lost in a gap.

Official organizational sponsorship of CoPs is proving to be an exceptionally valuable twenty-first-century tool for closing this gap. Organizations are proactively encouraging newcomers to form and participate in these mentoring and social networks by providing the networks with a time and place to meet, allowing interested individuals to attend, and providing management sponsorship, support, and facilitation as needed. To ensure the success of these networks, a customized form of basic training is proving effective at providing interested individuals with the capability to accomplish as much as the group agrees to pursue. And the big by-product of these collaborations is not only getting newcomers up to speed, but also creating networks of knowledge workers who are proactively creating, sharing, transferring, and reusing intellectual capital on behalf of the organization.

There are many barriers that must be overcome in order to form and sustain these CoP networks. Many companies have multiple product lines that end up becoming organizational stovepipes or silos of knowledge that are isolated from one another. In addition, the fact that people are located in different countries, cities, sites, plants, and buildings is a barrier to overcome, as are language and vocabulary differences. After all, people in those settings are outside the famous "water-cooler effect," the 30-foot-radius inner circle of knowledge learned around the water cooler or coffeepot. According to Wenger, McDermott, and Snyder, "Communities of Practice are groups of people who share a concern, a set of problems, or a passion about a topic and who deepen their knowledge and expertise in this area by interacting on an ongoing basis."[14]

This organized approach to forming and sustaining CoPs or "knowledge" social networks not only benefits the organization and its people in the ways already described, but also grows the core competencies needed for creating, transferring, sharing, and reusing intellectual capital knowledge so that it's a sustainable competitive advantage. In fact, several leading companies have formed a management oversight team to nurture their CoPs and ensure that each receives the support it needs. The fragile birth, life, and death of a CoP is usually not something that can be directed by upper management. The CoP is a living organization that does not show up on a traditional organization chart. Members of a CoP are volunteers and will participate only as long as they are getting value from doing so. Subject-matter experts are needed to infuse energy, vitality, and a sense that what's being done matters by adding validity and advanced leading-edge knowledge. Also, facilitation ensures that newer members are welcomed, oriented, and accepted fast, so that they're quick to be engaged, ask questions, challenge old assumptions, and add new perspectives. A CoP can meet weekly, biweekly, or monthly to cover subtopics that are of interest to the group. The CoP leader must be responsible for setting agendas, setting up meetings, communication, and capturing relevant knowledge to be shared among the group. Typical CoPs, for example, might be specialized engineering groups, marketing groups, librarians, and community relations managers.

From the experience at Raytheon, the basic eight rules to follow in starting a CoP are as follows:

1. Define the knowledge domains involved based on high value and passion. Define the boundaries that separate these domains.
2. Identify the subject-matter experts needed and seed them into the community.
3. Advertise the birth or existence of a CoP to gain participation.
4. Identify and dedicate a place and time for the CoP to meet regularly.
5. Identify and assign a coordinator/facilitator.
6. Permit the community to determine its agenda items.
7. Hold a kickoff meeting with management support.
8. Permit the CoP to determine its guidelines and rules and keep it spontaneous.

Many CoPs meet to exchange ideas, bring in outside speakers, review books on target subjects, and share their new learning experiences through conversations. Once the start-up has been successfully accomplished and friendships and trust have taken root, the real value and learning take place. One way to capture the tacit knowledge of the community and codify its explicit domain knowledge is for the CoP to start a "book of knowledge." The CoP can begin very simply by capturing the discussion of hot topics and consolidating thoughts and findings into mutual grounds for agreement. As this process matures, best practices and lessons learned should also be captured and shared so that standard work can be defined and reused to benefit the organization. "Shifting from sharing tips to developing a comprehensive body of knowledge expands the demands on community members, both in time and in the scope and of their interests."[15] One caution to the deployment manager: too much bureaucracy too soon will smother the fledgling CoP. In summary, author Nancy Dixon eloquently describes the creative potential of CoPs by saying: "Many innovative ideas could not have been created by a single individual; it took the diversity of minds and synergy of ideas to reach the prized goal."[16]

Finally, in the authors' view, instead of an age of individual "stars," this is now an age of teams, of which more and more are CoPs. There is undeniable growing value coming out of the creation and contributions of these vibrant communities. A leading organization in the knowledge transfer race will successfully recognize and reward these communities for their good work and thereby fill and expand its enterprise innovation pipeline. The historic design of rewards based wholly on individual star performances is an approach that has outlived its usefulness.

Summary

The best thing that can be learned from this chapter on new tools of the twenty-first century is that learning happens through aggressive study and research. There are many tools at current organizations' fingertips that were not available to prior generations, but because they are available now, all competitors have them also. So this is both an offensive set of tools to build competitive advantage and a defensive set of tools to catch up when a gap is identified. It determines how fast and how well you run the knowledge transfer race. By building a knowledge network composed of both people inside the organization and people outside the organization, and by gaining access to the myriad of excellent databases that have already captured and codified explicit knowledge, an organization can develop a real arsenal of tools that it can use to gain on the competition. In this chapter, various leading organizations have been identified that can assist the reader in developing her or his own knowledge network by attending conferences, meeting people, developing mutual relationships, and helping one another learn. Several have Web sites that offer access to databases for secondary research and sponsor conferences where knowledge is shared in a more primary research mode. The main goal is to enable the knowledge workers in each organization to be driven to aggressive learning and reusing of knowledge and to have the capability to know whom to ask and where to look for assistance.

The Bottom Line for People in Small Organizations

There are four tips from this chapter that are included in the summary of 55 tips for people in small businesses in Chapter 11. They are numbered 52 through 55, and in capsule form they are

- Pay attention to using new and simple tools like quick-turnaround benchmarking and database memberships that are easy to use.
- Use networking to learn about and try tool innovations.
- Use quick data searches to collect data for decision making.
- Use Table 10-2 and the other information in Chapter 10 to make quick-turnaround benchmarking successful.

Readers who are owners or managers of small businesses have good reasons to cheer because all the tools reviewed in this chapter are available to individuals like no other time in history. By using the Internet to do data searches, locate subject-matter experts, download knowledge content, and conduct quick-turnaround benchmarking, individuals have the capability and the power of a large organization. Managers and knowledge workers can join organizations that allow them to network and form CoPs with their peers, both in the same industry and in unrelated industries. Many of these networking opportunities will also enable participants to identify, contact, and sell to or buy from potential customers and suppliers. So there may be a triple payoff involved: improvement, sales to customers, and partnering with suppliers. Small organizations can make decisions, act, and implement changes much faster than large ones, so this ability should be used to advantage. In fact, the authors urge people in small businesses to make speed the mantra for accomplishing the action behind every important decision made.

Even a Balanced Scorecard and policy deployment tools are easier for small businesses to use. Owners, partners, or managers can set up five to ten key performance indicator (KPI) measures that will guide their business in the four key areas already discussed—customer perspectives, financial perspectives, internal business processes, and organizational learning and innovation—and every decision made will be aligned with the goals of the business. Often, when owners are trying to meet payroll or make a customer shipment, these strategic scorecard performance areas are neglected, but they don't have to be. They are all part of achieving long-term superior performance in a balanced way.

1. Particular attention should be given to new tools that simplify best practices benchmarking and knowledge searches, so they are well suited for resource-restricted small organizations. Quick-Turnaround Benchmarking and database memberships are simple and easy to use.

2. Networking greatly benefits people in small organizations so that they can learn about and try tool innovations that contacts are willing to share without charge in exchange for a similar favor at another time.

3. Quick Data Searches are greatly simplified with search engines like Google, Ask Jeeves, and Yahoo. The main problem is to pare down the results received to the "wheat" without the "chaff." Using additional search words and the PCF language or phrase descriptions for processes, often yields better results. A Web site named http://www.CEOExpress.com offers a wide range of information and data to satisfy most needs.

4. Quick Turnaround Benchmarking defines a rapid step-by-step process to do quick benchmarking studies. Information in Chapter Ten, along with Table 10-2, has been provided to aid the use of this quite successful process.

Endnotes

1. Robert S. Kaplan and David P. Norton, *The Balanced Scorecard: Translating Strategy into Action*, President and Fellows of Harvard University, 1996.

2. Ibid.

3. Robert C. Camp, *Benchmarking: The Search for Industry Best Practices That Lead to Superior Performance* (Milwaukee: Quality Press, 1989).

4. Robert C. Camp, *Business Process Benchmarking: Finding and Implementing Best Practices* (Milwaukee, ASQC Quality Press, 1995).

5. Interview of Kristen Smithwick, manager, *Best Practices, LLC*, by Mike English on Jan. 17, 2005.

6. Interview of Theresa Esposto, senior associate, *Best Practices, LLC*, by Mike English on Jan. 17, 2005.

7. Interview of Chris Bogan, chairman and CEO, *Best Practices, LLC*, by Mike English on Jan. 17, 2005.

8. Ibid.

9. From BMP Web site, http://www.bmpcoe.org.

10. Ibid.

11. Thomas A. Stewart, *Intellectual Capital* (New York: Doubleday, 1997), p. ix.

12. From the APQC Web site, http://www.apqc.org//portal/apqc/site/generic? path=/site/km/overview.

13. *Industry Week*, November 2004, p. 69.

14. Etienne Wenger, Richard McDermott, and William M. Snyder, *Cultivating Communities of Practice: A Guide to Managing Knowledge* (Boston: Harvard Business School Press, 2002).

15. Ibid., p. 97.

16. From Nancy Dixon, *Common Knowledge* (Boston: Harvard Business School Press, 2000), p. 157.

Chapter 11

The Conclusion: A Summary of 33 Key Points and Calls for Action, Along with 55 Tips for People in Small Organizations

By now, readers understand and have a mental picture of how their organizations are competing in a knowledge transfer race, whether or not their organizations' vision, mission, values, strategies, and leaders indicate it. It's a race that every twenty-first-century organization is in as a survival imperative. Some organizations, particularly MAKE Award recipients, are out in front in the race because they're mastering phases of the race and are already leveraging knowledge transfer and reuse. Figure 11-1 shows the picture that is emerging.

Everything that needs to be mastered is identified. And mastering each facet of the oval involving knowledge is synonymous with creating a sustainable competitive advantage.

But what is it about rapid knowledge transfer and reuse that qualifies it to be an advantage that is sustainable over competitors, anyway? Some say that every form of differentiation can be classified into one of three different strategies: (1) customer intimacy, (2) business performance excellence, or (3) lowest cost. Others contend that speed, or time-based competition, qualifies as a fourth differentiating strategy. Some counter the speed argument by saying that speed is crucial more as a means than as the be-all and end-all goal; and so it can be part of any of the three strategies already mentioned.

Yet another group of practitioners and academics, who see Senge's learning organization work as a breakthrough, contends that a fifth option is really the new battlefield for competitive advantage. They argue that successful organizations are

THE KNOWLEDGE TRANSFER RACE™

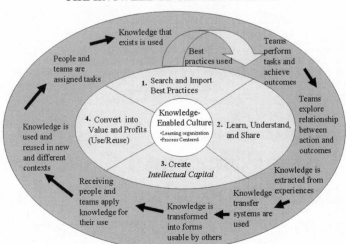

Figure 11-1   The knowledge transfer race.

developing a better capability for learning quickly. This fifth option is creating the capability for absorbing new knowledge more quickly and better than the competition. Missing from all five of these strategies, however, is accounting for the growing importance of intellectual capital. Also, pursuing speed does not necessarily exclude any of the other strategies.

The authors thus advocate a sixth option that integrates all the nuances of the learning organization and an emphasis on speed into a more robust concept that includes intellectual capital, which is described as rapid knowledge transfer and reuse. This concept is all about creating, learning, sharing, transferring, and reusing intellectual capital in ways that produce more and better customer value and profitability. This is a systematic approach that combines and integrates best practices knowledge that already exists; learning; speed; the creation, use, and reuse of intellectual capital; and managing by process. Cultural change is required in order to make the system permanent, although it's a dynamic, not a static, system because of its learning organization characteristic of having people and teams absorb new knowledge quickly and translate it into an agenda of managed change. People are valued as human beings and as human capital for how they create, in teams, better, faster, and less costly intellectual assets, which, in turn, are transformed by the organization into superior forms of customer value and profitability. And the insatiable business craving for speed turns the system into a twenty-first-century race.

It is the opinion of the authors that rapid knowledge transfer and reuse systems pass the tests of creating a sustainable competitive advantage and producing the most superior results. While there are pros and cons for each of the six strategies discussed, there seems to be a consensus that a strategy needs to pass at least a three-part test to legitimately claim that it provides a sustainable competitive advantage. First, it needs to be a permanent (rather than temporary), fully deployed, and continuously refined system. Second, it must not be easily replicated by competitors. Third, it must produce superior results for two to five and more years in the areas of (a) processes, (b) value for customers, and (c) profits. Because knowledge transfers and reuses are, by design, perpetual, systematic, and supported by necessary cultural changes, when they are accompanied by cycles of refinement and improvement, the system passes the first part of the test. Of course, senior managers have to demonstrate passion and commitment to the system, evidenced by an accompanying vision, strategy, policies, and behaviors. For the second part of the test, because of how the system is designed, the only way competitors can come close to replicating it is to make a total commitment to a similar approach requiring three to five years to implement.

What's open to dispute is whether rapid knowledge transfer can produce two to five and more years of superior results in the areas of (1) process performance, (2) producing products and services of the highest value for customers, and (3) having superior profits. In the case of superior processes, because becoming a process-centered or process-managed organization is a fundamental part of the system design, by definition, the system will optimize the performance of processes. For the same reason, outputs (products, services, documentation, and so on) will be of high value. Likewise, the learning organization features in the system design will, again by definition, translate into high-value output. What is inconclusive is how superior profitability (in comparison to competitors) will be attained. So far, perpetual MAKE Award winners Toyota Motor, IBM, BP, General Electric, Dell Computer, McKinsey & Co., Nissan Motors, Microsoft, Raytheon, and Buckman Labs have produced the two to five and more years of superior results in two or three of the three results categories and have become leaders in the knowledge transfer race. Not far behind are Amazon.com, Canon, Fuji Xerox, Honda Motor, IBM Japan, Intel, PricewaterhouseCoopers, Royal Dutch/Shell, Samsung, Siemens, and Xerox. In the end, rapid knowledge transfer systems rely on the origination of human capital, intellectual assets, and intellectual property to generate value and profits. Intuitively, the rapid knowledge transfer system design is compelling. The argument is equally compelling that such systems provide a sustainable competitive advantage. That is why organizations—whether they know it or not, whether they want to be or not—are in a knowledge transfer race.

Summary of 33 Key Points That Call for Many Actions

Throughout this book, the authors have presented the rapid knowledge transfer and reuse system as a metaphoric NASCAR race, repeatedly referred to as the knowledge transfer race. Depicted in a new light in Figure 11-1, the race involves how individuals and teams perform the tasks of the organization. After the fact, as they relate the action taken to the outcome achieved compared to the goals, they extract knowledge from the experience. In a serial sense, when the receiving team is also the originating team, the team learns and modifies its combined actions the next time around. Though speed is essential, there's no limit on the number of pit stops that can be taken, just as there's no limit on how often organizations need to create new policies, procedures, methods, and processes in order to move forward more effectively. Capability and capacity to do better in the future must be built. As competencies are built, the race will be mastered as well.

Figure 11-1 displays the knowledge transfer race in the different context of how, figuratively, the real-world, twenty-first-century information-age organization needs to perform. The illustration shows a closed-loop system of importing, creating, sharing, transferring, using, and reusing intellectual capital. Those who are overseeing knowledge-transfer and performance-excellence strategies are metaphorically compared to NASCAR race teams. Like NASCAR teams, knowledge transfer and reuse practitioners continually compare their organization's performance against the world's best. They are continually searching out and adapting best practices and making improvements to get in the lead and stay ahead of the competition.

There is a reason that best practices benchmarking has become the second most used management tool around the world. In the center of the race track, a knowledge-enabled culture is needed to stay in the race and master all phases of it. A knowledge-enabled culture is one that's grounded as a learning organization and has a focus on managing by process using the ASQC copyrighted PCF (Process Classification Framework), which is the equivalent of the Dewey Decimal System for processes and enables the deposit and retrieval of measurements, benchmarks, and best practices. Teams and people use every sharing method and display winning behavior from a litany of human capital systems. Just as a reservoir of fuel feeds energy to a race car, these systems supply a human capital framework that energizes and encourages people, as individuals and in teams, to learn, create, capture, share, and leverage knowledge in winning ways. By now, contestants have made at least one and probably several laps around the four phases of the race. This is a journey because it is a race without a finish.

Phase I: Search for and Import Best Practices

This phase involves reaching out via benchmarking to capture hundreds of gold nuggets called best practices from the outside world's stockpile of knowledge. A best practice fully satisfies customers, produces superior results in at least one operation, performs as reliably as any alternative, and can be adapted. There is no reason to reinvent what has already been invented several times over, which gives rise to the notion of reusing knowledge that already exists and reapplying it in new and different contexts.

Key points and actions called for are

1. *Best practices are forms of intellectual capital that usually need to be imported via benchmarking.* Forms of human capital do constitute best practices, but because they consist of tacit knowledge, they're troublesome to transfer or import. When codified, however, best practices become transferable intellectual assets. They are a practice that fully satisfies customers, produces superior results in at least one location, performs as reliably as any alternative, are documented, and can be adapted elsewhere. Every organization needs to capture, import, use, and reuse them.

2. *There are two types of best practices—process-practices and enabling–capability practices—and these are illustrated in Table 2-1.* Process practices correspond to those in the Process Classification Framework (PCF) presented in Chapter 4, which may be thought of as the Dewey Decimal System for processes. Enabling capabilities, which are given in the right-hand column in Table 2-1, have to do with leadership, strategic planning, measurement and analysis, policies, and governance (process management and rapid knowledge transfer).

3. *One of the biggest misunderstandings about best practices is the idea that, like Henry Ford's 1913 design of a moving assembly line, they must be extraordinary and unequaled anywhere in the world.* This is a mistake because it aims expectations too high; it is intimidating and makes the standard for what can be called a best practice almost unattainable.

4. *Another misconception is that a best practice is forever. Although it is sometimes difficult to accept this, change is inevitable.* Major advances in technology, business-cycle fluctuations, fierce competitor initiatives, changing governmental laws and regulations, mergers, shifts in customer expectations, and supplier policy changes together are bombarding the marketplace and altering the face of competition at an ever-increasing rate. Thus, all best practices have a life cycle.

5. *A common misuse of benchmarking is for managers to bring back to their organization a best practice to implement without first having done a reality check and getting buy-in from those who will have to implement the change.* Some sort of validation is needed to determine what enablers and what investment are required. Change management concepts also suggest that the team that is given responsibility for implementing the change should have firsthand experience of observing the practice in operation. Benchmarking is the systematic process of seeking out and adapting best practices and using benchmarks to set goals. According to Bain & Company's research, benchmarking, which Bain defines as, "Compares processes and performance to internal and external benchmarks; companies incorporate identified best practices to meet improvement

targets,"[1] is one of the two management tools that are most used in the world. Benchmarking has become sophisticated, as evidenced by the way Bank of America and Raytheon have aligned it to support Six Sigma projects. Raytheon people tap into current databases or Communities of Practice (referred to as CoPs inside Raytheon), which include the *Raytheon Six Sigma* Project Library, the Best Practice Knowledgebase, the Benchmarking Library, the Specialist Tracking System, Docushare repositories, and internal Web pages.

6. *The authors have created and are sharing an intellectual capital–oriented benchmarking framework, which is displayed in Table 2-8.* It consists of 14 steps in the five phases initiate, plan, import, formulate, and act. This framework was demonstrated in Chapter 2 using the example of Raytheon's strategic transfer of Six Sigma knowledge from AlliedSignal and GE to build *Raytheon Six Sigma*. A detailed checklist for conducting site visits was provided with the Benchmarking Code of Conduct.

7. *The insatiable craving for speed has turned knowledge creation, import, sharing, transfer, and reuse into a race.* Speed matters. It's a difference maker, and many times it's a key success factor. Thus, all other things equal, the organization that is fastest wins.

Phase 2: Learning, Understanding, and Sharing

This phase involves fast learning and sharing knowledge internally. According to Jeffrey Liker, author of *The Toyota Way*, "A learning organization does not only adopt and develop new business or technical skills; it puts in place a second level of learning—how to learn new skills, knowledge, and capabilities."[2] This second level of learning involves building the mental ability in people, individually and together, to acquire knowledge or understanding quickly, so that as each person or team performs the tasks the next time around, that person or team will be driven by opportunities to do better, including solving problems at their root cause—usually because of refined skills or more effective ways of behaving. What people learn through their individual experiences is shared with everyone else who is part of the involved team. Besides learning, to master phase 2, organizations must adopt sharing strategies and become proficient at using them, so that knowledge is systematically transferred.

Key points and actions called for about learning, understanding, and sharing are

8. *Becoming a learning organization not only is necessary to win the knowledge transfer race, but creates the kind of environment that is ideally suited for allowing employees to thrive, engage effectively in their work, and bring an organization's vision to life.* In Chapter 3, a learning organization was characterized as a place where people feel that they're doing something that matters. Everyone feels that his or her capacity to create is being enhanced. People become more

intelligent together in teams than they are apart as individuals. People treat each other with respect as colleagues. People also feel free to take risks by experimenting with potentially good ideas without the fear that someone is going to be prosecuted for making a mistake.

9. *Learning translates into people having the capacity to build on the knowledge gained from past experiences, so that performance is improved in future projects rather than having to start from scratch.* This same concept extends to knowledge reuse, where existing best practices knowledge is reused rather than reinventing from scratch something that's already been invented five, ten, or maybe 20 times. Thus, benchmarking helps those that want to be a learning organization because the process uncovers best practices that were already invented elsewhere. A barrier to this is the not invented here (NIH) syndrome, which TI offset with its Not Invented Here But I Did It Anyway (NIHBIDIA) Awards and Raytheon does with its Knowledge Sharing and Reuse Awards (KSARA).

10. *Systems thinking, personal mastery, mental models, building a shared vision, and team learning are the five learning disciplines of the Senge model of a learning organization.* The so-called fifth discipline, systems thinking, is at the heart of a learning organization. It enables people to grasp and improve the complex business and industry systems of the twenty-first century. It leads individuals to envision how all the subparts work together and minimizes the stovepipe thinking that leads to the suboptimization that is so prevalent in today's organizations. This fifth discipline is the conceptual cornerstone that underlies all five disciplines. As an organization builds its particular approach to being a learning organization, it must give consideration to all five learning disciplines.

11. *Toyota uses a "five whys" root cause solutions technique along with kaizen and hansei. Toyota was used as an example of a learning organization.* Kaizen is the Japanese equivalent to continuous improvement, which works best for Toyota when the involved process is stable (within variation limits) and standardized. *Hansei*, on the other hand, is the deeply rooted Japanese cultural concept involving self-reflection. It is a key part of Toyota's organizational learning. It is an adult version of the American "time-out" that parents use to discipline their children. The "five whys" technique is illustrated in Figure 3-3.

12. *Transformational learning was discussed, opening a discussion about how the mind plays a role in learning and how organizations may have to overcome the limitations on learning that mental images pose.* Transformational learning has tended to validate the use of teamwork to broaden the mental images of individuals to that of the entire team and thus better enable learning. There are principles that enable people and teams to learn: (1) *Frame* the knowledge being presented. (2) *Advocate* a use or reuse of the knowledge. (3) *Illustrate* the

knowledge so that it is easier to grasp. (4) *Demonstrate*, such as in a recipe, how the knowledge works.

13. *Author Nancy Dixon identified five types of team knowledge transfers that she named serial transfer, near transfer, far transfer, strategic transfer, and expert transfer, and all should be used.*[3] Dixon's work resulted from the study of ten organizations that are leaders in knowledge management. Dixon configured the key questions into a decision tree to aid the decision about which transfer method to use; this has been adapted in Figure 3-5, "The Dixon Decision Tree for Applying Five Types of Knowledge Transfer." Table 3-3 provides a matrix that displays the five types of knowledge transfers along with a definition, an example, and design considerations for each type. The case study in Chapter 2 of the Raytheon transfer of Six Sigma knowledge to create *Raytheon Six Sigma* is an example of strategic transfer. It behooves any learning organization to adopt the five types of knowledge transfer and to include the use of each in its approach.

14. *The authors have provided a "how to" list of actions that organizations may pursue to become faster at organizational and individual learning.* The list includes the following:

    14.1 *An organization's culture has to support rapid and continuous learning.* The culture needs to have the expectation that everyone's job is to continuously learn. Phrases such as "We've always done it this way" or "We're different" need to be treated as words to fight over, more for the attitudes they represent than for the words alone. Culture involves the kind and level of performance expected of individuals and teams and how they are evaluated, recognized, and rewarded.

    14.2 *The training provided for new tools and job performance techniques needs to be robust.* People need to know where to learn within their organization. For people to learn aggressively after college, many of the principles are the same, but the approach has to be adapted to the culture of the organization. Developing a knowledge network on the job is a choice and is not prescribed in the typical college curriculum of required courses. Yet the authors contend that it's a very effective way for a person to learn once he or she is on the job. Once a person is working, personal education, experience, and training need to be designed to support the type of employee job and aligned with competency and development needs.

    14.3 *Establish knowledge-sharing symposiums and internal meetings to elevate, highlight, and share knowledge.* Benchmarking will identify several very successful approaches to doing this that may be adapted to particular organizations. Several MAKE (Most Admired Knowledge Enterprise) Award recipients have an established record of doing this very effectively and have gone through several cycles of refinement and improvement. Use Communities of Practice (CoPs) to concentrate rapid learning among core business or technology groups.

14.4 *Provide recognition and rewards for sharing and reusing knowledge.* While achieving reuse is not easy, getting people to share knowledge regularly is even harder. Thus, addressing "what's in it for me?" right up front is advised. Once again, several MAKE recipient organizations serve as excellent role models and benchmarks.

14.5 *Obtain access to several of the splendid knowledge databases already available and use document-friendly software packages.* These tools are necessities for searches and learning, and they enable organizations to quickly document and update explicit knowledge content for training. Engage corporate librarians and information specialists to expand the knowledge network capabilities.

Creating a Knowledge-Enabled Culture

At the center of the knowledge transfer racetrack in Figure 11-1 is a circle labeled "Create Knowledge-Enabled Culture," which in business and industry consists of a unique combination of human resource systems that together determine what and how things are accomplished in any organization. It starts with a vision, includes a strategy, and involves a system of aligned human resource policies, tactics, processes, and practices. Together, all actions in a company form a system that should ensure that jobs are properly designed and staffed; appropriate performance measurements, goals, and evaluation processes are in place; and rewards (compensation, promotions, recognition, and so on) are sufficient to encourage and reinforce the behavior needed to achieve the organization's strategy and vision. In other words, culture has to do with structuring, empowering, training, and rewarding people, so that they bring to life the creation, sharing, transfer, and reuse of knowledge to create customer value and profitability.

Key points and actions called for are

15. *All value created by an organization comes from its processes.* As illustrated in Figure 4-1, processes are the mechanisms that organizations use to produce products and services that have value to customers. Superior processes create superior value. Therefore, it also makes sense to base the design of a best practices and knowledge repository system around a business process taxonomy or classification framework. But because processes are intangible, there are four things that need to be done to make them explicit, so that they can be managed and improved. First, each category—process, major process, subprocess, and activity—needs to be given a unique and corresponding name. Second, an architecture and common vocabulary, such as the PCF, is

needed. Third, input-processing-output (IPO) value-stream maps need to trace the value stream for processes, so that people can wrap their minds around what the processes are and how they create value. Finally, measurements for inputs, processing, outputs, and customer satisfaction need to be specified. For key performance indicators (KPIs), it's essential to have corresponding benchmarks as well.

16. *To counterbalance the shortcomings of functional organizations that will tend to optimize the performance of the functional groups (e.g., sales, finance, or human resources) at the expense of end-to-end process performance, the concept of a process-centered organization with an infrastructure of process owners has emerged.* Figure 4-2 has been provided to illustrate how an evolution takes place before an organization is "process-centered" and truly operated and managed by process.

17. *Through the collaboration of many international organizations, during 2005, version 3 of the Process Classification Framework (PCF) was issued by the American Productivity and Quality Center (APQC) and should be used.* It is a high-level, industry-neutral enterprise model that allows organizations to compare common processes against those of other organizations inside and outside of the industry in which they operate. It consists of twelve major categories of processes, five core and seven support. There are advantages to using the PCF, including the fact that it is becoming universally accepted, helps any organization to achieve its vision, enables pinpoint benchmarking exchanges, provides a classification scheme for knowledge, reflects the most recent business orientation, and will be continually refined by the Open Standards Benchmarking Collaboration.

18. *The PCF is an intellectual asset that the authors recommend be used and reused.* As long as it is credited as the source, the APQC has granted permission to any organization in any industry to use the PCF at no charge. The five core process categories are "1.0 Develop Vision and Strategy," "2.0 Design and Develop Products and Services," "3.0 Market and Sell Products and Services," "4.0 Deliver Products and Services," and "5.0 Manage Customer Service."

Phase 3: Creating Intellectual Capital

This phase is crucial because it involves creating intellectual capital, and the examination of it shows how crucial employees are, both as human capital and as the source of all intellectual assets. Employees and managers own human capital (the first of the three components of intellectual capital), which consists of the tacit knowledge in each person's mind. Human capital generally consists of each employee's experience, know-how, skills, and creativity. As employees codify or document knowledge that is of value, it becomes an enterprise's intellectual assets, which generally consists of the categories of programs, methodologies, inventions, documents, processes, drawings, databases, and designs. Intellectual property, on the other hand, is a subset of intellectual assets that consists of those assets that are legally protected (patents, copyrights, trademarks, and trade secrets)— hence the term *property*. And because of how crucial intellectual capital has become to the valuation and revenues of twenty-first-century organizations, the authors expect that CEOs will soon be reporting to shareholders regularly on how they are acquiring new knowledge and converting it into useful innovations of commercial value. Balanced Scorecards will contain ROI performance measurement results for investments in human capital and intellectual assets. Shareholders, themselves knowledge-enabled, will expect senior managers to provide them with results and the outlook for future performance. Best practices are forms of intellectual capital. Because knowledge is the fundamental ingredient of intellectual capital, the creation, sharing, transfer, and reuse of it not only is essential, but is of increasing importance.

19. *Human capital is the capacity to provide solutions to customers and is the source of an organization's new knowledge and intellectual capital creation.* A concise definition of intellectual capital developed by intellectual capital management (ICM) gatherings between 1995 and 1999 is "knowledge that can be converted into profits."[4] Figure 5-3 shows the importance of human capital for intellectual capital.

20. *Since 1998, the Most Admired Knowledge Enterprise (MAKE) Awards have embodied the best set of criteria to recognize those organizations that are the best at creating shareholder wealth by transforming both new and existing organizational knowledge into superior products, services, and solutions.* The MAKE awards are administered through the efforts of The KNOW Network, a global community of knowledge-driven organizations, and the consulting firm of Teleos, and are awarded for performance in five geographic regions of the world: Asia, Europe, Japan, North America, and Global.[5] Winners are judged against the following eight nominating criteria:

   ■ Creating an enterprise knowledge-driven culture
   ■ Developing knowledge workers through senior management leadership
   ■ Delivering knowledge-based products, services, and solutions
   ■ Maximizing enterprise intellectual capital
   ■ Creating an environment for collaborative knowledge sharing
   ■ Creating a learning organization
   ■ Delivering value based on customer knowledge
   ■ Transforming enterprise knowledge into shareholder value

21. *Winners of MAKE Awards are role models (i.e., benchmarks) that organizations are encouraged to study and learn from.* The winners for North America during 2005 were Buckman Laboratories, Dell Computers, Fluor, General Electric,

Google, Hewlett-Packard, IBM, McKinsey & Company, Microsoft, Raytheon, SAIC, Southwest Airlines, and 3M. In Japan, the 2004 winners, who have also consistently been winners in previous years, are Toyota Motor, Honda Motor, Kao, Nissan Motors, Canon, Sony, IBM Japan, and Fuji Xerox. The winners from the Europe, Asia, and global categories are listed in Chapter 7. A great deal can be learned from these winning organizations, and many case studies, examples, or illustrations involving MAKE Award recipients have been provided throughout this book.

22. *Because of its importance, organizations need to have strategies for managing human capital.* The authors' beginning list includes replacing less-qualified performers with people who are more qualified, investing in the current workforce to make it stronger by concentrating on activities that will help employees learn new technical and management skills that will increase the organization's intellectual capital, and outsourcing what cannot be done efficiently or effectively in-house or using a consultant who has the competence required. Sooner or later, most knowledge-based enterprises are likely to have to differentiate sets of employees by their contributions.

23. *To effectively create, import, share, and truly manage intellectual assets so that they're converted into the maximum value and profits, organizations need a customized version of a best practices intellectual asset inventory and management system.* Organizations need to have a vision and a strategy for converting the most valuable human capital into documented or codified intellectual assets. A system is needed to support this work as well as to keep inventory and track what qualifies for the protection or offensive action of patents, copyrights, trademarks, or trade secrets. There are issues to manage regarding intellectual capital, many of which are listed in Chapter 1.

24. *To illustrate the big payoff from reusing intellectual capital knowledge, an anecdote about aborigines trapped in an 1850 time capsule and two illustrations of MAKE Award recipients were provided.* In the aborigine story, the idea is to illustrate how much civilizations rely on knowledge transfer, sharing, and reuse. A Texas Instruments (the defense business, which has become part of the new Raytheon) example involved the leadership of the late CEO Jerry Junkins. Finally, the vision of Bob Buckman was highlighted to show how he transformed Buckman Laboratories into a perpetual MAKE Award winner and now a member of the MAKE Hall of Fame.

Phase 4: Converting Knowledge into Customer Value and Profits

This is the phase in which big payoffs result from mastering the reuse of existing knowledge and systematically transforming it into greater customer value and profits.

Rather than starting from scratch every time a solution is needed for customers, it makes much more sense to leverage knowledge that already exists. It's the mindset of reusing 75 percent of the knowledge that already exists, as in the example of the commercial version of the Hummer H2, originally a High Mobility Multi-Purpose Wheeled Vehicle (HMMWV) that American Motors General built for the U.S. Army for military purposes. The authors propose that organizations have campaigns such as "Reuse 75 percent of the knowledge that exists." The savings potential is huge. The time and cost of certain types of product developments and manufacturing may be reduced by 25 to 50 percent or even more. Key points and actions are

25. *Organizations are encouraged to create an "enterprise innovation pipeline" that consists of ideas from employees for reusing existing knowledge.* The pipeline includes the stages of evaluating and adopting ideas for reuse. Many ideas are aimed at correcting problems that customers unhappily experience. *Pipeline* is the term that describes the flow of ideas through a consideration process. Managers need to encourage the growth of the flow of ideas from a trickle to a gusher as they develop the full potential of the human capital knowledge base. The pipeline should become a key source of leading-edge innovations. Ideas focus on applications that customers are willing to pay to have, which means they have value.

26. *Three driving forces fill the "enterprise innovation pipeline".* The first is *necessity,* which is explained by the adage "necessity is the mother of invention." A second driving force is a *shared vision,* as employees who share the same vision as their organization tend to behave in ways that bring the vision to life. A third is the *encouragement and learning* brought about by the organizational capabilities created by benchmarking for best practices, being a learning organization, managing by process, and creating intellectual capital. Together, these capabilities help build a knowledge-enabled culture.

27. *The authors have established a starting-place list of knowledge reuse opportunities for programs and databases, inventions, processes, designs, drawings, documents, and methodologies.* This consists of

- Software reuse
- Portals for specific job classes
- Servlet reuse
- Database management systems
- Franchises
- Utility patent reuse
- Patent licensing
- Process Classification Framework (PCF) reuse (that may easily be free of charge)
- Architectural plans

- Engineering configurations
- Surveys
- Vehicle and machinery designs
- Document management systems
- Medical treatment (cures, vaccinations, medicines, and so on) reuse
- Agricultural knowledge reuse

28. *A partial list of the types of payback shows that reusing knowledge that already exists rather than reinventing new solutions from scratch is significant.* First, reuse creates greater profit, as illustrated by two examples from the Public Service Electric and Gas Corporation (PSEG). Second, reuse dramatically reduces the time required for product development, as evidenced by an example from Verizon Communications involving the reuse of existing best practices knowledge to make fast product development updates to its investor relations Web site nearly every week. Third, customer relationship management (CRM) reuses knowledge to broaden and deepen business with customers. The knowledge-enabled CRM axiom has become "know thy customer." An example was provided by the Ritz Carlton Hotel's customer intimacy approach. Fourth, reuse enables the success of strategic improvement and change management initiatives. Chapter 6 was devoted to the reusable intellectual assets embodied in the Baldrige criteria, the European Quality Award, the Shingo Prize, ISO 9000/TL9000, Six Sigma, and *Lean* Enterprise concepts. Knowledge sharing and reuse is the crucial element in achieving strategic change across an organization. Sharing the vision, goals, and detailed knowledge embodied in the aforementioned business excellence models is an outstanding reuse of intellectual knowledge that has been expressly designed for transfer and reuse. Fifth, knowledge reuse also reduces risk and enables quicker decisions. Sixth, despite the need to pay licensing fees, reuse of intellectual capital developed outside can speed innovation and leapfrog what one organization can do alone. Examples from Verizon's innovations in accounts payable were provided.

29. *To avoid a know-do gap, Pfeffer and Sutton identified eight themes that can help organizations avoid or prevent this source of problems.*[6] Organizations are urged to take advantage of this research by paying attention to and addressing these eight themes, which are

- Why before how: philosophy is important.
- Knowing comes from doing and teaching others how.
- Action counts more than elegant plans and concepts.
- There is no doing without mistakes.
- Fear fosters knowing-doing gaps, so drive out fear.
- Beware of false analogies: fight the competition, not each other.

- Measure what matters and what can help turn knowledge into action.
- What leaders do, how they spend their time, and how they allocate resources matter.

30. *Managing change is required in order to derive value from intellectual capital knowledge and is necessary to improve [for example, to go from the Three Sigma (3σ) to the Six Sigma operating level].* Gigantic change is involved in going from 93.32 percent defect-free output to 99.9966 percent. In addition, the knowledge regarding every relevant tool, technique, method, and technology that already exists should be reused, rather than starting from scratch to invent what will be needed to manage the colossal change involved. Knowledge reuse identifies best practices for managing change. It also helps to evaluate the impact of earlier changes.

31. *Six Sigma systems start with a focus on achieving the ultimate goal of 3.4 defects per million opportunities, but they have often neglected to use best practices benchmarking.* Other key characteristics include (a) a passion and commitment by the CEO and senior managers to undertake massive change and to stay the course; (b) process management and redesign as the improvement focus; (c) an infrastructure of process champions (or owners), such as Black and Green Belt facilitators, to guide and assist 6σ project teams and to manage change; and (d) the use of a data-driven DMAIC (define, measure, analyze, improve, and control) methodology to continually improve processes. Seeing a void, the authors have added "benchmark" to the DMAIC process to form the new DMBAIC process.

32. *In terms of achieving a Six Sigma strategy, five lessons have been learned so far from years of experience with knowledge-enabled organizations.* The authors provide a list of key success factors and pitfalls to avoid, as well as five lessons learned, which are

- *Integrate best practices benchmarking and internal knowledge management into Six Sigma approaches.* They provide the necessary learning and innovative adaptation to achieve the highest performance.
- *Speed up the cycle time for improvement projects.* Use of *kaizen* (like) blitzes, *Lean* Enterprise concepts, and fast-turnaround benchmarking will help. Avoid tendencies toward bureaucracy and "know it all" attitudes.
- *Create more focus on improvement projects that improve financial performance and competitiveness.* Strategic importance tests and better prioritization techniques are needed to ensure that enough of the right improvement projects are done correctly.
- *Six Sigma strategies and systems need to be simplified and made easier for small organizations, so that they can make a minimal investment and achieve a 100 percent payback in six months.* Because large organizations have

thousands of people at many locations using different vocabularies and have hundreds of suppliers, complexity has been added.

■ *Instead of worrying about whether they are at 3σ, 4σ, or 6σ, the ideal is for organizations to know how their performance compares and to keep filling up their "improvement pipeline" so that improvements can be made as fast as possible.* The reality is that every organization has to be driven by financial success. Thus, everyone in the organization needs to be on the lookout for and an advocate of new opportunities to fill the pipeline.

33. *In Table 8-4, the authors provide a process for achieving 6σ excellence.* In the first column is the traditional Six Sigma DMAIC process used in projects by the majority of Six Sigma organizations. The one exception is that, for obvious reasons, "benchmark," has been added to DMAIC to form DMBAIC. Raytheon's process is portrayed in the second column. The third column represents the authors' suggested process steps to achieve 6σ excellence. The authors' process starts with the DMAIC process and incorporates "Benchmark" (generic for best practices benchmarking) along with steps for "Plan," "Commit," and "Achieve," and substitutes "Sustain" for "Control." The key addition is step 5, "Benchmark," which is a generic term that incorporates any and all aspects of benchmarking to gain world-class knowledge before embarking on improvements. Table 11-1 pictures the nine process steps. The steps are like those of a ladder.

A Bottom-Line Summary of 55 Tips for People in Small Organizations

This book has paid particular attention to the needs of people in small organizations. While nearly every one of the 33 key points just reviewed involves actions

Table 11-1　Authors' Process for Achieving 6σ Excellence
(A Process for 6σ Project Teams to Follow)

								9. *Sustain*
							8. *Achieve*	
						7. *Improve*		
					6. *Analyze*			
				5. *Benchmark*				
			4. *Measure*					
		3. *Define*						
	2. *Commit*							
1. Plan								

that can be applied to small organizations (those with up to 75 employees), simpler solutions are needed for a good many such organizations. There are fewer people and far fewer resources available in small organizations. In addition, people in such organizations tend not to have developed a broad industry perspective. They also don't automatically follow technology trends. Next, these businesses can't afford specialized positions like full-time knowledge-sharing facilitators or librarians. Finally, any bad personal relationships can have bigger impacts. So trying to deploy certain types of actions that work for large organizations would be like trying to put a round peg in a square hole for a small organization. On the other hand, many actions do work in small organizations. In fact, some actions are easier for small organizations.

Indeed, there is an upside to being small. For one thing, everyone tends to be centrally located at one location. Small businesses don't have to deal with having many people at many different locations around the world, speaking different languages and working in different international time zones. They don't have as many cultural differences to contend with. Second, everyone knows everyone. This familiarity makes it easier for employees to relate to one another and to understand what other people are responsible for and what they do. Third, only broadly defined jobs exist, so people aren't siloed as they are in large organizations. Fourth, everyone easily identifies with the daily and weekly successes and disappointments of how the business is operating and sales are or aren't materializing. Small organizations also tend to be agile. Still, there are challenges.

And so the authors are obliged to begin a tradition in business books. A summary list of 55 tips for people in small organizations follows. These tips are broken down by chapter and boiled down to "bottom-line" ideas for applying simplified versions of the concepts put forth in this book. The tips are simplified in the form of bullet points in chapters 1-10, with no offense intended, like those used in many of the *Complete Idiot's Guides*. For ease of reference, we have numbered them in Chapter 11. The spirit of thinking here is, "Just keep it simple."

Chapter One

1. The responsibility for figuring out how to adapt the knowledge put forth in this book must be assigned and rotated among people as secondary focal-point roles [or as subject-matter experts (SMEs)], on top of their primary job responsibilities. People must wear multiple hats and be generalists because the scarcity of resources doesn't permit having specialists. Consequently, the responsibility for acting on the knowledge presented in this book must be shared and people rotated in and out of the key roles involved. This can succeed only if the owner, manager, partners, or CEO become totally absorbed with all the concepts in this book. And because "jack of many trades" type

jobs are a necessity in a small business, it is suggested that the duties of a focal-point or subject-matter expert be assigned as add-on responsibilities and then rotated every six months or so. This also makes people believers.

2. Any business that is coming in the door of a small business has priority over implementing any specific action item in this book. However, this does not mean that action can be postponed indefinitely, as that would constitute a "know-do" gap. The eight know-do gap avoidance principles covered in Chapter 9 apply.

3. Unavoidably, there is key human capital (in the form of a critical few people who have knowledge in their head) that is not backed up. Thus, these people may be or are almost indispensable. This characteristic places a burden on the owners, requiring them to make key people partners or vest them with equity positions in order to safeguard against losing their key skills, experience, know-how, and creativity.

4. Use the ability to change on a dime as an advantage when decisions justify it. Difficulty in making quick decisions and implementing the changes fast are big disadvantages for large organizations. So small organizations should use their ability to move fast to their advantage.

5. It is essential that at least a minimum effort to codify absolutely essential knowledge be sustained. There is more tacit than explicit knowledge, so a plan is needed to capture (codify) essential knowledge.

6. Document the deliverables expected from people in plain and simple job descriptions, along with their monthly schedules of knowledge capture and transfer. Documenting the deliverables expected for each employee position is recommended. Use of ISO 9000, an international quality standard discussed in Chapter 6, is also recommended. Also, processing steps should be documented as a living document to help small companies align inputs, processing steps, and outputs with customer specifications and requirements [using input-process step-output (IPO) charts, for example] for every key product or deliverable. These simple documents will go a long way to reduce the loss of knowledge as employee losses occur. To offset losses of knowledge, it is all the more important that small organizations make a commitment to importing best practices using simple and cost-effective forms of benchmarking.

7. Deploy a systematic approach to rapid improvement (a Balanced Scorecard), and use best practices benchmarking to create an agenda for improvement. Instead of a TQM, Baldrige criteria, European Quality Award, or Shingo Prize undertaking (although none of these should be ruled out for future use), it is recommended that the first steps be as follows: first, establish and fully deploy a systematic and fully deployed approach to rapid improvement; second, establish a Balanced Scorecard that contains at least three performance goals for knowledge creation, transfer, sharing, and reuse; and third, selectively use best

practices benchmarking to identify performance gaps that drive a rotating "top 10 list" of improvement opportunities. There will always be needed new actions.

8. Take steps to keep the start-up mentality so that speed of learning is emphasized as part of being a learning organization. Focus on best practices that help leverage market niches and on using innate agility to grow horizontally just as well as vertically.

9. Concentrate the capture, transfer, sharing, use, and reuse of knowledge on innovating solutions to customer needs and problems, usually in the form of better, faster, and cheaper products and services. This ensures a better and quicker return on investment.

10. As people necessarily multitask, emphasize that they should have an attitude of "I can learn from anyone," and ask questions like, "How do we compare?" and "Who's the best at doing this today?" This way, people will have humility and the desire to learn. The example of what Google has done was shared in Chapter 1. Eventually, after the question about who's the best is answered, it should be followed by, "If it's not us, what are we going to do about it?"

Chapter Two

11. To simplify Six Sigma project work, a Black or Green Belt facilitator may be brought in quarterly to generate more ideas to make the project work more simply and easily. As it is, the project work tends to be too complicated for people who can be away from their desk for only two days at time. Periodic outsourced experts can help people analyze key processes and be "just in time" to develop root cause solutions that prevent defects and disconnects, and improve the value stream.

12. To develop the needed Six Sigma mentality, have hats made with hatbands with the inscription "Benchmarking to Reduce Defects and Variation." Since people must perform several jobs because specialists are unaffordable, they need a Six Sigma mentality so that, just as driving a car becomes automatic, they automatically apply ingrained Six Sigma principles. Also, print DMBAIC (define, measure, benchmark, analyze, improve, and control) on notepads or on forms so that, in the same way, problem-solving steps may be applied. Consider three hours of classroom training for everyone each month.

13. Normally, what 6σ project teams in large organizations accomplish in weeks must be resolved in a day or two in a small organization. The cycle-time expectation is "here and now."

14. When best practices are discovered, share them with everyone. The medium may be e-mail, a memo, a poster board, or a bulletin. The medium used should depend on what works best in any particular organization or situation. Try to build a culture of sharing and reusing knowledge that already exists.

15. As growth occurs, take steps to retain the "I can learn from anyone" mindset. As organizations grow, there will be people who will think that benchmarking, improvement initiatives, and the other facets of knowledge creation, transfer, sharing, and reuse are someone else's job because it's not in their job description. Make it everyone's job.

Chapter Three

16. The learning organization concept is just as valid for small businesses and needs to be designed into the structure in the way that makes the most sense. If it's built into the organization's vision, values, and strategy with senior management commitment, it will take form. Toyota's "five whys" technique will help orient people to be focused on root causes.

17. Of the five types of knowledge transfers (serial, near, far, strategic, and expert), serial and expert transfer should be implemented immediately. Serial transfers will have an immediate positive impact on the organization's bottom line. Expert transfers will be the most friendly and effective. Use the others selectively in experiments.

18. The transformational learning principles apply to small businesses but may be simplified to one-page handouts to coach people to make better verbal and written presentations. The concepts are to frame, advocate, illustrate, and demonstrate.

19. An organized, yet informal, *water-cooler effect* may be a very effective method of sharing information in a bull-pen manner. Perhaps there are regular times that people can plan to gather for planned Q&A sessions. Impromptu gatherings can be called when there's time-sensitive information to share. Piggybacked work-group meetings may follow to take action on matters that were discussed. Besides, if the usual water-cooler effect results in insiders being well informed compared to those who are not insiders, why not be inclusive and have company management bring everyone into one insider group?

20. Recognize those who reuse best practices knowledge that already exists and encourage others to do the same. Arrange learning and sharing meetings where people can speak out about what has been learned recently and is being reused in a new context.

21. Make it a company value to ask for help and to give suggestions. Because employees in small companies have many broad and varied responsibilities, they may be more receptive to continual learning. Reinforce this.

Chapter Four

22. All the value of a small organization comes from its processes, so those processes need to be made explicit in order for them to be managed and

improved. Start with the top three to five core processes and make them explicit via input-processing-output (IPO) mapping and analysis, measurements, and goals. This is a stair-step approach to keep it simple, so that employees comprehend and engage in the work.

23. Process management needs to be implemented by everyone. Employees need to receive a minimum level of education and training, and to be given practice in spotting, correcting, and heading off disconnects and breakdowns. People need to be familiar with tools for optimizing end-to-end performance. Simplify everything to the level where people easily incorporate what's needed into the way they do their daily tasks, just as they drive a car without thinking about it.

24. Dispense with the huge infrastructure that large organizations use to manage processes and instead push for one to three measurements for the inputs, processing throughput, outputs, and customer satisfaction. Do include at least one or two benchmarks. Monitoring performance against goals for each measurement will guide the actions that are required.

25. Use portions of the Process Classification Framework (PCF) for the three to five processes selected to be made explicit. Adopt the PCF because it is a valuable reuse of an existing and free best practice intellectual asset. Another advantage of the PCF is that its clear language and common definitions make it easier for people to communicate with people inside and outside the company and be understood.

26. It is suggested that small organizations grow into adoption of the 12 process categories of the PCF provided in Figure 4.3 and listed in detail in Chapter 4. This action alone will leverage learning and save more than $30,000 in equivalent value of outside consulting work. The PCF helps owners of small businesses think about their business in process terms and in ways that help them define, limit, and refine their knowledge searches to maximize the benefit.

27. Use of off-the-shelf software to help in managing processes is suggested. Such software enables the definition and mapping of processes, identifying inputs, processing steps, outputs, customers, and customer evaluation results. One good source for software and other off-the-shelf materials is the online bookstore operated by the American Society of Quality (ASQ) at http://qualitypress.asq.org. In addition, organizations may visit such organizations as Best Practices, LLC, online at http://www.benchmarkingreports.com or the American Productivity and Quality Center International Benchmarking Clearinghouse at http://www.apqc.org to purchase and benefit from researched off-the-shelf best practices.

28. Rather than create a best practices and knowledge repository from scratch, people are encouraged to visit commercial Web sites such as http://www.bmpcoe.com and http://bestpracticedatabase.com and reuse the

information at prices that make sense for knowledge that already exists. Once there, inexpensive memberships may be obtained and the knowledge gained can be leveraged rapidly to create and continuously improve business processes. This is a cost-effective alternative to what large organizations spend and invest in gaining knowledge and transferring it across their organizations.

29. A careful look should be taken at outsourcing portions of major processes or subprocesses when that is a more effective and efficient alternative. One fear is that the marbling of levels of bureaucracy works against agility. Such subprocesses as "manage human resource information systems (HRIS)," "manage and administer employee benefits," and "create and manage employee orientation program," to mention just a few, may be carried out better and at lesser cost through outsourcing when the process is not considered a core competency that provides a competitive advantage.

30. Leverage, in every way possible, the age-old and still-thriving approach called *social networking*. It is still one of the best ways to benchmark and collect best practices data and performance metrics. This can be done through contacts at local chambers of commerce, industrial cooperation groups, neighbors, old friends, professional associations, and industry leadership groups.

31. When doing benchmarking comparisons, don't underestimate what's involved in normalizing data comparisons. If precise definitions are not addressed up front, it can skew data comparisons to the point that invalid conclusions may be reached.

32. Networked contacts are more apt to be willing to help a struggling "friend" than an unknown "outsider." So devote time to networking. Time and time again, the authors have found that having a network of contacts can be of enormous help.

Chapter Five

33. The MAKE Award criteria are just as applicable to small companies as to large ones. This means that full deployment of scaled-down approaches is needed for (1) creating an enterprise knowledge-driven culture, (2) developing knowledge workers through senior management leadership, (3) delivering superior knowledge-based products, services, and solutions, (4) maximizing enterprise intellectual capital, (5) creating an environment for collaborative knowledge sharing, (6) creating a learning organization, (7) delivering value based on customer knowledge, and (8) transforming enterprise knowledge into shareholder value. Managers and employees need to learn and use the criteria.

34. Because people are indispensable from a knowledge standpoint, it is all the more important that small organizations have human capital strategies that focus on increasing intellectual capital and preventing its loss. Therefore, a

simple intellectual asset inventory and management system is needed. It starts with having a short one-page vision and strategy that includes being a learning organization.

35. Having a commonly shared knowledge system for new product launches has proved successful for some organizations and helped them to put emphasis on developing competitive advantages. To do this, people must collect and learn knowledge regarding the characteristics of rival products. Once this knowledge is routinely collected and commonly shared, it will enable better future product launches.

36. The owner/manager is crucial in the creation and transfer of intellectual capital as the firm grows and expands. That person must have passion and must make a personal commitment to being knowledge-enabled as a way of conducting business. He or she must also promote and build a culture of continuous learning, so that everyone adds to the collective brain trust.

37. If only one thing can be emphasized, make it *reuse of best practices that already exist*. This means that a modest form of best practices benchmarking needs to be undertaken to identify best practices that may be reused in different contexts.

Chapter Six

38. Take advantage of business excellence models. Although undertaking the use of the Baldrige criteria, European Quality Award criteria, Shingo Prize, *Industry Week*'s Best Plants, or ISO 9000 is an enormous undertaking, these are free-of-charge valuable intellectual assets that have been designed for reuse. The challenge is dividing their use into manageable parcels that generate "as-you-go" paybacks that equal or exceed the time and cost investment.

39. Experience has shown that these self-assessment criteria are excellent barometers for identifying and prioritizing the highest-priority improvement opportunities. The issue is how to allocate limited resources in ways that make the most sense.

40. As organizations grow using these low-cost business performance excellence self-assessments, it also helps to identify what the enterprise's core competencies are or need to be in the future. Once these core competencies have been identified, performance in these areas may be compared to that of leaders in the industry or to key competitors. Core competencies may involve unique processes and/or emerging technologies that may be radically affected by future developments. This study will lead the owner/manager to look at industry best practices, technologies, and opportunities, so that he or she can chart the future course of the enterprise.

Chapter Seven

41. Small organizations that want to market products and services internationally have to anticipate communicating in several languages and meeting the ISO 9000 quality management standard. Taking these proactive actions while operating from one home base can be easier than for a company like Siemens, which has 417,000 employees and operates in 190 countries.

42. Culture and networking need attention. Encourage the formation of networks that bring people together to share and learn. Face-to-face meetings are needed at least once a year to build familiarity and trust. People will generate enthusiasm about a topic, and ideas and Communities of Practice can flourish. These can be both inside and outside the organization. The international consortiums are examples of this approach. If organizations have the funds to join the APQC's International Benchmarking Clearinghouse, Best Practices, LLC's Global Benchmarking Council, or Teleos's the KNOW Network, they should go ahead; the money will be well spent.

43. Use the MAKE criteria to one's advantage; they're free. Concentrate on making it easy to capture tacit know-how and share it, making certain that there are knowledge transfer and reuse methods that are well understood and used by everyone.

44. Study and learn from the masters—the perpetual winners of the MAKE Awards for Japan, Europe, Asia, North America, and the global category. Such multiyear recipients as Toyota Motor, Honda Motor, Canon, Buckman Labs, HP, IBM, Raytheon, Microsoft, and Siemens are masters at the creation, sharing, transfer, and reuse of intellectual capital. Learn from them.

Chapter Eight

45. Six Sigma strategies have become too complicated for small organizations, having the same effect as an underfinanced expedition trying to climb Mount Everest. In fact, from the authors' list of what's been learned so far, Six Sigma needs to be simplified and made easier for small organizations, so that they can make a minimal investment and achieve a 100 percent payback in six months. Therefore, the authors suggest that, rather than undertaking Six Sigma, small companies adopt the authors' process for achieving 6σ excellence, which is displayed in different forms in Tables 8-4 and 11-1. Otherwise, pursuit of the other concepts already mentioned (best practices benchmarking, becoming a learning organization and process managed, conducting a Baldrige self-assessment, and so on) is enough to undertake.

46. Rather than adopting the usual Six Sigma methodology of define, measure, analyze, improve, control (DMAIC), people in small organizations are urged

to add a benchmarking step (DMBAIC), as shown in Tables 8-4 and 11-1. Without benchmarking, an organization is flying blind in a storm.

Chapter Nine

47. Designate a "lead" person to help formulate and deploy a strategy for the single most important concept to emphasize: reuse of the intellectual capital that already exists. Depending on the organization and its leadership philosophies, this may be a subject-matter expert (SME), a person designated as a "focal point," or the lead person. In any case, this person helps formulate strategy (through policies, procedures, illustrations, communications, awards, and so on) and helps people learn, share, and reuse knowledge. And since this is part-time and an add-on to the full-time responsibilities this person will have, it is suggested that the lead responsibility be rotated every six months or whenever it's ideal. Hopefully, people will line up for the opportunity to perform this role.

48. The CEO or owner must be personally involved in designing the plan and strategy to make knowledge reuse become systematic. A simple approach is having the lead person conduct two-hour meeting-discussions about how to reuse knowledge and recognize those who were involved in recent examples of this. The CEO or owner must be present to signify his or her personal endorsement and to "walk the talk." The emphasis is always on applying existing knowledge in different contexts to solve present-day problems.

49. The notion of filling an "enterprise innovation pipeline" is straightforward but requires a well-developed, best practices–like methodology that, while simple, manages the life-cycle stages of evaluation and adoption of knowledge reuse. The process should encourage, not discourage, idea generation and submittal. The paperwork needs to be scaled down so that it is simple. Brainstorming sessions are a valid approach, too, and ideas for reusing knowledge may be refined by piggybacking on earlier suggestions or ideas. The list for a start-up company will be different from that for a company that has existed for several years.

50. There needs to be a bias for action to avoid a "know-do" gap. The size of the pipeline may depend on the extent to which a given organization is knowledge-enabled and what opportunities for reuse exist. There should be a quick or speedy process to decide to adopt or reject ideas.

51. Software reuse needs to be explored, including brainstorming about applications of commercial off-the-shelf (COTS) software, which has proved successful where math routines, screen formatting, graphics, data visualization, and database building are involved.

Chapter Ten

52. Particular attention should be given to new tools that simplify best practices benchmarking and knowledge searches, so that they are well suited for resource-restricted small organizations. Quick-turnaround benchmarking and database memberships are simple and easy to use. Quick-turnaround benchmarking consists of a defined, rapid, step-by-step process to accomplish fast benchmarking studies that produce reliable results. Information has been provided in Chapter 10 to help readers learn how to use this quite successful process.

53. Networking greatly benefits people in small organizations, enabling them to learn about and try tool innovations that contacts are willing to share without charge in return for a similar favor at another time.

54. Quick data searches are greatly simplified with search engines like Google, Ask Jeeves, and Yahoo. The main problem is to pare down the results received to get the "wheat" without the "chaff." Using additional search words and the PCF language or phrase descriptions for processes often yields better results. A Web site named http://www.CEOExpress.com offers a wide range of information and data to satisfy most needs.

55. Communities of Practice (CoPs), though not new, have become an exceptional tool for mentoring newcomers, so that they get up to speed more quickly, don't get lost trying to fit in, and are able to contribute sooner. Some CoPs are becoming knowledge-based networks, and they are proving successful at building employee competencies. CoPs are discussed in Chapter 10, along with Raytheon's eight rules for creating and supporting them.

Endnotes

1. "Management Tools and Trends 2003," slide presentation of Bain & Company dated June 2003, slide 36;, obtained from Dan Pinkney of Bain & and Company with permission for use on June 26, 2003.

2. Liker, Jeffrey K. Liker, *The Toyota Way,* (New York: McGraw-Hill, New York, 2004), p. 251.

3. Dixon, Nancy M. Dixon, *Common Knowledge: How Companies Thrive by Sharing What They Know,* (Boston: Harvard Business School Press, Boston, 2000), pp. 17–20.

4. Sullivan, Patrick H., *Value-Driven Intellectual Capital: How to Convert Intangible Corporate Assets into Market Value,* (New York: John Wiley & Sons, Inc.: New York, 2000), pp. 16–17.

5. See the Web site www.knowledgebusiness.com. The KNOW Network is a global community of knowledge-driven organizations dedicated to networking, benchmarking, and sharing best practices leading to superior performance.
6. Pfeffer, Jeffrey, and Sutton, Robert I., *The Knowing-Doing Gap: How Smart Companies Turn Knowledge into Action*, Harvard Business School Press, Boston, MA, 2000.

Index

About the Authors

 ## Michael J. English

Since 1983, Michael has worked passionately at "pushing the envelope" as far as he could to achieve superior customer-focused business performance excellence. During his 26 year career at GTE (now Verizon), he mastered applications of customer satisfaction measurement, Total Quality Management, self-directed teaming, ISO 9000, process management, unconditional service guarantees, customer relationship management, and benchmarking. Michael is one of the founding partners of Best Practices, LLC, which provides access and intelligence to its clients for achieving world-class excellence.

As director of quality and customer service, Michael led GTE Telephone Operations' 1989 Malcolm Baldrige application and site visit teams. In 1990 he published the article "Service Quality Surveys in a Telecommunications Environment" to demonstrate how customer satisfaction surveying needed to focus on inspiring customer loyalty. In the years that followed, he gained approval for deploying service guarantees, benchmarking, supplier report cards, Baldrige assessments, and a team-based GTE culture.

Michael served for four years (1993–1996) as an examiner for the Malcolm Baldrige National Quality Award. During that period he shaped the TQM system of GTE Directories Corporation and played a key role in that company's winning of the 1994 Baldrige Award. In 1994 he published the articles "Evolution: Quality Means Value" and "Baldrige Examiners, They're Winners, Too." During 1995 he cochaired the team that researched and developed a master plan for continuously improving all the key processes of GTE Telephone Operations.

In collaboration with Christopher Bogan, during 1994 they wrote the McGraw-Hill book *Benchmarking for Best Practices: Winning Through Innovative Adaptation*. Published in four languages, the book is highly regarded by performance improvement practitioners around the world.

For three years ending in 1998, Michael served on the U.S. Quality Council V, an organization focusing on the next wave of improvement after the year 2000. He was cochair of the council during 1998. He is a senior member of the American Society for Quality (ASQ) and in 2004 was the program chair for the Dallas ASQ TL9000 Special Interest Group, the business excellence track moderator for the 2003 and 2005 Dallas ASQ Fall Conferences, and the chair-elect for 2005–2006. In 2002, he published *Not Forgotten*, a historical novel that reveals how war can affect families. Michael earned a Master of Arts degree in economics from California State University at Sacramento in 1976.

William H. Baker, Jr.

William "Bill" Baker recently retired as the Knowledge Management and Benchmarking Champion for the Raytheon Company. He was responsible for awareness, training, coordination, and identification of benchmarking and knowledge management activities in order to deploy *Raytheon Six Sigma*™ throughout the company. His previous experience includes manufacturing and operations management on various missile programs, geophysical exploration, space exploration and space propulsion. He contributed heavily to Texas Instruments Defense Systems Electronics Group's winning application for the Malcolm Baldrige National Quality Award in 1992. Bill had been with the company since 1971 and had been benchmarking champion since 1990. He led the major 2002–2004 activity, the Knowledge Management Deployment Team in Raytheon.

He was instrumental in Texas Instruments receiving the American Productivity and Quality Center's (APQC) 1994 Award for Excellence in Corporate Benchmarking, and TI also received three APQC Study Awards for Outstanding Benchmarking Studies in 1994 and 1996 under his leadership. He was a key member of the Texas Instruments knowledge management design and deployment teams known as "Best Practice Sharing," implemented in 1995 and recognized in the 1998 book *"If Only We Knew What We Know."* The Raytheon knowledge management process was recognized in 2000 and again in 2004 by APQC as a best practice.

Bill is a Director in the Association for Manufacturing Excellence (AME)—Southwest Region, a senior member of the American Society for Quality, and a senior member of the American Institute of Aeronautics and Astronautics. He was the program chairman for the 1997 and 2002 AME Annual International Conferences, which drew over 1,000 attendees each. He is currently the conference chair for the AME 2005 International Conference in Boston. He has served on the associate staff of the Boston College Center for Corporate Community Relations; he has contributed articles to the *National Productivity Review*, *Target*, and *Quality Progress*; and his work has been featured in numerous books. He was the author of Raytheon's "Knowledge Management Handbook," Raytheon's "Benchmarking Handbook," and Raytheon's "Metrics Guide for Managers." He is publishing a series of articles with others in *Target* magazine on knowledge management based on your organization's approach to life. He is cited in *The Complete Guide to Knowledge Management* and *The Knowledge Evolution* and is a frequent speaker on benchmarking, performance measurement, knowledge management, Raytheon Six Sigma, and the Lean Enterprise.

Bill received his Bachelor of Science in Mechanical Engineering from the University of Mississippi in 1963 and his Masters in Business Administration from Southern Methodist University in 1973.